Keep this book. You will need it and use it throughout your career.

About the American Hotel & Lodging Association (AH&LA)

Founded in 1910, AH&LA is the trade association representing the lodging industry in the United States. AH&LA is a federation of state lodging associations throughout the United States with 11,000 lodging properties worldwide as members. The association offers its members assistance with governmental affairs representation, communications, marketing, hospitality operations, training and education, technology issues, and more. For information, call 202-289-3100.

LODGING, the management magazine of AH&LA, is a "living textbook" for hospitality students that provides timely features, industry news, and vital lodging information.

About the Educational Institute of AH&LA (EI)

An affiliate of AH&LA, the Educational Institute is the world's largest source of quality training and educational materials for the lodging industry. EI develops textbooks and courses that are used in more than 1,200 colleges and universities worldwide, and also offers courses to individuals through its Distance Learning program. Hotels worldwide rely on EI for training resources that focus on every aspect of lodging operations. Industry-tested videos, CD-ROMs, seminars, and skills guides prepare employees at every skill level. EI also offers professional certification for the industry's top performers. For information about EI's products and services, call 800-349-0299 or 407-999-8100.

About the American Hotel & Lodging Educational Foundation (AH&LEF)

An affiliate of AH&LA, the American Hotel & Lodging Educational Foundation provides financial support that enhances the stability, prosperity, and growth of the lodging industry through educational and research programs. AH&LEF has awarded hundreds of thousands of dollars in scholarship funds for students pursuing higher education in hospitality management. AH&LEF has also funded research projects on topics important to the industry, including occupational safety and health, turnover and diversity, and best practices in the U.S. lodging industry. For information, call 202-289-3180.

Managing Beverage Service

Educational Institute Books

Managing Beverage Service

Lendal H. Kotschevar, Ph.D.
Ronald F. Cichy, Ph.D., CFBE, CHA, CHE

EDUCATIONAL INSTITUTE
American Hotel & Lodging Association

Disclaimer

This publication is designed to provide accurate and authoritative information in regard to the subject matter covered. It is sold with the understanding that the publisher is not engaged in rendering legal, accounting, or other professional service. If legal advice or other expert assistance is required, the services of a competent professional person should be sought.

—From the Declaration of Principles jointly adopted by the American Bar Association and a Committee of Publishers and Associations

The authors, Lendal H. Kotschevar and Ronald F. Cichy, are solely responsible for the contents of this publication. All views expressed herein are solely those of the author and do not necessarily reflect the views of the Educational Institute of the American Hotel & Lodging Association (the Institute) or the American Hotel & Lodging Association (AH&LA).

Nothing contained in this publication shall constitute a standard, an endorsement, or a recommendation of the Institute or AH&LA. The Institute and AH&LA disclaim any liability with respect to the use of any information, procedure, or product, or reliance thereon by any member of the hospitality industry.

Contents

Donation

About the Authors

Dr. Lendal H. Kotschevar, a former Distinguished Professor in the School of Hospitality Management at Florida International University and the author or co-author of 15 texts, was a pioneer in establishing the discipline of hospitality management.

His broad and distinguished career began when he was trained as a chef by his grandfather, Chef Louis Belanger. Later, in World War II, he served as Director of the U.S. Navy's Commissary Schools. After World War II, he became Civilian Director of the U.S. Commissary Research and Development Facility, where he and his staff were instrumental in food planning research that helped pave the way for the atomic submarine. He left that position to take his doctorate at Columbia University, then went to the University of Montana to become Director of Housing and Foodservices and Chair of the Department of Home Economics. In the early 1960s, he went to Michigan State University as Professor of Food Service Management. He left Michigan State after nine years to devote more time to writing. Dr. Kotschevar served as visiting professor to such schools as the University of Hawaii, the University of Nevada at Las Vegas, Haifa University in Israel, and the Centre International de Glion in Switzerland.

In addition to teaching and writing, Dr. Kotschevar has lectured widely and has served as a consultant to Pope Paul, the Food and Agriculture Organization of the United Nations, and a number of hospitality suppliers. In recognition of his contributions and outstanding service to education, he received the Meek Award from the Council on Hotel, Restaurant and Institutional Education (CHRIE). He is also a diplomate of the Educational Foundation of the National Restaurant Association.

Dr. Ronald F. Cichy is the Director of and a Professor within *The* School of Hospitality Business at Michigan State University. Previously, he was the Director of Educational Services for the Educational Institute of the American Hotel & Lodging Association. Dr. Cichy has also served on the faculties of the University of Denver and Lansing Community College. He has earned a Ph.D. from MSU's Department of Food Science and Human Nutrition, and an MBA and a BA from the university's School of Hotel, Restaurant and Institutional Management.

Dr. Cichy earned the designations of Certified Food and Beverage Executive (CFBE) and Certified Hotel Administrator (CHA) from the Educational Institute in 1983, and the Certified Hospitality Educator (CHE) designation in 1992. In 1996 he was named an Outstanding Alumnus by MSU's

College of Human Ecology. His industry experience includes positions in lodging and food service operations as a hotel manager, food and beverage manager, banquet chef, and sales representative.

Dr. Cichy has written more than 125 articles for food service and lodging audiences. In addition to co-authoring *Food and Beverage Service,* he is the author of *The Spirit of Hospitality* and *Quality Sanitation Management,* and is the co-author, with Dr. Lewis J. Minor, of *Foodservice Systems Management.*

Active professionally, Dr. Cichy is a member of the Educational Institute's Board of Trustees, serves on the Institute's Executive Committee, and is a member of the Institute's Presidents Academy Board of Regents. He is a member of the Board of Directors of the Michigan Restaurant Association and the Michigan Hotel, Motel and Resort Association. He has served as a consultant for lodging and food service operations, and has traveled extensively throughout the United States, Australia, Canada, Europe, and Japan to conduct training programs, present seminars, and participate in conferences.

Chapter 1 Outline

Process of Beverage Service
    Beverage Selection
    Beverage Preparation
    Beverage Service
Types of Beverage Establishments
    Free-Standing Bars and Lounges
    Bars in Restaurants
    Bars in Hotels
    Bars in Other Venues
Types of Beverages
    Malt Beverages
    Spirits
    Liqueurs
    Wines
    Non-Alcoholic Beverages
Beverage Staff Positions
    Beverage Server
    Bartender
    Bar Back
    Beverage Manager
Keys to Success
    The Essentials of Beverage Service
    Responsible Service
    Teamwork

Competencies

1. Outline the process involved in beverage service, describing each of the three main steps. (pp. 3–6)

2. List the types of beverage establishments and distinguish between them. (pp. 6–13)

3. Describe the major types of beverages served in beverage establishments. (pp. 13–15)

4. Identify the major beverage staff positions found in most establishments and their responsibilities. (pp. 15–19)

5. Explain what the keys to success are for any beverage establishment. (pp. 19–20)

1

The Basics of Beverage Service

THE KEY TO BEVERAGE SALES in a beverage establishment is service. The guests expect to be treated in ways that make the experience delightful and memorable. Successful beverage establishments have selected, trained, and retained staff members who are deeply committed to beverage service.

The levels of service bartenders and beverage servers create and deliver depend on their skills, knowledge, and attitudes. They are essential staff members who directly interact with the guests. Beverage product and preparation knowledge, service skills, and an attitude of genuine hospitality all combine to give bartenders and beverage servers opportunities to serve guests and exceed their expectations.

Beverage service is rewarding for the staff members providing the service, since they immediately see how the service positively affects the guests receiving it. Guests welcome beverage service, since receiving service from a professional beverage server or bartender makes guests feel special and helps them enjoy the experience. Beverage service is one of the ways that a beverage establishment generates profits that can be invested in staff wages, improvements for the business, and in the local community.

This chapter covers the process for the service of alcoholic beverages, the types of beverage establishments, the types of beverages, the positions in a beverage establishment, and the keys to success in beverage establishments. It sets the stage for beverage service throughout an establishment.

Process of Beverage Service

The service of beverages, both alcoholic and nonalcoholic, is really part of the larger process that begins with the selection of the beverage based on the needs, wants, and expectations of guests. It is the guests who drive the selection of beverages, and until the selection of beverages is made, no beverages can be prepared and served. Exhibit 1 illustrates the process for beverage service.

Beverage Selection

Beverage selection involves determining which beverages to purchase and offer for sale in the beverage establishment. Beverage selection relies on knowledge of the guests and knowledge of the products. The manager who selects beverages must have knowledge of guests and their beverage needs, wants, and expectations. Some guests have the *need* to experiment by sampling new drinks, while others *need* to order their usual beverage cocktail when they are in a beverage

3

Exhibit 1   Process for the Service of Beverages

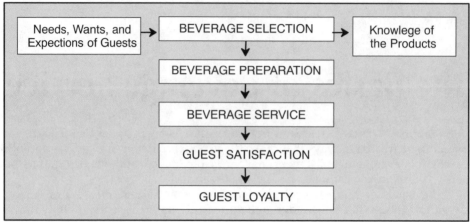

establishment. Other guests *want* their beer served iced, while still other guests *want* to sip a martini on the rocks with two olives and a cocktail onion. Some guests *expect* the beverage server to approach the table and offer a drink refill even before the first beverage is empty, while some other guests *expect* a large selection of wines by the glass to complement the various food courses available on the menu.

Needs, wants, and expectations may vary from guest to guest of the same beverage establishment. For example, one guest of a college bar may enjoy consuming a light beer, while another may order Belvedere vodka on the rocks. Some guests associate beverages with certain activities such as a date, a night out with friends, celebration of a special event, or other relaxing activities. Beverage selections are always made with the guest foremost in mind.

Beverage Preparation

Some say that the difference between simply serving a beverage and creating a memorable experience is in the preparation of the beverage. Think about it. All establishments have basically the same products available from their suppliers, the source of beverage products. That is to say, the manager responsible for purchasing at Lounge A can select the same beverages as the manager's counterpart at Lounge B. In that regard, the products are the same and there is no product differentiation in the minds of the guests. Granted, the staff, décor, service, and guest experiences are likely to differ between the two lounges, but the products are basically the same, given the same manufacturers and suppliers.

So where does the differentiation begin? It begins with product preparation. Product preparation can range from simple to complex, from being completed in a matter of seconds to being done with more flair and being more time consuming.

A simple preparation is opening a bottle of beer. A more complicated process of preparation is opening that same bottle of beer and pouring it into a frosted glass. Someone had to think ahead and place a clean glass in a machine that chills it

Source: Bittersweet Bistro. For more information about this operation, visit the restaurant's Internet site at www.bittersweetbistro.com.

so it becomes frosted. Some cocktails require more time-consuming assembly and mixing of ingredients. Other beverages require the bartender to float certain liqueurs on top of others to arrange them colorfully in a glass. Wines may not require any additional preparation, yet the bottles that they are purchased in still must be opened and many guests like to see certain wine service rituals observed. After-dinner drinks may require specialized glassware (such as a brandy balloon or snifter). Sometimes preparation is done in front of the guest; other times it is done at the bar out of the guests' view. Preparation begins the differentiation of beverages and leads to beverage service.

Beverage Service

Beverage service is the step following beverage preparation. Beverage service is the key to a successful beverage establishment. The ways that you carry out your role as a bartender or beverage server directly affects the satisfaction of the guests and their loyalty. For the most part, the skills necessary to be an effective beverage server or bartender are learned skills that include the ability to keep your composure and deliver delightful service even when the rush of business tries to make you do your tasks efficiently, yet with little regard for guest interaction and satisfaction. Part of the essential skills of beverage service also includes product knowledge so that a consistent product can be consistently served to guests, regardless of who the bartender or server is.

Responsible beverage service requires a thorough knowledge of the legal requirements for serving alcohol with care. Essential parts of these requirements are the techniques for properly checking age identification, as well as intervening when a guest has had too much to drink. An understanding of proper drink recipes and carefully following procedures for not over pouring or under pouring has responsible beverage service implications and also affects guest satisfaction and the establishment's profitability.

In some beverage establishments, bartenders are expected to supervise service staff, including beverage servers. Sometimes this also includes staff training in product knowledge, responsible service, and skills for satisfying guests through the creation and delivery of delightful service. When staff supervision is included in the bartender's responsibilities, an understanding of the proper ways to train, and the knowledge, skills, and behaviors necessary to effectively deliver beverage service are also needed.

Types of Beverage Establishments

There are many ways to categorize beverage establishments, based on the guests that they serve, the location, the setup and layout, and the service styles. Before we do so, consider the changes occurring in the guests that frequent beverage establishments. In general, guests are more sophisticated and they have more disposable income and more mature tastes than in the past. While guests may be consuming lower quantities of alcoholic beverages, they generally do so with premium and super-premium (translated: more expensive) beverages. Champagnes, 100 percent agave tequilas, Irish whiskys, vodka from French grapes single malt Scotch, and single barrel bourbons are very popular with these guests. So, too, guests are ordering cognacs and vintage ports as they view these "small indulgences" as rewards and part of the good life.

Some of the whiskey-based retro drinks (e.g., Manhattan) have resurfaced in popularity to join the martini. When these are made from premium and super-premium brands of whiskey, the guests perceive them as having a higher value. The retro drinks have led the way for retro mixers (e.g., Dr. Pepper, grape juice, root beer, and Squirt) that guests specify as key ingredients in cocktails. Retro drinks are being served in signature glassware in the shapes of fish bowls, cactus, figurines, and other impressive and unique shapes. One establishment features speciality drinks in a plastic goblet glass and a plastic "ice cube" which both glow with a light green. For those who wish to indulge, but not with alcoholic drinks, beverages without alcohol such as designer teas, energy drinks, flavored bottled waters, fruit smoothies, gourmet coffees, and lemonade continue to be popular.

Free-Standing Bars and Lounges

Free-standing bars have always been popular with segments of the guest population.

Gritty McDuff 's Portland Brew Pub

When Gritty's Portland Brew Pub opened in 1988, it became Maine's first brew pub since Prohibition and a leader in the state's microbrew revolution. Since then, locals of every stripe and visitors from around the world have been enjoying fine, small-batch ales brewed on-premise, great pub fare and a real Old World pub atmosphere.

Gritty's Portland Brew Pub is the perfect place to experience the ambience of Portland's Old Port. Our Fore Street location is right in the heart of the historic district.

Pull up a chair at our copper-topped bar, strike up a conversation at our beer hall style tables, or take in street life on the cobblestones of Wharf Street from our basement Brewery Bar patio.We're open everyday and you're always welcome.

Gritty's has become a Maine institution, garnering many awards for Best Bar, Best Brew Pub and Best Beer. Stop in, have a pint and see where the legend began. Cheers!

Gritty McDuff 's Portland Pub Brewery

Gritty's first brewery was designed and manufactured in 1988 by Peter Austin & Partners in Ringwood, Hampshire, England. All subsequent renovations and expansions of our brewery have remained true to the original, classic style of the English pub brewery. The copper-domed, brick faced brew kettle is the showpiece of the brewery and sits in a tiled room behind large viewing windows in our Wharf Street basement brewery bar. The pub brewery produces our five classic ales (Sebago Light, Portland Headlight Pale Ale, McDuff's Best Bitter, Best Brown Ale, Black Fly Stout) and many seasonal ales depending on the time of year. From its inception, our brewery has been producing award-winning ales, and production has grown at a rate of thirty percent per year. We use only the finest hops, English barley malt, and a special English ale yeast and water to produce hand-crafted ales that are all-natural and always fresh.

Source: Gritty McDuff's Brew Pub, Portland, Oregon. For more information visit the operation's Internet site at: www.grittys.com.

Brewpubs started in Colorado and the Pacific Northwest, although their popularity has spread out from there to other regions (i.e., Southeast, Midwest, and Northeast). Brewpubs promote quality craft beer brewed on premises. Brewpubs offer guests an alternative to casual theme restaurants and are perceived as having a more entertaining ambience. The popularity and growth of brewpubs is in part due to guests drinking fewer, but higher quality, beverages. Some brewpubs also distribute their microbrews to other area beverage establishments for sale. One of the keys to longevity in a brew pub is to sell high quality food to complement the beer. While beer may initially attract guests, it is the food that keeps them coming back (and bringing their friends) time and time again.

Cigar bars have been introduced in various venues from arenas to racetracks to stadiums to hotels, as well as in free-standing cigar bars. While some of the popularity has diminished due to government warnings about the potential perils of cigar smoking, cigar aficionados treasure cigar bars where they can relax and enjoy their smoke. Some cigar bars in private clubs maintain member-owned humidors. Many cigar bars feature a large selection of single malt Scotches that appeal to cigar smokers. The Dalmore Cigar Malt was the first single malt Scotch, created in 1998, specifically to complement a premium hand-rolled cigar. Other cigar bars are promoting cognacs specifically blended to accompany a high quality cigar.

Service bars are those that do not serve guests directly, but instead prepare beverages for beverage servers who then deliver them to guests. Service bartenders do not directly prepare beverages for guests. Most beverage establishments have service bars designed to accurately, efficiently, and quickly prepare guests' beverage choices. The key component of a service bar is the design for efficiency and speed. The cocktail station must be correctly configured to assist the bartender's speed and efficiency, including the placement of blender stations (for blended drinks), soda guns (for the quick and easy dispensing of mixers), ice storage chests, easily accessible bottles of spirits stored in "speed rails," glass storage, and the glass-washing area. The health department may also require a hand sink with soap and paper towels next to the glass-washing station. Certain specialty drinks (e.g., ice cream-based drinks) require other specialized equipment in the service bar. Bartenders can help beverage servers set up their trays, thus speeding service. It is important to keep the bar neat and clean because it is easier to operate an organized bar with equipment, products, and supplies in the proper places.

Sports bars feature a sports décor and often a number of televisions tuned to different sporting events. Some sports bars are at stadiums and may be quite strictly regulated in terms of the products (i.e., beer only, beer and wine) that may be sold, as well as whether seating is permitted. Some sports bars have tried to lose the image of burgers-and-beers by offering menus that are more sophisticated, accompanied by rather extensive wine lists. One such sports bar offers wild-game menu items, particularly in colder months, and fresh local ingredients. These bars usually promote their products and services to a much broader market than simply those fans attending a sporting event.

Wine bars are another kind of free-standing bar. The London Wine Bar in San Francisco bills itself as the first wine bar in the United States, but other wine bars have proliferated around the country. Wine bars sell whole bottles of wine, half

Source: Seau's The Restaurant, San Diego, California. For more information about the operation, visit the restaurant's Internet site at: www.seau.com.

bottles, wines by the glass, and tastes of wine in 250- or 500-milliliter decanters. They usually feature dozens of wines by the glass. In some cases, the wines are offered in flights, that is, a selection of different wines in relatively small quantities produced from a certain grape (e.g., Merlot). In many ways, the flight offers a "tour" of the wine world as it features several different wines made from the same grape, yet from different countries. Two of the keys to a successful wine bar are the careful care of opened bottles of wine, and the knowledge of the staff. Once opened, a bottle of wine must be kept cool; inert gas should be sprayed inside the bottle to displace the oxygen that rapidly deteriorates the wine. Beverage servers should be trained to promote wines by the glass from bottles that are already open. Some wine bars offer free splashes of wine so guests can decide for themselves whether to order a full glass of the wine. The overall goal of wine bars is to make wine fun and approachable for guests. The successful wine bars do not simply rely on wines; they also promote high quality food items and are usually known for their delightful service. These wine bars offer two or three wines to pair with each menu item from appetizers to desserts.

Bars in Restaurants

Bars in restaurants add to the profitability of the overall business. Compared to food products, on average, beverage products have relatively low inventory costs (on a per unit basis) and less labor requirements to produce and serve in the operation. Casual dining restaurants with bars continue to market their beverages to boost sales and guest satisfaction. Some offer large selections in bound drink menus as thick as textbooks. Others offer wine samples to guests who are waiting to be seated in the dining room. Still others have dramatically increased

Source: 750 ml Bistro and Wine Bar, Portland, Oregon. For more information, visit the operation's Internet site at www.750-ml.com.

their selections of wines, particularly wines available by the glass, and offer suggestions for wine and food pairings on the menu. One such establishment promotes a two-hour island vacation by coupling food and beverages to encourage guests to take a mini-getaway without having to pack their luggage and board an airplane.

Sometimes restaurants offer a different menu in the bar. These menus are designed to encourage guests to eat and drink. A bar menu may contain a selection of the same items found on the restaurant menu, yet in smaller portions with different sauces or different presentations. For example, a shrimp martini may be featured on a bar menu instead of the shrimp cocktail on the restaurant menu. Guests waiting for a table in the restaurant may enjoy an appetizer with their drink in the bar. Other guests may simply want to eat a full meal made up of two or three bar menu selections. When bar menus are focused on appetizers, it encourages guests to make multiple orders of menu items. Usually the average check is higher because the guests drink more in the bar, sometimes stimulated by the increased spices used in bar menu items. Bars in restaurants also usually have a less formal environment that appeals to younger, hipper, more casual guests. The

Source: Great Slates, an entertainment restaurant and bar in Cambridge, Maryland, offering live music, billiards, and state-of-the-art video games. For more information about this operation, visit the restaurant's Internet site at: www.cweb5.com/greatslates.

menu items may be priced lower due to the reduced portion size and this may attract younger guests than the restaurant does.

Often when wine selections are increased, the restaurant offers wine flights, a sampling of small pours of a selection of wines for a very reasonable price. Still other restaurant bars have added signature drinks (e.g., margarita) and are selling them in larger glassware that increases the size and the price of the drink. Some bars in restaurants have intentionally been redesigned to locate the bar off to the side of the restaurant, giving the feel of an intimate, separate bar room that appeals to those who simply want to enjoy a cocktail after work. This design also is appealing to families who may not want to see the bar as the focal point when they first walk into a restaurant.

Bars in restaurants, hotels, and clubs may be either public bars or private bars. Public bars are those where the guest may approach, order a drink, and pay for the drink either with cash, credit card, or a guestroom charge. Private bars, on the other hand, are not for use by the general public. Private bars are usually arranged and underwritten by the host of a group (e.g., meeting, wedding, other private banquet) and only invited guests are permitted to use the services of the private bar. Sometimes these guests have to pay for their own drinks. Other times the guests' drinks are charged to a master account that is later paid by the host.

Source: Nedley's Restaurant & Sports Bar, Richardson, Texas. For more information about the operation, visit the Internet site at www.nedleys.com.

Bars in Hotels

Hotel bars have undergone a transformation due to their historic lack of profitability, proliferation of liability issues, and the increasing challenges in finding and retaining qualified beverage servers. Some hotel bars, however, run counter to this trend. These successful establishments have boosted their profitability by expanding drink menus, adding innovative food selections, and using compelling promotions to attract both hotel and local guests. The secret to a successful hotel bar is to establish a separate identity around an attractive theme. At the Hard Rock Hotel in Chicago, the theme is focused on rock music and rock groups.

Hotel bars that have made the transition identify carefully guest requirements in the form of their needs, wants, and expectations. Then they undergo an assessment of the bar's foodservice menus, food and beverage pricing strategies, drinks promoted, operating hours, and whether entertainment is needed. A good source from which to begin gathering this information is the hotel bar's staff, those who interact regularly with guests in the bar. Staff members can help improve the products and services offered in the hotel bar and when they are involved, they will be more likely to recommend the hotel's beverage operations when or before a guest asks.

Fundamentally, a hotel bar must offer value, based on the products, services, and pricing. And this value must be in the eyes of the guests and the staff alike.

Friendly and courteous well-trained beverage service staff members are critically important to providing memorable service experiences in a hotel bar. Sometimes, wineries or beer manufacturers are interested in participating in joint promotions with hotel bars. These promotions can offer additional value and interest to guests.

Hotel bars that have transformed themselves into trendy gathering places have seen bar profit margins soar. When viewed as other than a necessary amenity, a hotel bar can change its image to a feeling of the guest's "living room" where guests are encouraged to gather. Sometimes outside food and beverage operators own or manage these hot spots. The hotel must be careful in that case to make sure hotel guests continue to receive superior guest service.

Bars in Other Venues

Beverage establishments are, of course, in other venues such as private clubs and on cruise ships. Private clubs are for use by members and their guests. Sometimes the bars and lounges in private clubs give away appetizers in the hope of attracting more members to the bar or lounge who then purchase alcoholic beverages. Sometimes portable bars are driven to certain holes on a golf course during a tournament. Cruise ships often have bars throughout the vessel, and may even have a bar in the swimming pool that guests swim up to and enjoy the cocktail of their choice.

Types of Beverages

The types of beverages offered for sale in a beverage establishment are fundamentally determined by the guests' needs, wants, and expectations. The broad categories include malt beverages, spirits, liqueurs, wines, and non-alcoholic beverages.

Malt Beverages

Malt beverages contain 0.5 percent or more of alcohol, are brewed or produced from malt, wholly or in part, and include beers, ales, stouts, and porters, as well as bock and sake. These beverages have malt barley as a main ingredient. Malt beverage ingredients also include hops, water, yeast, adjuncts (e.g., corn, rice, wheat, soybean flakes, potato starch, and/or sugar), and additives (e.g., preservatives and/or enzymes). **Beers** may be:

- Pilsner: a light rich, and mellow lager

- Bavarian: light in body and darker than pilsner

- Dortmunder: dark color and full body

- Malt liquor: more pronounced malt flavor and slightly darker than regular beer

- Steam beer: high carbon dioxide content and a creamy foam

Ale contains more hops than beers, giving it a characteristic bitter taste. Porter is produced from malt roasted at high temperatures. Stout is higher in alcohol content with a more "hop-like" taste than porter. Bock is a German beer that is richer, darker, and higher in alcohol content than regular 3.2 percent beer. Sake is produced from rice. Near beers are non-alcoholic beverages produced with the same ingredients; however, the alcohol is removed prior to bottling.

Spirits

Spirits are alcoholic beverages that contain a significant amount of distilled ethanol. The five major groups of spirits are grain, plant, fruit liquors, liqueurs, and bitters. Whiskeys, vodka, grain neutral spirits, and compounded liquors such as aquavit and gin are produced from grains. Flavored vodka options are available today as stand-alone drinks or for use in cocktails. Apple, citrus, cranberry, peach, pepper, raspberry, tangerine, and vanilla vodkas are all choices today. While some flavored spirits are purchased from manufacturers, others are made-from-scratch fruit infusions. Whiskeys include Scotch whisky and American whiskeys (bourbon, rye, corn whiskey). The major plant liquors are rum and tequila. The most important fruit liquors are brandies. Highly flavored spirits containing bitter substances such as quinine are aromatic or fruit bitters.

Liqueurs

Liqueurs are also known as cordials. Cordials and liqueurs are produced from grains, plants, or fruit spirits, or a combination. They are compounded spirits flavored with a variety of substances including coffee, fruits, herbs, licorice, mint, and spices. The basic ingredients, processing methods, and the amounts and quality of the added flavorings directly affect the flavor of the finished liqueur. Most liqueurs are produced from grain neutral spirits. All liqueurs are aged so the flavor develops. Cordials are either added as ingredients when producing blended drinks (e.g., Triple Sec added to a margarita) or they are consumed as is, usually at the end of the meal. Spirits and cordials are being combined into drinks that feature a rainbow of colors. When exotic and dramatic garnishes are added, the potential to increase beverage revenues and profits rises. Retro drinks, such as mai tais and grasshoppers, are also being introduced to a new generation of guests.

Wines

Wines are produced by fermenting grapes. The basic wine classifications include table wines, natural and fortified wines, aperitif and dessert wines, and sparkling wines. **Table wines** are the largest category and are suitable to accompany food. They may be further classified based on color as red, white, or rosé. **Natural wines** include most table wines because the product is the result of grape fermentation without the addition of alcohol or sugar. In contrast, **fortified wines** have alcohol, usually in the form of a brandy distilled from wine and added during fermentation. This produces a sweeter wine higher in alcohol content. **Aperitif wines** are fortified, flavored with herb ingredients, and are usually served before a meal as an appetizer or cocktail. **Dessert wines** are fortified and are served following a meal as dessert or with dessert. **Sparkling wines** are usually produced by fermenting them a second time and trapping the resulting carbon dioxide gas which adds the appealing effervescent bubbles.

Some beverage operators are promoting "undiscovered gems," that is, unknown wines from little known, unheralded wine growing areas across the United States. These handcrafted, vibrant wines from younger American producers represent great value for guests, as well as the beverage establishment. Guests are also ordering more wines from around the world, for example merlots from Australia. Other guests are willing to experiment and try new wines that offer value.

Wines by the glass give the guest a higher perceived value provided that the wines are fairly priced. Some believe that the price of a glass of wine should not exceed the price of a premium beer. Some beverage establishments are featuring super-premium wines by the glass at remarkably low prices. Wine flights featuring 2-ounce pours of a number of samples encourage the guests to experiment with expensive wines that they may not choose to purchase by the bottle. Half bottles of wine are becoming a more popular option since they permit two guests to pair two or three wines with two or three separate food courses, as well as enjoying a variety of wines without over-consuming alcohol. Guests today are more often ordering the softer, easier to drink wines that match well with food menu items, particularly fresh fish, in casual-dining establishments.

Another wine option is to develop and feature private-label wine selections, capitalizing on the power of the establishment's brand. These proprietary labels bear the visible and exclusive stamp of the beverage establishment in which they are being sold. The advantages to doing so include marketing opportunities, pricing freedom, enhanced perception of the brand by the guests, and the guests' perception that the wine is special and exclusive since they can only obtain it at the beverage establishment with the name on the brand. An example of the copy of the proprietary wine label resulting from a collaborative effort on the part of the Musser Family of Grand Hotel on Mackinac Island, Michigan and the Trinchero Family of Napa Valley, California is presented in Exhibit 2.

To effectively add value to the guests' experience, the private-label wines must be priced within the "comfort zone" of the guests. Guests who believe that the proprietary wines are too pricey, that is they do not represent value, simply will not order them.

Non-Alcoholic Beverages

Non-alcoholic beverages include designer teas, energy drinks, flavored bottled waters, fruit smoothies, gourmet coffees, and lemonade among others. Fresh fruit and herbal sodas are popular summertime non-alcoholic beverage options. Alcohol-free refreshers such as ginger lemon, cherry, lemon verbena, passion fruit chili, and tarragon flavors are more appealing choices than iced tea. They are usually produced by combining natural herb and fruit concentrates with sugar, resulting in a drink base that is added to soda when the drink is prepared immediately prior to service.

Beverage Staff Positions

While the number of beverage staff positions varies among establishments, there are common job skills for the positions of beverage server and bartender. Most

Exhibit 2   Proprietary Wine Label from Grand Hotel, Mackinac Island, Michigan

Front of the label

The Trincheros of Trinchero Family Estates and the Musser Family of Grand Hotel together present this distinctive private label vintage bottled exclusively for Grand Hotel. Crafted from grapes grown in California's cool coastal climates, this distinctive collaboration proudly boasts the heritage and time-honored traditions of both families.

TRINCHERO   1999
Grand Hotel   Estate Bottled
                  Petit Verdot
                  Napa Valley

Back of the label

Welcome to the Wine Cellars of Grand Hotel. Each year Grand Hotel Chef Hans Burtscher and I research, study or taste over 500 wines from the world over, searching for the finest. A few of the wines we find are of such exceptional quality and value that we have them specifically bottled under our name through Grand hotel Cellars. Hopefully you will enjoy these wines, as we believe they are reflections of the standards we have set for all aspects of Grand Hotel.

Produced & Bottled by   (signed)
Trinchero Family Estates   R. D. Musser III
St. Helena, Napa County, CA 94574   President

establishments list these job skills in a job breakdown for each position, along with a list of equipment and supplies needed to perform the task, the steps to perform the task, and how-to's and tips to perform the task both efficiently and effectively.

Beverage Server

The beverage server is the staff member who takes and serves guests' beverage orders. Since the beverage server is the staff member who most frequently interacts directly with guests in a beverage establishment, the beverage server in many ways most directly influences whether the guests truly enjoy the experience and become satisfied, or have a rotten experience and leave vowing to never return. The beverage server must do everything possible, within reason, to make each guest's experience exactly as the guest wants it to be. And whenever possible, the beverage server should exceed the guest's expectations.

Beverage servers are responsible for:

- Preparing for service

- Greeting guests

- Taking the order

- Serving the order

- Creating a friendly atmosphere where guests can enjoy themselves

- Closely monitoring guest alcohol consumption
- Completing service
- Helping co-workers as needed

It is important that beverage servers view themselves as part of a team in the establishment. Other team members may include bartenders, kitchen staff, bus persons, and supervisors. By working together as a team, all can contribute to positive guest experiences. In addition to teamwork, beverage servers are responsible for serving alcohol with care, helping to keep the bar area and tables clean, being certain that glassware is clean and free from chips and cracks, serving each beverage in a clean glass, being familiar with the food menu (if applicable), acknowledging guests soon after they are seated, greeting guests warmly, delivering the guests' orders promptly, demonstrating professional behavior, and adhering to other performance standards as specified by the management of their particular beverage establishment.

Beverage servers encourage guests to buy beverage and food products through suggestive selling or upselling. Suggestive selling includes the suggestion of an appetizer to go with a beverage. Upselling occurs when a beverage server encourages a guest to purchase a call brand spirit, say a Bombay Sapphire gin martini, rather than a martini made from a house brand of gin. It is essential that beverage servers know standard drink ingredients and garnishes if they are to upsell and provide superior service.

Beverage servers must also understand the special terms for equipment used in bars, as well as the right glass for each beverage. Sometimes, beverage servers are also required to know correct china, silverware, linens and napkin folding, depending on the extent and variety of food products available to the guests.

Bartender

Just like beverage servers, bartenders may interact directly with guests. Bartenders prepare and serve drinks to bar guests, and sometimes serve food as well. Bartenders also prepare beverages for beverage servers to deliver to their guests. As service professionals, bartenders are responsible for:

- Monitoring guests' alcohol consumption
- Controlling alcohol risks effectively
- Ensuring that drinks are prepared consistently and to quality standards every time
- Knowing how to use bar equipment efficiently and safely
- Helping control waste and costs
- Maintaining bar sanitation
- Preparing drinks promptly
- Accommodating taste preferences of individual guests

- Making drinks look attractive

- Promoting the establishment's facilities

Experienced bartenders usually also help train new bartenders and beverage servers. They may also test new drink recipes.

Just like other beverage professionals, bartenders are responsible for working as a team with their associates. Together, the team delivers superior service to guests. Many of the performance standards for bartenders are the same as those for beverage servers. Additionally, bartenders are responsible for serving alcohol with care as specified by state and local regulations, controlling keys to limited access areas (e.g., cash bank, alcohol storerooms), upselling and suggestive selling, understanding the terms and uses for bar equipment, knowing how to develop and test a beverage recipe, being able to convert beverage recipes to prepare batches of the beverages, knowing the standard setup for a portable bar for banquets and receptions, and adhering to other performance standards as specified by their particular beverage establishment. Some bartenders are also required to maintain the par stock system. Par is the number of each of the supplies needed to get through one work shift.

Bar Back

The bar back is a position in larger beverage establishments that assists bartenders with replenishing products and supplies during busy periods, and maintaining the cleanliness of the bar and equipment. Usually bar backs are found in higher volume establishments. A bar back's duties vary but may include the filling of ice chests, helping with opening sidework, cutting of fruits and vegetables for drink garnishes, washing bar glassware and utensils, replacing empty draft beer kegs with full kegs, restocking bottled beer in coolers in the bar area, restocking other alcoholic beverages and bar supplies, taking dirty dishes or glassware to the kitchen dishwashing area, assisting the bartender in setting up service bars and portable bars for banquets and catered events, emptying trash containers behind the bar, cleaning bar areas, and sweeping, mopping, and vacuuming. The bar back assists the bartender so the bartender can focus on the primary responsibilities of preparing beverages, controlling cash, and interacting with guests.

Beverage Manager

The beverage manager, like other beverage professionals, is fundamentally responsible for exceeding guests' expectations. Effective beverage managers realize that they are not the primary person responsible for creating and delivering superior guest service in the beverage establishment. Rather, it is those who more frequently come into contact with guests, such as beverage servers and bartenders, who more directly influence the guests' experiences in the beverage establishment. Effective beverage managers, then, see their main role as one of assisting and facilitating the development of others, so that these others can create and deliver memorable service.

Just like beverage servers and bartenders, beverage managers are encouraged to interact directly and regularly with guests. This interaction gives beverage managers a sense of:

- Who are the guests?

- What are their requirements?

- How are we doing, individually and collectively, in meeting those requirements?

- What needs to change to better meet the requirements?

As service professionals, beverage managers are responsible for:

- Developing and training beverage staff members (including beverage servers, bartenders, and bar backs) to understand the skills, knowledge, and behaviors essential for superior guest service

- Supervising other beverage service professionals

- Scheduling other beverage service professionals

- Monitoring guests' alcohol consumption

- Controlling alcohol risks effectively

- Controlling cash, charge cards, costs, and inventory

- Monitoring payroll records

- Establishing standard recipes for beverages to be prepared consistently and based on established quality standards every time

- Knowing how to use bar equipment efficiently and safely

- Establishing procedures for controlling waste

- Establishing and monitoring bar sanitation standards

Beverage managers often help train new bartenders and beverage servers. They may also test new drink recipes.

Just as other beverage professionals, beverage managers must work as a team with others. Effective beverage managers set the team spirit in the establishment by modeling the behavior that is desired in other team members.

Keys to Success

The keys to success in a beverage establishment are an understanding of the essentials of service, serving alcoholic beverages responsibly, and teamwork.

The Essentials of Beverage Service

Beverage service essentials focus on understanding the needs, wants, and expectations of the guests. Once these are understood, a beverage professional can anticipate them and take action to satisfy the guests before the guests have to ask. This is called anticipatory service and it is found in the way that guests are treated in organizations that truly value guest service, guest satisfaction, and guest loyalty.

Anticipatory service includes greeting the guest with a smile and a warm welcome as soon as the guest is seated. Some establishments have a standard greeting time of 60 seconds or less. Then the guest is informed of the specials of the day. During this interaction, the goal is to determine the guests' needs, wants, and expectations. Sometimes, despite a professional's best efforts, guests are unhappy. When guests are dissatisfied, it is essential that staff members listen to them, apologize, take appropriate action to eliminate the source of dissatisfaction, and thank the guest.

Responsible Service

Responsible beverage service includes monitoring guests' alcohol consumption and controlling alcohol risks effectively. Controlling risks means asking for and carefully checking identifications from all guests who look like they are under the age of 30, monitoring alcohol consumption of guests and changes in guests' behavior, and intervening when necessary if a guest becomes intoxicated.

Teamwork

Teamwork in a beverage establishment is critical to the delivery of delightful service for guests. Effective team members understand that they are responsible for giving both guests *and* associates superior service. Excellent team players help their co-workers and guests whenever possible, and ask associates for help when needed so guest service doesn't suffer, and all staff members can focus on guests' needs. Effective team members also say "hello" to guests and associates, use their names when they greet them, and say "please" and "thank you" to guests and co-workers. They also share supplies, always clean up after themselves, and take pride in their work.

Excellent team players think about the effect that they have on other departments in the establishment. They turn in food orders promptly to the kitchen to prevent last-minute rushing for everyone involved. They also pick up orders in the kitchen promptly when they are prepared to avoid quality deterioration and backlogs. They report repairs to the appropriate department (e.g., engineering in a hotel) using the correct forms. And they provide the same superior service to associates (your internal customers) that is provided to guests.

References

Battaglia, Andy. "Raising the Bar: Casual Chains Uncork New Beverage Tactics." *Nation's Restaurant News.* May 1, 2000. 34(18): 53.

Bertagnoli, Lisa. "Raising the Bar." *Restaurants & Institutions.* April 1, 2001. 111(9): 97.

Bounds, Wendy and Higgins, Michelle. "She's Stepping on my Spreadsheet—Hotel Bars, Once Serene Spots to Conduct Business, Turn Boisterous—and Profitable." *The Wall Street Journal.* January 21, 2000. p. B.1.

Bryant, Katherine. "Exclusively Yours." *Restaurant Business.* August 15, 2003. 102(13): 28, 30, 34.

Durocher, Joseph. "Lounge Acts." *Restaurant Business.* August 10, 1993. 92(12): 182.

Gaiter, Dorothy J. and Brecher, John. "Tastings: Wine Bars Get Another Round—Chic in the 1970s, They're the New Thing Again; Touring the World for $8." *The Wall Street Journal.* May 16, 2003. p. W.6.

O'Brien, Tim. "Sports Bars Added at Texas Stadium; Sheriff Baylock's Chili a Huge Hit." *Amusement Business.* June 15, 1998. 110(24): 17.

Plotkin, Robert. "Bar Management 101." *Restaurant Hospitality.* July 1990. 74(7): 158, 160, 162.

Plotkin, Robert. "Bar Management: New Millennium Trends." *Restaurant Hospitality.* September 1999. 83(9): 83.

Scarpa, James. "Bottle Rockets." *Restaurant Business.* August 15, 2003. 102(13): 22, 26.

Scarpa, James. "Clearly Flavorful." *Restaurant Business.* August 15, 2003. 102(13): 76, 78.

Schaffer, Athena. "Venues Find Cigar Bar Trend More Than a Passing Fad." *Amusement Business.* September 10, 2001. 113(36): 15.

Sheridan, Margaret. "Rainbows by the Glass." *Restaurants & Institutions.* November 1, 2001. 111(26): 89.

Walkup, Carolyn. "Brewpub Popularity Hops Across the US." *Nation's Restaurant News.* August 28, 1995. 29(34): 3.

Walkup, Carolyn. "Operators Decant Wine Bars to Tap Savvy Clientele." *Nation's Restaurant News.* February 21, 2001. 35(7): 1.

Walkup, Carolyn. "Upscale Outpost Scores Amid Neighborhood Sports Bars." *Nation's Restaurant News.* July 7, 2002. 37(27): 20.

Warner, Grace. "The Hotel Bar." *Lodging Hospitality.* December 1993. 49(13): 55.

Key Terms

ale—A malt beverage with more hops than beers. It has a bitter taste.

aperitif wines—Wines that are fortified, flavored with herb ingredients, and are usually served before a meal as an appetizer or cocktail.

beer—A drink brewed from malt as a main ingredient.

beverage selection—The process of determining which beverages to purchase and offer for sale in an establishment.

bock—A German beer that is richer, darker, and higher in alcohol content that regular beer.

brewpubs—Establishments that brew craft beers on the premises and serve them, usually with a selection of high quality food.

cigar bars—Bars in which cigar aficionados can smoke cigars and drink beverages that complement the cigars.

dessert wine—Wine that is fortified and served following a meal as dessert or with dessert.

fortified wines—Wines that have alcohol added during fermentation.

liqueurs—A compounded spirit produced from grains, plants, or fruit spirits and flavored with a variety of substances.

natural wines—Wine that results from grape fermentation with the addition of alcohol or sugar.

near beer—A non-alcoholic beverage that is made the way beer is but the alcohol is removed before it is bottled.

porter—A drink produced from malt roasted at high temperatures.

sake—a malt beverage brewed from rice.

service bars—Stations at which service bartenders prepare drinks for beverage servers to take to guests.

sparkling wines—Wines that are fermented a second time and the resulting carbon dioxide gas is trapped inside.

spirits—Alcoholic beverages that contain a significant amount of distilled ethanol.

sports bar—Establishment featuring a sports décor and televisions.

stout—A malt beverage with a hop-like taste that is high in alcohol content.

table wines—Wines that are suitable to accompany food. May include red, white, or rose.

wine bar—A free-standing bar that sells whole bottles of wine half bottles, wines by the glass, and tastes of wine.

Review Questions

1. What are the steps in the beverage service process?
2. What types of establishments are classified as free-standing bars and lounges?
3. What type of transformation have hotel bars undergone in the past several years?
4. What are three types of malt beverages?
5. What is a spirit?
6. What are liqueurs made of?
7. What are the basic classifications of wine?
8. What type of non-alcoholic beverages are growing in popularity in beverage establishments?
9. What are four key staff positions in a beverage establishment?
10. What are the keys to success for a beverage establishment?

Internet Sites

For more information, visit the following Internet sites. Remember that Internet addresses can change without notice. If the site is no longer there, you can use a search engine to look for additional sites. Many alcohol-related sites require users to be of legal drinking age to enter.

Adams Beverage Group
www.beveragenet.net/links/links.asp

All Drinks List
www.alldrink.com/

Bartender Zone
www.bartenderzone.com/

Coffee Universe
www.coffeeuniverse.com/

Happy Hours
www.happyhours.com/

Hotel Resource
www.hotelresource.com/

Just Drinks
www.just-drinks.com/index.asp?c=1

Sante Magazine: The Magazine for Restaurant Professionals
www.santemagazine.com/

Silver Spirits Monthly
www.silver-spirits.com/

Wine.com
www.wine.com/

Chapter 2 Outline

Types and Forms of Alcohol
    Beer
    Spirits
    Wine
    House Brands and Call Brands
    Standard Drink Abbreviations
    Standard Drink Ingredients and
        Garnishes
Tools of the Beverage Service Trade
    Bar and Lounge Equipment Terms
    Glassware, China, and Silverware
    Linens and Napkin Folding
Beverage Requisition/Issue
    Establishing Bar Par Inventory Levels
    Beverage Issuing Steps
    Bottle Marking
    Additional Concerns for Beverage
        Control
Safety and Security for Servers
    Kitchen Safety
    OSHA Regulations
    Heimlich Maneuver and First Aid
    Sanitation
    Health Department Regulations
Making an Establishment Work: Policies
    and Procedures
    Last Call
    Restaurant Menus
    Point-of-Sale Equipment
    Tipping Policies
    Par Stock System
    Telephone Courtesy and Reservations

Competencies

1. Identify the types of alcohol commonly served at beverage establishments. (pp. 25–31)

2. Explain how establishments standardize brands, abbreviations, and recipes for drinks. (pp. 31–35)

3. List the tools needed for excellent beverage service. (pp. 35–41)

4. Describe the steps establishments take to ensure safety and security for their staff members and guests. (pp. 41–45)

5. Identify how policies on such things as last call, menus, tipping, point-of-sale systems, par stock levels, and telephone courtesy help an establishment run more effectively. (pp. 45–51)

2

Beverage Service Operations

THE ALCOHOLIC PRODUCT alone constitutes only part of the beverage experience that guests seek when they come to a beverage establishment. The service—the human contact, how a drink is poured, the condition of the glasses, and the knowledge of a server—is an equally important part of the beverage experience that guests expect. These service expectations can be met only with well-trained and talented servers who understand the beverages served, the tools of the trade, how to work safely, and how to deliver excellent service.

This chapter focuses on the knowledge that front-line beverage servers need, whether they are bartenders, servers, or beverage supervisors. It explains the primary types of alcoholic beverages served in establishments—beer, spirits and wine. It also explains how establishments categorize beverages and how staff members communicate orders to each other. It then goes on to explain important equipment terms, define the types of glassware and silverware often used, and briefly explains how different napkin folds can enhance the experience a guest has in an establishment.

Safety and security are also major concerns for anyone who serves alcohol. Servers and bartenders must be aware of things which threaten the safety of guests, themselves, and the establishment—whether it be through overconsumption of alcohol, sanitation risks, accidents or illness, or chemical hazards.

Finally, the chapter will address some of the policies that various establishments might enact regarding last call, their menus, the point-of-sale equipment, tipping, the par stock system, and telephone courtesy.

All of this knowledge makes up the basic foundation that anyone serving alcohol in a beverage establishment needs to know.

Types and Forms of Alcohol

While the intricacies of content, price, and packaging may be the realm of knowledge for alcohol manufacturers, purchasers, and establishment owners, those who serve alcohol must also possess a hefty amount of knowledge about the beverages they serve. Bartenders and beverage servers make recommendations, answer guest questions, and keep track of the amount of alcohol consumed and how it contributes to intoxication levels. They must know such details as a 12-ounce glass of beer, a 4-ounce glass of wine, and a 1-ounce serving of 100-proof liquor all have approximately the same amount of pure alcohol (see Exhibit 1).

Bartenders and servers need to learn the basic types of alcohol and what the difference is between such common beverages as beer, wine, and distilled spirits.

Exhibit 1   Alcohol Equivalencies

The following beverages have almost exactly the same percentage of alcohol:

| 12 oz. of beer | 4 oz. of wine | 1 ¼ oz. of 80-proof liquor | 1 oz. of 100-proof liquor |

Typically, each of these equals one standard drink and contains approximately one-half ounce of alcohol.

They also need to understand the difference between house and call brands, standard drink abbreviations, and standard drink ingredients and garnishes.

Alcoholic beverages are an important part of most restaurants' and lounges' service. They can bring in a lot of profit, and they can make guests' dining experiences more enjoyable. An alcoholic beverage is a drink that has 0.5 percent or more alcohol content. The amount of alcohol in a beverage is measured by **proof.** Proof is double the percentage of alcohol in the beverage. For example, a drink that is 40 percent alcohol is measured as 80 proof. This use can be traced back to early days when the "proof" of a whiskey used in barter was to mix it with gunpowder to see if it contained enough alcohol to burn.

There are three general types of alcoholic beverages: beer, spirits (also known as liquor), and wine.

Beer

Beer is a beverage made from fermented grain. It has the lowest alcohol content, the highest food value, and the shortest life span of the three types of alcoholic beverages. There are two class of beer: ale, which is top-fermented at warmer temperatures and not aged, and lager, which is bottom-fermented and aged at colder temperatures.

Other beer terms that beverage servers and bartenders need to know are:

Draft beer: Beer drawn from a keg or a cask to a glass.

Dry beer: Beer that is less sweet, with little or no aftertaste.

Light beer: Beer with one-third to one-half fewer calories than regular beer.

Nonalcoholic beer: Beer with few calories and less than 0.5 percent alcohol. The alcohol is removed after brewing, or the fermentation process is stopped before alcohol forms.

Exhibit 2   2001 Beer Consumption

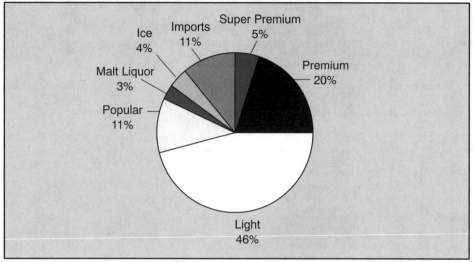

Source: Cheers, Adams Beverage Research Group. For more information, visit the company's Internet site at www.beveragenet.net/home.asp.

Head: The foam that forms at the top of a glass when beer is poured. The ideal head on a beer should be one-half to one-inch thick.

Keg: An aluminum or wooden container for storing beer.

Tap: A beer faucet used to pour beer from a keg, or the process used to set up a beer keg for service.

There are many different categories of beer. Exhibit 2 shows the 2001 beer consumption of consumers in the United States. Some additional types of beers that might be served at an establishment include:

- Bock beer
- Malt liquor
- Pilsner
- Porter
- Stout
- Ice beer

Operations that offer specialty beers must make sure that the servers know the style, origin, and unique characteristics of each beer, along with which foods they best complement. Beer suppliers are a good source of information for training programs. Beer sales can increase when servers are well trained and are given incentives to sell more beer. Exhibit 3 shows BeerMaster, an Australian course available online or over the Internet that was designed for beer services.

Exhibit 3   BeerMaster

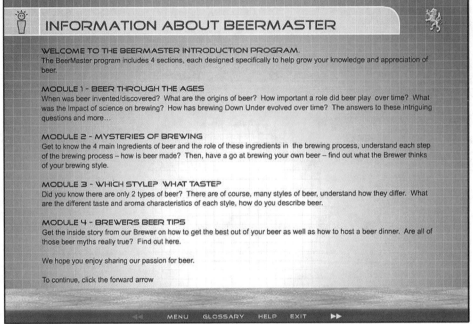

Source: BeerMaster. For more information, visit the Internet site at www.beermaster.com.au/.

Spirits

Distilled **spirits** are any alcoholic beverage that is made by distillation rather than fermentation. Both beers and wines are made through fermentation. All spirits start out colorless and completely clear, their browns and other hues show up in the aging process.

According to the Distilled Spirits Council of the United States there are currently more than 4,000 brands of distilled spirits on the market in the United States. These spirits contribute more than $26.9 billion in economic activity and more than 530,000 jobs to the U.S. economy.

Spirits differ depending on what they are made from and what flavorings are added. For example, brandy is made from fruit; rum is made from sugar cane or molasses; and gin is made from grain and flavored with juniper berries. Spirits have the highest alcohol content of the three types of alcoholic beverages. Some common types of spirits are:

- Gin—a colorless spirit made by distilling or redistilling rye or other grain spirits and adding juniper berries or aromatics as flavoring.

- Vodka—originally distilled from fermented wheat mash, but now also made from a mash of rye, corn, or potatoes. Vodka has been the largest selling distilled spirit in the United States for more than 25 years, and one in every four alcoholic drinks consumed in the world is vodka or vodka-based.

- Rum—distilled from cane juice, or from the scummings of the boiled juice, or from treacle or molasses.

- Brandy—distilled from wine or fermented fruit juice.

- Tequila—distilled from the fermented juice of the plant Agave tequilana.

- Whiskey—distilled from grain, potatoes, or corn.

There are many types of whiskey, which is made from grain. The type of whiskey depends on the grain used. **Straight whiskeys** are made from only one kind of grain; **blended whiskeys** are made from a combination of straight whiskeys.
     Some of the most popular whiskeys are:

- Bourbon: American whiskey made from corn.

- Irish whiskey: Whiskey made in Ireland from barley.

- Rye: Whiskey made from rye.

- Scotch: Single or blended whiskey from Scotland.

     Some other spirits that an establishment might carry are:

Bitters: Spirits flavored with herbs, bark, roots, and other cogeners (flavorings). Bitters are usually used as a cocktail ingredient.

Cognac: The most prestigious blend of brandy.

Liqueur or cordial: Spirits redistilled with fruits, flowers, or plants, or their juices or extracts. They are usually sweet, with a high alcohol content.

Schnapps: In Europe, an herb-flavored dry spirit. In the United States, a sweet, usually fruit-favored liqueur.

Sherry: A dessert wine with grape brandy added.

Spirits are especially popular in many establishments because they are used to make mixed drinks, or cocktails. For example, a martini marries gin and vermouth and is typically garnished with an olive. A Long Island Ice Tea mixes equal parts of vodka, tequila, rum, gin, and triple sec with sweet and sour mix and cola. Exhibit 4 gives a sample cocktail recipe.
     Cocktails give bartenders a chance to indulge their artistic nature once they learn basic bartending skills such as shaking, straining, stirring, muddling, blending, building, and layering.

Wine

Wine appreciation is an ancient art. Many guests may know a great deal about wine while others are interested in learning more. Therefore, beverage service staff need to know the basics of wine service.
     Wine is made from fermented grapes, other fruits, or flowers, and is usually classified according to color. Red wines have a purple color and are served at a cool room temperature. White wines have a pale color ranging from straw to gold and are served chilled. Blush wines (roses) are pink and are served chilled. These

Exhibit 4   Cocktail Recipe

A perennial favorite for summer is ice tea. The Whiskey Tea Smash is a very simple recipe, and weighs in at around 160 calories! Brew some of your favorite tea and then chill for a personal touch.

Recipe

Ingredients: 1$^1/_2$ oz. Bourbon, $^1/_2$ oz. Simple Syrup, 3 oz. iced tea, 2 pieces of ripe peach and 2 wedges of lemon.

Preparation: Muddle (or mash) a piece of peach and a wedge of lemon with the $^1/_2$ oz. simple syrup in the bottom of a mixing glass. Add 1$^1/_2$ oz. Bourbon and 3 oz. iced tea and shake well with ice. Strain the drink into a rock glass filled with ice. Garnish with a slice of peach and a lemon wedge.

Source: Distilled Spirits Council of the United States. For more information, visit the Internet site at www.discus.org/.

Exhibit 5   Wine Temperatures

Serving Temperatures

Wine Type	°F	°C
Sparkling Wine	42–54	6–10
Rosé Wine	48–54	9–12
White Wine	48–58	9–14
Sherry (Light)	48–58	9–14
Red Wine	57–68	13–20
Fortified Wine	57–68	13–20
Sherry (Dark)	57–68	13–20

For more information, visit the Internet site at www.tasting-wine.com/html/serving.html.

three types of wines are also known as table wines. Exhibit 5 shows ideal serving temperatures based on wine type. Generally speaking, cooler wines can mask imperfections while warmer wine allows for a better expression of any complex characteristics of an older or more expensive wine. Wine tends to warm at the rate of four degrees Fahrenheit or two degrees Celsius for every ten minutes left at room temperature, though the temperature of the room will affect this speed.

Many customers will want to know about the wines they order, so beverage servers and bartenders need to be familiar with the following terms that apply to wine tasting and drinking:

Aging: Storing wines before bottling.

Aroma: The odor of a young wine, usually fruity or flowery.

Bouquet: The complex smell of a mature wine.

Body: The feel and weight of a wine in the mouth.

Dry: Not sweet.

Vintage: The year a wine's grapes were harvested and wine-making was begun.

Some other wines that may be served in an establishment include:

- Aperitif wine. Wine with spirits added and flavored with herbs and spices. Example: Vermouth.

- Dessert wine: Wine with spirits added, but with no herbs or spices. Port, sherry, and Madeira are dessert wines.

- Port: Dessert wine that normally ages at least 20 years.

- Sake: Japanese rice wine

- Sparkling wine: Wine containing carbon dioxide, which produces bubbles when the wine is poured. Champagne is a sparkling wine produced from grapes grown in Champagne, France.

- Still wine: Wine with no carbon dioxide or bubbles.

Pairing wine with food has always been a matter of taste. While lighter wines generally complement lighter foods and heavier wines complement heavier foods, many restaurants now recognize that whatever the guest desires is appropriate. Dining service staff are trained to react positively to any wine orders that guests place. To help guests unfamiliar with wine, some restaurants develop wine lists with specific food recommendations or make wine suggestions on the food menu. Exhibit 6 lists several Web sites that offer advice and suggestions on food and wine pairings.

Wine tasting should be part of server and bartender training so that servers can make informed suggestions to guests. A question or comment about wine by the server can provide a strong incentive for guests to order the product.

Pour still wines toward the center of the glass and sparkling wines against the side to preserve bubbles. Twist the bottle slightly as you tilt it upright to control drips. Also, fill the glass no more than two-thirds full to allow guests to swirl the wine, smell the bouquet, and examine the wine's "legs." Exhibit 7 explains how wine forms legs or "tears."

House Brands and Call Brands

Guests will often ask what brands of alcohol an establishment serves. Beverage servers and bartenders can provide excellent service by explaining the difference in brands. Alcoholic beverage brands can be grouped into various categories.

House wines are usually inexpensive wines the establishment sells by the glass. They may be bought in large bottles, jugs, or plastic containers. Many restaurants limit their house wines to a Chablis, a Burgundy, and a rosé or blush wine.

Spirits may be grouped according to the quality of the brand name. **Well brands,** also known as house brands, are used when a guest does not ask for a specific alcohol brand. For example, if a customer orders a rum and cola, the bartender would use the well brand of rum, or use upselling and ask whether the

Exhibit 6   Wine Pairings Web Sites

The following Web sites offer advice on pairing food and wine:

DrinkWine
http://www.drinkwine.com/wine_guide/pairing.html

Eat, Drink, Dine (must be of legal drinking age to access site)
http://www.eatdrinkdine.com

Food and Wine Pairing Wheel
http://www.bi-lo.com/Learn/Departments/Wine/pairings.cfm

German Wine and Food Pairing Guide
http://www.germanwineusa.org/foodguide.htm

Gourmet Sleuth.Com
http://www.gourmetsleuth.com/cpairing.htm

Hannaford
http://www.hannaford.com/instore/wine_cellar/wine_pairings.htm

Learn Vino
http://students.depaul.edu/~egruenth/final/learnvino/pairings/

Novus Vinum Food and Wine Pairing
http://www.novusvinum.com/pairings/pairing.html

Star Chefs
http://starchefs.com/wine/html/index.shtml

Sutter Home Food and Wine Pairing Wheel
http://www.sutterhome.com/guide/winewheel.html

Wine Answers
http://www.wineanswers.com/Food_categories.asp

guest prefers Bacardi or another premium rum. Well brands are the first quality level, with the lowest prices, minimal packaging and processing, and average-quality ingredients. **Call brands** are used when a customer specifies a brand by name, such as a Bacardi and cola. Call brands are usually of higher quality and price than well brands. **Premium brands** have the best taste, packaging, and ingredients. They are also the highest priced of all brands. The establishment may have several levels of premium brands, including super premium, select premium, and the top level—ultra-premium.

Standard Drink Abbreviations

There are nearly as many types of drinks as there are guests' tastes. Beverage establishments probably get orders for every type of mixed drink ever concocted. Because of this, beverage servers and bartenders use standard drink abbreviations. These abbreviations help them provide better service to their co-workers and guests.

Without standard abbreviations, a bartender might prepare a Bloody Mary for a guest who orders a Black Monk because the server mistakenly used the abbreviation "BM"—the typical abbreviation for a Bloody Mary.

Exhibit 7   Wine Legs

A lot of myths have evolved about what the "legs," or more properly called "tears," observed in a glass of wine represent. They do not represent a wine's quality or its glycerol content. They represent a wine's alcohol content. The more alcohol, the more legs. However, wines would have to have about a five percent difference in alcohol level to notice a significant difference. Often the cleanliness of the glass can override this difference.

James Thompson, a British physicist, explained the formation of tears in 1855. His work was overlooked, however, and Marangoni, who published in 1871, is credited with the explanation, and tears are therefore called the Marangoni effect.

The forces involved in producing tears are:

- Surface Tension: The attractive forces between molecules of the liquid that hold the liquid together.

- Interfacial Tension: The attractive forces between molecules of the liquid and the molecules of a solid surface.

If the interfacial tension is greater than the surface tension, molecules of the liquid will adhere to the glass and continue to wet areas higher and higher on the surface until the weight of the clinging liquid equals the interfacial forces trying to lift more liquid. In a pure liquid, this action stops, a meniscus forms, and no tears develop.

Wine, however, is a mixture of alcohol and water. The alcohol evaporates faster and has a lower surface tension (about 1/3). As a film of wine climbs up the side of the glass, the alcohol evaporates faster from the film surface, increasing the water concentration and thereby the surface tension and the film is pushed higher.

This increased surface tension effect compensates by transferring more alcohol-laden wine to the rising film to lower the surface tension. More alcohol then evaporates and the water concentrated film is pushed ever higher until gravity takes over.

When gravity prohibits more wine from rising, the only way the liquid has to decrease its surface tension and energy state is by beading, whereby the surface water molecules are strongly pulled into the body of the water, aiming to achieve the lowest energy state, which is a spherical shape.

The beads grow until the forces of gravity are stronger than the interfacial forces holding the drop to the glass and it flows down the glass as tears.

Source: www.thewinemerchantinc.com/educational/LegsTears.html. Used with permission.

Each individual establishment may also use additional abbreviations before a drink to identify whether the drink is dry, sweet, perfect, double, or frozen. Other abbreviations identify house liquors, mixes, requests for ice or glass types, and garnishes. Exhibit 8 gives sample abbreviations that an establishment might use.

Standard Drink Ingredients and Garnishes

Have you ever heard of a Zombie, White Russian, or Mimosa? As a cocktail server, you probably recognize these as types of drinks, but do you know what's in them? While most drinks have a major ingredient as part of the name, a lot of drink names, such as those mentioned here, give no clue as to what the drink is made out of. That's where the drink knowledge of the beverage server or bartender comes in.

Exhibit 8   Sample Standard Drink Abbreviations

Bourbon	B/	Wild Turkey 80	Turk 80/
Brandy	Br/	Drambuie	Dram/
Gin	G/	Irish Mist	Mist/
Rum	R/	Coffee	/Cof
Scotch	S/	Black Russian	Bl Russ
Tequila	T/	Bloody Mary	Mary
Vodka	V/	Dry Martini	Dry/Mari
Bacardi Select	Bac Select/	Long Island Iced Tea	Tea
Bushmill's Irish	Bush/	Tom Collins	Tom
Jack Daniel's	Jack/	White Russian	Wh/Russ
Seagram's V.O.	VO/		

Exhibit 9   Common Bar Measurements

Term	Standard	Metric
Dash	1/32 oz.	0.9 ml.
Teaspoon	1/8 oz.	3.7 ml.
Tablespoon	3/8 oz.	11.1 ml.
Splash	$1/2$ oz.	14.8 ml.
Pony	1 oz.	29.5 ml.
Jigger	1 $1/2$ oz.	44.5 ml.
Wineglass	4 oz.	119 ml.
Split	6 oz.	177 ml.
Pint	16 oz.	472 ml.
Fifth	25.6 oz.	750 ml.
Quart	32 oz.	944 ml.

The **standard pour** is typically set by each establishment. It is the amount that is set as a single shot. It might be 1¼ ounces, 1½ ounces, or even larger. Other measurement terms that are used in standard recipes are defined in Exhibit 9.

Guests usually ask about the ingredients in a drink, especially if the drink is new or has an unusual name. Staff members at an establishment are prepared to answer any questions a guest might have about drinks. They learn the ingredients that go into every drink on the menu.

Either the beverage server or the bartender will add garnishes to drink orders. Garnishing is an important part of service. What's a martini without the olive? A Margarita without the salt? A Manhattan without the maraschino cherry?

Garnishes add color, elegance, and flavor to drinks. Without them, drinks are not complete. Standard recipes will indicate what garnish should be used—unless a guest requests a substitute, at which point the guest request should be honored if possible and reasonable.

Tools of the Beverage Service Trade

Like any trade, beverage service has its own tools. Some are unique to beverage service while others are common to many businesses and even private home kitchens and bars. Beverage operations with comprehensive training programs help their servers get up to speed quickly by introducing them to the equipment found in their operation and how it is used. These servers are then able to provide better guest service by always providing the right glassware and silverware and by being able to use the time-saving tools that the operation has available.

Bar and Lounge Equipment Terms

Beverage servers and bartenders make use of a large variety of tools to execute excellent beverage service. They quickly learn how to use each piece of equipment to produce the best result. Some of the equipment commonly found in beverage service establishments are:

Beverage tray: A small, round, plastic tray (often 12 inches in diameter), usually lined with rubber or cork, used to carry food and beverages.

Bus tub: A large tub, usually plastic, in which soiled dishware is placed and taken to the dishwashing area.

Chafer: A metal holder that keeps food hot using Sterno. Chafers are usually made of stainless steel, silver, or copper.

Decoy system: Bus tubs and dish racks with one dirty dish, glass, etc. in them to show where to place dirty items.

Drip bucket: A bucket that collects drips of water produced by ice melting in a food and beverage display.

Glass froster: A cold storage unit, like a small refrigerator, that cools glasses so that they frost when you take them out.

Glassware: Tumblers, wine glasses, champagne flutes, beer steins, water glasses, etc.

Jigger: A measuring receptacle used to mix cocktails.

Linen roll-up: Silverware rolled up in a linen napkin.

Metal shaker: A metal cup that is placed over a mixing glass in order to shake cocktail ingredients with ice.

Order pad (captain's pad): A pad of paper, often with carbon copies, on which guest orders are written before they are entered into the precheck machine or POS system.

Exhibit 10   Glassware

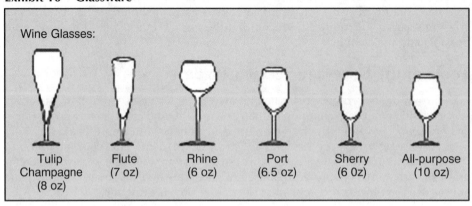

Wine Glasses:

Tulip Champagne (8 oz)   Flute (7 oz)   Rhine (6 oz)   Port (6.5 oz)   Sherry (6 Oz)   All-purpose (10 oz)

Oval tray (service tray): A large plastic tray, usually lined with rubber or cork, used to carry food and beverages.

Portable bar: A cabinet on rollers used to store and serve beverages, glassware, napkins, stirrers, etc.

Ramekin: A small receptacle used to hold butter and sauces.

Speed rail: A rack that holds bottles of a restaurant's most popular brands of liquor and the restaurant's house brands.

Tray jack: A wooden or metal stand that oval trays are placed on when serving food or drinks.

Underliner: A plate set under teapots or condiments. Underliners may be covered with napkins or paper doilies.

Glassware, China, and Silverware

Beverage establishments use many different types of glasses for the beverages they serve. Guests expect that wine will be served in a stemmed glass and beer in a pilsner glass. Exhibit 10 shows several types of glasses and what they are used for.

Different types of alcohol are served in different glasses. Many guests feel that the shape of a wine glass, for instance, affects the taste of the wine. White wine glasses are generally tulip shaped, red wine glasses are more rounded and have a larger bowl, and sparkling wine flutes are tall and thin. Some wine aficionados insist that an all-purpose wine glass should hold ten ounces, be transparent, and have a slight curve in at the top to hold in the bouquet.

Beverage servers exhibit professionalism by properly caring for glassware and following the following basic steps when serving beverages:

1. Make sure they have the right glass for the beverage.

2. Pour beverages only into sparkling clean glasses without cracks, chips, or spots. Throw away glasses with cracks or chips. Return potted glasses to the dish room.

This Dominick and Haff antique hammered silverware set includes a luncheon knife, luncheon fork, salad fork, dinner knife, teaspoon, soup spoon, citrus spoon, iced tea spoon, demitasse spoon, sugar spoon, tablespoon, olive spoon, and butter knife. Source: www.imperialhalfbushel.com/FlatwareServices.htm.

3. When pouring at a table, leave the glasses on the table. Never pick up a glass to pour unless there is no other way to pour without spilling.

4. Pour from the right side with their right hand.

5. Never add ice to a hot glass.

6. Always use an ice scoop or tongs—not their hands or a glass—to pick up ice.

An establishment's china—its plates, bowls, cups, saucers, and serving pieces—tell a lot about the type of place it is. China tells whether an establishment is casual, formal, trendy, or traditional. An establishment chooses its china very carefully to present a certain image to guests.

Beverage servers and bartenders enhance that image by inspecting all china to make sure it is spotless and free of cracks and chips. They return spotted china to the dishwasher and tell their supervisor about china with cracks or chips. The damaged china may get thrown out, recycled, or replaced. Beverage servers and bartenders are also careful to use the correct items for the food they are serving.

Silverware are the tools that guests need to eat their meals comfortably. At home, the basic "tools" such as a knife, teaspoon, and dinner fork may be enough.

Exhibit 11   Napkin Folding

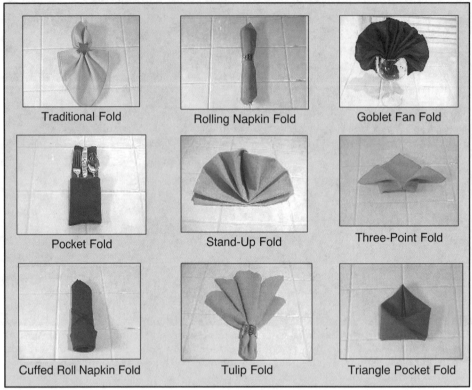

Traditional Fold	Rolling Napkin Fold	Goblet Fan Fold
Pocket Fold	Stand-Up Fold	Three-Point Fold
Cuffed Roll Napkin Fold	Tulip Fold	Triangle Pocket Fold

But there are more than 40 additional types of silverware, and guests expect beverage servers and bartenders to bring the right silverware with their orders.

Washable silverware, such as forks, knives, and spoons, is typically made of stainless steel. True silverware, which is made of silver, is extremely expensive and rarely used.

Linens and Napkin Folding

Fresh, clean linens and crisply folded napkins are a necessary and important part of professional food presentation, whether guest are having a glass of wine and a snack or an entire meal. Some common linen types are napkins, tablecloths, cleaning cloths, and aprons. Replace ripped, stained, or worn linens—do not use them in the restaurant or lounge.

Every beverage operation wants to create an atmosphere that is appealing to its guests—no matter which market segment they are targeting. Part of creating an appealing atmosphere is the attractiveness of the table. Napkins are used to create a striking look at each table. There are a multitude of different folds that can be used and each establishment will train their servers and bus persons in how to make their fold. Some types of napkin folds can be found in Exhibit 11.

Beverage Requisition/Issue

Beverages, by their nature, are very susceptible to employee theft, so there are several special procedures which are incorporated into transferring beverages from storage to production.

Establishing Bar Par Inventory Levels

Beverages are issued only in the quantities needed to re-establish bar par inventory levels. A **bar par** is an established number of bottles of each type of beverages that is always kept in behind-the-bar storage areas. A bar par is established for each type of liquor and wine kept behind the bar. Some food and beverage operations also set pars for bottled beer. Bar pars are established on the basis of the number of bottles of each beverage type used during a busy shift. For example, if an average busy shift uses four bottles of house brand Scotch, the beverage manager may be conservative and set the bar par at five bottles—four full bottles in behind-the-bar storage and one opened bottle in the speedrail or back-bar display area.

The number of empty bottles at the beginning or end of each shift—preferably the end—determines the number of full bottles needed to replenish the bar par. If then, for example, the bar par is five bottles for house Scotch and two bottles are empty, then two bottles will be issued to maintain the bar par. An important rule is that empty bottles must be presented before full bottles are issued.

Beverage Issuing Steps

The beverage issuing process typically includes the following steps:

1. At the end of each shift, the bartender places the bottles emptied during the shift on top of the bar.

2. The bartender completes a beverage requisition form (Exhibit 12), recording the name of each type of liquor or wine emptied (column 1), the number of empty bottles (column 2), and the size of the bottle (column 3). Depending on the specific operation, the bartender may also record the unit cost (column 4). Information for this column comes from the invoice cost marked on the bottle at the time it was placed in storage.

3. The beverage manager checks the number and type of empty bottles on the bar against the information on the beverage requisition form. If there are no problems, he or she signs or initials the "OK to Issue" section of the sheet.

4. The bartender or manager takes the empty bottles and the beverage requisition to the beverage storage areas. The person responsible for issuing: (a)compares empty bottles with the data on the issue requisition, (b)bottle-for-bottle, replaces empty bottles with full ones, and (c) signs or initials the "issued by" section of the sheet. At the same time, the bartender or manager, who returns full bottles to the bar, signs or initials the "received by" section.

Exhibit 12   Beverage Requisition Form

		Beverage Requisition		

Shift: ___A.M. (Lunch)___   Date: ___8/1/XX___

Bar: ___Main___   Bartender: ___John Smith___

Liquor	Number of Bottles	Size	Unit Cost	Total Cost
Col. 1	Col. 2	Col. 3	Col. 4	Col. 5
B. Scotch	3	750 ml	$12.50	$37.50
B. Gin	2	750 ml	11.75	23.50

Total Bottles: ___12___   Total Cost: ___$118.75___

OK to Issue: ___JN___

Issued by: ___GC___

Received by: ___JS___

Check one:
- ☐ low price
- ☑ reg. price
- ☐ high price

$118.75 ÷ $593.75 = 20%
(cost)   (revenue)   (beverage percent)

5. Empty bottles are broken or otherwise disposed of according to local or state laws, or as specified by the operation's control requirements designed to prevent re-use.

6. Total cost calculations (column 5) and the beverage cost percent calculations at the bottom of the requisition form are normally completed by management or secretarial/bookkeeping personnel, not the bartender or storeroom issuing staff. Except in large operations with storeroom personnel, management office staff should maintain perpetual inventory records for beverage products.

Bottle Marking

Bottle marking identifies an bottle before it is issued. It may simply identify the bottle as house property, or it may also contain information about the bottle's cost and/or date of issue. If an operation has only one bar, the bottle can be marked when it is placed in storage. If, however, there is more than one bar in an operation, each bottle should additionally be marked with the site to which it is issued.

Frequently, the bottle mark is an adhesive-backed label or hard-to-remove ink stamp, with a logo or symbol difficult to duplicate. Since the **bottle mark** identifies the bottle as house property, it helps supervisory staff ensure that all bottles behind the bar belong to the operation. There is less likelihood that bartenders can bring in bottles and steal from the operation by selling their own liquor and keeping the revenue.

Bottle marking is important for two other reasons. First, if the cost, from the daily receiving report or delivery invoice, is recorded on the bottle, it is easier to complete the issue requisition form as well as the physical inventory form. Second, if the date of issue is recorded on the bottle, it is easier to keep track of the rotation of bottles behind the bar.

The bottle mark, or at least the cost and date of issue, should not be easy to notice. Sometimes special situations require making exceptions to bottle-marking practices. Bottles going to the table, such as wine, might be marked on the bottom.

Additional Concerns for Beverage Control

Finally, several additional control concerns about issuing beverages should be noted. When beverages behind the bar frequently run out, bar par levels should be re-examined and increased. Guests do not want to wait while another bottle is brought from the storeroom. Similarly, there may not be time to complete a beverage issue requisition in the middle of a rush period, so information about beverage costs and reduced perpetual inventory balances is lost. To avoid these problems, managers should carefully assess the need for behind-the-bar inventories during the operation's busy periods, and issuing times and bar par quantities should be planned accordingly.

When the bar is not in operation, all bar par inventories should be locked to discourage staff member theft. In addition, keys to beverage storeroom areas should not be left with bartenders. In small operations, the key can be sealed in an envelope placed behind the bar. If it must be used when a manager is not immediately available, it will be available. However, the opened envelope will show that the storeroom has been entered. An immediate comparison of perpetual inventory records with physical count may then be in order.

Safety and Security for Servers

Providing security and maintaining safety mean protecting people—guests, staff members, visitors, and others who have a lawful reason to be at the establishment. Safety and security also include protecting items that belong to these people and to the establishment.

Beverage servers and bartenders are key parts of the property's security system. As they work, they watch for people who seem suspicious or out-of-place, and look for unusual situations. One of the most important responsibilities they have is to monitor how much alcohol guests have had. Drunken guests can be a cause of personal injuries and property damage, both on and off the property.

They are also alert to and report dangerous situations such as burned-out light bulbs, broken windows and locks, and other problems or possible problems.

Kitchen Safety

A kitchen is likely to be the busiest place in an establishment—and the spot with the highest potential for accidents. Beverage servers and bartenders follow these guidelines to help keep themselves, their associates, and their guests safe:

- Avoid spilling beverages by watching for sudden movements or gestures made by those around you.

- Do not put hot ashes into the same trash bin as papers or other flammable objects.

- When walking close behind someone, call out "behind you." This way the person is less likely to make a sudden turn or stop.

- Use the correct door when entering or leaving the kitchen service area. Wipe up all spilled liquids or foods at once. Leave the area clean and dry. If it is not possible to completely dry it, cover the area with a chair.

- When glass or china breaks, use a damp paper towel to pick up all slivers and pieces of glass.

- Put broken glass or china into separate trash containers.

- Throw out food if there is any chance that broken glass or china may have gotten into it.

OSHA Regulations

The **Occupational Safety and Health Administration** (OSHA) is a federal agency that helps keep employees safe by regulating sanitation, safety, and first aid in the workplace. OSHA regulations cover a variety of areas that concern food and beverage staff members.

OSHA regulations deal with such areas as hallways, storerooms, and service areas. These regulations require that work areas be kept clean, neat, and sanitary. Regulations also require that hallways, passageways, and stairways have guardrails and railings.

OSHA regulations require special signs for safety reasons. Three different types of signs are generally needed at a beverage establishment:

- **Danger signs** (red, black, and white)—used only in areas where there is an immediate hazard, such as where a caustic cleaning liquid has been spilled.

- **Caution signs** (yellow and black)—used to warn against a possible hazard, such as a wet floor.

- **Safety instruction signs** (green and white or black and white)—used to give general instructions, such as to tell staff membes not to eat in storage areas.

The OSHA **Hazard Communication Standard** requires all U.S. employers to tell their employees about hazardous materials that employees may be required to handle to do their jobs. The standard is commonly referred to as HazComm or OSHA's right-to-know legislation. **Material Safety Data Sheets** (MSDSs) must be collected for each hazardous chemical used, and must be filed where staff members may read them at any time. MSDSs are forms that list a product's hazardous components, health hazard data, and spill or leak procedures, as well as special precautions or protective gear required when using the product.

The MSDS form that OSHA developed has a section labeled "Health Hazard Data" that specifies first aid procedures for accidents involving different chemicals. For instance, the form may say to flush a person's eyes with water for one to five minutes if a certain cleaner splashes into that person's eyes. These forms are useful for all accidents involving hazardous chemicals.

Beverage establishments use a variety of chemicals that make HAZCOM compliance important. For example:

- Ammonia-based cleaners

- Chlorine-based cleaners

- Abrasives

- Acids, such as vinegar, which are used to clean glass and stainless steel

- Pesticides

- Disinfectants

Each chemical has an individual set of hazards to avoid.

The MSDS form developed by OSHA has a section labeled "Health Hazard Data" that specifies first-aid procedures for accidents involving different chemicals. For instance, the form may tell staff members to flush a person's eyes with water for 15 minutes if a certain cleaner splashes into that person's eyes. Refer to these forms for all accidents involving hazardous chemicals. OSHA also regulates the number of first-aid kits an establishment must have.

Heimlich Maneuver and First Aid

Emergencies and accidents can happen anywhere. Beverage servers and bartenders can help save lives by being trained in proper first-aid procedures. This training helps them give first aid to anyone in the restaurant who needs it.

Choking is one of the most common restaurant accidents that require first aid. Common steps for helping a guest who might be choking are:

- Find out whether the person can breathe, talk, or cough. If he or she can, do not give first aid.

- If the person cannot talk, breathe, or cough, a staff member should call the establishment's emergency number immediately and ask for help.

- If the guest is conscious and the staff member has been properly trained, he or she gives the Heimlich maneuver, which consists of grasping a person around the waist and thrusting on the person's abdomen to force any blockage out of the airway.

Staff members who have not been properly trained in first-aid procedures such as the Heimlich maneuver or CPR do not try to give them. Instead, they get help immediately. Trying to perform first-aid procedures without training can do more harm than good. For example, improperly performing the Heimlich maneuver could drive food farther down the airway and damage lungs and ribs.

Sanitation

One of the most important responsibilities of beverage staff members is to practice good sanitation procedures. Many diseases can be transmitted to guests by unsanitary food handling.

Many establishments have specific personal hygiene guidelines which represent a crucial component of sanitation. In general, food and beverage staff members:

- Stay home when sick
- Cover cuts, burns, sores, and abrasions with a tight, dry, antiseptic bandage
- Shower or bathe daily
- Keep clothes or uniform clean at work; change apron if it becomes soiled
- Follow the establishment's policies about jewelry
- Keep hair clean and tied back
- Use soap and plenty of hot water to wash hands frequently, especially after performing activities that might contaminate foods, such as:
  - Touching eyes, mouth, ears, nose, or hair
  - Smoking
  - Eating or drinking
  - Using the rest room
  - Sneezing or coughing
  - Using a tissue or handkerchief
  - Handling raw food, such as unwashed fruits or vegetables or uncooked meat
  - Taking out the trash
  - Touching any dirty surfaces, such as wash rags, money or credit cards, or soiled dishes or linens

If food and beverage staff members wear latex utility gloves, they wash their gloved hands as thoroughly as they would wash their bare hands. Gloves can spread germs just as easily as bare hands. In addition, food and beverage staff members never wash their hands in sinks used for preparing food.

Food and beverage staff members help make sure germs don't get into food by keeping it at the proper temperature. Most germs can survive and multiply only between the temperatures of 41 and 140 degrees Fahrenheit (4 and 60 degrees Celsius)—the **Temperature Danger Zone**. If food and beverage staff members are responsible for maintaining soup, bread, or other hot items, they make sure they are held above 140° F (60° C). If they are responsible for maintaining salads, salad dressings, or other cold items, make sure they are held between 32° F and 40° F (0° C and 4° C). By keeping hot foods hot and cold foods cold, food and beverage staff members can prevent staph and other germs from spreading.

There are many other work habits that staff members can follow to protect themselves and guests:

- Always use tongs, serving utensils, or scoops when necessary. Always serve ice with a scoop. Never touch ice or prepared food with hands.

- Never touch food-contact surfaces, such as the rims or inside of cups, or the tines of forks.

- If a food item has already been served, reuse it only if it is an individually wrapped item, such as crackers or bread sticks.

- Wipe up spills promptly.

- Never stack plates of food to carry them to the table. Contaminants on the bottom of plates might be transferred to the food on the plate below.

- Wash hands after clearing tables and before touching clean tableware.

- Wash hands twice after using the rest room.

- Cover mouth when coughing or sneezing, and then wash hands.

- Wash all dirty tableware immediately after use.

- Wash all raw fruits and vegetables before preparation.

Health Department Regulations

Every food and beverage location must follow local health department regulations. These regulations, which are meant to make food service as safe and sanitary as possible, cover everything from making sure can openers are clean to using only health department-approved cleansers. Health department regulations vary depending on the area.

The health department conducts regular inspections to make sure an establishment is following regulations. Some food and beverage outlets consider health department regulations only when it's time for an inspection. However, successful establishments are led by successful managers and successful staff members who know that following the regulations is part of everyone's daily responsibilities.

Making an Establishment Work: Policies and Procedures

A plethora of federal, state, and local laws govern beverage establishments. These laws cover everything from the hours that alcohol can be served, who can be served, sanitation rules, worker protection laws, and even menu language. On top of that, each establishment has policies for staff members regulating how to use point-of-sale equipment, how tips will be shared, what the par stock system is, how to take reservations, etc.

Last Call

Each state has its own laws for when an establishment must close. Even in states where alcohol can be served 24 hours a day, many establishments have a set closing time and a "last call" period before that closing time. Typically, beverage staff members will issue a last call at least 20 minutes before closing. Some guests may ask staff members to keep the establishment open later or to sell items after closing. Staff members must be vigilant about not selling any alcohol after the closing time specified by their liquor license.

Staff members execute last call by telling their guests that it is last call and asking whether they would like to have another beverage before the establishment closes. They do not offer or serve alcohol to guests who are intoxicated or who are almost intoxicated. They also do not serve double orders during last call. Typically beverage servers will each be assigned a section of guests that they are in charge of. If guests in their section resist closing, the servers are pleasant, but simply tell guests that closing time is set by management and that they must comply. If necessary, they ask a manager or security to help them with any guest problems.

During this time, they are especially alert for:

- Guests who try to leave without settling an open check.

- Guests who appear intoxicated and should not be allowed to drive.

- Guests who may need assistance to their rooms.

- Guests who harass associates to go out with them after closing.

- Guests who try to take alcohol with them in open containers, if this is illegal in the area.

Restaurant Menus

A successful beverage establishment begins with the menu. Much planning and design goes into deciding what food and beverages an establishment will offer to its guests. In fact, the menu is the first and best marketing tool an establishment can have. It tempts guests with its offerings, and sells guests with its scrumptious descriptions. The menu dictates what resources are needed and how they must be expended. Typically, the more complex and varied the menu, the more expensive and elaborate the operation.

When planning a menu, managers consider the following factors:

- What is the target market (i.e., guests)

- What type of food, beverages, and services will be offered

- Location of the establishment

- Transportation and parking accommodations and facilities

- Competition

When planning a menu, it is also necessary to determine how the menu will affect the following:

- Labor—an adequate number of qualified staff members with the appropriate skills are required to produce all menu items.

- Equipment—equipment must be available to produce all items required by the menu.

- Space—adequate square footage is required for all equipment and for receiving, storing, serving, clean-up, and other needs.

- Layout and design—the menu affects space and equipment necessary for efficient production.

- Ingredients—recipes, which specify necessary ingredients, are important. All ingredients should be readily available at costs that support anticipated product selling prices.

- Time—the menu will affect timing of food production and service.

- Cost implications—equipment, space, personnel, and time concerns can all be translated into costs. The menu will also affect expenses for utilities and supplies.

The menu can be viewed as the directions or the owner's manual for the establishment staff. They read it and become familiar with it. It is their job to know all of the items on the restaurant's menu. Guests will often ask questions about the beverages on the menu. All food and beverage staff members are able to answer the following questions about any item offered:

- What are the ingredients?

- How is it prepared?

- How large are the portions?

- What goes with it?

- What does it taste like?

- What may guests substitute for this item?

- What cannot be substituted for this item?

Staff members make a point to sample as many of the items offered on the menu as possible. If they try something and like it, it is easier to suggest that item to a guest. Staff members also explain any words on the menu that a guest may not understand.

Menus change regularly. Successful staff members ask the chef or head bartender about any new items or changes in recipes. Guests often are interested in chef and daily specials because they offer an added value. Staff members tell guests what specials are offered without making them wait. They also know which drinks are considered house specialties. Guests will often try these if they are described well.

During busy times, the establishment may run out of a popular item. Food and beverage staff members track what's not available before approaching a table to take an order and are prepared to suggest another item instead.

Beverage prices change from establishment to establishment. Most drink prices are set according to the drink's:

- Size

- Ingredients

- Amount of alcohol

- Quality of alcohol

Point-of-Sale Equipment

A **point-of-sale (POS) system** is made up of a number of POS units, usually found in the an establishment's restaurants, gift shops, room service stations, and front desk area. Point-of-sale units are like cash registers. They add up guest charges and print a bill.

The majority of POS systems at most restaurant, club, and bar operations today are computerized. At these establishments, the computerized POS system is used for all money activities or billing transactions.

Computerized POS units in different food and beverage outlets may be linked to each other, or they may be linked to POS units at the front desk. With these units, a guest's restaurant check can be transferred and automatically added to a guest's folio.

Most establishments program the keys on point-of-sale units according to standard prices for all items offered in the restaurants or lounges. This makes food and beverage staff members' jobs easier, because they don't have to enter prices.

Most computerized point-of-sale units require staff members to sign onto the system at the beginning of a shift using a three-digit number called a server number. Then, whenever they open a new guest check, add orders to an open guest check, or total a guest check, they enter their server number. At the end of their shift, they must sign off the system. At that time, the system may automatically print a report summarizing their shift transactions.

Tipping Policies

Sharing tips among staff members is one way to recognize that excellent service is impossible without the efforts of *all* staff members. Everyone in an establishment depends on each other to provide excellent service to all guests.

Every establishment has its own tipping policies. A few of the more common ways that restaurants handle tips are:

- Staff members are allowed to keep all of their individual tips.

- Servers share their tips with a few specific co-workers, such as the server, bus person, and bartender.

- All servers combine their tips, which are then evenly divided.

Establishments are required to report to the Internal Revenue Service tips that servers earn. There are two basic ways to report tips: via the Tip Rate

Determination Agreement (TRDA) or the Tip Reporting Alternative Commitment (TRAC).

TRDA requires operations to establish a tip rate for various positions in the restaurant. Each employee must sign a tip reporting agreement with the employer. If the employee doesn't report tips at or above the agreed-upon rate, the employer must give the IRS the names of the employees, their social security numbers, job classification, sales, hours worked, and tips reported.

TRAC does not require a tip rate be set, but it does require employers to give employees a written statement of charged tips, have a procedure for employees to verify and correct the statement, adopt a method for indirectly tipped employees to report their income, and process a monthly statement reflecting all cash tips attributed to employees.

Employees are required to report to their employer 100 percent of all tips in any month that they received more than $20. All tips must be reported on federal tax returns. The IRS encourages employees to keep a daily log of tips that they've received.

Par Stock System

Having enough supplies on hand keeps an establishment running smoothly. A **par** is the number of supplies an establishment needs to get through one work shift. For example, a lounge may need 100 beverage napkins to get through a dinner shift. This is the dinner par for beverage napkins.

Restaurants and lounges set a standard for how many pars to have on hand for each shift. For instance, using the example above, if an establishment's standard par level is three, they would keep 300 beverage napkins on hand at the start of the dinner shift. This way, there are enough extra supplies on hand for emergencies. Staff members typically restock items at the beginning or end of their shift so that standard par levels are met.

Telephone Courtesy and Reservations

Staff members try to make every caller feel important by being friendly, polite, and professional on the phone. The following techniques help them leave a good impression with each caller. Beverage staff members:

- Smile when they talk. A smile helps them sound more relaxed and pleasant.

- Speak clearly into the receiver. They avoid slang, technical terms, or hospitality words that callers may not understand.

- Use proper grammar and diction. They avoid "yep," "uh-huh," "not too shabby," and "OK." Instead, they use "yes," "certainly," or "absolutely."

- Answer the phone within three rings. A phone that rings more than three times gives a caller the impression that the establishment doesn't want to take the call.

- Always tell the caller their name, the operation's name, and their department. Each operation may have a specific way for staff members to answer the phone.

- Give the caller a friendly greeting, such as "Good morning" or "Good evening," and ask how they can help him or her.

- Give the caller their complete attention. They pretend the guest is standing right in front of them.

- Talk only to the person on the phone, not to anyone around them.

- If the call is for a manager, they ask the caller if they may put him or her on hold. Then they get the manager immediately, or take a message if necessary.

- If the caller is looking for a guest, they ask a co-worker to help them locate the guest. If they can't find the guest within one or two minutes, they take a message.

- If a work-related call is for a staff member, they ask the caller if they may put him or her on hold and then get the staff member.

To take a message, they write down the caller's name, the time and date of the call, the message and their name as the message-taker in case there are any questions. Most of the time, callers will leave voice mail messages.

Sometimes, to take care of a request, beverage staff have to put callers on hold. Providing good guest service means they always ask callers first if it is all right to put them on hold. If a caller gives permission, they take care of the request quickly and then thank the caller for waiting when they return to the line.

Each phone call is ended with a sincere "Thank you for calling." They offer to be of assistance in the future, and let the caller hang up first. The end of the call is the last chance to leave a good impression with a potential guest.

Successful restaurants can get very busy. It is helpful if all food and beverage staff members are familiar with taking reservations. This helps the staff work better as a team and it helps make everyone's job easier and more enjoyable.

When taking a reservation, food and beverage staff members:

- Greet the guest warmly. If it's a phone reservation, they answer within three rings, and use proper phone etiquette. If someone is making a reservation in person, they welcome him or her to the restaurant.

- Find out:

  - The name the reservation will be under

  - Whether the guest wants a booth or table, if both are available

  - The date and time of the reservation

  - The number in the party

  - Whether there are any special requests

  - The guest's phone or room number

  - Whether a smoking or nonsmoking table is desired (if it is legal to smoke in a public food establishment in the state)

- Repeat the information back to the guest to make sure it is correct. Spell names for the guest to ensure correct pronunciation.

- Thank the guest for calling. They initial the reservation in case someone has questions about it later.

Key Terms

aging—Storing wines before bottling.

ale—Type of beer which is top-fermented at warmer temperatures and not aged.

aroma—The odor of a young wine, usually fruity or flowery.

bar par—The established number of bottles of each type of beverages that is always kept in behind-the-bar storage areas.

beer—A beverage made from fermented grain.

beverage tray—A small, round, plastic tray (often 12 inches in diameter), usually lined with rubber or cork, used to carry food and beverages.

bitters—Spirits flavored with herbs, bark, roots, etc. Bitters are usually used as a cocktail ingredient.

blended whiskey—A whiskey made from a combination of straight whiskeys.

body—The feel and weight of a wine in the mouth.

bottle mark—An adhesive-backed label or hard-to-remove ink stamp, with a logo or symbol difficult to duplicate.

bouquet—The complex smell of a mature wine.

bourbon—American whiskey made from corn.

bus tub—A large tub, usually plastic, in which soiled dishware is placed and taken to the dishwashing area.

call brands—Brand served when a guest asks for a specific brand by name.

caution signs (yellow and black)—Used to warn against a possible hazard, such as a wet floor.

chafer—A metal holder that keeps food hot using Sterno. Chafers are usually made of stainless steel, silver, or copper.

cognac—The most prestigious blend of brandy.

danger signs (red, black, and white)—Used only in areas where there is an immediate hazard, such as where a caustic cleaning liquid has been spilled.

decoy system—Bus tubs and dish racks with one dirty dish, glass, etc. in them to show where to place dirty items.

draft beer—Beer drawn from a keg or a cask to a glass.

drip bucket—A bucket that collects drips of water produced by ice melting in a food and beverage display.

dry beer—Beer that is less sweet, with little or no aftertaste.

dry—Not sweet.

glass froster—A cold storage unit, like a small refrigerator, that cools glasses so that they frost when you take them out.

glassware—Tumblers, wine glasses, champagne flutes, beer steins, water glasses, etc.

Hazard Communication Standard—A law that requires all U.S. employers to tell their employees about potentially hazardous materials that employees are required to handle.

head—The foam that forms at the top of a glass when beer is poured. The ideal head on a beer should be one-half to one-inch thick.

house wines—Inexpensive wines an establishment sells by the glass.

irish whiskey—Whiskey made in Ireland from barley.

jigger—A measuring receptacle used to mix cocktails.

keg—An aluminum or wooden container for storing beer.

lager—Type of beer which is bottom-fermented and aged at colder temperatures.

light beer—Beer with one-third to one-half fewer calories than regular beer.

linen roll-up—Silverware rolled up in a linen napkin.

liqueur or cordial—Spirits redistilled with fruits, flowers, or plants, or their juices or extracts. They are usually sweet, with a high alcohol content.

Material Safety Data Sheets—Forms that list a product's hazardous components, health hazard data, and spill or leak procedures, as well as special precautions or protective gear required when using the product.

metal shaker—A metal cup that is placed over a mixing glass in order to shake cocktail ingredients with ice.

nonalcoholic beer—Beer with few calories and less than 0.5 percent alcohol. The alcohol is removed after brewing, or the fermentation process is stopped before alcohol forms.

Occupational Safety and Health Administration—A federal agency that helps keep employees safe by regulating sanitation, safety, and first aid in the workplace.

order pad (captain's pad)—A pad of paper, often with carbon copies, on which guest orders are written before they are entered into the precheck machine or POS system.

oval tray (service tray)—A large plastic tray, usually lined with rubber or cork, used to carry food and beverages.

par—The number of supplies an establishment needs to get through one work shift.

point-of-sale system—A number of POS units, usually found in an establishment's restaurants, gift shops, room service stations, and front desk area. Point-of-sale units are like cash registers. They add up guest charges and print a bill.

portable bar—A cabinet on rollers used to store and serve beverages, glassware, napkins, stirrers, etc.

premium brands—Brands that have the best taste, packaging, and ingredients. They are the highest priced drinks.

proof—Measurement of the amount of alcohol in a beverage. It is double the percentage of alcohol.

ramekin—A small receptacle used to hold butter and sauces.

rye—Whiskey made from rye.

safety instruction signs (green and white or black and white)—Used to give general instructions, such as to tell staff members not to eat in storage areas.

schnapps—In Europe, an herb-flavored dry spirit. In the United States, a sweet, usually fruit-favored liqueur.

Scotch—Single or blended whiskey from Scotland.

sherry—A dessert wine with grape brandy added.

speed rail—A rack that holds bottles of a restaurant's most popular brands of liquor and the restaurant's house brands.

spirits—Any alcoholic beverage made from distillation rather than fermentation.

standard pour—It is the amount that represents a single shot and varies by establishment.

straight whiskey—A whiskey made from only one kind of grain.

table wines—Red wines, white wines, and blush wines.

tap—A beer faucet used to pour beer from a keg, or the process used to set up a beer keg for service.

temperature Danger Zone—The temperature at which most germs can survive and multiply—between 41 and 140 degrees Fahrenheit (4 and 60 degrees Celsius).

tray jack—A wooden or metal stand that oval trays are placed on when serving food or drinks.

underliner—A plate set under teapots or condiments. Underliners may be covered with napkins or paper doilies.

vintage—The year a wine's grapes were harvested and wine-making was begun.

well brands—The spirit served when a guest does not ask for a specific brand. Also known as a house brand.

wine—Beverage made from fermented grapes, other fruits, or flowers.

 Review Questions

1. What is a proof?

2. What are the two classes of beer?

3. What type of alcoholic beverage typically has the highest alcohol content?

4. What is a call brand?

5. Why is it important for servers to use standard drink abbreviations?

6. What should servers be alert for during last call?

7. What factors are considered when setting a price for a drink?

8. Describe the two different systems for reporting tips.

9. What information should a staff member ask a guest for when taking a reservation?

Internet Sites

For more information, visit the following Internet sites. Remember that Internet addresses can change without notice. If the site is no longer there, you can use a search engine to look for additional sites. Many alcohol-related sites require users to be of legal drinking age to enter.

Alcohol Problems and Solutions
www2.potsdam.edu/alcohol-info/

Ardent Spirits
www.ardentspirits.com/

Bar Products
www.barproducts.com/

Beer Advocate
beeradvocate.com/

Beverage Net
www.beveragenet.net/home.asp

The Distilled Spirits Council of the
United States
www.discus.org/

Drink Boy
www.drinkboy.com/

Extreme Bartender
www.extremebartending.com/

GlasTender
www.glastender.com

iboozer
www.iboozer.com/

Wine, beers, and spirits of the Net
www.ryerson.ca/~dtudor/wine.htm

Webtender: Online Bartender
www.webtender.com/

World of Beer
worldofbeer.com/

Chapter 3 Outline

Beverage Server
    Suggestive Selling and Upselling
    Preparing for Service
    Taking Orders
    Serving Drinks
    Maintaining Tables
    Guest Checks
    Clearing Tables
    Last Call and Closing
Bartender
    Key Control
    Standard Drink Recipe Development
    Converting Recipes
    Standard Portable Bar Setup
    Opening Sidework
    Wash Bar Glasses
    Prepare Beverages
    Prepare Orders for Room Service
    Clean Bartop and Lounge During
      Service
    Balance Bank, Make Shift Deposit, and
      Collect Due-Backs
    Clean and Secure the Bar and Lounge
Specific Beverage Service Procedures
    Coffee
    Tea
    Beer
    Wine and Champagne
Conclusion

Competencies

1. Describe the duties of a beverage server. (pp. 57–69)

2. Explain the role that a bartender plays at a beverage establishment. (pp. 69–81)

3. Identify the rituals and procedures associated with the service of coffee, tea, beer, wine, and champagne. (pp. 82–90)

3

Beverage Service Responsibilities

A CERTAIN MYSTIQUE has grown up around beverage service over the centuries. A plethora of rituals and ceremonies are brought to each beverage sale. Even those who serve the beverages do not escape the expectations of the guests. Some expect staff members to be chummy confidantes or elegant sommeliers.

Given the allure of beverage service, the staff members who provide it hold important roles in a beverage establishment. The two positions that are most often responsible for serving alcoholic beverages to guests are the beverage server (sometimes called a cocktail server) and the bartender. Both of these positions have a high amount of guest contact and must be thoroughly trained in and knowledgeable of the establishment's beverages, service styles, standards, and policies.

Beverage Server

A beverage server could be defined as someone who takes and serves guests' beverage orders. While this definition is technically correct, it leaves out the heart of a beverage server's job. A better definition might be: A food and beverage internal customer who does everything possible, within reason, to make each guest's experience at least exactly what he or she wants it to be, and who exceeds guest expectations whenever possible.

Beverage servers are responsible for:

- Preparing for service

- Greeting guests

- Taking the order

- Serving the order

- Creating a friendly atmosphere where guests can enjoy themselves

- Closely monitoring guest alcohol consumption

- Completing service

- Helping other staff members as needed

One secret of a beverage establishment's success is that everyone works together as a team to give guests great service. Beverage servers are part of a service delivery system. They must give guests and associates great service for the system to work.

To be an excellent team player, beverage servers can:

- Help their associates and guests whenever possible
- Ask associates for help when they need it so guest service doesn't suffer and all employees can concentrate on guests' needs
- Say "hello" to associates and guests when they see them, and use their names if they know them
- Say "please" and "thank you" to guests and associates
- Share supplies
- Take pride in their work
- Always clean up after themselves
- Immediately removing from tables the items guests do not need anymore
- Clearing and resetting tables
- Restocking side stations so that supplies are always available
- Writing drink orders clearly and completely
- Asking guests all necessary questions when they place beverage orders, such as, "Do you want that 'up' or 'on-the-rocks'?"
- Turning in drink orders promptly
- Picking up drinks promptly
- Properly sorting and stacking used glasses, china, silverware, etc.

The quality of the food, drinks, and service at a restaurant, club, and lounge should enhance each guest's overall experience. Providing excellent service, beverages, and meals at a reasonable price is each establishment's ultimate goal. One way to achieve this goal is to set superior performance standards.

Beverage servers help to meet these superior performance standards. What are some of these standards? They must make sure:

- Alcoholic beverages are served in accordance with state and local laws, ordinances, rules, and regulations
- The bar and lounge area is clean and attractive
- Table and bar surfaces are free of spills, spots, chips, cracks, and warping
- Glasses are clean, sparkling, and free of chips and cracks
- Each beverage is served with a clean glass and a new beverage coaster or napkin
- A nonalcoholic beverage menu is available
- Servers are familiar with all restaurant menus and food and drink offerings
- Servers demonstrate professional behavior

- Guests are acknowledged within at least two minutes after being seated

- Servers quickly approach guests and greet them warmly

- Servers introduce themselves to guests, and use their names whenever possible

- The initial order is delivered within five minutes or less

Suggestive Selling and Upselling

Suggestive selling encourages guests to buy additional food and beverages. An example of suggestive selling is suggesting an appetizer to go with beverage orders. **Upselling** means suggesting more expensive and possibly better quality items.

Suggestive selling and upselling require tact and good judgment. If guests know exactly what they want, servers don't try to change their minds. Instead, they suggest additional items that will improve the guests' experience. And they pick up on when guests want suggestions.

Suggestive selling makes some servers nervous. This is probably because selling reminds them of a pushy salesperson they've known. Using suggestive selling and upselling techniques, however, is not being pushy. These techniques are part of providing good service.

The key to effective selling is a good knowledge of the menu. Servers have to know all of the products the lounge or restaurant sells. When they are completely familiar with the menu and how each item is prepared, they can suggest dishes confidently and professionally.

Beverage establishments also encourage servers to suggest the most popular call brands when a guest does not specify a brand. When a guest is not sure what to order, servers can suggest a specialty drink to suggestively sell. Other suggestive selling techniques include asking guests whether they would like a glass of wine or a nonalcoholic drink when they defer on cocktails. Servers can also always suggest specific alcoholic and nonalcoholic drinks such as a Beefeater gin and tonic, a sparkling water, or a strawberry daiquiri.

Here are some techniques servers use for more effective suggestive selling and upselling:

1. Develop a selling attitude.

2. Be enthusiastic. It's easier to sell something they're excited about.

3. Make beverages sound appetizing. Use words like "fruity," "icy," and "thirst-quenching" when describing them.

4. Ask questions. Find out if guests are unhurried or only have time for a quick drink; whether they like sweet or tart beverages; if they feel like having something hot or cold.

5. Suggest specific menu items. Don't simply ask: "Would you like soup with your drinks?" Instead, point out: "A cold bowl of borscht would go nicely with your martini on a hot day like this."

6. Suggest personal favorites. Try as many beverages as possible, and tell guests they've tried them: "You'll like the rum punch; it's one of my favorites here." But they are honest — they don't say that something is their favorite if it isn't.

7. Offer a choice: "Would you like Smirnoff's or Absolut in your vodka and tonic?"

8. Suggest the unusual. People go to bars and lounges to get away from their routines, and most guests don't know what they want to order when they arrive.

9. Suggest foods and beverages that naturally go together —beer and pizza, wine and cheese, margaritas and nachos.

10. Compliment guests' choices. Make guests feel good about their choices even if they don't order what servers suggest.

And finally, they ask for the sale. After they suggest and describe a beverage, they ask if the guest would like it. A good way to do this is to describe several items and ask which the guest would prefer.

Beverage servers must always keep responsible beverage service techniques in mind when they sell. A beverage server should never attempt to sell alcoholic beverages to an intoxicated guest or encourage a guest to drink more alcohol then that person wants to have. Rather, the beverage server should focus on selling other non-alcoholic drinks and food when a guest is nearing intoxication or is intoxicated.

Preparing for Service

Servers work with bus persons to set up tables in their area. They make sure that each table in their section is perfect. This includes checking:

- Silverware

- Glasses

- Napkins

- Salt and pepper shakers or grinders

- Sugar bowls or caddies

- The tablecloths

- The evenness of place mats

- The condiments

- Chairs and booths

- Flower arrangements

- Table lamps

- Floor and carpets

- Overall table appearance

- Ice buckets

Most lounges or restaurants provide servers with an opening duty checklist that lists all of the tasks they must complete before the lounge opens for service. Some of these tasks may include vacuuming—if housekeeping does not do it, cleaning tables and chairs, checking table lamps, checking flower arrangements, adjusting drapes and blinds, supplying lounge tables with appropriate items, restocking guest checks, and setting up a cash bank.

Side stations store extra supplies that help eliminate trips to the kitchen for beverage servers. This means more efficient service for guests.

The **sidework checklist** lists sidework tasks and the servers who are assigned to complete each task. These tasks are important to the smooth operation of a bar and lounge. Common sidework tasks include folding napkins and filling salt and pepper shakers.

Taking Orders

Beverage servers are encouraged to greet guests as soon as they are seated. Many properties have a standard greeting time of two minutes or less. Some have only a 60- or 30-second greeting time. Servers who are unable to greet their guests within that time are told to at least stop by the table and let the guests know they'll be back soon. Then they apologize for the wait when they return.

During the greeting, beverage servers tell the guests about the specials. They also attempt to read their guests right away. **Reading guests** means determining what type of service they need. They are alert to guests who may have been drinking and who may become intoxicated quickly.

When guests order alcoholic beverages, beverage servers verify that they are of legal drinking age by checking identification of anyone who looks under the age of 30. The server examines the ID and politely asks for another form of identification if it appears the first one has been tampered with or is a false identification.

Most establishments use an order-taking system to take orders. Frequently, beverage servers will place a beverage napkin in front of each guest as they take orders to help keep track of who has ordered. They place the napkin so that any logos are facing the guests. If guests are not ready to order, leaving a beverage napkin at the table will let other servers know that someone has checked with the guest. It is another way to use teamwork to provide excellent guest service.

Beverage servers write orders on the guest check or order pad according to how the guests are seated, following a clockwise direction. By using a standard order-taking system, anyone can serve guests without having to annoy them by asking who ordered which items. Servers will typically assign a number to each chair at a table. Chair number one at each table is typically the one closet to the door or some other landmark in the lounge. All beverage servers use the same reference point as a starting point. Exhibit 1 shows a sample point-of-sale printout.

Beverage servers then write the order for the guest in chair number one on the first line of the guest check or order pad. They write the order for the guest in chair number two on the second line of the guest check or order pad and continue until

Exhibit 1   Sample Point-of-Sale Printout

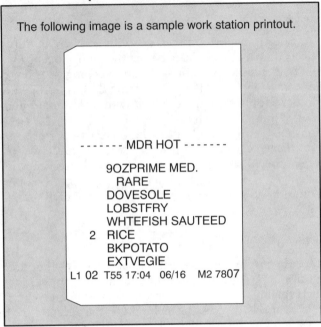

The following image is a sample work station printout.

```
- - - - - - - MDR HOT - - - - - - -

       9OZPRIME MED.
        RARE
        DOVESOLE
        LOBSTFRY
        WHTEFISH SAUTEED
    2   RICE
        BKPOTATO
        EXTVEGIE
  L1 02  T55 17:04  06/16    M2 7807
```

all guests have ordered. At some operations, beverage servers write the orders on the back of a guest check and the point-of-sale equipment prints the orders neatly on the front side.

Orders are taken using standard drink and food abbreviations. While taking the orders, servers listen carefully to each guest's order and repeat the order and details. Any special requests are noted on the guest check or order pad. Because each guest may have wildly different preferences for drinks, servers need to ask what their preferences are for such things as "on-the-rocks" or "straight up."

After taking drink orders, beverage servers often bring complimentary food to guests. Some types of food, such as pasta or pretzels, increase the absorption of alcohol into the bloodstream. Foods high in fat, such as fried cheese, slow the absorption of alcohol into the bloodstream.

If complimentary food is offered on an hors d'oeuvres table, servers:

- Offer to bring items to the guests.

- Select four to six items from the hors d'oeuvres table and place them on a small service plate for each guest.

- Bring the appropriate silverware and present it to each guest on a dinner napkin. For serving food in the bar or lounge, silverware may be wrapped in linen napkins in advance. These are typically called **roll-ups.**

If complimentary food is not offered, servers try to sell appetizers such as shrimp cocktails or nachos, along with each drink order.

Exhibit 2   Standard Drink Calling Order

A standard calling order for drinks is:

- Frozen drinks
- Highballs
- Cognacs
- Liqueurs or cordials
- Mixed drinks
- Blended drinks
- Cream drinks
- Plain sodas and juices
- Wine by the glass
- Beer

Placing orders. After taking orders, beverage servers must place the orders with the bartender. This might be done through either point-of-sale systems or by clipping the guest check to a rail.

Many beverage operations ask the beverage servers to set up glasses for drink orders. If so, they set up the glasses in the order in which they will "call" the drinks. They place the glasses near the edge of the bartender's side of the service bar. They also fill glasses with ice for drinks that require it.

One way beverage servers help associates is by being organized when giving drink orders to bartenders. This means combining drink orders for more than one table and calling the drinks in a specific order to the bartender. To call a drink, servers use a clear voice and say "Ordering," and then tell the bartender the drink orders, including any special instructions. A **calling order** is necessary because some drinks take longer to prepare than other drinks or do not hold up as well as other drinks. Exhibit 2 shows a standard calling order for drinks.

After calling the drinks, the written order is placed where the bartender can refer to them. The beverage server then places one beverage napkin for each glass on the beverage tray and inserts stirrers or straws if needed.

Serving Drinks

Mixing, pouring, garnishing, and serving drinks the same way every time is the mark of a quality operation. To help create this quality, beverage servers check each beverage to make sure they are complete as ordered before serving them. If something is amiss, they fix it before serving it. They check each beverage by asking themselves:

- Is it the correct beverage?
- Is it in the correct glass?
- Is the garnish correct?
- Have special instructions been followed?

Sommeliers deliver outstanding wine experiences for guests.

- Has anything spilled over the side?

- Should it have a chaser?

Beverage trays. Beverage trays are lined with a linen napkin to improve the look of the tray and to avoid spills and moisture. Typically, there are two types of trays. A 12- to 14-inch beverage tray is used only for serving beverages or serving food to a single guest. A large restaurant service tray, usually 27 inches long and oval in shape, is used for serving food to a party of more than one and for clearing tables. Many establishments use cork-lined trays so glasses don't slip. Beverage servers also often keep an extra pen and extra beverage napkins on the tray. They center glasses on the tray so that it will be balanced. Heavy or tall glasses are put in the center of the tray. Servers must also keep in mind the order in which they will serve the drinks so that the tray will be balanced until the last drink is removed.

Safe work habits come into play whenever servers carry trays. When filled with beverages, the trays are often heavy and potentially treacherous. Safe lifting and carrying involves bending at the knees and lowering the shoulder below the tray. Servers then pull the tray with one hand onto the palm of the other hand. They balance the tray at shoulder level on their fingertips, not on their forearms. If the tray is carried on the forearm, it may tip over. They then keep their back straight as they stand up and steady the tray with their free hand.

Serving beverages. Traditionally, servers have served women first and the host of the group last. In a no-host situation, they simply serve women first and men last. The first step is to place a beverage napkin on the table in front of the guest, unless they have already placed one. They then move around the table and serve every guest from the guest's right side with the server's right hand when possible. They avoid reaching across guests.

Servers handle glasses away from their rim or lip. Stemmed glasses are handled by the stem or base. Hands warm drinks when they touch the outside of the glass and it is unsanitary to put fingers inside a glass.

A sign of a quality establishment is that beverage servers know who ordered which drink and they do not have to ask who ordered what. They also repeat the name of the drink and any special requests as they serve each drink so that they can ensure all is correct.

At some beverage establishments, beverage servers pour bottled beer into a glass at the table, while at other establishments, guests pour their own beer from the bottle.

Maintaining Tables

The beverage server's job does not end with the delivery of a single round of drinks. Guests will frequently want refills. Also, when dirty items are quickly cleared away, the entire establishment looks neater and the guests can have a more relaxing time with a less cluttered table.

Maintaining a table typically involves:

- Changing ashtrays often.

- Clearing items such as dirty tableware, linens, and any other items that are not being used.

- Keeping the bar and lounge area neat at all times.

When a guest's glass is half to three-quarters empty, beverage servers will ask guests whether they would like another beverage. They suggest alcoholic drinks only to guests who are not intoxicated or nearing intoxication. This means that servers must count the number of drinks each person has had and what type of drink they've had. The amount of alcohol in a mixed drink with one ounce of alcohol is about equal to one beer or to one glass of wine. Drinks are served only to guests who want them. Servers do not simply bring another round for everyone' if some guests do not want another drink. Also, as establishments allow, they'll provide nuts, buttery popcorn, or other high-fat snacks to slow the absorption of alcohol into the bloodstream.

Bartenders and beverage servers work together to provide superior guest service.
(Courtesy of Luxor Resort & Casino, Las Vegas, Nevada.)

When writing the second order on the order pad or guest check, servers typically draw a line under the first order and write the new order below the line. They write "repeat" on the order pad or guest check if all guests in a party order the same thing for the next round.

Servers clear empty glasses and beverage napkins before serving additional beverages. They always bring a fresh glass with each fresh bottle of beer.

Guest Checks

Prompt service in processing payment is the guest's last impression of a beverage establishment. It is a key service point for all beverage servers. The exact procedures for totaling guest checks and presenting the check to guests will vary among establishments and will often be dictated by the point-of-sale system.

If guests get up to leave before beverage servers present the check, they ask, "Are you ready to settle your tab?"

Most establishments present checks in a check folder. Check folders keep checks clean and provide a place for guests to put their money or credit cards. It is also an ideal place for establishments to put comment cards.

Cash. When guests pay by cash, the servers take the money to the point-of-sale system and then present change in the guest check folder. They do not claim a tip until guests leave. If the guest leaves while the server is settling the check, the change is then taken as a tip. Establishments should always provide a receipt with the change.

Traveler's check. Traveler's checks must be signed in the presence of the beverage server. If the server was not present, he or she must ask to see a driver's license and compare the signatures on the two documents.

Credit card. Beverage servers must always get an approval code when taking payments by credit card. If a credit card is declined, they can politely ask the guest for another card or form of payment. If necessary, a beverage server might ask the guest to step away from his or her group to avoid embarrassment.

Typically, servers will imprint the card on the back of the guest check and on a credit card voucher. They may be asked to underline the account number and the expiration date on the imprint. If the card is expired, they return it and ask for another form of payment. They then complete the voucher by entering the date, their name, the guest check number, which credit card is being used, the approval code, and the amount of the purchase. The voucher is then presented with a pen to the guest. The guest totals and signs the voucher. Guests will often include a tip before signing the voucher. Servers return the card along with the guest's copy of the credit card voucher.

House accounts. Guests who are staying at a lodging property with approved credit accounts may charge restaurant meals and drinks to their room. This is called a "house account." These guests print their names and room numbers on the guest checks and sign them. Often establishments will ask guests to present their room key as identification. In addition to guests, some associates, such as sales staff members or managers, may also have house accounts.

City ledger accounts. Some local guests may have charge accounts. This allows them to be directly billed each month. Such local accounts are called "city ledger accounts." When settling guest checks charged to city ledger accounts, servers ask guests to print the company name or group name on the check. They also ask for the city ledger account number and then have the guests sign the guest check. They then provide a receipt showing the charge.

Personal checks. It is extremely important that beverage servers get as much information as possible from the guest who is settling the check by a personal check. This information helps assure that a personal check is good or can be traced if it is returned for non-sufficient funds.

Coupons, vouchers, or gift certificates. Each establishment will have its own policy for each type of coupon, voucher, or gift certificate. For example, many establishments do not give change for gift certificates and coupons. However, guests may receive smaller gift certificates in place of change. Servers carefully read any document they are given to determine whether it is valid and unexpired. They also check to see which charges are covered as some coupons might exclude alcoholic beverages or particular meals. If the document is valid, servers treat it the same as cash. They collect the balance of the account if the document doesn't cover the full amount. They then put the receipt and any change or smaller gift certificates in the guest folder and return it to the guest.

Transferring checks. If an establishment has a separate lounge and restaurant, there may be times when a guest transfers his or her bar charges into the restaurant and pays both at the end of the visit. This is possible only if the establishment's point-of-sale system allows it, otherwise the servers must settle checks before the guests move into the restaurant. However, transferring a bar tab to the restaurant is one way to show guests that an establishment's first priority is service.

Also, beverage servers may offer to deliver unfinished drinks to the restaurant after guests are seated. This must be done promptly so that the ice does not melt and ruin the drinks.

Clearing Tables

While most restaurants have server assistants (or bus persons), it is common for beverage servers to clear lounge tables after the guests have left. A sign of quality in an establishment is to have the tables cleared within five minutes of guest departure. This helps to seat other guests quickly and keeps the establishment looking good.

When clearing tables, servers place a service tray on a nearby tray jack or bring out a bus tub. They place all dirty tableware on the tray or in the bus tub, being alert to broken glass, personal articles left behind by guests and missing items that belong to the property. They are also careful to not put their fingers in glasses. Clearing the table also involves removing all used napkins, soiled ashtrays, and debris. When possible, servers avoid stacking plates in front of guests.

After the table is cleared, it must be cleaned and sanitized. Crumbs can be brushed into a beverage napkin and sanitizing solution is kept at each side station. Servers also clean chairs by brushing crumbs off, wiping the seats with a clean, damp cloth, and placing the chairs so that the seats are even with the table edge.

Once the tables are cleared, servers reset them so that the tables are as neat and attractive as they were when the establishment first opened. Every table in an establishment should look the same whether it was set before the lounge opened or right after the last group of guests left the table. When tables are set consistently, it shows guests that the staff cares about providing a quality dining experience. Table setup specifications may change with the time of day. All soiled equipment and debris are taken to the service area.

Last Call and Closing

Many states and localities require beverage establishments to stop alcohol service at a particular time. Where this is the case, an establishment will often issue a "last call" at least 20 minutes before closing.

Beverage servers are typically the ones who deliver the last call message. They typically tell guests it is the last call and ask whether they would like another beverage before the bar closes. They do not offer to serve alcoholic beverages to guests who are intoxicated or who are almost intoxicated. They also don't serve double orders during last call.

After the last drink is served, beverage servers prepare the lounge for closing by cleaning and storing equipment.

Exhibit 3   Last Call Alerts

During last call, beverage servers are especially alert to:

- Guests who try to leave without settling an open check.
- Guests who appear intoxicated and should not be allowed to drive.
- Guests who may need assistance to their rooms.
- Guests who harass employees to go out with them after closing.
- Guests who try to take alcohol with them in open containers if this is illegal in the establishment's area.

Guests may ask servers to keep the establishment open later or to sell items after closing. It is important that no alcohol is sold after the closing time the establishment's liquor license specifies. Beverage servers are in charge of the guests in their section. If guests resist closing, they are pleasant but simply tell them that management sets closing time and they must comply. Exhibit 3 lists some of the things that servers watch for during last call.

Closing duties vary with different establishments. Typically an establishment will have a closing duty checklist. If the beverage servers have cleaned throughout the shift, they will have less work to do at closing time.

Common closing duties include:

- Cleaning tables and chairs
- Taking soiled tableware to the dish room
- Emptying ashtrays and cleaning them
- Cleaning out and storing ice buckets
- Cleaning service trays
- Storing food
- Removing flowers from tables
- Cleaning the side station
- Vacuuming carpets
- Turning in guest checks
- Removing all trash and relining trash cans

Bartender

Bartenders prepare and serve drinks to bar and lounge guests and sometimes serve food as well. They prepare beverages for beverage servers, restaurant servers, and room service attendants to bring to their guests.

On May 11, 1911, H. L. Mencken described bartenders in the *Baltimore Evening Sun*:

Bartenders create drinks with artistry and appeal.
(Courtesy of Norwegian Cruise Line.)

The average bartender, despite the slanders of professional moralists, is a man of self respect and self possession; a man who excels at a difficult art and is well aware of it; a man who shrinks from ruffianism as he does from uncleanliness; in short, a gentleman...the bartender is one of the most dignified, law abiding, and ascetic of men. He is girt about by a rigid code of professional ethics; his work demands a clear head and a steady hand; he must have sound and fluent conversation; he cannot be drunken or dirty; the slightest dubiousness is quick to exile him to the police force, journalism, the oyster boats or some other Siberia of the broken.

Today, bartenders are as likely to be women as men, but many of the traits Mencken describes continue to hold true. Bartenders are responsible for:

- Monitoring guests' alcohol consumption
- Controlling alcohol risks effectively

- Ensuring that drinks are prepared consistently and to quality standards every time
- Knowing how to use bar equipment efficiently and safely
- Helping control waste and costs
- Maintaining bar sanitation
- Preparing drinks promptly
- Accommodating taste preferences of individual guests
- Making drinks look attractive
- Promoting the establishment's facilities

In addition, experienced bartenders may help train new bartenders and beverage servers, and they may test new drink recipes.

Bartenders contribute to the establishment's team by:

- Helping co-workers and guests whenever possible.
- Turning in food orders promptly to the kitchen to prevent last-minute rushing for everyone involved.
- Picking up food from the kitchen when beverage servers are busy.
- Conducting inventories according to the inventory schedule to ensure that other bartenders won't run out of supplies.
- Reporting repairs to engineering using a maintenance request system, and filling out a maintenance request form, if necessary.
- Providing the same excellent service to associates that they provide to guests.

Key Control

Bartenders use many different keys. At any given establishment, they might control keys to the cash bank, alcohol storerooms, bars, and other limited-access areas. All bartenders have to be trained in proper key control to protect these areas.

Key control guidelines for bartenders include:

- Following procedures for signing keys in and out.
- Never leaving keys in a door's lock and never setting them down. They keep keys with them or secured in a cash drawer at all times.
- Always turning in any keys before leaving the establishment for any reason.
- Reporting any lost keys immediately to the manager-on-duty.

Standard Drink Recipe Development

Every standard drink recipe an establishment uses has been thoroughly tested. Typical testing procedures include:

- A skilled bartender creates a tested recipe or one is selected from a published source.

Exhibit 4   Recipe Conversion

Most standard drink recipes make one drink. To convert a recipe, simply count the number of guests ordering the drink, and multiply the ingredients by the number of guests. For example, if five guests have ordered Margaritas, you will multiply all of the ingredients in your recipe by five:

Margarita for 1			**Margarita for 5**
1 ounce Tequila	× 5	=	5 ounces Tequila
½ ounce Triple Sec	× 5	=	2 ½ ounces Triple Sec
1 ounce lime juice	× 5	=	5 ounces lime juice

When you make several drinks in a batch, always be sure to use equipment large enough to accommodate the amount of your ingredients.

- Several people prepare and test the drink. Guests participate in the testing. The bartender collects feedback about the flavor, color, and strength.

- Adjustments are made to the recipe based on the feedback, and testing continues until the recipe produces a perfect result.

- Preparation testers consider the difficulty of the recipe, how the guest will like it, potential service problems, and how many servings might be sold.

- Final adjustments are made.

Although individual bartenders may find some ingredients or methods odd, they are instructed to follow the exact recipe so that the drinks are consistent no matter who mixes the drink.

Converting Recipes

When several guests in the same party order the same type of drink, most bartenders will make the drinks in a batch to save time. Making drinks in batches involves converting drink recipes. Bartenders must be well trained in converting drink recipes as if they convert incorrectly, they end up wasting ingredients or not having enough drinks for their guests.

Most standard drink recipes make one drink. To convert a recipe, simply count the number of guests ordering the drink, and multiply the ingredients by the number of guests. For a sample conversion, see Exhibit 4.

When several drinks are made in a batch, bartenders must use equipment large enough to accommodate the amount of their ingredients. Some drinks—such as layered drinks, in which lighter ingredients are floated on top of others—must be made one at a time and cannot be made in a batch.

Standard Portable Bar Setup

Bartenders may work anywhere from a lounge, a restaurant, a banquet, or a reception. In such service areas as banquets and receptions, bartenders prepare and

Exhibit 5   Receipt of Cash Bank

By signing on the last unsigned line below, I acknowledge receipt of cash in the amount of $_____ to be used as a cash register bank. The total amount is due and payable before checking out at the end of the shift.

Name	Date of Shift	Returned (Signature of Manager on Duty)

serve drinks from a portable bar. Being able to easily find the correct spirits, mixers, glassware, napkins, and other items conveys an image of professionalism and quality service to guests.

Bartenders stock the bar for the number of people they will be serving, plus an additional percentage. The number of people that will be served is typically available on a banquet event order.

Opening Sidework

Like beverage servers, bartenders have several tasks that fall under opening sidework. These tasks include:

- Picking up, verifying, and setting up a cash bank.
- Setting up and locking the cash drawer.
- Setting up the point-of-sale equipment.
- Setting up guest checks.
- Reviewing the bar logbook.
- Reviewing the daily function sheet.
- Picking up and transporting liquor and food issues from the storerooms.
- Storing items.
- Preparing the bar area.
- Preparing mixes and garnishes.
- Preparing service areas.
- Completing other tasks according to the opening duty checklist.

Picking up, verifying, and setting up a cash bank. Bartenders must be given a cash bank at the beginning of their shifts. In many establishments, a bartender completes a form similar to the one shown in Exhibit 5. In this way, the bartender certifies that the cash bank has been received and that he or she is responsible for the amount of cash in the bank until the bank is returned at the end of the shift.

Setting up the point-of-sale equipment. Bartenders start their shift by taking preshift readings on the point-of-sale (POS) units and recording those readings on the cashier's report. This reading establishes a starting point for sales during the shift. As POS units become more sophisticated, such sales records are able to be further broken down.

Set up guest checks. Every person at a beverage operation is accountable for his or her own checks. They pick up and sign for these checks when they pick up the cash bank, unless the point-of-sale unit produces guest checks. If the latter is the case, then the establishment will not distribute guest checks. Often, bartenders will be responsible for issuing guest checks to beverage servers. When this is the case, they record the range of check numbers on the checks servers receive. Depending on how busy the establishment is, the bartender may bundle servers' checks in batches of 15, 25, or 35 to save issuing time.

Review the bar logbook. Bar logbook entries are extremely important—if the establishment is ever sued in any matter related to alcohol service, the entries are legal records. The logbook keeps bartenders informed about important events and decisions that happened during previous shifts. Some of the incidents that might be noted about in the bar logbook are:

- Service is cut off for an intoxicated guest.

- A dissatisfied guest is compensated in any way, including complimentary service.

- An associate is harassed by a guest.

- Something is spilled on a guest.

- An accident or injury involves guests or employees.

- A sick guest requires medical help.

- Bar products or money is stolen.

- Bar equipment breaks down.

- A guest demands a service that the establishment cannot provide.

- Food and beverages are unavailable.

- A foreign object is found in a food or beverage item.

Review the daily function sheet. The daily function sheet tells bartenders what activities and meetings are taking place at the establishment. These are most common in establishments that are attached to lodging properties.

Pick up and transport liquor and food issues from storerooms. Bartenders pick up the exact type and quantity of items listed on the food requisition and beverage requisition and sign for it. At some establishments, storeroom personnel may be responsible for delivering items.

Store items. Bartenders rotate old stock to the front and new stock to the rear. As they rotate the stock, they check expiration dates and inform their supervisor about any items that have expired or are about to expire.

Prepare the bar areas. To start the shift, bartenders set up portable equipment such as mixers or blenders. The supplies and portable equipment used at each establishment will vary according to menus and service styles. Some common equipment and supplies include: heavy-duty blenders, spindle drink mixers, ice picks, cocktail shakers, bar spoons, corkscrews, ice buckets, ice scoops, cork-lined beverage trays, bar glassware, coffee cups and saucers, ashtrays, matches, stir sticks, tall straws, beverage straws, round toothpicks, beverage napkins, linen napkins and silverware roll-ups, cutting boards, paring knives, zesters, salt shakers, pepper shakers, and others.

When setting up liquor, bartenders create a speed rail for house brands. Many establishments will have a standard speed rail setup for house brands. Otherwise, a common order is:

- Vodka
- Gin
- Rum
- Whiskey
- Scotch
- Bourbon
- Sweet vermouth
- Dry vermouth
- Brandy
- Grenadine
- Lime juice

Next, bartenders set up display bottles of call brands. Depending on the bar setup standards, all beer coolers will be filled. Bartenders will assemble and setup draft-beer and soda-dispensing equipment. They will also check pre- and post-mix tanks and beer kegs, changing them as needed. Clean glasses are set up according to type and in the amounts the establishment sets. Bartenders also set up manual glass-washing equipment for the washing of bar glasses.

Next, bartenders set up for coffee service and make sure the ice bins are clean and filled with fresh ice. In some establishments, the bartenders may also set up food such as popcorn machines or hors d'oeuvres tables. Finally, they sanitize the bar and counter by spraying an approved sanitizing solution and wiping it with a clean, foodservice-safe cloth.

Prepare mixes and garnishes. To provide more efficient service, bartenders often prepare some mixes and garnishes ahead of time. If there are leftover mixes or garnishes, they check it for freshness and appearance, discarding anything doubtful or unusable. Mix and garnish ingredients range from types of juices to fruits and vegetables to sugar and salt.

Prepare service areas. Along with the beverage servers, bartenders will check the lounge tables. Table cars and displays are sometimes used to promote food or drink items. Displays may be used to promote wines or champagnes. Bartenders will make sure this material is neat and in good shape, replacing whatever is worn. They'll also refuel table lamps or replace candles and make sure that table cards, chairs, and stools are clean and arranged properly.

Wash Bar Glasses

Many bars will hand wash some of the bar glasses—especially those glasses in which beer will be served.

To wash glasses, bartenders fill the washing sink with water that is at least 110 degrees Fahrenheit (43 degrees Celsius). The washing sink is the one with brushes mounted in the bottom. A thermometer is typically kept on hand to check water temperature. A detergent is added to the first sink and the center sink is filled with clean, clear rinse water that is at least 120 degrees Fahrenheit (49 degrees Celsius). The third sink is filled with clean, clear water and a sanitizing solution. The temperature of the water will depend on the type of sanitizing solution being used and will typically be provided with the manufacturer's guidelines.

When hand washing bar glasses, each glass is moved up and down 12 to 15 times on the brush mounted on the bottom of the sink, making sure to clean away all lipstick and residue. Each glass is then thoroughly rinsed in the rinsing and sanitizing sinks.

It is necessary to test and change the sanitizing solution often. The detergent residue from glasses will break down the sanitizer. Footed glasses are hung on a rack to dry and unfooted glasses are placed on a stainless steel drain board. If the rinse water is hot and changed often, the glasses should drain and air dry without spots. After drying, they are moved to shelves.

Bar glasses are not hand dried or polished. Drying and polishing violates the health code because it puts germs on the glasses from your hands and the towel. Glasses are stored upside-down to prevent contaminants from falling into them.

Prepare Beverages

Standard recipes keep drinks consistent. Bartenders make it their goal to memorize the standard recipes used at their establishment. Those who have not memorized the recipes are advised to read all recipes twice before preparing drinks.

Once bartenders have read the recipe, they gather all ingredients and needed equipment. Each time they prepare a drink, they measure all the ingredients. Exhibit 6 gives several standard measurements. Some bartenders think they are doing guests a favor by over pouring, however, a strong drink is not necessarily a quality drink. Many establishments have automated liquor guns for pouring well-brand liquor. These guns will pour a standard shot of alcohol whenever used. Certain mixes, such as water or soda, may also be poured from a gun. This speeds service and provides additional cost control for the bar.

Exhibit 6　Measurement Cross-Check Chart

Mixologist's Measurement Cross-Check Chart

	Dash	Barspoon	Tsp	Tbsp	oz	Jigger	Wine Glass	Cup
Dash	1	$1/3$	$1/6$	$1/18$	$1/36$	$1/54$	$1/144$	$1/288$
Barspoon	3	1	$1/2$	$1/6$	$1/12$	$1/18$	$1/48$	$1/144$
Teaspoon	6	2	1	$1/3$	$1/6$	$1/9$	$1/24$	$1/48$
Tablespoon	18	6	3	1	$1/2$	$1/3$	$1/8$	$1/16$
Ounce	36	12	6	2	1	$2/3$	$1/4$	$1/8$
Pony	36	12	6	2	1	$2/3$	$1/4$	$1/8$
Jigger	54	18	9	3	$1^1/2$	1	$3/8$	$3/16$
Wine glass	144	48	24	8	4	$2^2/3$	1	$1/2$
Cup	288	96	48	16	8	$5^1/3$	2	1

Measurement Relationships—American Units

8 oz	=	2 gills	=	1 cup	=	$1/2$ pint		
16 oz	=	4 gills	=	2 cups	=	1 pint	=	$1/2$ quart
32 oz	=	8 gills	=	4 cups	=	2 pints	=	1 quart	=	$1/4$ gallon
		16 gills	=	8 cups	=	4 pints	=	2 quarts	=	$1/2$ gallon
		32 gills	=	16 cups	=	8 pints	=	4 quarts	=	1 gallon
$15^3/4$ gallons		=	1 keg	=	$1/2$ barrel	=	$1/4$ hogshead
$31^1/2$ gallons		=	2 kegs	=	1 barrel	=	$1/2$ hogshead
63 gallons		=	4 kegs	=	2 barrels	=	1 hogshead

Metric System Measures for Distilled Spirits

Old Bottle Size	U.S. Measure	New Metric Measure	U.S. Measure	Servings per Bottle ($1^1/2$)
Miniature	1.6 oz	50 ml	1.7 oz	1
Half pint	8 oz	200 ml	6.8 oz	$4^1/2$
Pint	16 oz	500 ml	16.9 oz	$11^1/4$
Fifth	25.6 oz	750 ml	25.4 oz	17
Quart	32 oz	1 Liter	33.8 oz	22
Half gallon	64 oz	1.76 l	59.2 oz	$39^1/2$

Wine Bottle Measures

Name	Metric Measure	U.S. Measure	Servings per Bottle ($4^1/2$ oz)
Split	187 ml	6.3 oz	$1^1/2$
Tenth	375 ml	12.7 oz	3
Fifth	750 ml	25.4 oz	6
Quart	1 Liter	33.8 oz	8
Magnum	1.5 l	50.7 oz	12
Double magnum	3 l	101.4 oz	24

Bartenders shake or blend drinks with a mixing glass and shaker.

Good drink recipes specify the type of glass needed for each drink. The bar glass sizes at each establishment are related to the pour size (the standard amount of liquor poured for each drink recipe) and the prices charged for drinks.

Special cautions must be given to ice handling when preparing drinks. Guests consume ice, especially after it melts, so sanitary guidelines must be followed. The ice bin is cleaned each day before ice is added. Bartenders use a clean ice scoop or tongs to handle ice and do not scoop it with a glass or their hands. Cubed or cracked ice is used for stirred or shaken drinks. Crushed ice is used for mists. If glass breaks in the ice bin or anything spills into the ice bin, the bartenders empty all ice, clean the bin, and refill it with fresh, clean ice.

Stirred drinks. To prepare stirred drinks, bartenders place all ingredients in a mixing glass. If several guests order the same stirred drink, the drinks are prepared in a batch. If the beverage is mixed with fruit juices or aromatics, it is stirred with a spoon and a scoop of ice is added. The drink stirred three to four times to mix and chill it. Bartenders must be careful not to over stir or the alcohol will be watered down by the melting ice. After stirring, the ingredients are strained from the mixing glass into the correct serving glass. If drinks are being made in a batch, drinks are strained so that each glass is filled to the midpoint. Then the remainder is evenly divided among the glasses.

Shaken or blended drinks. Preparing drinks in a shaker is one way many bartenders add artistic flair to their work. Some bartenders hold the mixing glass and shaker over their head and shake vigorously to put on a show for guests. This type of showiness works well in a noisy "action" bar, but would be in poor taste in a quiet, intimate bar and lounge. Good bartenders match their bartending style to their bar.

Ice is placed in a mixing glass, followed by the nonalcoholic ingredients and then the alcohol. A metal shaker is placed firmly upside down on top of the mixing glass. Holding the two securely together, the bartender shakes hard and fast. After shaking, the drink is strained into the correct glass and garnished according to the recipe.

Frozen drinks. Frozen drinks include daiquiris and Margaritas. Bartenders begin by placing a scoop of ice in a blender cup and adding the other ingredients. The mixture is placed on an electric blender and blended until the ice is crushed and the ingredients are pureed. Pureeing is the process of reducing to a pulp and then rubbing through a strainer. Bartenders must be careful not to over blend frozen drinks. They then pour the drink from the blender cup into the correct glass and garnish as the recipe directs.

Building drinks. Some drinks are prepared using what is called a "build" method. To make drinks in this fashion, bartenders place ice in the correct serving glass. They then add the liquor. Next, they add the correct amount of mixer, the garnish, and a swizzle (stir) stick. The drink is served without mixing, stirring, or shaking.

Layered drinks. A layered drink involves pouring each beverage on top of the previous one in layers to form multicolored stripes in the glass. Some layered drinks have only one alcoholic beverage, and sweet cream (whole cream, not whipped) is "floated" on top. Ice is not used for layered drinks. The heavier ingredients are poured first so that the lighter ingredient will float on top of the heavier layer. If a recipe calls for floating an ingredient off the back of a spoon, the ingredient is poured over the rounded part of a spoon into the glass. The spoon method reduces the chance of disturbing the layer below.

Coffee drinks. Coffee drinks can be a good seller in cold weather, especially as an after-dinner drink. With the increasing growth in popularity of coffee shops, specialty coffee drinks are being ordered more frequently. Most drinks are begun by pouring fresh hot coffee into the correct glass or mug. The other ingredients are added according to the recipe. A bartender gently stirs the ingredients with a bar spoon and adds whipped cream as called for by the recipe.

Prepare Orders for Room Service

Bartenders who work at lodging properties may help prepare drinks for room service. Most small properties will provide beverage service from a main bar rather than from a separate room service bar.

A room service attendant typically picks up prepared drinks. There will usually be some sort of covering for the glass, either plastic wrap or a paper covering.

Many properties use a control procedure called red-lining. This involves bartenders drawing a red line under the last beverage listed on the order. Establishments will also have control procedures to account for full-bottle sales. Tight controls are required for all beverage activities. These controls help to properly charge revenue to the appropriate departments.

Clean Bartop and Lounge During Service

Bartenders and beverage servers work together to keep the bar and lounge neat at all times. This involves:

- Removing glasses, napkins, food plates, and silverware that are not being used.

- Clearing empty plates from guest tables

- Picking up any popcorn or snacks on the floor

- Changing ashtrays

While smoking is being banned from many food establishments, exceptions are often made for bars and lounges. Ashtrays should be changed whenever there are one or two used cigarettes in them. The "capping" method prevents ashes from falling on guests, the bartop, or the table as ashtrays are removed. This method involves turning a clean ashtray upside down and placing it over the dirty ashtray on the bar or table. Both ashtrays are then picked up and the dirty one is placed on a tray or behind the bar. The clean ashtray is then returned to the table.

Balance Bank, Make Shift Deposit, and Collect Due-Backs

A **cash bank** is the smallest amount of cash that allows bartenders to do their business. It is individual to each bartender and each individual should be the only one using his or her own cash bank.

Bartenders are responsible for maintaining security over their cash bank at all times. This involves counting their cash bank money at least twice before starting the shift. The count should be in a private place away from the public. Most establishments will ask bartenders to sign a cash-bank contract assuming responsibility for the bank when it is issued. The cash bank is locked in a safe-deposit box between shifts and the bartender must maintain key control over the safe-deposit key.

At the end of each shift, bartenders prepare a deposit and cashier's report. They begin by counting any vouchers for tips paid out as cash since that amount will be reimbursed as a due back. In a safe, private location, bartenders count the money in the deposit, and list cash, change, checks, traveler's checks, gift certificates, coupons, credit vouchers, and other forms of income on a cashier's report. They then place the deposit in a deposit envelope along with the cashier's report. They seal the envelope and sign their names across the seal. The deposit envelope is then placed in a drop safe with a witness present. The bartender and the witness sign the drop safe logbook.

Bartenders prepare due-back vouchers for the total amount of money they paid out of their cash bank during the shift. A **due back** is a receipt for any money that is paid out of the bank. It could cover change or small purchases made with a manager's approval. It might also reimburse the bartender for any cash paid out to associates for tips on credit cards or house accounts. The cash bank must never be used for personal loans. Most establishments will have unannounced audits of cash banks.

The bartender documents due-backs with copies of credit card vouchers, charge tips, and a tips-paid-out voucher signed by each staff member who was paid out tips. Bartenders then take the due-backs to the general cashier, along with the backup vouchers, and receive reimbursement for their banks. When the general cashier is not available, they put the tips-paid-out vouchers in the safe-deposit box until the next shift they work. They are then turned in for reimbursement.

Clean and Secure the Bar and Lounge

Bartenders have a number of specific tasks that they must do to help clean and secure the bar and lounge. The exact tasks and procedures will vary among establishments, but they generally include:

- Closing out guest checks and point of-sale equipment. This is often the first task in establishments connected to a lodging property. It helps the night auditor begin his or her work on time.

- Separating cash bank from shift receipts.

- Washing, sanitizing, and storing all glassware and small utensils.

- Recording all empty liquor bottles (type, size, quantity) on a beverage requisition. Sometimes this task is performed as part of opening duty.

- Storing and locking displayed liquor in the proper cooler or cabinet.

- Storing leftovers. Bartenders discard unusable fruit garnishes, cover fresh garnishes, label and date containers, refrigerate leftover garnishes, and discard unusable mixes.

- Preparing the food requisition for items needed for the next day.

- Cleaning dispensing equipment.

- Emptying trash and washing and relining trash cans.

- Emptying and washing ashtrays.

- Cleaning and sanitizing portable equipment and work areas. The closed bar should be clean and in order.

- Doing a final check of the area.

Specific Beverage Service Procedures

Whether it is the beverage server or the bartender preparing and bringing to the table the drinks, there are certain procedures that apply to different beverages. This chapter will briefly look at the rituals and procedures involved with serving:

- Coffee

- Tea

- Beer
- Wine

Coffee

Coffee has long been a popular drink in the United States and specialty coffee drinks are a trend which continues to strengthen. As heated coffee quickly goes bad and can be bitter if improperly brewed, it is important to prepare coffee correctly.

Coffee pots need to be clean before they are used. One common problem is coffee residue. This forms when a stainless steel or glass pot was left on a burner too long. Servers must keep careful eyes on pots as coffee evaporates quickly, scorching the residue. This makes the pots difficult to clean. If an empty pot is left for too long on a hot burner, the pot may explode. Steps for removing coffee residue are to place a scoop of ice in the pot along with a half cup of table salt and a squeeze of lemon juice. The pot must not be hot, or it might explode. The ice is swirled in the pot for several minutes and then emptied and taken to the dishroom for washing.

To prepare coffee, follow these steps:

- Remove the grounds holder from the coffee maker. If necessary, throw away the grounds and rinse the holder.
- Remove the sanitary wrapping from a pre-measured filter pack of fresh coffee. Shake the filter pack to evenly spread the coffee.
- Place the filter pack in the grounds holder, seam-side down.
- Replace the grounds holder in the coffee maker.
- Place a clean coffee pot under the grounds holder. Use the correct pot for the type of coffee being brewed (regular, flavored, or decaffeinated).
- Pour water into the coffee maker from a measured pitcher or a clean coffee pot. Press the "start" button, if necessary.
- If using an automatic coffee urn, connected to a direct water source, press the "brew" button.
- Allow all water to pass through the ground coffee before serving any coffee.
- Turn on the reserve burner. Move the full pot of fresh coffee to the reserve burner.
- Remove the grounds holder and throw away the grounds.
- Rinse the holder and replace it in the machine.
- After each shift, clean the nozzle head on the grounds holder, and the area around the nozzle head.

Coffee strength **layers** as the water passes through the ground coffee. The first third of the pot will be too weak, the second will be too strong, and the last third will be too weak. To get the right flavor, let the full pot drip to blend the layers and arrive at the desired strength.

Coffee begins to go bad immediately after it is brewed. The oils in the coffee break down and a foul odor and taste will develop. Establishments avoid serving coffee that has been held for longer than 30 minutes. It gives off an offensive odor that will spread through the establishment. If a coffee pot is one-quarter full or less, most bartenders will start a fresh pot. Do not combine the contents of two partially full coffee pots. This spoils the taste of the coffee.

Anyone serving coffee frequently refills it—typically as soon as a cup of coffee is less than half-full. Coffee cools quickly and guests expect the server to keep their coffee hot and fresh. Most servers will not ask whether guests want a refill but will pour them until guests signal that they have had enough.

Tea

Tea can be made with loose tea or tea bags. When making tea, the water should be at the boiling point when it is poured over the loose tea or the tea bag. The teapot/cup should be kept hot and the tea should be allowed to steep for no more than five minutes. It should be served immediately.

Hot tea is usually brewed by the two-cup pot or by the individual cup. Most guests prefer to place their own tea bags into the hot water. While tea usually takes eight to ten minutes to brew, some guests may prefer more or less time.

Beverage servers typically preheat ceramic pots by filling it with boiling hot water and letting it stand while they set up the beverage tray. On the beverage tray they put cream, sugar, a spoon, a mug or cup and saucer, a tea bag, and a lemon wedge. They then fill the teapots with hot water from the coffee maker. When using ceramic pots, they empty the water used to preheat it and then refill it with hot water.

Tea drinkers like refills but are often overlooked. Staff members can show their commitment to superior service by offering to bring more hot water at frequent intervals.

Iced tea is often prepared with one-ounce tea bags immersed in water that has reached the boiling point. The normal proportion is two ounces of tea to one gallon of water. Like hot tea, iced tea should steep for no more than five minutes and then be poured into a glass with ice. When this is impractical, tea should be pre-cooled and ice should be added to the glass when the tea is served. Since ice will dilute the tea, it should be made stronger than hot tea.

Beer

Draft beer is beer that is served from a keg. The servers hold the glass near its base and then tilt it slightly (about 30 degrees) under the tap so the first few ounces of beer will pour down the side of the glass. The servers do not pour all of the beer down the side of the glass as a direct pour down the center releases carbon dioxide and will result in a smoother tasting beer. The servers open the beer tap dispenser quickly and completely. If they try to hold the tap in a half-open position, they will draw too much air. This creates too much head and changes the taste of the beer.

Exhibit 7   Food and Wine Pairing Guidelines

1. Drink light-bodied wines with lighter foods and fuller-bodied wines with heartier, more flavorful foods.

2. Food preparation methods affect wine pairings. A delicate sauce on a food should be paired with a delicate wine while a grilled chicken breast might call for a heartier wine.

3. Sweet foods make wines seem drier than they are, so pair them with a sweeter wine.

4. High acid foods go well with wines that have a higher acidity.

5. Bitter and astringent foods make a wine's bitter flavor more pronounced, so try pairing the food with a full-flavored fruity wine,

6. Taste both the wine and food separately and then together to determine whether it would make a good pairing to recommend.

They then tilt the glass to an upright position as it fills. They pour the beer directly into the center of the glass to form a head about one-half to one-inch thick. If the beer doesn't develop a head, they change the keg before serving any beer. Beer that will not develop a head may have gone bad in the keg. Age or a leaking keg can result in a loss of carbon dioxide and flat beer. It is helpful to check that the carbon dioxide tank is full. Finally, they close the tap quickly and completely.

Bottled beer is typically served with a glass—many times a frosted glass. At some establishments, beverage servers will pour bottled beer into a glass at the table, while at other establishments, guests pour their own beer from the bottle.

Wine and Champagne

Ordering wine and champagne is fun for many people and staff members can help their guests enjoy it. Over the centuries, an etiquette and rituals have been developed concerning the service of wine. There are many guests who will want to have the ritual as part of their dining experience. These rituals include wine and food pairings, glassware, the temperature at which wine is served, how to open bottles, and how to pour.

Selecting wine. Beverage servers present the wine list to guests upon arrival. If possible, they open the wine list before presenting it. Servers should be prepared to suggest one or two wines or champagnes.

The general rule is that white wines go best with white meats and seafood, and red wines go best with red meats and game. Rose and blush wines and champagnes go with any type of food. Regardless of the general rule, the guest is never wrong in his or her selection of a wine. Good servers allow guests to make their own selections and always support the guest's preference. Some additional guidelines are listed in Exhibit 7. Some Web sites, such as the Sutter Home Winery (http://www.sutterhome.com/guide/winewheel.html) have a wine wheel to suggest food and wine pairings.

Exhibit 8   Glassware Shapes

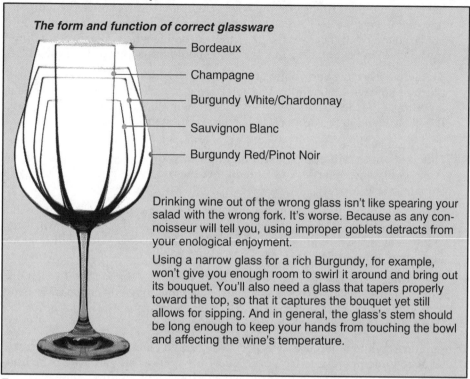

The form and function of correct glassware

— Bordeaux

— Champagne

— Burgundy White/Chardonnay

— Sauvignon Blanc

— Burgundy Red/Pinot Noir

Drinking wine out of the wrong glass isn't like spearing your salad with the wrong fork. It's worse. Because as any connoisseur will tell you, using improper goblets detracts from your enological enjoyment.

Using a narrow glass for a rich Burgundy, for example, won't give you enough room to swirl it around and bring out its bouquet. You'll also need a glass that tapers properly toward the top, so that it captures the bouquet yet still allows for sipping. And in general, the glass's stem should be long enough to keep your hands from touching the bowl and affecting the wine's temperature.

For more information, visit www.epicurious.com/c_play/c04_victual/glasses/glasses.html.

Many establishments will have suggestions for specific wines for each of their main dishes either printed on the menu or offered to servers during their training. This helps the servers to make suggestions. Wine and food pairing can be a complicated task of which many people have devoted a great deal of research and thought.

Servers can ask guests about their preferences to help them arrive at a suitable choice. They answer any specific questions about the wines or champagnes on the list. Most establishments will have frequent wine tastings for the staff so that team members can accurately describe a wine's taste and features.

Glassware. Each establishment may have several different types of wine glasses. The size and shape of a wine glass can affect how the wine tastes. Some guests will prefer a certain type of glass and may request it. These requests should be honored wherever possible. Exhibit 8 shows some of the different glass shapes for different wines.

Still wines are typically served in transparent glasses so that guests can see the wine properly. Sparkling wines are often served in crystal glasses.

Factors that affect glassware include:

- **The stem.** The stem should be long enough so that guests can hold it without having to put their fingers on the bowl. Their hands can change the temperature of the wine if they have to hold it by the bowl. However, the stem should not be so long that it causes the glass to be unstable when wine is poured into the bowl. Many experts say that the stem should be as long as the bowl is tall.

- **The bowl.** The size and shape of the bowl determine the intensity and complexity of the wine's bouquet. The bowl of the glass should be round and long, tapering at the top so that when the wine is swirled, it can be held in the glass. It will also hold in the aroma that is released by swirling the wine.

- **The rim.** The shape of the rim determines where the wine lands on the tongue. Different wines will appeal to different parts of the tongue depending upon their acidity and other factors. The thinner the rim, the less the glass distracts from the wine.

- **Size.** Generally, glasses for red wine are larger than glasses for white wine. Red wine glasses typically have a 12-ounce capacity, though that will vary. White-wine glasses will be slightly smaller. Champagne flutes will hold six and a half ounces or more.

- **Cleanliness.** Glasses need to be clean so that nothing interacts with the wine except air and the glass itself. Sparingly use mild detergents on glassware and either air dry it or dry it with a lint-free cloth. Stemware should not be loaded in the dishwasher with other grimy dishes.

Temperature. White wines are designed to be served chilled while red wines are served at room temperature. However, guest preferences should always be honored—even if they want ice in their red wine or room temperature white wine.

How cold is "chilled"? Dry white wines are best served between 45 degrees Fahrenheit to 50 degrees Fahrenheit and sweet whites at 40 degrees Fahrenheit to 50 degrees Fahrenheit. It is better to serve a drink slightly colder than needed as the wine will quickly warm up once it is poured and served.

White wines can be chilled by placing them in a bucket of ice water. There should be enough ice and water in the bucket to cover the shoulder of the bottle. This is usually means a server will fill a bucket half full with ice and then pour water in to just cover the ice. The ice bucket and ice bucket stand are placed to the right of the person who ordered the wine or champagne. A clean linen napkin is threaded through the ring of the bucket.

Room temperature refers to the wine cellar temperature of most European wine cellars—which is around 64 degrees Fahrenheit. Full-bodied and mature red wines are best at 60 to 65 degrees Fahrenheit while young reds do better around 55 to 60 degrees Fahrenheit. As most room temperatures are actually warmer than that, many establishments will chill a wine for a few minutes to lower the temperature to a cool room temperature. However, it is not served with an ice bucket unless the guest requests it.

Opening. Wine and champagne service is a ritual that has been handed down for centuries. By following these rules, staff members impress their most knowledgeable guests and help inexperienced wine and champagne drinkers develop an

Exhibit 9   Corkscrew

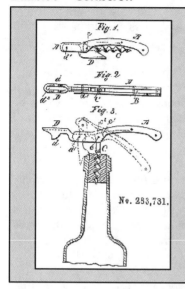

Carl Wienke invented the "waiter's corkscrew" and patented it in Germany on May 26, 1882. It was brought to Great Britain and France in 1883. It was nicknamed the "waiter's cork-screw" or "butler's friend" because of how easy it was able to remove and replace a cork. It is still used today by many beverage servers and bartenders.

The drawing on the left was submitted as part of the patent application in the United States in 1883.

appreciation for this service. The bottle is first presented to the guest who placed the order. The bottle is held wrapped in a linen napkin with the label displayed to the guest who placed the order so that he or she can read the label. Champagnes and sparkling wines are held gently with the corks protected as they are under pressure from carbonation. When the guest approves, the server may proceed.

To open still wines, the wine bottle is set on the edge of the table and the server holds it firmly at the shoulder. Using the blade on his or her corkscrew, the server cuts the foil capsule cleanly around the rim of the bottle. Servers cut low enough so that the wine won't touch the foil when they pour. The capsule is then removed and placed in their pockets. A clean linen napkin is then used to wipe the lip of the bottle. That also removes any mold or mineral salts that may have accumulated.

The servers insert the tip of the corkscrew slightly off-center of the cork. (A sample waiter's corkscrew is shown in Exhibit 9.) The corkscrew is twisted, with the servers directing it vertically through the center of the cork. They continue twisting until all spirals of the corkscrew have entered the cork. The cork can break if the corkscrew is not deep enough. They stop twisting before the corkscrew comes out of the bottom of the cork. If they insert the corkscrew too far, bits of cork fall into the wine.

Servers remove the cork by placing the corkscrew lever on the lip of the bottle and holding it firmly with their thumb and forefinger. They never put the bottle between their legs to pull out the cork. With their other hand, they slowly and steadily pull upward to remove the cork. If the cork breaks, they pull out the loose pieces and insert the corkscrew into the remaining cork. They then use the lever to pull up the cork with their free hand until only a half inch of the cork remains in the neck of the bottle. They grasp the cork with their thumb and forefinger and ease it out of the bottle.

The cork is removed from the corkscrew and placed near the guest who ordered the wine. The server does not smell the cork. The cork is shown to the guest to prove that the wine has been stored correctly. Wines should be stored on their sides, and the cork should be wet.) You can judge a wine only by the smell of the wine itself—not by the smell of the cork.

Many red wines benefit from the opportunity to breathe (be exposed to air). Younger wines usually need little to no time to breathe while older wines might need ten to fifteen minutes. Some experts even recommend that red wines be allowed to breathe for 30 minutes to allow oxygen to bring out the wine's full aroma and flavor. Servers ask the host whether he or she would like the wine to breathe before it is served. If the guest says yes, the open bottle is left on the table and is not poured.

Sparkling wines require a slightly different opening procedure. Champagne service is fun, but it requires attention to details and special care to protect guests from a flying cork. The bottle is placed on the corner of the table or to the right of the host in his or her full view. Working under a linen napkin, servers use the blade of the corkscrew to cut the foil hood just below the retainer wire. They keep their thumb on the cork. The cork is secured by a wire hood because of the pressure inside the bottle. Servers must always protect the cork from flying out and must make sure the cork is never pointed at a guest. As servers become more familiar with the wines on their wine list, they will learn which sparkling wines are more bubbly—and more likely to pop a cork. Servers remove the foil and place it in the trash or in their pocket. They do not place it on the table or in the ice bucket.

Servers then hold the bottle firmly by the neck with one hand with their thumb still securely on top of the wire. They untwist the wire. If they feel the cork moving against their thumb, they keep a napkin wrapped tightly over the cork and bottle until they are sure the bottle is not going to overflow. They then carefully remove the wire and put it in the trash or in their pocket.

The servers then hold the bottle at a 45-degree angle, pointing it away from guests. They grasp the cork firmly and twist the bottle—not the cork. They allow the pressure to force the cork out gently, without popping. Some pressure may be released around the cork to prevent overflow. By tilting the bottle, the server increases the amount of air space within the bottle and reduces the pressure at the small neck of the bottle. They continue to hold the bottle at a 45-degree angle for a few seconds to reduce the chance of the contents foaming out. If the sparkling wine foams to the top of the bottle, the server pours a small amount into the host's glass to prevent a spill.

Pouring. Wine pouring takes some practice, but competent wine service sells wine. Servers always stand up straight when pouring and pay attention to what they are doing. They wipe the lip of the opened bottle with a clean napkin to remove any cork pieces or mold. While pouring, they continue to hold the clean linen napkin in their left hand to wipe the bottle of drips, moisture, or water from the ice bucket.

Holding the bottle firmly by the wide portion, with the label in full view of the guests, servers lower the lip of the bottle to about one inch above each glass. They do not pick up the glasses. They pour a taste (about one-half inch) for the guest who ordered the wine or champagne. The guest may then sniff and taste the wine

Proper beverage service enhances the guest dining experience. (Courtesy of the Tides Inn, Irvington, Virginia.)

or champagne and give approval. If the host says the wine or champagne is unsatisfactory, the server apologizes, takes it away, and informs his or her supervisor immediately. If the host approves, servers pour wine or champagne for women first, then men, moving clockwise around the table and ending with the host. Wine or champagne is served from the right side of each guest, holding the bottle in the server's right hand.

Depending on the size of the glass, each glass is filled about half-full with wine or champagne. By filling the glasses half-full, guests are better able to smell more bouquet or aroma from the wine.

Champagne and sparkling wines are poured in one of these motions:

- Pour about one-third of a glass and let the foam settle. Then pour more.

- Fill each glass to about half-full.

Servers lift the bottle as they pour so that when they finish, the bottle is about six inches above the glass. They give the bottle a slight twist as they finish pouring. This will help prevent dripping.

Guests often toast a special occasion with wine or champagne. Servers step back as soon as they have served everyone so they do not interfere with these festivities. They then place red wine bottles on the table to the right of the person who ordered them. White, blush, rose, and sparkling wines are placed in the ice bucket, with the server making sure the ice water covers the shoulder of the bottle. The clean linen napkin is placed in the ring on the side of the bucket or draped over the top of the bucket.

Servers typically get five or six 6-ounce to 8-ounce glasses of wine from a 750-milliliter bottle. If the party is large and one glass each almost empties the bottle, servers will ask the person who selected the wine or champagne whether they should chill another bottle and have it ready, or open another bottle to allow it to breathe.

As needed, the server will refill guests' wine or champagne glasses. If a guest places his or her hand over the glass, it means they do not want a refill and are not given one.

When guests order additional bottles of wine, servers provide a fresh glass for the host to taste each new bottle. Servers also bring fresh glasses for everyone if a different wine or champagne is selected. The complete ritual is followed for each bottle served.

Conclusion

No matter what the style of an establishment is—formal, casual, trendy, or night-club—the staff members will be the ones who communicate the image. They will be the ones who will have the most control over whether a guest has an enjoyable experience and wants to return. It is their expertise and competence that will help an establishment create loyal guests and succeed.

Key Terms

cash bank—An amount of cash that a bartender has for making change and performing other business-related tasks.

draft beer—Beer that is served from a keg.

due back—A receipt for any money that is paid out of the cash bank during a shift.

layers—A term describing what happens with coffee strength when it is brewed. The first third of the pot will be too weak, the second will be too strong, and the last third will be too weak. The full pot must drip to blend the layers and arrive at the desired strength.

reading guests—A process by which a staff member determines what type of service each individual guest needs.

roll-ups—Silverware that is wrapped in linen napkins in advance of service.

sidework checklist—A to-do list that lists the sidework tasks and which servers are assigned to complete each task.

suggestive selling—A sales method that encourages guests to buy additional beverages and food.

upselling—A sales method that suggests more expensive and possibly better quality items to guests.

Review Questions

1. How can beverage servers work as a team with other beverage establishment staff members?

2. What is the difference between suggestive selling and upselling?

3. Why do servers follow an order-taking system?

4. What are the different ways that guests can settle a bill?

5. What are the most important tasks that bartenders perform?

6. How are standard drink recipes developed?

7. What type of incidents might be noted in a bar logbook?

8. How are blended drinks prepared?

9. What reports does a bartender prepare at the end of the shift?

10. How long can coffee be held before serving?

11. What should a bartender or server do if draft beer does not develop a head?

12. What factors should be considered when determining which glass to serve wine in?

13. What temperature is white wine usually served at? Red wine?

Internet Sites

For more information, visit the following Internet sites. Remember that Internet addresses can change without notice. If the site is no longer there, you can use a search engine to look for additional sites. Many alcohol-related sites require users to be of legal drinking age to enter.

The Bartender Foundation
www.bartenderfoundation.org/

Bartender Jokes
www.workjoke.com/projoke86.htm

Bartender Magazine
www.bartender.com/home.htm

Cellar Notes
www.cellarnotes.net/index.html

Dale Degroff's Cocktail Corner
www.bevaccess.com/cocktail_
corner.html

Extreme Bartending
www.extremebartending.com/

Happy Hours
www.happyhours.com/

iboozer
www.iboozer.com/

Internet Wine Guide
www.internetwineguide.com/
index.htm

Into Wine
www.intowine.com/enjoy.html

King Cocktail
www.kingcocktail.com/

List of Bartending Schools
www.bartenderzone.com/
bartending%20schools.htm

Miss Charming
www.miss-charming.com/

Sasky.com
www.sasky.com/

Tasting Wine
www.tasting-wine.com/html/
etiquette.html

United States Bartender Guild
www.usbg.org/new/index.cgi?find=
index

The Webtender
www.webtender.com/index/
Bartending/Bartending_Schools/

Wine Education.com
www.wineeducation.com/home.html

Wine Lovers Page
www.wine-lovers-page.com/

The Virtual Bar
www.thevirtualbar.com/

Chapter 4 Outline

Competencies

1. Identify legal restrictions and liability issues affecting the service of alcoholic beverages. (pp. 95–101)

2. Describe steps to take when checking identification of guests. (pp. 101–103)

3. Explain the physical effect of alcohol in relation to the strength of drinks and the body's rate of absorption. (pp. 103–107)

4. Identify signs of intoxication and explain how a "traffic light" system is used to monitor and control guests' alcohol consumption. (pp. 107–111)

5. Describe steps to take when stopping alcohol service to intoxicated guests. (pp. 111–112)

4

Serving Alcohol With Care

Throughout history, people have used alcohol to celebrate special times. Guests frequent taverns, bars, and establishments and order drinks for many reasons:

- To celebrate special events such as weddings, reunions, and births

- To create a feeling of fellowship among friends

- To make their meals more enjoyable

Unfortunately, people also drink to deal with loneliness, to "drown their sorrows," or to "get wasted." Guests who drink for the wrong reasons are more likely than others to drink too much alcohol. In the wrong hands, alcohol can become a fatal weapon, contributing to traffic accidents and fatalities, boating accidents, drowning deaths, and other mishaps.

Alcohol can also be a fatal poison. Each year many people die from overdoses of alcohol or alcohol in combination with other drugs. When its effects are not fatal, inappropriate use of alcohol can contribute to violent acts as well as serious accidents (slips and falls). It can also interfere with normal fetal development, resulting in fetal alcohol syndrome or other birth defects.

Society is increasingly concerned with alcohol abuse, and courts are increasingly holding establishments responsible for serving intoxicated guests. Groups like MADD (Mothers Against Drunk Driving), SADD (Students Against Drunk Driving), and BADD (Bartenders Against Drunk Driving) are on the rise. Exhibit 1 presents sample statistics and resources on the effect of drunken driving available from MADD's Web site. Exhibit 2 shows the kind of designated driver and alternate transportation programs promoted by sectors of the beverage industry.

Servers of alcoholic beverages have legal responsibilities. What happens when establishments violate the laws regarding alcohol service?

- Owners, managers, servers, and bartenders can be sued if someone is injured because of irresponsible alcohol service.

- Managers, servers, and bartenders can lose their jobs.

- Establishments can lose their liquor licenses.

- Owners can lose their businesses.

When servers of alcoholic beverages understand their legal responsibilities, they:

- Develop better judgment and confidence when serving alcohol.

- Enhance guest service and safely promote hospitality.

- Reduce injuries and deaths caused by drunken driving accidents.

Exhibit 1   Statistics on Drunk Driving

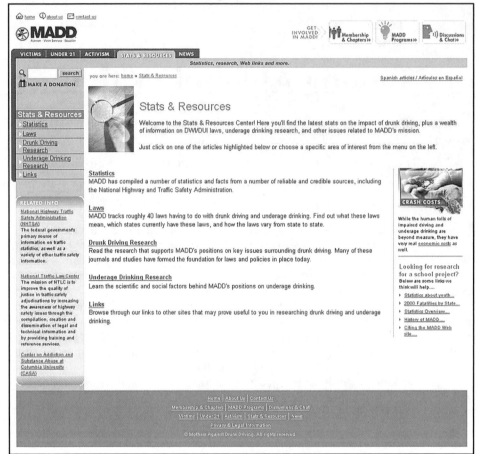

Source: Mothers Against Drunk Driving (MADD). For up-to-date statistics and resources about drunk driving, browse the organization's Web site at: http://www.madd.org.

Regardless of legal considerations, bartenders and servers have an ethical duty to see to it that people are not hurt because of the failure to serve alcohol with care.

Alcohol Service and the Law

Under the Twenty-First Amendment of the U.S. Constitution, each state has the right to control the sale of alcoholic beverages within that state. In states that permit the sale of alcoholic beverages, sales are governed by alcoholic beverage control laws, rules, and regulations of the state liquor authority. While alcoholic beverage control boards in each county generally have specific powers and responsibilities, the final control usually rests with the state liquor authority. Every establishment serving alcoholic beverages should have a copy of the rules and

Exhibit 2   Designated Driver and Alternate Transportation Programs

Source: Anheuser-Bush Inc. For more information about responsible alcohol programs, browse the company's endorsed Web site at: www.designateddriver.com.

regulations of its State Liquor Authority. The laws in every state (and often every county) are different with regard to the on-premises and off-premises sales of alcoholic beverages.

Establishments must be licensed to sell alcoholic beverages and the license must be renewed every year. Applications for a license are made to the local county Alcoholic Beverage Control Board or directly to the State Liquor Authority. Three types of licenses for on-premises consumption are:

- Beer license

- Liquor license (includes sale of wine and beer)

- Wine license (may or may not include the sale of beer)

Before granting an on-premises license, the Alcoholic Beverage Control Board inspects and approves the establishment. Once granted a license, the establishment must obtain approval from the Board for any planned increases (or decreases) in the size of premises or any change in equipment. In many states, no retail licensee for on-premises consumption may deliver or give away any liquors or wines for off-premises consumption.

Alcoholic Beverage Control Boards also regulate the hours of the day during which an establishment may not sell alcoholic beverages. For example, in some areas it is illegal to sell alcohol from 2 a.m. to 11 a.m. It may be illegal to sell alcohol on Sundays, or Sunday sales of alcohol are legal only after noon. Some areas prohibit the sale of alcohol on voting days when the polls are open. In a few areas, it is always illegal to sell all or most types of alcohol. These areas are said to be "dry," although they may allow some type of alcohol sales, such as beer with less than three percent alcohol by volume.

State laws usually require every retail licensee for on-premises consumption to maintain records of daily sales and purchases of alcoholic beverages. Purchase records must generally include the sellers' names, license numbers, and places of business.

In some states, a licensed establishment is prohibited from employing any person under the age of twenty-one as a host, server, bartender, or other staff position whose duties require them to sell, dispense, or handle alcoholic beverages.

Illegal sales of alcoholic beverages may well result in the suspension or revocation of a liquor license. This would cause at least the loss of some jobs and possibly the closing of the business. Alcoholic beverage control laws generally prohibit sales to minors, to habitual drunkards, or to visibly intoxicated persons. It is up to individual states to determine who is a minor (that is, who is too young to drink) and who is legally intoxicated. States classify a person as legally intoxicated based on blood alcohol concentration (BAC). Each state determines a minimum BAC level at which a person in that state is legally intoxicated.

Blood Alcohol Concentration (BAC)

When you drink an alcoholic beverage, some of the alcohol enters your bloodstream. The amount of alcohol in your bloodstream is your **blood alcohol concentration**, or BAC. In most areas, if you have a BAC of 0.08 percent (8/100 of 1 percent), you are legally drunk.

It is important to understand that someone who doesn't look or even act drunk may, in fact, be legally intoxicated. A BAC of 0.10 is equivalent to one drop of alcohol in 1,000 drops of blood. While this may not seem like a lot, a BAC of 0.30 percent may cause a coma, and a BAC of 0.40 percent can cause death.

How can you tell what someone's BAC is? You can't—unless you have special equipment such as a breathalizer. Bartenders and servers must rely on a guest's behavioral signs and on the amount of alcohol a guest consumes to gauge the guest's level of intoxication.

Liability

Anyone who serves alcohol at an establishment can be sued for injuries or damages caused by illegal alcohol sales. That includes establishment owners, managers, servers, and bartenders. Two basic types of laws determine liability in alcohol sales cases:

- Dram shop acts (legislative acts passed by a state's legislature)

- Common law (negligence)

Dram shop acts are referred to as third-party liability laws. The state legislature enacts them into law. In order to understand how these laws work, you must understand what is meant by the terms "first party," "second party," and "third party." The "first party" is the person buying the alcohol; the "second party" is the person or establishment selling or serving the alcohol; the "third party" is someone outside the alcohol sales transaction. The key statutory words in most states are: the establishment's liability follows the service of alcohol to a minor and/or an obviously and visibly intoxicated individual, who then is involved in a drunken driving accident injuring others.

Liability Under Dram Shop Acts. Under many dram shop acts, a plaintiff (the person suing) must prove an unlawful sale of liquor or other alcoholic beverages (beer or wine) to an intoxicated person which causes injury to another party. Dram shop acts date back to the 1800s and were enacted to protect family members from habitual drunkards. Each state has the right to legislate its alcohol liability laws. Today, one must read the state's dram shop act of their location, as each state's third-party liquor liability statute may differ. For example, the statute in Florida will differ from the statute in New York.

While dram shop acts vary from state to state, they generally provide consistent guidelines about who is responsible when third parties suffer because of an intoxicated person's actions. Let's assume something like this happens in a state where there is a dram shop act:

> A man comes into a bar and drinks four Manhattans in an hour. Even though he is slurring his words and trips over a chair on his way to the bar counter, the establishment serves him two more Manhattans. When the man leaves the bar, he gets into his car and has a head-on collision with a van. He and the woman driving the van are both injured.

Under a dram shop act, the woman in the van (the third party) will probably have a successful suit against the bar. The potential liability of taverns, restaurants, hotels, and other establishments is usually tremendous. The owners may be directly liable to the injured or deceased party or parties for various damages including medical expenses, property damages, damages for pain and suffering, support for spouse and dependents, lost wages, funeral expenses, and perhaps punitive damages.

All establishments serving liquor should obtain insurance to cover these potentially devastating amounts of recoverable damages. As the frequency and amounts of awards in favor of third parties increase, liquor liability insurance rates rise. Strict adherence to responsible service procedures, documentation of service, and training efforts may help establishments obtain insurance rate discounts— some as high as 15 percent.

The Model Alcoholic Beverage Retail License Liability Act of 1985, or the "Model Dram Shop Act," establishes consistent, equitable, and uniform guidelines for the application of alcohol-server liability. The act created the "Responsible Business Practice Defense" to provide an establishment with a means of protection from liability. The establishment is protected if it can be proven that, at the time of service, a licensee or server was adhering to "those business practices which an ordinary, prudent person would follow under like circumstances." By permitting a defendant to assert a defense of responsible business practices, the act encourages licensees and servers to conduct themselves in a responsible manner toward their guests. The practices and policies cited in the act include:

- Actively encouraging guests not to become intoxicated if they are consuming alcoholic beverages on the premises.

- Promoting alternative, non-alcoholic beverages and making food readily available to guests.

- Actively promoting an alternative, "safe" means of transportation to prevent guests from driving while intoxicated.

- Prohibiting staff members from consuming alcoholic beverages while on duty.

- Providing a comprehensive, ongoing training program for servers in alcohol awareness, the responsible service of alcohol, and how to effectively interact with intoxicated guests.

Common Law Liability. A person who is injured by the acts of an intoxicated individual may also have the **common law** right to bring a lawsuit against the owners of a restaurant or bar where the person causing the injuries was served intoxicating beverages. Such suits may be based on a common law theory of negligence—independent of any claim under a state's Dram Shop Act. A lawyer representing an injured party in a drunken driving accident case may opt to sue in common law negligence. "**Negligence**," as defined under common law, means the failure to exercise the type of reasonable care used by a prudent person under similar circumstances. "Reasonable care" is a somewhat vague term, but it is crucial for an establishment's defense, to be able to show they have exercised reasonable care with alcohol service.

In the earlier head-on collision example, under common law, the woman could argue that the bar was negligent in serving the man, who was obviously drunk. When an establishment is negligent, it means that its staff members failed to do what any sensible person ought to have done under the circumstances: stop service when the man showed signs of intoxication and provide alternate transportation home, possibly a taxi cab. If the drunk is not driving, there is no drunken driving accident. Training should focus on methods to spot the intoxicated guest, and preventing him or her from driving. Stopping alcohol service to the intoxicated guest is not enough.

Checking Identification

Establishments avoid serving alcohol to minors by developing various procedures for staff to follow when the checking identification documents of guests. Some establishments may check identification at the door and not allow minors to enter. Others may allow minors to enter, but use a method (such as hand stamps) to distinguish guests of legal drinking age from minors. Others may have staff check guests' identification as they order alcoholic beverages. Some establishments use an identification register—a book signed by guests who appear to be underage but have identification documents. If a guest's identification is fake and he or she signs the register, liability may transfer from the establishment to the guest.

Typically, a valid identification must have a photograph, statement of age (such as date of birth), and the signature of the person named on the document. Commonly accepted types of identification include:

- Valid driver's license issued by any state

- State-issued identification card

- International driver's license

- United States military identification

- Valid United States passport

Checking guests' identification can be uncomfortable, but it is one of the most important responsibilities staff members of alcohol service establishments face. If the establishment's policy for checking identification is posted at the entrance, guests may be more comfortable showing their identification. For example, a sign could say, "If you look younger than 30 years of age, please be prepared to show identification." If guests see that everyone is treated equally and that it is the establishment's policy to check identification, they may be less likely to object if asked to show identification. Some older guests may even feel complimented.

Regardless of whether an establishment checks identification at the door, a server should always ask to see the identification of anyone he or she suspects is not of legal drinking age before serving the person alcohol. Servers can't ignore guest relations when checking identification. Ensuring that guests are of legal drinking age is like other services they provide. Servers should always be courteous and polite. Basic procedures include:

- Smile, look directly at the guest, and greet him or her: "Hello. Welcome to the Pub."

- Politely ask to see the person's identification: "May I please see your identification?"

- If the person does not remove the identification from his or her wallet, politely ask: "Could you please remove the identification from your wallet?" Never remove an identification from a person's wallet or purse yourself.

- Look at the birth date on the identification. Is the person of legal drinking age?

- Check whether the photograph appears to be that of the person handing you the identification. Look at the physical description on the document, especially the height and weight. Do they fit the person?

- Check the expiration date to ensure that the identification is valid. All drivers' licenses have an expiration date.

- Check the state seal to ensure that it is the right size and in the proper location.

Sometimes, minors obtain fake identification. When checking documents, you may find one that is altered, counterfeit, or borrowed/stolen from a person of legal drinking age. When checking an identification that you think may be false:

- Feel the surface to make sure a new layer of lamination has not been added.

- See whether the type has been tampered with.

- Examine the official information such as the state seal, number of digits in the driver's license number, borders, and colors.

- Examine the identification with a light behind it to more clearly see any cuts, erasures, or other alterations.

- Look at the picture and physical description on the identification and compare them to the person presenting the document.

If you have any doubts that the person presenting the identification is the legal owner, ask the person questions he or she should be able to answer immediately, such as:

- "What is your address?"

- "What is your middle name?"

- "How do you spell your last name?"

If the person hesitates before answering or behaves in other ways that make you suspicious, ask the person to sign his or her name. Compare the signature to that on the identification. They should match.

If you suspect that an identification is fake, ask for a second identification document. If you still have doubts, you should follow your establishment's procedures and refuse to admit the person or refuse to serve the person alcohol. If you deny someone entrance or service, it's best to be firm and polite, but never pushy or rude. For instance, depending on the establishment's policies, you might say:

- "I'm sorry, but if I let you in without seeing a valid identification, I'll lose my job."

- "I'm sorry, but it's against the law for me to serve you alcohol."

- "I'd be happy to bring you something else, but I can't serve you alcohol."

You should avoid saying anything to embarrass the minor, such as:

- "You're underage, and I'm not going to let you in."

- "Just what are you trying to pull here? I could have you arrested."
- "You're too young to drink alcohol, and I'm certainly not going to serve you any."

Establishments generally have a policy about confiscating false identification documents and also about detaining minors who present them. If a staff member confiscates an identification document or detains a minor, he or she should always complete an incident report as soon as possible after the occurrence. An incident report documents the facts of an occurrence and explains actions taken and the reasons for the particular actions.

Sometimes minors may get alcohol, even if you have refused to serve them. For example, legal drinkers may give alcoholic beverages to minors who are with them and parents may give their children alcoholic beverages. Different states have different laws regarding minors who are with of-age guests. In states in which it is illegal for minors to drink no matter whom they are with, most establishments tell servers to call a manager to handle the situations described above. The manager will likely take the legal-age drinker aside and discuss the situation.

Alcohol and Its Physical Impact

True or False?
Alcohol is a depressant.

> True. Alcohol is a depressant that deadens the area of the brain that controls a person's inhibitions. That is why people sometimes seem to be more open and friendly when they drink alcohol. However, as alcohol levels increase, other areas of the brain become numb, and people can quickly become withdrawn and sad or irritable and disorderly.

True or False?
Alcohol decreases body temperature.

> True. Alcohol causes the small blood vessels in the skin to expand and this causes a loss of body heat. A person feels the heat on the skin and thinks he or she is getting warmer, but in fact the body is cooling off.

True or False?
How much you drink—not what you drink—causes hangovers.

> True. Hangovers are caused by how much alcohol a person drinks, not by the type of alcohol consumed. When a person drinks alcohol, the liver cannot perform its regular function of maintaining the body's blood sugar levels. It must instead break down the alcohol. As a result, the sugar level in the blood drops, causing headaches, extreme thirst, and other symptoms of a hangover.

True or False?
Time is the only factor that can restore sobriety.

> True. The only way to increase sobriety is to wait for the liver to break down all the alcohol in the body into waste products. Coffee, cold showers, exercise, and other activities do not increase the liver's rate of breaking down alcohol.

True or False?
Alcohol is high in calories.

> True. Alcohol provides more calories per gram than carbohydrates or protein. Therefore, alcohol has more calories than most bread, potatoes, meat, cheese, and other foods that are high in carbohydrates and protein. Alcohol has only slightly fewer calories than pure fat.

Drink Strength

Beer and wine are examples of alcoholic beverages made when certain plants (such as grains, berries, and fruits) undergo a chemical change known as fermentation. Scotch, bourbon, gin, vodka, and rum are examples of beverages made when alcohol is distilled. Distilling alcohol creates stronger, more potent alcohol.

The strength of alcohol is measured in term of "proof." The percentage of alcohol in a beverage is one-half the beverage's proof. For example, a 100-proof beverage contains 50 percent alcohol.

The following beverages have almost exactly the same percentage of alcohol:

- 12 ounces of beer

- 4 ounces of wine

- 1 ¼ ounces of 80-proof liquor

- 1 ounce of 100-proof liquor

Typically, each of these equals one standard drink and contains approximately one-half ounce of alcohol. Different establishments may use different glass sizes to serve common drinks. For example:

- Some establishments pour four ounces of wine as a standard drink, while others pour six ounces.

- Some establishments use glasses that hold 12 or more ounces of beer, while others use glasses that hold 8 or fewer ounces of beer.

- Some establishments serve beer and other alcoholic beverages by the pitcher.

The same type of alcohol is sold in different strengths. Not all brands of beer have the same percentage of alcohol; not all types of wines have the same percentage of alcohol; and not all brands of the same liquor have the same percentage of alcohol. For example, some vodka is 80 proof while other vodka is 100 proof. Exhibit 3 summarizes the alcohol potency of common types of alcoholic beverages.

Also, the way an alcoholic beverage is prepared can affect its alcoholic potency. Suggesting drinks with low-alcohol content is an effective way to help guests drink in moderation. For example:

- A drink served over ice is less potent than one with the same amount of alcohol served straight-up (no ice), because, as the ice melts, it dilutes the strength of the alcohol.

Exhibit 3   Alcohol Potency

- Most liquors range between 80 and 86.9 proof, except gin, which ranges from 90 to 94.6 proof. Some vodka is 100 proof and some rum is 151 proof.
- Most American beers range from approximately 6.4 to 10.5 proof.
- Imported beers range from about 7 to 26 proof.
- Some American beers made in micro-breweries are also as strong as 26 proof or more.
- Dessert wines and sherry, port, and other aperitifs have a higher percentage of alcohol than other wines.

- A drink blended with ice, such as a margarita, daiquiri, or other frozen drink, is more diluted and therefore less potent than a drink served on-the-rocks (with ice) or straight-up.

- A "tall" drink, such as a vodka and orange juice (served in a 12-ounce, rather than in a 6-ounce glass), is less potent than a standard drink. Although the same amount of alcohol is used in both, the taller glass requires more ice and mixer, resulting in a weaker proportion of alcohol to non-alcohol ingredients.

Rate of Absorption

Food has a significant effect on the absorption rate of alcohol. Most food causes alcohol to move slowly from the stomach and small intestine into the bloodstream. This gives the liver more time to break down the alcohol in the body.

Certain types of food slow intoxication more than others. Fatty foods are difficult to digest and therefore remain in the stomach, along with any alcohol present, for a longer time than other foods. However, foods high in carbohydrates such as pretzels, vegetables, fruits, and pasta are quickly digested and may actually speed the absorption rate of alcohol into the bloodstream.

An effective way to reduce the rate of alcohol absorption is to eat foods high in fat. High-fat foods to suggest to guests who are drinking alcohol include:

- French fries
- Deep-fried items
- Cheese
- Pizza
- Chips and dip
- Nachos
- Any beef items (hamburgers, meat balls, beef tacos, etc.)

Intervention

Intervention involves more than stopping alcohol service to guests who are intoxicated. It consists of everything servers, co-workers, and managers do to influence

Exhibit 4   Sample BAC Card

KNOW YOUR LIMITS

Chart for responsible people who may sometimes
drive after drinking!

Approximate Blood Alcohol Percentage

Drinks	1	2	3	4	5	6	7	8
100	.04	.09	.13	.18	.22	.26	.31	.35
120	.04	.07	.11	.15	.18	.22	.26	.29
140	.03	.06	.09	.13	.16	.19	.22	.25
160	.03	.06	.08	.11	.14	.17	.19	.22
180	.02	.05	.07	.10	.12	.15	.17	.20
200	.02	.04	.07	.09	.11	.13	.15	.18
220	.02	.04	.06	.08	.10	.12	.14	.16
240	.02	.04	.06	.07	.09	.11	.13	.15

Body Weight in Pounds

Influenced	Possibly	Definitely
Rarely		

Subtract .01% for each 40 minutes or .03% for each 2 hours of drinking. One
drink is $1\frac{1}{4}$ oz. of 80-proof liquor, 12 oz. of beer, or 4 oz. of table wine.

SUREST POLICY IS . . .
DON'T DRIVE AFTER DRINKING!

This chart is provided for information only. Nothing contained in this chart
shall constitute an endorsement by the Educational Institute of the
American Hotel & Lodging Association (the Institute) or the American
Hotel & Lodging Association (AH&LA) of any information, opinion,
procedure, or product mentioned, and the Institute and AH&LA disclaim
any liability with respect to the use of such information, procedure, or
product, or reliance thereon.

Source: Distilled Spirits Council of the United States, Inc.

guests' attitudes and behaviors as they drink alcohol. In fact, not letting guests
become intoxicated is just as important as not serving alcohol to guests who are
already intoxicated.

Intervention techniques can help you serve alcohol responsibly, discourage
overconsumption, and manage guests who, despite your efforts, become intoxicated. Your first responsibility in intervention is to talk with guests as they arrive.
This will establish good guest relations and help you discover who may be more
likely than others to become intoxicated.

There are many devices that can help you determine a guest's blood alcohol
concentration after drinking certain amounts of alcohol. These devices, similar to
the sample shown in Exhibit 4, contain tables that show estimated BAC for various

Exhibit 5   Factors Affecting BAC and the Impact of Alcohol

Rate of consumption
Alcohol potency
Rate of absorption
    Food
    Water and carbonated beverages
    Emotional factors
Drugs or medicine
Physical characteristics of the person consuming alcohol
    Body size
    Body fat
    Gender
    Age
Environment in which alcohol is consumed

body weights per ounce of alcohol consumed within a specific period of time. However, variables in addition to body weight and the number of drinks consumed affect a guest's BAC. Drink tables and BAC cards have limited practical application, and you should only use them as basic guidelines by which to judge a guest's level of intoxication. Exhibit 5 lists other factors that affect BAC and the impact of alcohol.

One way to monitor a guest's rate of alcohol consumption is to keep track of the number of alcoholic beverages he or she consumes. Some drinks contain more alcohol than others and should be counted as more than one drink. Frequently used drink recipes should be standardized to help staff members more accurately count drinks. Everyone at the establishment should make these drinks exactly the same way, with exactly the same amounts of alcohol.

What a guest is drinking and how quickly it is consumed are also important items to note. All establishments should have procedures to help bartenders and servers count the number of drinks served to each guest. When guest checks are used, servers can note the time and the person ordering the drink each time an order is placed. When guest checks are not used, drink-tracking records are used (similar to the one presented in Exhibit 6) to count the number of drinks served to each guest and to rate each guest's level of intoxication.

Signs of Intoxication

In addition to counting drinks, servers can control alcohol risks more effectively by recognizing changes in behavior that may indicate guests' levels of intoxication. When talking with a guest, ask yourself the following questions:

- Does the guest appear stressed, depressed, or tired?

- Is the guest drunk or determined to get drunk?

- Is the guest dieting?

- Is the guest taking any medication or other drugs?

Exhibit 6 Sample Drink-Tracking Record

Table # / Guest #	Drink #	Time		Table # / Guest #	Drink #	Time		Table # / Guest #	Drink #	Time
Table 21 / Guest 1				Table 21 / Guest 1				Table 21 / Guest 1		
Table 21 / Guest 2				Table 21 / Guest 2				Table 21 / Guest 2		
Table 21 / Guest 3				Table 21 / Guest 3				Table 21 / Guest 3		
Table 21 / Guest 4				Table 21 / Guest 4				Table 21 / Guest 4		
Table 22 / Guest 1				Table 22 / Guest 1				Table 22 / Guest 1		
Table 22 / Guest 2				Table 22 / Guest 2				Table 22 / Guest 2		
Table 23 / Guest 1				Table 23 / Guest 1				Table 23 / Guest 1		
Table 23 / Guest 2				Table 23 / Guest 2				Table 23 / Guest 2		
Table 23 / Guest 3				Table 23 / Guest 3				Table 23 / Guest 3		
Table 23 / Guest 4				Table 23 / Guest 4				Table 23 / Guest 4		
Table 24 / Guest 1				Table 24 / Guest 1				Table 24 / Guest 1		
Table 24 / Guest 2				Table 24 / Guest 2				Table 24 / Guest 2		
Table 24 / Guest 3				Table 24 / Guest 3				Table 24 / Guest 3		
Table 24 / Guest 4				Table 24 / Guest 4				Table 24 / Guest 4		

Rating: **g** = green **y** = yellow **r** = red

Exhibit 7   Behavioral Changes That May Indicate Intoxication

Relaxed Inhibitions	Impaired Judgment	Slowed Reaction Time	Decreased Coordination
• Personality changes such as a quiet guest becoming overly friendly or an outspoken guest becoming quiet and withdrawn • Anti-social behavior such as leaving a group of friends and drinking alone • Uncontrolled emotional displays or outbursts • Noisy or rowdy behavior such as speaking too loudly or "showing off" • Obnoxious behavior such as suddenly using foul language or making offensive comments	• Complaining about drink strength, preparation, or price after consuming one or more of the same type of drink without complaining • Drinking faster; ordering shots or doubles • Being careless with money by leaving it unattended or offering to buy drinks for strangers or employees • Making irrational or nonsensical statements • Starting arguments or fights	• Glassy, unfocused eyes; dilated pupils • Drowsiness • Loss of concentration such as inability to finish sentences • Altered speech patterns such as slurred speech • Difficulty lighting cigarettes or having two cigarettes burn at once	• Difficulty handling coins or selecting money from a wallet or purse • Clumsiness, such as spilling drinks • Loss of balance, staggering, bumping into people, furniture, walls, etc., falling down • Falling asleep

Alcohol may affect guests in any of these situations more quickly or severely than it affects other guests.

Guests can exhibit various signs of intoxication. Exhibit 7 shows four general types of changes in behavior that occur when guests drink alcohol and provides examples of each type of behavior.

Changes in behavior are more important than the behavior itself. For example, a loud guest may not signal that the guest is intoxicated—the guest may simply be a loud person. However, it may be a sign of intoxication if the guest was quiet and reserved at first and then became loud and rowdy after a few drinks. Similarly, a guest complaint about the strength of a drink may not be a sign of intoxication. However, if a guest complains that his or her drink is weak after drinking one or more of the same alcoholic beverages without complaining, this would be a sign of intoxication because it indicates a change in behavior.

Traffic Light System

The traffic light system is an easy-to-use method of recognizing and rating guests' levels of intoxication. The system is based upon the colors of a traffic light. When guests drink alcohol, they can change quickly, just like a traffic light. Guests can also be in the green, yellow, or red when they enter your establishment.

Green—Go.
The guest is sober. Actions to take include:

- Encourage food with drinks, if appropriate at your establishment.

- Explain any designated driver specials (such as free non-alcoholic beverages) that the establishment may provide.

- When a guest asks for a drink served straight-up, bring a glass of water along with it. If it's acceptable at your establishment, serve water with all drinks.

- Serve only one drink at a time to each guest.

- Don't bring a drink to someone who doesn't want one.

Yellow—Caution.
The guest is becoming intoxicated. Actions to take include:

- Take the situation seriously; it's much easier to deal with a guest at this stage than if the guest is in the red.

- Advise a manager about the situation to help prevent the guest from moving into the red, if appropriate at your establishment.

- Strongly encourage the guest to eat, if appropriate at your establishment.

- Strongly suggest non-alcoholic or low-alcohol beverages in place of the alcoholic beverages being consumed.

- Wait for the guest to reorder—don't suggest or encourage the purchase of more alcoholic beverages.

- Remove the guests' used glass before bringing a new drink when the guest reorders.

- Ensure that the guest will be safe when he or she leaves by telephoning a taxi, suggesting that the guest telephone for a ride, assuring that someone in the guest's party will drive, or suggesting that the guest stay at an adjacent lodging property.

Red—Stop!
The guest is intoxicated. Actions to take include:

- Get a second opinion from a co-worker or manager before stopping alcohol service.

- Ask a manager or other staff members to help; dealing with guests in the red is a team effort.

- Deny or stop alcohol service by following the establishment's policies and procedures.

Developing a network of staff members that monitor and control alcoholic consumption is a responsible business practice that may lower the risk of alcohol-related incidents at an establishment. It's important to train all staff members—including valet attendants, door attendants, cashiers, and others in guest-contact positions—to spot signs of intoxication and to alert a supervisor or manager to the problem.

Stopping Alcohol Service

Denying or stopping alcohol service is never an enjoyable task. However, it is an extremely important one. When dealing with an intoxicated guest, the guest's well-being and the safety of others depend upon the actions you take. General guidelines for denying or stopping alcohol service include:

- Ask a co-worker to watch as you refuse to serve alcohol to a guest. You may appreciate the co-worker's help.

- Move the guest away from others.

- Calmly and firmly state your establishment's policy: "I'm sorry, but I've served you all the alcohol that my manager will allow."

- Do not judge the guest, make accusations, or argue. Don't say: "You're drunk" or "You've had too much to drink."

- Repeat your establishment's rules: "We care about your safety, and I can't serve you any more alcohol" or "The local police are really cracking down, and I can't serve you any more alcohol or we'll both get in trouble."

- Remove all alcohol from the reach of the person—even if it is his or her drink.

- Get a doorperson or manager to help you, if required at your establishment.

- Try not to let an intoxicated guest drive away—or even walk away—even if that means calling the police. It's better to risk making the guest angry than to risk lives.

- Make sure the guest has all of his or her personal belongings when he or she leaves.

- Fill out an incident report to describe the situation and to record all actions taken.

Other Situations

Some situations require special alcohol service procedures. For instance, banquets, meetings, receptions, and other special events make it more difficult to control alcohol risks effectively.

Lodging facilities face additional challenges because guests may drink in their rooms, in hospitality suites, lounges, restaurants, and other areas. In addition, lodging staff members must make sure intoxicated guests do not leave the property. It's not enough to escort an intoxicated guest from the restaurant or lounge to a guestroom. Staff members must then make sure the guest does not later leave the hotel.

In these types of situations, it's extremely important for servers to use the traffic light system and work as a team with other staff members to monitor and control alcohol consumption. Staff members such as guest service representatives, uniformed service staff members, and others must be part of the effort to control alcohol risks effectively.

Key Terms

blood alcohol concentration (BAC)—Expresses the weight of alcohol per unit of blood, usually in grams per 100 milliliters (or per deciliter).

common law—A system of unwritten law not evidenced by statute, but by traditions and the opinions and judgments of courts of law.

dram shop laws—Statutory third-party liability laws which make dispensers of alcohol liable if they dispense alcohol irresponsibly, that is, to minors, to anyone who is obviously intoxicated, or to an anyone who becomes intoxicated because of such service.

negligence—As defined under common law, the failure to exercise the type of reasonable care used by a prudent person under similar circumstances.

Review Questions

1. What is the role of state liquor authorities in regulating the sale of alcoholic beverages?

2. What types of licenses do operations need to sell beer, liquor, and wine?

3. What is BAC and how is it determined?

4. Why are Dram Shop Acts referred to as third party liability laws?

5. How is "negligence" defined under common law?

6. What are the commonly accepted types of guest identification?

7. What actions could you take if you feel that a guest is presenting a fake identification?

8. How is the strength of a drink determined?

9. How is a "traffic light" system used to monitor a guest's consumption of alcohol?

10. What actions could you take to deny or stop the service of alcohol to intoxicated guests?

Case Studies

Responsible Alcohol Service: A Rose Between Two Thorny Situations

It was just after 9:00 P.M., at the end of a long Saturday shift, when Rose Wheaton, a server at Vic's Restaurant, noticed a group settling into one of her tables by the bar. Although she had been at Vic's less than a month—and had yet to receive all of her server training—she recognized four of them as some of the restaurant's best guests. There were six people in the group: two older couples that were Saturday-night regulars whom she called by name, and a younger man and woman she did not know.

"Hey, Rose!" one of the men called out. "Sure looks busy tonight."

"Never too busy for you and your friends, Mr. Grove," Rose said, smiling as she reached their table. "How are you doing this evening?"

"We're fine. Just waiting for a table." Mr. Grove reached over and put his arm around the young man beside him. "This here's my son, Tommy. He's been away at college, but he's finally going to graduate next weekend. And this is Gwen, his fiancée. We're out for a kind of two-for-one celebration—graduation and engagement."

"That's great," Rose said. "What can I get for you while you wait for your table?"

"I think champagne is in order," Mr. Grove said. "And six glasses."

Rose glanced up from her pad at Tommy and Gwen. She quickly remembered that she had been 22 years old when she graduated from college. And Tommy and Gwen looked young. Were they even able to drink legally?

"I'll bring your champagne right out," she said. She moved around the table toward the younger couple. "Could I please see your driver's licenses?" she asked the couple.

"You've got to be kidding," Tommy said.

"We card everybody that looks really young."

Tommy's face flushed deep crimson as he turned to Gwen. "Do you have yours?"

"I left my purse at your parents' house," she said.

"Along with my wallet," Tommy said, staring back at Rose. "What about a passport? I've got mine out in the car."

Rose shook her head. "It's got to be a driver's license."

"That's crazy. What if we didn't drive a car?"

"Look, I don't make the —"

"I swear, we're both 22. We're getting married, for Pete's sake. Trust us."

"I do trust you, but, you know, it's not up to me. It's my boss's rule. He says that unless you have a driver's license, you can't drink alcohol here. The last thing we need to deal with is a bunch of drunk teenagers!" she said with a laugh.

"What? I—"

"It's okay, son," Mr. Grove interrupted, looking up at her with a smile. "You just bring us four glasses, Rose, and we'll be fine here."

"But, Dad—"

"It's okay," he said with a wink.

Ten minutes later, Rose was picking up a round of beers for a bowling league having a shouting match at table 7 when Gary Hammond, the bartender, called her over. "Did you card those two at table 5?" he asked, nodding toward the Grove party.

"Of course," she said. "They didn't have their I.D.s, but it's okay. They're not drinking."

"You could have fooled me," Gary said. "See for yourself." She looked in time to see Mr. Grove refill four champagne glasses—and two "water" glasses sitting in front of the engaged couple.

Rose shook her head. The bowlers were hollering for their beer. "Gary, I don't have time to play games with these people. Where's Vic?" she asked, referring to the restaurant's owner/manager. When she found Vic overseeing the dinner production in the kitchen, she quickly explained the situation and asked him to come out and talk to the Grove party.

When Vic approached the table, he immediately greeted the four adult regulars by name and asked how they were doing. Everyone seemed to be in especially fine spirits, though he noticed that the young man and woman suddenly weren't drinking their "water."

"May I talk with you for a moment, Ted?" he asked Mr. Grove. The two stepped over to the bar for a private conversation. "Ted," Vic began quietly, "people without a valid photo I.D. cannot be served alcohol here."

"They weren't," Mr. Grove said, his smile starting to fade. "Well, not really, anyway. Rose said you wouldn't allow it, but I didn't see why you couldn't do us a little favor."

"It isn't a matter of favors, Ted, it's a legal requirement for running a restaurant in this state. You know that we trust and respect you and your guests, but this isn't about that. It is simply a matter of obeying the law. Now, I understand you're out for a celebration tonight, and I certainly don't want to rain on that. But, to avoid any further embarrassment, I do have to take the champagne away from your son and his fiancée. I also need to ask that you not give them any more."

"Is that all?" Mr. Grove said glumly.

"Well. . ., no. Because this is a special night for your family and friends, I want to offer you a complimentary appetizer platter. Your table in the dining room should be ready in about five minutes, and I'll have the appetizer delivered hot from the kitchen the minute you all sit down."

"Really? Well, thanks, Vic. I appreciate that." As the two men headed back to table 5, Mr. Grove approached Tommy and Gwen, explained the law, and asked for their glasses. He handed them over to Vic, along with an apology and another "thank you" for the offer of the appetizer platter. Vic took the glasses back to the bar, where Gary was prepping a platter of five 23-ounce beers.

"Nice work, boss," Gary said. "I wish you could handle every problem that comes up like that."

"What do you mean?"

"Look at table 7. Or maybe I should say, listen to table 7. It's the Bolingbrook Bowling League again. They must start drinking at the bowling alley. And for some reason they always come in with their volume stuck on 10."

"How long have they been here?"

Gary checked his watch. "Forty minutes. And this is round two of large beers."

That meant the five bowlers had each consumed the equivalent of four beers within forty minutes. And who could know how much they may have had to drink before they arrived? "Who's serving table 7?"

"It's Rose's table, but I told her I'd cover during her break. I could be wrong, but I'd say there are a couple people there moving straight into the yellow," he said, referring to the cautionary zone between sobriety (green) and inebriation (red). "Even though they started loud, they seem to be getting even rowdier. And for a while they were telling everyone around them that we're watering down the beer. Unless I'm misreading the signs or they start slowing down, this round will turn the whole table yellow."

"All right. Take five waters along with these beers. You might also ask if anyone would care for coffee. Keep a close eye on them and fill Rose in when she comes off break. I don't think she's ever had to deal with a situation like this before."

"So I'm not cutting them off?"

Vic shook his head. "They're obviously feeling good—and loud—but they still seem to be under control to me."

Fifteen minutes later, Rose was back at the bar with an order for another round of beer for table 7. "That's some wild group," she said, rubbing her temples. "Another round of these and they'll be bowling me across the restaurant."

"That's it, then," Gary said. "You need to cut them off. Offer them coffee, soda, sparkling juice, whatever—but let them know that you cannot serve them any more alcohol."

"Are you serious?"

"Absolutely."

Rose nervously approached the table, but instead of finding five bowlers, she now discovered eight people squeezed around the table.

"Come over here, little lady, and meet some of our new friends!" one of the bowlers said, grabbing her arm and yanking her toward the table.

"Hey," another one spoke up, "where's our brewskies? I succinctly remember ordering another brewskie."

"You did," Rose said, "but it's obvious that you've all had enough. In fact, I'd say it's obvious to every other person in this restaurant. I'm cutting you off. Now, if you'd like something else to drink, or something to eat, I'd be happy—"

"But what about us?" one of the newcomers asked. "We just got here, and we want something to drink."

"'Course you do, buddy," chimed in one of the original five, slapping the man hard across the back. "You got catching up to do. Lots. Nobody's cutting anything off as long as I'm here."

"Are you saying we have to sit here nursing a soda pop or something while our friends are drinking real drinks? You've got to be joking!"

"Look, missy, you're new here, so you probably don't have any idea how much money we spend in this place," another added.

Rose looked up helplessly at Gary behind the bar. Where's Vic now? she silently asked.

Discussion Questions

1. What mistakes did Rose make in her handling of the Grove party? the Bolingbrook Bowling League?

2. What steps can a server take to effectively manage someone in the yellow zone?

3. What could Vic have done to better prepare his staff for responsible alcohol service?

Case Number: 3494CA

The following industry experts helped generate and develop this case: Christopher Kibit, C.S.C., Academic Team Leader, Hotel/Motel/Food Management & Tourism Programs, Lansing Community College, Lansing, Michigan; and Jack Nye, General Manager, Applebee's of Michigan, Applebee's International, Inc.

Chapter 5 Outline

Competencies

1. Describe four leadership styles and identify situations that may be appropriate to each. (pp. 119–121)

2. Describe steps supervisors take when communicating change to staff members. (pp. 121–124)

3. Identify supervisory responsibilities in relation to human resource functions. (pp. 124–137)

4. Explain how managing time, delegating tasks, and controlling stress increase the personal effectiveness of a supervisor. (pp. 137–141)

5

Fundamentals of Supervision

First and foremost, supervisors are leaders within their organizations. **Leadership** is the ability to attain objectives by working with and through people. A leader creates conditions that motivate staff members by establishing goals and influencing the staff to attain those goals.

Supervisors cannot be everywhere at once, peering over the shoulders of staff members, policing procedures, and correcting behaviors. In service-driven operations, like bars and lounges, the most important decisions and actions of supervisors are those that help staff members become more effective in serving guests on their own. Traditional management functions of directing, controlling, and commanding give way to new responsibilities of enabling, empowering, and supporting.

Supervisors enable staff members by providing the training necessary to help them become competent in performing the fundamental tasks of their positions. Training is absolutely essential to delivering quality service to guests and is most effective when it provides staff members with the "why" behind the "how-to" of their positions.

Empowering staff members means that supervisors must influence individuals to accept greater responsibility and exercise more control over the way they perform their jobs. Responsible alcohol service requires that bartenders, servers, and other staff members are properly trained and empowered to make decisions while serving guests. However, before exercising more control over their positions, staff members will want assurances from their supervisor that he or she values their ideas, has confidence in their judgment, and will support their efforts.

Supervisors support staff members by backing up the good decisions and actions they take on the front lines and serving guests as best they can at each point of guest contact. If a staff member makes a truly poor service choice, the supervisor points out the mistake, but still shows support by coaching the staff member and providing retraining if necessary.

The sections that follow examine basic leadership styles and explore the role of the supervisor as a change agent. Supervisory responsibilities in relation to human resource functions are also addressed. The closing sections focus on increasing personal effectiveness as a supervisor through better time management, delegation, and stress-coping techniques.

Leadership Styles

Leadership styles are the tools for creating the conditions in which staff members become motivated to achieve the establishment's goals. Ideally, an effective supervisor adopts the leadership style most appropriate to the situation at hand. In practice, however, this is hard to achieve because a variety of factors generally limit your ability to move easily among very different leadership styles.

Your personality, knowledge, values, and experiences shape your feelings about and reactions toward staff members. Some supervisors feel comfortable in freely delegating work and like to involve the staff in a team approach to defining and resolving problems. Other supervisors like to do everything themselves. Simply put, your feelings about appropriate leadership are important in determining the specific leadership style you will use. Also, the success you may have achieved with a particular style may affect your willingness to adopt a different style.

Staff members are individuals with differing personalities and backgrounds. Like their supervisors, they, too, are influenced by specific factors. Staff members who want independence or decision-making responsibility, who identify with the organization's goals, and who are knowledgeable and experienced in their positions may work better when guided by a specific leadership style. On the other hand, staff members with different expectations and experiences might require a very different leadership style from their supervisor.

Autocratic Leadership

The **autocratic leadership style** is one of the oldest approaches to management. Supervisors adopting this style make decisions without input from their staff members. They generally give orders without explanations, and expect those orders to be obeyed. When practiced in the wrong situations or with the wrong type of staff members, this leadership style can be disastrous. Low staff morale, high absenteeism and turnover, even work stoppage could result. However, there are times when this leadership style is both necessary and effective.

Consider, for example, the situation when business at the bar unexpectedly doubles the forecasted volume during a night shift. The bar staff would need fast, specific instructions on how to vary accepted procedures in order to properly serve all of the guests. In this type of situation, staff members might expect the supervisor to adopt an autocratic leadership style and tell them: "This is what we need to do. Here is how we can do it. Now let's get it done." Autocratic leadership techniques can also be successful when:

- The supervisor knows how to do the work of the staff.

- There are a number of new, untrained staff members who do not know which tasks to perform and/or which procedures to follow.

- A staff member does not respond positively to any other style of supervision.

Bureaucratic Leadership

The **bureaucratic leadership style** is one in which a supervisor focuses on rules, regulations, policies, and procedures. These supervisors manage by the rules and rely on higher levels of management to make decisions about issues not covered "by the book."

A bureaucratic supervisor is more a police officer than a leader. Normally, this enforcement style is adopted only when all other leadership styles are inappropriate, or when staff members can be permitted no discretion in the decisions to be made. For example, it is important that rules and procedures are followed to the letter when staff check guests' identification, monitor guests' alcohol consumption, or stop alcohol service to intoxicated guests. A bureaucratic leadership style may also be appropriate in many situations in which procedures are established for staff members performing routine or repetitive tasks, such as inventory procedures and restocking products at the bar.

Democratic Leadership

The **democratic leadership** style is almost the reverse of the autocratic style. The democratic supervisor keeps staff members informed on all matters that directly affect their work, and shares decision-making and problem-solving responsibilities. This type of supervisor emphasizes the staff members' roles in the operation, and provides opportunities for staff members to develop a high sense of job satisfaction. The democratic supervisor seeks the ideas and opinions of staff members and seriously considers their recommendations. For example, before implementing a special drink promotion, a bar supervisor may ask for ideas from staff members. Feedback from staff could help the bar supervisor to increase the staff's knowledge of the products to be promoted and to set realistic sales goals for the promotion. The democratic leadership style may be most appropriate to use with highly-skilled or experienced staff members. This style can be effective when implementing operational changes or resolving individual or group problems.

While this leadership style may seem vastly more appealing than autocratic or bureaucratic approaches, there are limitations and potential disadvantages to consider. For example, it may take longer to reach a decision or solution when a number of staff members are involved in the decision-making or problem-solving process. Some situations call for more prompt action. Also, it may not be cost effective to involve the entire staff in matters that are straightforward and easily resolved by the supervisor.

Laissez-Faire Leadership

The **laissez-faire leadership** style refers to a hands-off approach in which the supervisor actually does very little leading. The supervisor provides little or no direction and allows staff members as much freedom as possible. In effect, the supervisor gives all authority (power) to the staff members, and relies on them to establish goals, make decisions, and resolve problems. The basic motto of this type of supervisor is "don't rock the boat." While there are relatively few times when this approach can be effectively used, it may be appropriate to use with highly-skilled or experienced staff members who have been trained in decision-making and problem-solving techniques.

The Supervisor as Change Agent

Yesterday's solutions may not solve today's problems and today's solutions may not solve tomorrow's problems. Change is a constant in the fast-paced world of beverage operations. Not only do the needs, wants, and expectations of guests change, but also the laws and regulations affecting alcohol service. Mixology changes with new, creative types of drinks to offer. Changes in technology affect how orders are placed and sales are reported. Change is everywhere and the agent of change is often the beverage supervisor. A **change agent** is the person responsible for planning, implementing, and evaluating changes within the work environment.

Change can be difficult to implement when staff members feel comfortable with what they are doing and want to maintain established routines. As a supervisor, you need to find out why staff members might resist a proposed change so you can develop strategies to overcome their resistance to change. Anticipating resistance to change begins with knowing your staff and using this knowledge to modify your leadership styles to meet the needs of the situation. How would you feel about a proposed change if you were a staff member? What could make you feel differently about the need for change?

It is important for individual staff members to become involved in the change process. Involvement begins when changes are first considered (staff members may have ideas about alternatives), continues to the actual decision-making process (staff input can help ensure the best decision is made), and concludes with the staff's involvement in the implementation, modification, and evaluation process. The level of involvement is often determined by the kind of change being implemented. But, it's up to you, as the supervisor, to involve the staff whenever possible. If you want staff to take pride in their work, give them a voice in planning changes that affect their work.

Perhaps the most important factor in implementing change successfully is for you to develop and maintain an atmosphere of trust and respect in all of your interactions with staff members. A history of honesty, fairness, and concern for staff members influences the development of a positive attitude toward you; as this occurs, the relationship will carry over in the acceptance of change.

The following sections review some of the change principles previously discussed and focus on basic steps in communicating change to staff members as outlined in Exhibit 1.

Step 1—Explain the Details. To avoid suspicion, anxiety, and unnecessary rumors, give your staff as much information as early as possible: the "who, what, where, when, and why" behind the proposed change. You will be able to strengthen trust if you communicate often and as completely as possible, even when you have to say, "I don't know," in response to some concerns. Suppose, for example, you will be installing new point-of-sale technology throughout the establishment. Begin by explaining how the beverage staff will benefit from this change. The fundamental question in many staff members' minds will be: "What's in it for me?" or "How will I be affected by this change?" The benefits you highlight should be the ones important to your team. For example, the new technology might make the ordering process more efficient, or it might make it easier for servers to cover each other stations, or it might reduce drink preparation errors. It's important to focus on the direct benefits for the staff members before addressing overall benefits for the operation. Be sure to communicate what will not be affected by the change. You can help calm fears and reduce stress by emphasizing what is stable in the situation.

Exhibit 1   Steps in Communicating Change

Step 1—Explain the details.
    Emphasize how staff members benefit from the change.
    Stress to staff members what will *not* change.

Step 2—Ask for opinions/listen for feelings.
    Respond to a staff member's negative feelings without becoming defensive.
    Demonstrate acceptance of a staff member's feelings:
        Listen and observe.
        Reflect the staff member's feelings and opinions.
        Check for understanding.

Step 3—Solicit ideas on how to accomplish the change.

Step 4—Ask for commitment and support.
    Ask for help.
    Emphasize positive past performance.
    Offer help and support yourself.
    Express confidence in the staff member's ability to adapt.

Step 5—Follow up.

Step 2—Ask for Opinions/Listen for Feelings. Staff responses to proposed changes are often more emotional than rational. Be prepared to deal with emotional reactions. When asking staff members for their opinions and feelings, you may encounter negative kinds of feedback that could trigger defensiveness on your part. Avoid becoming defensive but don't ignore the feelings and emotions expressed. Bring the issues out into the open where you and the staff member can address them. Demonstrate your acceptance of a staff member's feelings. Acceptance demonstrates understanding—not agreement. What you are accepting is the reality of the staff member's reaction.

Step 3—Solicit Ideas. Whenever possible, ask staff members for suggestions regarding a proposed change. For example, if a change affects how beverage servers order drinks from bartenders, ask both beverage servers and bartenders for their ideas. If you do, they are more likely to support and help implement the change. Keep the focus on areas of the change that can be affected by their input.

Step 4—Ask for Commitment and Support. A direct request for commitment and support can be extremely powerful. When you express confidence in your staff members' abilities to adapt to a change, you exert a powerful influence on their behavior. If informal leaders exist and were not involved earlier, this is a good opportunity to enlist their help.

Step 5—Follow Up. Too often, a change is communicated, implemented, and then assumed to be working satisfactorily. Actually, the time following a change can be stressful for staff members as they adjust to the "newness" of the change. Reinforcing even small improvements with positive feedback not only increases staff motivation and self-confidence after the change, but also helps create a receptive climate for future change.

Human Resource Functions

As a supervisor, you perform several important human resource functions. Proper recruitment, selection, orientation, and training can significantly improve staff productivity, prevent performance problems, and even lower an operation's turnover rate. Your day-to-day supervision of staff performance will be much easier if you recruit and select the best people for the positions you have to fill, make new staff members feel welcome, and train them thoroughly according to the standards of your operation. Setting goals with staff members and evaluating staff performance keeps everyone on track and is key to successful operations. As a supervisor, you also need to know how to take disciplinary actions to correct, strengthen, and improve the performance of staff members. The following sections address these key human resource functions and special supervisory concerns related to sexual harassment in the workplace.

Recruitment and Selection

Before you can hire people, you have to know what you want them to do and what skills they'll need to get the job done. It's helpful to have clearly written job descriptions before you start recruitment and selection activities. A **job description** is a written summary of the duties, responsibilities, working conditions, and activities of a specific position. Besides tasks and qualifications, the description should include wages, benefits, hours, and working conditions. Easily understood job descriptions become useful human resource tools that can help you to:

- Know what the work involves and, therefore, what kind of person to look for.

- Write better employment advertisements or position postings.

- Focus the job interview on matching the applicant's knowledge and skills with the position to be filled.

- Set performance goals for the applicant you eventually hire.

- Protect yourself and the operation from later claims that a staff member didn't understand what was expected.

Assess the usefulness of the job descriptions currently in place by answering the following questions:

- Is this job description up to date? Does it reflect any changes in duties, pay and benefits, hours, and working conditions?

- Does the job description include the most important qualities the operation wants staff members to have?

- Does the job description express the establishment's goals and values?

- Have current staff members been asked if there are other knowledge, skills, and behaviors important to performing the job?

- Is the job description clear and complete, without a lot of jargon and unnecessary words?

- Does the job description meet legal requirements, such as those in the Americans with Disabilities Act (ADA)?

Many beverage operations recruit internally as well as externally. **Internal recruiting** aims to fill positions quickly with applicants from within the operation. **External recruiting** aims to fill positions with applicants from outside the operation. There are advantages and disadvantages to each of these strategies.

Internal recruiting can improve the morale of current staff members as they see future opportunities for themselves. However, there is also the possibility for lowered morale for those staff members who apply but are not selected. Internal recruits can be appealing since supervisors can often better assess the recruits' abilities because performances have been observed over time. However, supervisors must be careful that internal transfers and promotions are not viewed by current staff members as acts of favoritism.

External recruiting can bring new ideas and skills into the operation and may avoid the kind of political problems associated with internal recruiting. However, external recruiting can be expensive and time consuming, and can lower productivity over the short run as the new staff members are brought up to speed on policies and procedures of the operation.

Before interviewing job candidates, review their job application forms. These forms typically ask applicants to report on their employment history, educational background, work preferences, personal references, and other personal data. Questions on application forms must relate to bona fide occupational qualifications. Therefore, questions that require applicants to reveal their gender, age, birthplace, race, marital or family status, sexual preferences, religion, military record, or convictions or arrests not related directly to the position at hand are all illegal.

Prepare for the interview by making a list of questions you'll ask all applicants. This helps you listen to their answers instead of thinking about what to ask next. Be sure to ask both closed and open-ended questions. Closed questions call for very brief responses (usually "yes" or "no") and are used to verify facts, such as information the person provided on the application form. Open-ended questions are broad and allow the applicant to respond in a free and unstructured way. These types of questions enhance your opportunity to obtain meaningful information from the applicant. Examples of open-ended interview questions include:

- "What do like and dislike about your present job?"

- "Can you describe a typical day at your last job?"

- "What do you like most (or least) about working in a beverage establishment?"

- "If you are successful, what will you be doing three or four years from now?"

During the interview, be very specific about the position, what you expect the person to be able to right away, and what's expected after additional training. As

Exhibit 2   Tips for Conducting Better Interviews

Watch out for halos.
> The "halo effect" simply means that you let one outstanding trait over-shadow other characteristics that will affect performance.

Check it out.
> Check out the references and other information provided. Some job applicants lie about their education, experience, and other information asked on employment application forms.

Listen more than you talk.
> The objective is to learn about the applicant. Seventy-five percent of the interview time should be taken up with the applicant talking and with you listening.

Keep an open mind.
> Remember, a hiring decision is a business decision, not a personal decision. Avoid violating federal or state employment laws.

Be considerate.
> Most applicants are nervous, even if they don't show it. Put the applicant at ease. A simple question like, "How did you find out about us?" may be a good way to begin the interview.

Take good notes.
> You may think you'll remember what was said, but after a few interviews it's easy to get applicants mixed up in your mind.

Understand that the hiring process is mutual.
> While you're interviewing candidates, they're also looking you over and deciding whether they want to work for you.

Send applicants away with a good feeling.
> Some candidates are potential guests, and all of them will talk to other people about their impressions of your establishment.

Make the hiring decision promptly.
> If possible, at the end the interview, tell the applicant when you plan to make your decision. After you have made the decision, telephone or write all the candidates to thank them for applying. It's not just the considerate thing to do, it's also good public relations for your establishment.

you talk with the applicant, ask yourself whether the person has the knowledge and skills you need. For example, if you want an outgoing, cheerful person as a bartender, don't hire a shy, quiet individual just because he or she has more experience than other applicants. Remember, skills usually can be taught; it's a lot harder to change someone's personality. Additional tips for interviewing appear in Exhibit 2.

Orientation and Training

If you've ever read Alice in Wonderland, you may remember the Caucus-race in which players ran around in a circle without a starting or stopping point. At the end of the race, everyone asked, "'But who has won?" If you fail to orient and train new staff members, you're essentially asking them to run a Caucus-race—that is, play a game in which they don't know the rules and can't win.

Orientation is the process of introducing new staff members to the establishment and their positions. New staff members should be given a thorough orientation that begins with the first day they arrive for work. Many new staff members arrive with a great deal of enthusiasm about their position. This presents an ideal opportunity for supervisors to instill pride in the establishment and its goals. Exhibit 3 contains a sample checklist that you can use to plan an orientation for new staff members.

In order to meet the performance standards of your establishment, new staff members need training and current staff members often need retraining. Training benefits everyone. Training provides an opportunity for staff members to succeed not only by preparing them to perform their jobs effectively, but also by:

- Improving their self-confidence
- Increasing their motivation
- Improving morale
- Preparing them for promotion

Guests benefit from a well-trained staff because they receive high-quality products and services, their visits are more pleasant, and they feel they are getting value for the dollars they spend. The beverage operation benefits as training helps to:

- Increase productivity
- Build repeat business
- Reduce costs
- Build a strong staff team
- Decrease absenteeism
- Reduce turnover

Many supervisors use a four-step training method to train both new and experienced staff members. This method is a basic training model that can be used to implement on-the-job training programs. The four steps are:

1. Prepare to train.
2. Conduct the training.
3. Coach trial performances.
4. Follow through.

Preparing to train begins with knowing skills required for a particular position and conducting a job analysis. Job analysis involves creating a job task list and developing breakdowns for each job task. A **job task list** itemizes every task that a staff member in a certain position must perform. The **job breakdown** provides

Exhibit 3   Orientation Checklist

Name of Staff Member:_____ Position:_____

Department:_____ Supervisor:_____

For each item below, place a check in the box and record the date the activity is completed or the information is provided.

Part I — Introduction

☐_____Welcome to the new position (give your name, find out what name the
       employee prefers to be called, etc.)

☐_____Tour of the establishment

☐_____Tour of department work area

☐_____Introduction to fellow employees

Part II — Discussion of Daily Procedures

☐_____Beginning/ending time of work shift

☐_____Break and meal periods

☐_____Uniforms (responsibilities for, cleanliness of, etc.)

☐_____Assignment of locker

☐_____Parking requirements

☐_____First aid and accident reporting procedures

☐_____Time clock or sign-in log requirements

☐_____Other (specify):_____

Part III — Information about Salary/Wages

☐_____Rate of pay

☐_____Deductions

☐_____Pay periods

☐_____Overtime policies

☐_____Completion of all payroll, withholding, insurance, and related forms

☐_____Other (specify):_____

Part IV — Review of Policies and Rules

☐_____Safety

☐_____Punctuality

☐_____Absenteeism

Exhibit 3   *(continued)*

☐ _____ Emergencies

☐ _____ Leaving work station

☐ _____ Packages

☐ _____ Fires, accidents, and emergencies

☐ _____ Maintenance and use of equipment

☐ _____ Illness

☐ _____ Use of telephone

☐ _____ Smoking/eating/drinking

☐ _____ Vacations

☐ _____ Other (specify)_____

Part V — Staff Member Handbook/Related Information

☐ _____ Received and reviewed

☐ _____ Review of employee appraisal process

☐ _____ Review of organizational chart

☐ _____ Review of job description

☐ _____ Review of department's responsibilities

☐ _____ Review of all benefit plans

☐ _____ Discussion of performance standards

☐ _____ Discussion of career path possiblilties

Part VI — Miscellaneous Orientation Procedures

(Review all other areas covered with the new staff member)

☐ _____   _____

☐ _____   _____

☐ _____   _____

☐ _____   _____

☐ _____   _____

I certify that all of the above activities were completed on the date indicated.

Staff Member:_____   Date:_____

Trainer:_____   Date:_____

Exhibit 4   Sample Job Task List and Breakdown

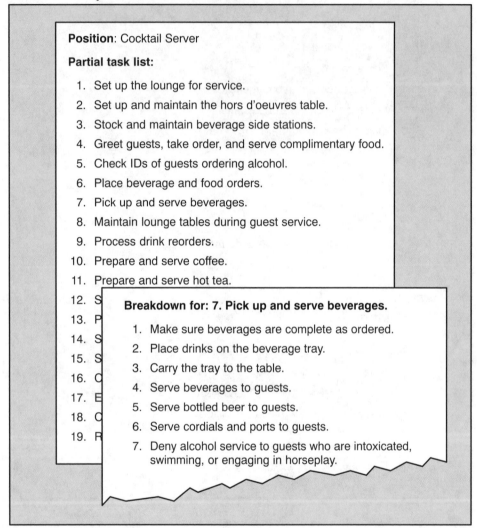

Position: Cocktail Server

Partial task list:

1. Set up the lounge for service.
2. Set up and maintain the hors d'oeuvres table.
3. Stock and maintain beverage side stations.
4. Greet guests, take order, and serve complimentary food.
5. Check IDs of guests ordering alcohol.
6. Place beverage and food orders.
7. Pick up and serve beverages.
8. Maintain lounge tables during guest service.
9. Process drink reorders.
10. Prepare and serve coffee.
11. Prepare and serve hot tea.
12. S
13. P
14. S
15. S
16. C
17. E
18. C
19. R

Breakdown for: 7. Pick up and serve beverages.

1. Make sure beverages are complete as ordered.
2. Place drinks on the beverage tray.
3. Carry the tray to the table.
4. Serve beverages to guests.
5. Serve bottled beer to guests.
6. Serve cordials and ports to guests.
7. Deny alcohol service to guests who are intoxicated, swimming, or engaging in horseplay.

information that tells how to perform each task on a task list. A sample job task list and breakdown are shown in Exhibit 4. Task lists and job breakdowns are used to train new staff members and to assess the training needs of current staff members. Materials developed in the job analysis process help in ways other than training. For example, job analysis:

*   Helps you explain the job to applicants and helps you find the right person for the position.

*   Provides guidelines for performance reviews and keeps those reviews objective.

- Can help you develop standard operating procedure manuals that communicate your expectations to staff members.

- Helps you see how the work in your area is distributed among staff members and how to adjust the workload when appropriate.

Conducting the training entails using the job breakdowns as a training guide and following the sequence of each step in each job breakdown. For each step, show and tell staff members what to do, how to do it, and why the details are important. As you explain the steps, demonstrate them. Encourage staff members to ask questions whenever they need more information. Be patient if staff members don't understand right away. Go over all the steps at least twice. When you show a step a second time, ask staff members questions to see whether they understand. Repeat the steps as many times as necessary.

When coaching trial performances, have staff members demonstrate each step of the task presented during the training session. This tells you whether they really do understand. Resist the urge to do the tasks for the staff members. Compliment staff members immediately after correct performance. Gently correct them when you observe problems. Bad habits formed at this stage of the training may be very difficult to break later. Be sure that staff members understand and can explain not only how to perform each step, but also the purpose of each step.

Following through means coaching staff members on the actual on-the-job application of what has been learned in the training sessions. As a coach, you challenge, encourage, correct, and positively reinforce the knowledge, skills, and attitudes learned during the training session. Coaching staff members provides helpful feedback on how well they are performing.

Goal-Setting and Evaluating Performance

Setting goals and developing action plans with your staff members is a little like taking a trip. Goals represent a destination—where you want to go. An action plan is like a road map—the steps you need to take to reach the destination. All staff members need both goals and action plans in order to do good work, and staff members will likely be more motivated to become top performers if they have a say in what the goals will be and how they can be accomplished.

The number of performance goals that you set with individual members of the staff is important. Generally, a staff member can work on no more than five to nine performance goals at one time. This range has proven effective because there are enough goals to capture the complexity working in a beverage operation, but there are not so many that staff members become confused or think they are being asked to accomplish too much. Exhibit 5 offers helpful guidelines for setting performance goals with staff members.

Performance evaluations provide feedback to staff members, telling them how they are doing on a regular basis. Regular feedback prevents misunderstandings. For example, if you provide no feedback at all, staff members might believe anything from "I must be doing very badly" to "My performance must be perfect." A well-conducted performance review helps to identify the strengths of a staff member as well as areas for improvement.

Exhibit 5 Guidelines for Setting Performance Goals

Specify the objective or task to be completed.
Objectives that are too general, such as, " I will do better at my job," are not specific enough.

Establish attainable goals.
Be sure to establish goals that will require effort, yet be attainable.

Specify how performance will be measured.
Be specific about whether the measures will include productivity, observations of changed behavior, or other measures.

Specify the outcome to be reached.
Discuss with the staff member exactly what outcome you expect.

Set a deadline.
Allow enough time for the goals to be accomplished.

Set priorities if there are multiple goals.
Reach agreement with the staff member on which goal or goals are the most important.

Establish an action plan.
A step-by-step action plan makes goal attainment much easier. Since the steps of an action plan often represent "mini-goals," accomplishing them can encourage staff members to keep progressing toward their goal.

A performance review should be a two-way communication process that permits you to help the staff member develop goals to reach by the next evaluation. At the end of the session, you and the staff member should agree about areas in which the staff member is performing well, areas that need improvement, and specific action plans for improving performance. You should also make it clear to the staff member what you, as his or her supervisor, can do to help and whether additional evaluation sessions should be scheduled. Exhibit 6 offers guidelines for conducting performance evaluations.

Disciplining

In general, supervisors take disciplinary action when a staff member was able to do what he or she was supposed to do—but chose not to. Before deciding to take disciplinary action, consider the following:

- Is the situation important enough to spend valuable time to correct?

- Did factors beyond the staff member's control cause the problem?

- Did the staff member know better?

In every potential disciplinary situation, you should look at yourself and your operation to assess whether causes of the problem are, or are not, within the staff members' ability to control. Unacceptable behavior that is within the control of the

Exhibit 6   Conducting Performance Evaluations: Guidelines

1. Interview in a setting that is informal, private, and free of distraction.
2. Provide a courteous, supportive atmosphere.
3. Encourage the staff member to participate actively.
4. Clearly explain the purpose of the interview.
5. Explain problem areas thoroughly but tactfully.
6. Listen when the staff member talks; don't interrupt.
7. Criticize job performance, not the staff member.
8. Criticize while you're calm; never become angry.
9. Avoid confrontation and argument.
10. Emphasize the staff member's strengths, then discuss areas which need improvement.
11. To set goals for improvement, focus on future, not past performance.
12. Assume nothing; instead, ask for clarification.
13. Ask questions to gather information, not to "test" the staff member.
14. Assume the staff member will disagree; be prepared with documentation and/or examples.
15. Try to resolve differences; don't expect total agreement.
16. Avoid exaggerations (such as "always" or "never").
17. Help the staff member maintain self-esteem; don't threaten or belittle.
18. Keep your own biases in check.
19. Allow the staff member to help you set goals for improvement.
20. Assure the staff member that you will help him/her reach the goals.
21. Maintain appropriate eye contact.
22. End on a positive note.

staff member must be managed through effective disciplinary action procedures. However, unacceptable behavior beyond the control of the staff member is really your problem. You must do a better job of helping staff members meet job requirements.

A staff member who is constantly late for work or who takes too much time for breaks is troublesome for a supervisor and may affect the morale and productivity of co-workers. This staff member usually knows better. So the problem isn't normally a lack of knowledge of the operation's policies and regulations that can be resolved by simple correction through training. Disciplinary action would be in order.

The objective in disciplining a staff member is not to punish, but to change his or her behavior. Disciplinary sessions should be conducted to determine why a situation occurred and how to best resolve the difficulty. The most effective way to do

Exhibit 7   Managing the Disciplinary Process

Define the performance gap
>   Describe the unacceptable behavior
>   Specify the performance standard—the acceptable behavior
>   Restate relevant policies
>   Summarize previous discussions
>   Avoid general statements
>   Don't threaten, argue, or display anger
>   Explain how you feel

Identify the cause of the problem
>   Ask why the unacceptable behavior occurred
>   Actively listen
>   Encourage the staff member to provide more information
>   Ask probing questions
>   Avoid loaded questions
>   Reach agreement on probable cause

Agree on a solution
>   Ask the staff member for improvement ideas
>   Add your own suggestions
>   Agree on a specific solution
>   Set a timetable with specific target dates for improvement

State the disciplinary action
>   State the immediate action to be taken
>   Explain future actions, if behavior does not improve
>   Be specific
>   Next disciplinary action should not be a surprise

Set a follow-up date
>   Set a specific date and time for a follow-up meeting
>   Regularly observe staff member's behavior
>   Summarize the improvement plan in writing

End on a positive note
>   Offer support
>   Express confidence in staff member's ability to improve
>   Shake hands
>   Communicate again with the staff member before the end of the day

---

this is to gain the staff member's involvement and commitment to change—which is not achieved by criticizing, blaming, or attacking the person. Exhibit 7 outlines the steps to follow in managing the disciplinary process.

Sexual Harassment Issues

Today, sexual harassment in the workplace receives significant attention. Title VII of the Civil Rights Act of 1964 and similar state laws focus on this issue. The Equal Employment Opportunity Commission (EEOC) has confirmed that sexual harassment is a violation of Title VII and has presented information about conduct that constitutes unlawful sexual harassment.

While the laws and interpretations may change, some principles appear established. You and/or your employer will probably be held liable for sexual harassment if a staff member is deprived of a tangible job benefit—for example, if a staff member is fired for refusing a supervisor's sexual advances. If a staff member's work environment is negatively affected (in the staff member's opinion) by the sexual harassment of a supervisor or co-worker, and if the employer knows or should have known of this conduct and does not take immediate action, the employer will probably be held liable. You and the beverage operation could also be found liable for the harassment of staff members by guests and vendors if unwanted activities occurred, you were aware of them, and did not take immediate corrective actions.

Sexual harassment can take many forms; some are easier to identify than others. Managers and supervisors are learning that a wide range of activities can be labeled as sexual harassment. The EEOC identifies sexual harassment acts as unwelcome sexual advances, requests for sexual favors, or other verbal or physical conduct of a sexual nature. These acts constitute sexual harassment if:

- Employment decisions are made or threatened based on acceptance or rejection of sexual conduct.

- A person's job performance is adversely affected by sexual conduct.

- Sexual conduct creates an intimidating, hostile, or offensive work environment.

Sexual harassment does not necessarily involve sexual contact or overt sexual advances or suggestions. Harassment can occur when one staff member, supervisor, or manager, stares provocatively at another staff member, supervisor, or manager. Graffiti, vulgar and abusive language, suggestive jokes, references to sexual activity, unwelcome or repeated flirtation, and unwelcome comments about appearance have been considered by courts of law to be forms of sexual harassment.

Workplace sexual harassment does not just occur between a male boss and a female staff member. Offenders can be supervisors, co-workers, guests, vendors, or suppliers. Harassment may take the form of:

- Peer harassing peers

- Staff members harassing supervisors

- Women harassing men

- Same-sex harassment

How individuals perceive and respond to particular situations plays a big role in defining harassment. What one person thinks is friendly and harmless behavior may be unwelcome or offensive to another. Sexual harassment is not normally friendly interactions, or non-offensive joking, or behavior that would not offend a reasonable person.

Beverage operations must exercise reasonable care to prevent sexual harassment. General strategies include:

- A written and distributed policy statement prohibiting sexual harassment

- A reasonable and well-publicized grievance procedure for reporting and processing sexual harassment allegations

- Ongoing training for supervisors and managers to make sure they are aware of their responsibilities to guard against sexual harassment

All supervisors should make sure that staff members know the operation's policy on harassment. Your operation's harassment policy should be posted in staff member areas. You should review this policy when orienting new staff members and periodically during staff meetings. Be a positive role model. Always conduct yourself in a businesslike manner. Your behavior sets an example. Listen to staff members and observe their behavior. If you observe behavior that could be offensive to others, express your strong disapproval and restate your operation's policy. Take concerns, suggestions, or complaints seriously. Keep a record of all complaints and report complaints to your operation's human resources area. If it is your responsibility, be sure to investigate each complaint immediately. Monitor and correct offensive situations as they occur. Don't wait for a complaint before correcting a situation. If there is graffiti in the workplace, have it erased.

If a staff member lodges a complaint, act immediately and appropriately. Do not simply direct the staff member to the human resources area. Once you receive a harassment complaint, it is your responsibility (not the staff member's) to follow through and make sure the complaint reaches the appropriate management representative. Keep the facts and other information concerning the issue private. Do not discuss the situation with others unless you are the one to conduct an investigation into the complaint. If you are investigating a complaint:

- Interview the accuser, the accused, and any witnesses.

- Set a professional tone for each interview.

- Get detailed answers to the who, what, when, where, and how questions that are specific to the investigation.

- Whenever possible, protect everyone's privacy by maintaining confidentiality.

Take corrective action by stopping the harassment. Failure to take corrective action in response to sexual harassment places you at risk of contributing to the harassment environment. Correct the effects of harassment and ensure the harassment does not recur. Disciplinary measures should be proportionate to the seriousness of the offense and consistent with the discipline administered in similar situations. Measures to stop the harassment may include:

- Oral or written warning

- Transfer or reassignment of the harasser (not the victim)

- Demotion

- Reduction of wages

- Suspension
- Discharge

Follow up immediately reporting back to the victim about the actions you have taken. Also, after an appropriate period of time, check with the victim to make sure the situation has been corrected and retaliation has not occurred. Follow up with the accused to reinforce improved behavior or to counsel further, if necessary.

Personal Effectiveness

The work you do is important, but you must also have adequate time for your family and friends, for professional growth, and, of course, some time for leisure activities. Supervisors who manage their time wisely, delegate effectively, and control stress lead well-rounded lives. Those who cannot may become workaholics—working during time they should spend on other activities. If you can learn to manage your time well, you'll accomplish more personally as well as professionally, and, at the same time, experience less stress and feel better about yourself.

Time Management

Interruptions can come from many different sources: your boss, your staff members, other supervisors and managers, even from your family and friends. Interruptions can be particularly draining on your time when you enjoy the "people" part of your job best. So when a staff member comes to you with a problem, or another supervisor asks you for advice, or your boss stops by to chat, it's easy to let the visit take up more time than it should.

Whenever you're interrupted, you might spend up to twice as long "recovering" from the interruption (getting back to the task at hand) as the interruption itself took. This means interruptions take more time than you think. Consider Orlando's situation:

> Orlando manages the Season's Room, a busy, upscale lounge at the Seasons Inn. This morning, he sets aside an hour to review the applications of job candidates he'll be interviewing later in the day. During that hour, he's interrupted three times:
>
> - Tony, the general manager, stops by and asks, "Say, Orlando, got a minute? I need you in a meeting this afternoon. Here's what we'll discuss." The visit takes four minutes.
>
> - Megan, the supervisor in marketing and sales, drops in. "What do you know about the meeting Tony's called for this afternoon?" she asks. Orlando tells Megan about the visit from Tony. Their conversation takes eight minutes.
>
> - Orlando's son calls: "Have you seen my brown sweater? I want to wear it to the football game, and I can't find it." "Did you look in your brother's closet?" asks Orlando. "Hold on," says his son. The call takes three minutes.

> At then end of an hour, Orlando has hardly made a dent in his stack of paperwork. Here's why: Orlando has set aside 60 minutes to review the applications. His interruptions total 15 minutes, but his recovery time eats up another 15 or 30 minutes. At best, that leaves him with 30 minutes to review the stack of job applications.

Just about every supervisor knows someone who "pops by just to say hello" and ends up chatting for half an hour, or someone who wants to discuss something "for just five minutes" and ends up going on for almost an hour. If you're a "people person" like most hospitality supervisors, you can draw on your tact and natural courtesy to wrap up these interruptions quickly and politely. For example, you can signal that a conversation is over with verbal cues and body language:

- Stand up and start to move toward the door while saying, "I hope I don't seem rude, Jerry, but I have to finish my budget report this afternoon. Let's talk another time."

- Sit on the corner of your desk and say, "Sounds like you had a great vacation. Let's get together for lunch on Wednesday and you can show me more photos."

- Look at your watch and say, "I'm on my way to a meeting. Tell me what you need me to do while I walk to the conference room."

Delegation

One of the most effective ways to make more time for important supervisory activities is to delegate jobs to your staff. Delegation does not mean dumping unpleasant work on others, or assigning work to staff members and abandoning them, or assigning work and then hovering over them every step of the way.

Delegation is entrusting work to staff members and giving them the right to make some decisions for you. However, even when you delegate a task (or parts of a task), you are responsible for your staff members' performances. If they fail to accomplish a task that you delegate to them, it will be your failure as well. Being responsible or held accountable for the actions of their staff members is one of the hard facts of organizational life for supervisors and managers.

Delegation is not the same as assigning work. Assigning work is asking a staff member to do a specific task that is part of that person's job. Delegation means first looking at what tasks you perform, as a supervisor, that can be delegated to a staff member, and then seeing how you can help that staff member successfully complete the delegated task. The benefits of delegation are many. Effective delegation can:

- Increase the time supervisors have for other tasks and responsibilities.

- Build skills, competence, and confidence among staff members.

- Develop a strong foundation for staff empowerment.

- Improve staff morale and self-esteem.

- Create a better team approach to work.

- Improve efficiency in the department and operation.

Unfortunately, inexperienced supervisors refuse to delegate. Reasons they offer for resisting delegation include:

- "I can do this faster (better) than my staff; after all, that's why I'm the supervisor."
- "I don't have time to train the staff to do this."
- "If my staff messes up, I'll get blamed; if my staff does well, they'll get the credit."
- "My staff doesn't have time to take on new responsibilities."
- "I know my staff could handle this, but I enjoy doing it."
- "If I show someone how to do this, I won't be needed anymore."

Actually, when supervisors delegate, they reap rewards for themselves, their staff members, and their operations. Successful delegators often share similar traits. They can live with the imperfections of others, as well as their own. They don't feed their egos at the expense of their staff. They are patient teachers, coaches, and mentors and give constructive, positive feedback. Most important, they know how to choose the right staff member for the job.

Delegating work to staff members does not have to be an elaborate process. But, you can't delegate on a moment's notice, either. If you do, you've set everyone up for failure. To delegate effectively, you must plan, carry out, and follow up.

Planning the delegation involves deciding in advance what tasks to delegate, how much to delegate, and to whom you will delegate. To decide what tasks to delegate, make a list of all the tasks you perform. Cross off tasks that you cannot delegate (such as performance reviews), put a question mark next to tasks you could delegate, and star those you definitely can delegate. Choose one of the starred items to start. You may decide to delegate all or part of the task to a staff member, depending on how elaborate the task is. In a partial delegation, a staff member gathers information for you or recommends a decision. If you delegate the entire task, the staff member is empowered to make decisions and inform you of the decisions. When you choose a staff member to delegate a task to, consider his or her job skills, reliability, independence, interpersonal skills, and initiative.

Carry out the delegation by explaining the task to the staff member and ask if he or she is willing to take on the responsibility. Be sure to express your confidence in him or her, explain the benefits of delegating the task, and stress that you'll be available to help with problems. Train the staff member to perform the task. If possible, let the staff member watch you do the task while you explain each step as you do it. Then ask the staff member to do the task, explaining each step to you. Coach by offering corrections, suggestions, and positive feedback.

Following up the delegation does not mean hovering over the staff member or abandoning him or her altogether. Instead, check back occasionally to see how things are going. Expect and accept some mistakes. Encourage the staff member to ask for help, and be positive and supportive if he or she does so. Also, as the staff member progresses, evaluate the effectiveness of the delegation. Decide whether the delegation has saved you time and whether the staff member is performing the task satisfactorily.

Managing Stress

The atmosphere of beverage service operations is often meant to be fun and exciting. The environment generally encourages guests to interact and relax with friends and companions. Working in this atmosphere can also be fun, exciting, and fast-paced. However, as with any work environment, managers, supervisors, and staff members can experience stress.

Some kinds of stress are expected and can actually raise the level of excitement, such as those busy nights when the lounge is full of guests. However, if a busy beverage operation is consistently short-staffed, the excitement and challenge of the job wears thin and work becomes truly stressful. Left unmanaged, excess stress takes its toll on you as a supervisor and also on your staff as well as the overall beverage operation. For example, stress can:

- Reduce guest satisfaction and lower staff morale—stressed-out staff members dread their work and often complain to other staff members or, even worse, to guests or in front of guests.

- Reduce staff productivity—stressed-out staff members don't work as accurately or efficiently as they normally do, and absenteeism may increase.

- Stifle new ideas—staff members under stress are doing all they can to handle business as usual; they don't have the energy or the morale to approach problems creatively.

- Increase the cost of health benefits—staff members suffering from stress-related health problems may need to take medication or seek counseling; this can hinder efforts to control heath costs.

- Increase staff turnover and training costs—if stress continues for a long time, staff members may quit and the operation not only loses seasoned staff members but also must pay to train replacements.

If you don't have time to recover from stress, burnout occurs. The word "burnout" may paint a mental picture of someone who can barely sit up or keep his or her eyes open. But appearances can be deceiving. Burned-out supervisors may say things like:

- "This place would fall apart without me."

- "If I weren't here, I'd be at home worrying about not being here."

- "I can't afford to take a vacation or personal time."

Even though burned-out supervisors look busy, the quality of their work is likely not up to par and they could be stressing their staff members. Stress is often contagious.

Some people don't believe in stress. They believe "stress" is an excuse for not working hard enough. People like these, unfortunately, become a source of stress for others. As a supervisor you need to handle people at work that cause stress.

Exhibit 8   Common Stress Safety Valves

- Break your workday in half and take a mini-break between halves, even if it's just a 15-minute walk outside or around the property.

- Take an after-work break—jogging, mountain biking, walking, listening to music on the ride home—to help you put the stress of the workday behind you.

- Develop a talent like roller-blading, woodworking, cooking, or gardening that affirms your creativity and abilities.

- Acquire a hobby that's always interested you.

- Pursue an interest (literature, music, politics) that gives you an appreciation for the larger world beyond work.

- Maintain close friendships with people you don't work with and who share and affirm your interests and insights.

- Volunteer to coach a youth sport's team.

- Set aside one night a week for a "date" with your spouse or companion.

These people could be guests, staff members, other supervisors, vendors, and even your boss.

Managing your own stress means developing stress "safety valves." A stress safety valve is anything in your life outside of work that helps you get away from your job mentally as well as physically. Stress experts say that a safety valve can be a relatively simple thing, like listening to music. The important thing is to make time for yourself on a regular basis. Exhibit 8 lists common stress safety valves. Other actions you can take to control stress include:

- Plan a vacation that you'll really enjoy—and then take it. You've worked for it, you deserve it. Don't let others pressure you into a vacation that will simply increase your stress levels.

- Be realistic. You're human and you make mistakes. Learn to accept that fact and ask yourself: "What will this mistake mean a week from now?" Most of the time, the answer is "not much."

- Eat and drink sensibly. Too many cups of coffee, cola drinks, and candy bars don't make you more energetic; they make you more nervous. Also, don't eat on the run or skip meals. No one expects you to work so hard that you don't have time to eat.

- Exercise regularly. It sounds like a contradiction, but to have energy, you have to use energy. When stress makes you tired, pep yourself up after work with a walk, run, or workout. If you're going to do strenuous activity, check with your doctor first.

- Get enough sleep. A simple but effective form of torture is depriving a victim of sleep. If you feel tired all the time, learn to stop torturing yourself with long hours or sleep-depriving worry.

🗝 Key Terms

autocratic leadership style—A leadership style in which the supervisor retains as much power and decision-making authority as possible.

bureaucratic leadership style—A leadership style in which the supervisor "manages by the book" and enforces rules, policies, regulations, and standard operating procedures.

change agent—The person responsible for planning, implementing, and evaluating changes within the work environment.

delegation—The supervisory task of assigning authority to staff members to perform tasks or make decisions for which the supervisor is still accountable.

democratic leadership style—A leadership style in which the supervisor involves staff members as much as possible in aspects of the job that affects them.

external recruiting—A strategy to fill positions with applicants from outside the operation.

internal recruiting—A strategy to fill positions quickly with applicants from within the operation.

job breakdown—Provides information that tells how to perform each task on a task list.

job description—A written summary of the duties, responsibilities, working conditions, and activities of a specific job.

job task list—Itemizes every task that a staff member in a certain position must perform.

laissez-faire leadership style—A leadership style in which the supervisor maintains a hands-off policy and delegates to staff as much discretion and decision-making authority as possible.

leadership—The ability to attain objectives by working with and through people. A leader creates conditions that motivate staff members by establishing goals and influencing staff members to attain those goals.

orientation—The process of introducing new staff members to the property and their jobs.

❓ Review Questions

1. How does autocratic leadership differ from bureaucratic leadership?

2. Why wouldn't all supervisors adopt a democratic leadership style for every situation?

3. What are the dangers of adopting a laissez-faire leadership style?

4. Why is it important to ask for staff members' opinions and listen for their feelings when implementing change?

5. What are ways to involve staff members in the change process?

6. What are the advantages and disadvantages of internal recruiting and of external recruiting?

7. What are some guidelines for setting performance goals with staff members?

8. How should you respond if a staff member complains to you about being sexually harassed on the job?

9. How does delegation differ from assigning work?

10. What "safety values" would you use to managed stress on the job?

Mini-Case Studies

Just Joking

Jake and Judy are beverage staff members who have become good friends during the six months they have worked together. One day, you overhear Jake and Judy making jokes at the expense of some of their co-workers. During the course of their conversation, you hear them refer to various co-workers as "Emotional Cripple," "Old Fogey," and "Hot Mama." No one else was around to hear the jokes, and no one has complained about Jake and Judy's behavior in the past.

Discussion Questions

1. Should this behavior be considered harassment, even though the co-workers who are the subject of the jokes were not aware of the jokes?

2. Since no one has complained about Jake's and Judy's jokes in the past, is there a need for the supervisor to get involved?

3. What would be the appropriate course of action for the supervisor to take?

Upward Delegation

Mary, the bartender in the Seasons Room, has always ordered bar supplies. After reviewing the expenses for the lounge, however, Orlando, the bar manager, decides he should do the ordering himself.

"I think our costs are too high," he tells Mary. In the process of doing the ordering himself, Orlando finds several ways to cut costs. "Look at this," he excitedly tells Mary one evening, "I can save $300 worth of supplies in the first quarter of this year. I can't imagine why you ever ordered so much before."

Orlando now asks Mary to resume ordering the bar supplies, using his techniques. "I think you should continue to order the supplies," Mary tells Orlando. "I don't feel comfortable doing it anymore."

Discussion Questions

1. How did Orlando mishandle the situation?

2. How could he have handled the situation better?

3. What can he do now to persuade Mary to resume the ordering?

The Domino Effect of Stress

Hans, the evening bartender, is due for a performance appraisal. Orlando, the bar manager, is especially unhappy about doing Hans's review because Hans still has a problem coming to work on time. Orlando likes Hans and his work is good. But Orlando feels he should "lay down the law" to Hans about arriving late to work. He knows there will be an unpleasant scene.

Orlando is hoping Hans just won't mention that his review is due. In fact, Orlando has been going out of his way to avoid Hans, hoping Hans won't ask about it. Whenever he sees Hans, Orlando gets nervous and heads in the opposite direction.

One day, Hans sees Orlando working with Cindy, one of the beverage servers. Orlando can't get away before Hans comes up and says, "Hi, boss. Say, it's about time for my performance review, isn't it? I'm hoping for a big raise this year."

Orlando now feels a bit angry, knowing that Hans is expecting a big raise even though he's been coming to work late. "Well, I do have other things on my mind besides your review. And I guess you'll get that raise when you can show up on time," Orlando snaps.

Hans is shocked. He doesn't know what to say. Orlando walks off feeling very upset. He can't stop thinking about how he shouldn't have snapped at Hans.

Meanwhile, Hans goes back to the bar, thinking about what Orlando said. "Maybe he's going to fire me," Hans thinks.

A guest at the bar interrupts Hans's train of thought: "Hey," says the guest, "This drink's got too much ice in it."

"It's the same amount of ice I put in your last drink," Hans retorts. "How come you didn't complain before?"

Discussion Questions

1. Who experiences stress in the scenario? How does their behavior show they are under stress?

2. What problem is the root cause of the stress experienced those in the scenario?

"Why Haven't You . . ."

Orlando, the bar manager, has just put in a difficult three weeks getting ready for a big party held in the lounge last night. He'd like things to get back to normal soon, but his budget report is due in two days. In addition, he needs to interview candidates for a bartender's position that should have been filled a week ago. "Just one more week and things will get back to normal," he tells himself.

Tony, the general manager, comes in as Orlando is beginning to work on his budget report. "Say, seeing that report reminds me I'm going to need it this afternoon so I can fax it to the corporate execs before the big meeting, day after tomorrow," says Tony. "And by the way, why haven't you hired somebody for that bartender's position yet?"

Discussion Questions

1. How would you feel if you were Orlando?

2. What would you say to Tony?

Balancing Work with Life

"Most people complain about stress," says Orlando, the bar manager. "But I really thrive on it. My workday lasts about ten hours, on average, but I can honestly say the time just flies. I enjoy my work a lot. Most of my friends are in the business, and we're always talking about it. On my days off, I usually show up once or call the manager on duty just to see how things are going."

Discussion Questions

1. While Orlando would deny it, what signs of stress and potential burnout do you find in this scenario?

2. What could Orlando do to balance work with life?

Chapter 6 Outline

Families of Beer
Alcohol Content
Beer Ingredients
    Water
    Malt
    Hops
    Yeast
Making Beer
    Malting
    Mashing
    Brewing
    Fermenting
    Maturing
    Packaging
Storing and Handling Beer
Serving Beer
    Pouring Beer
    The "Beer-Clean" Glass
Taste Talk

Competencies

1. Distinguish ale from lager. (pp. 147–150)

2. Identify the basic ingredients of beer. (pp. 150–151)

3. Explain the stages in the process of making beer. (pp. 151–156)

4. Identify storing and handling concerns in relation to beer. (pp. 156–157)

5. Identify appropriate glassware and temperatures for serving different styles of beer. (pp. 157–160)

6. Explain how to pour beer from bottles and from taps. (pp. 160–161)

7. Describe specific taste characteristics of common styles of beer. (pp. 161–164)

6

Beer

BEER IS ONE OF THE MOST POPULAR alcoholic beverages consumed in bars, lounges, restaurants, hotels, and resorts around the world. It is also considered to be the oldest alcoholic beverage. About 13,000 years ago, Mesopotamians and Sumerians recorded a beer-making process on clay tablets. **Beer** is an alcoholic beverage obtained through the fermentation of grains. Modern beer is flavored with hops and carbonation. Today, there are many styles and numerous brands of beer, each made with a unique blend of basic ingredients and with brewing techniques that enhance the fundamental beer-making process.

How much do bartenders and beverage servers need to know about beer? Probably at least enough to respond to questions that guests may ask about beer, such as:

- Why won't you serve my fourteen-year-old some non-alcoholic beer?
- Why are some beers light and others dark?
- What's the difference between a porter and a stout?
- Is this beer "light" because it has less alcohol or because it has fewer calories?
- What makes beer skunky?
- How can I know if this beer is fresh?
- Why isn't all beer pasteurized?
- Why can't I get a quality collar of foam when I pour this same beer at home?
- What does bock beer taste like?

Topics covered in this chapter will help you answer these questions and others as well. Volumes have been written on the history of beer and it would take some time and effort on your part to become fully informed about the events and techniques forged by brew masters over the centuries. In terms of the growth and development of today's beer industry, there are three significant milestones: refrigeration, pasteurization, and the invention of metal kegs. Before refrigeration, beer was produced only during the winter months because the fermentation process required cooler temperatures and because beer would spoil when exposed to heat. Refrigeration enabled year-round beer production. Pasteurization brought a method of purifying the brew, extending its shelf life up to 120 days. This also allowed packaged beer to be stored at room temperature. Metal kegs greatly enhanced the packaging, transport, and service of beer. They could withstand the build-up of pressure through further fermentation better than wooden barrels, and they proved easier to tap.

This chapter focuses on the most popular types of beer consumed: lager and ale. These beers are made from barley malt (sometimes mixed with other grains). During beer production, starch from barley malt is broken down into simple sugars that yeasts consume during fermentation, producing alcohol and carbon dioxide. While there have been vast improvements since the Mesopotamians and Sumerians, the fundamentals of fermentation remain the same.

After identifying the main ingredients of beer and presenting the fundamentals of making beer, this chapter addresses the care, handling, and service of beer. The chapter closes by introducing you to the language of **tasting beer**—differentiating styles of beer in terms of aroma, appearance, flavor, and body.

Families of Beer

Most beer can be defined as either lager or ale. Around the world, lager is by far the most popular style of beer. Lagers are of a German tradition and were brewed in the Alpine caves of Bavaria and other parts of Europe where cooler temperatures prevailed. Ales were traditionally brewed in the British Isles.

Exhibit 1 shows some of the many distinct styles of beer within the ale and lager families. Pilsner is one of the most popular lager styles. Modern brands of lager include Budweiser, Miller, Sam Adams, and Coors. Porter and stout are popular styles of ale. Modern brands of ale include Bass, Red Hook, and Anchor Steam. In addition, there are an increasing number of micro-brews produced by relatively small breweries. Styles of both ale and lager beer vary in relation to color (from light to dark) and in the amount of alcohol by volume. The difference between lagers and ales is created by the type of yeast used in the brewing process and by the temperature of the fermentation. Bottom-fermenting yeast produces lagers; top-fermenting yeast produces ales.

Ales are often served warmer than lagers. **Ales** are typically fermented warm (at about room temperature) with yeast that rises to the top of the beer near the end of fermentation. They typically have a pronounced malty and bitter taste because ale recipes often contain a larger amount of hops and roasted malts than do lagers. Ales generally have a hearty, robust, and sometimes fruity taste. The warmer fermentation temperature also lends a distinctive nutty and spicy character to ales.

Lagers typically ferment more slowly than ales and at colder temperatures. They are fermented with yeast adapted to low temperatures. At the end of the fermentation, lager yeast settles to the bottom where it is collected and used again. Lagers are stored at lower temperatures and usually for longer times than ales. This low temperature process combined with a bottom-fermenting yeast results in distinctively milder and fruitier aromas as well as a cleaner, crisper taste than ales.

Beers are sometimes mixed with each other or with other alcoholic beverages. For example, stout is blended with ale to make a "black and tan," while stout and champagne creates a "back velvet."

Alcohol Content

Throughout this chapter, the alcohol content of beer is discussed in terms of its percentage by volume. **Alcohol by volume** is a measure of the space the alcohol in a

Exhibit 1   Lager and Ale Families of Beer

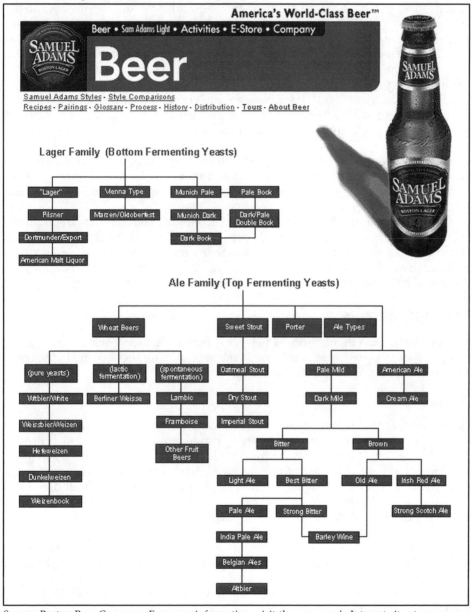

Source: Boston Beer Company. For more information, visit the company's Internet site at: www.sam adams.com.

beer takes up as a percentage of total space. **Alcohol by weight** is also a measure of the amount of alcohol content. Here the measure is the amount of weight the alcohol in a beer has as a percentage of total weight.

Today's popular beers generally contain alcohol levels of 3 percent to 7 percent alcohol by volume. There are also several brands of non-alcoholic beer on the market. Many people believe that these beers are called "non-alcoholic" because they don't contain alcohol. But actually, they do contain low levels of alcohol—usually 0.5 percent by weight, although the amount varies by brand. While this is a very small amount of alcohol, many beverage establishments will not serve non-alcoholic beer to anyone under the age of 21.

Designations of "light" beer vary among countries. In the some countries, light beer is defined by a low amount of alcohol, usually between 2.6 percent and 4 percent alcohol per volume. In the United States, the number of calories defines a type of beer as "light." Light beers typically contain around 100 calories in a twelve-ounce serving (compared to 135–170 calories for regular beer.) Light beer brewers use a special process to break down more sugars during fermentation, creating a beer with fewer calories but with alcohol content comparable with regular beer.

Ice beers contain 15–20 percent more alcohol by volume than traditionally brewed beers. Ice brewed beers are super-chilled before the final filtration at the end of the maturing stage. Lower than freezing temperatures can be used because of the high alcohol content of ice beer. Ice brewing clarifies the beer by removing unwanted proteins and also helps preserve freshness.

Beer Ingredients

The four basic ingredients from which most beer is made are water, malt, hops, and yeast. Each ingredient contributes to the beer-making process and to the overall flavor and appearance of the beer.

Water

Historically, as the mineral content of the water supply varied from location to location, so local brewers were limited to producing certain styles of beer. For example, the water supply used to produce lager beers generally had a low mineral content. If the local water supply had a high mineral content, brewers would be smart to steer clear of lagers. In the past, brewers sometimes built breweries only in areas where the right type of water could be found. Today's modern water treatment techniques enable brewers to meet the mineral content of almost any beer. However, large brewers often use water that meets the highest standards of quality. They use extensive water filtering systems to remove impurities or flavors that may be present even in the locally approved water supplies. These filtering systems are adjusted to produce the same standard of water, regardless of the quality and flavor of locally available water. Micro-breweries, on the other hand, use characteristics of the local water to create their distinctively flavored micro-brews.

Malt

Except for brews made from wheat, all malt beverages are made from barley. In beer production, the term **barley** actually refers to the grains (seeds) of the barley plant. These grains are typically high in starch content, low in protein, and have little taste. Two-row barley produces two rows of grains on each stalk; six-row barley produces six. Two-row barley usually produces a smooth, sweet tasting beer, while six-row barley generally creates a crisp, snappy flavor. Brewers often adjust portions of each to produce the balance they seek.

Hops

Hops are cone-shaped clusters of blossoms (fruit) from the vine-like hop plant. Over a hundred varieties of hops are grown throughout the world and the care taken in growing hops for beer matches the care taken in growing grapes for wine. The soil, climate, and care given to the vines create unique characteristics in the hops that produce the eventual flavor (a refreshing bitterness) and aroma of beer. Hops are often referred to as the "spice" of beer. Blending hop varieties during the beer production process creates unique flavors and aromas in different beers. Blossoms of the hop vine are harvested, dried, packed in sealed bags, and stored cold in order to preserve their freshness.

Yeast

Yeast is the living microorganism that consumes the sugars from the brew of grains, water, and hops and produces alcohol and carbon dioxide in the fermentation process. Yeast also helps create flavors and aromas of beer. As living microorganisms, yeast can change its characteristics. To ensure consistency, cultures of unique yeast strains are grown in laboratory-controlled environments. Anheuser-Busch stores its cultured yeast in liquid nitrogen and can trace its Budweiser yeast to the original strain used by Adolphus Busch in the late 1800s.

Making Beer

Many variations of the beer-making process exist. Exhibit 2 offers a condensed diagram of the basic stages. Depending on the type of beer being made (ale or lager) and on the length of the maturing stage, beer production may take anywhere from a few weeks to six months.

The basics of making beer have not changed significantly. Exhibit 3 presents a more detailed diagram of a brewing process used in the 1950s. Virtual tours of modern beer-making processes are usually available at the Internet sites of major breweries. The following sections examine beer production in relation to a six-stage process:

1. Malting

2. Mashing

3. Brewing

4. Fermenting

5. Maturing

6. Packaging

Exhibit 2   A Snapshot of Making Beer

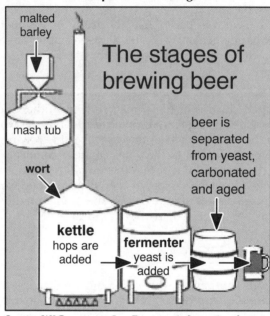

Source: W3Commerce, Inc. For more information, browse the company's Internet site at: www.history-of-beer.com.

Malting

Malt refers to any type of grain that is allowed to sprout and then is dried to prevent further development. The malting stage begins with cleaning the barley grains. Next, water is added, enabling the grains to germinate. Starting barley seeds to sprout activates enzymes that convert the proteins and starch of the grains into fermentable sugars. The sprouted barley is kilned (heated in a controlled manner) to stop the germination process. Malt determines the color, flavor, and body of the eventual beer. Malt is roasted according to the brewer's standards. The length and intensity of roasting develops unique flavors and deeper colors. Some brewers make their own malt; others purchase malt in a dried or roasted form.

In beer production, malt refers to barley seeds that have been allowed to start germination and are then heated, dried, or roasted. The grains of roasted malt look like very small coffee beans. **Milling** the malt crushes the husks and exposes the starches found in the kernels, preparing the malt for the mashing process.

Other grains (such as rice, corn, or wheat) are sometimes used in addition to barley malt in the production of beer. These additional grains are called **grain adjuncts**. During the malting stage, these other grains are separately ground and cooked to increase the size of the starch they contain and are combined and heated with barley malt during the mashing process. Many of the popular qualities of beer in the United States that are light in color and flavor are produced with these additional grains, particularly rice. A brewer's form of corn syrup is sometimes used to produce a beer with a light color and taste.

Exhibit 3   Brewing in the 1950s

The following is reprinted from a 1950s brochure entitled "Brewing In Brief," published by the United States Brewers Foundation.

1. The careful, unhurried brewing process begins at the *malt and cereal storage bins,* where malt, made from quality barley, is precisely measured. Extreme cleanliness is vital to the whole process.

2. In the *mash tub,* the malt is mixed with heated, sterilized, and filtered water. This is stirred until the malt proteins are broken down.

3. A cereal mash of other grains is boiled in the *cooker* and then is added to the malt mash. Cooking changes the malt and grain starches into fermentable sugars.

4. After this mixture is filtered through the *Lauder tub,* spent grains are removed and are shipped out as livestock feed. The remaining liquid is called "wort" (pronounced "wurt").

5. The wort flows into *brew kettles,* where it is boiled with hops to give the beer or ale its pleasant, tangy flavor. The hops are then strained off.

6. Distinctively flavored, the wort now is pumped to a *wort-collecting tank.*

7. The wort then flows through *coolers,* where the temperature drops from about 212 degrees F. to about 50 degrees F.

8. Pumped into the open *starter tank,* the wort receives a portion of carefully cultured yeast and fermentation begins.

9. Now the wort and yeast go into *fermenting tanks,* where they remain about a week. Beer is made by a "bottom-fermentation" process, ale usually by "top-fermentation."

10. Fermentation over, the beer is then pumped into *aging tanks* and remains in them for many weeks to age properly.

11. After carbonation and a final filtering, beer or ale to be served on draught goes to the *racking room* to be put into barrels which have been scrupulously cleaned.

12. Beer and ale to be packaged goes to the *bottling or canning plant* where it is pasteurized after automatic machinery has filled and closed the surgically sterile containers.

Finally, the beer or ale leaves the brewery on its way to hundreds of thousands of places where beer is sold in this country.

Source: American Brewery History Page. For more information, browse the Internet site at www.beerhistory.com.

Mashing

During the **mashing** stage, milled malt, water, and pre-cooked grain adjuncts (if appropriate) are measured and mixed in a kettle (or tun). The mixture is mashed (stirred and heated) in a controlled time and temperature cycle. This reactivates malt enzymes that break down grain starches to sugars.

The mixture is transferred to a filtering device called a **lauter tun**. "Lauter" is a German word meaning to clarify or to make clean. At this filtering point, the **mash** liquid is separated from the malt husks and grain particles. The resulting sweet liquid is called **wort** (pronounced as "wurt"). The wort is circulated and strained before being transferred to huge copper or stainless steel brewing kettles.

Brewing

Brewing is a flavoring stage at which the wort is boiled and hops are added. Hops provide flavor and aroma to the eventual beer. Boiling sterilizes the wort and extracts flavors from the hops. The length of the boil helps define the color and grain flavor characteristics of the eventual beer. After boiling, the wort is sent to whirlpool tanks (or other kinds of straining or filtering devices) to settle out the hops and tiny particles of solids remaining in the wort. Then the wort is cooled—for ales 50° to 70° F (10° to 21° C) and for lagers 37° to 49 degrees F (3° to 9° C). Cooling and evaporation remove unwanted flavor compounds and bring the wort to an optimum temperature to start fermentation.

Fermenting

During the fermenting stage, filtered and cooled wort is transferred to fermenting tanks and yeast is added. During **fermentation**, **yeast** consumes sugars from the wort and creates alcohol and carbon dioxide. The type of yeast used determines the kind of beer produced. One type of yeast rises to the top during the fermenting process and is used to produce ales, porters, or stouts. Fermentation for ales may be complete within a week. Bottom-fermenting yeast is used to product lagers. Fermentation for lagers occurs at lower temperatures than for ales and may last over a month. Some brewers capture and store the carbon dioxide produced during fermentation for further carbonation of the beer during the maturing stage.

Maturing

During the **maturing** stage, lagers are pumped into conditioning or aging tanks in which many lagers undergo a second fermentation, known as **krausening**, to deepen the flavor and texture of the beer and to naturally carbonate the beer. The fully fermented beer from the first fermentation is moved into aging tanks and small amounts of freshly yeasted wort are added. The sealed aging tanks enable carbon dioxide gas to build and the result is natural carbonation of the beer. This second fermentation may take up to three weeks. There may be a short maturing stage for ales. After fermentation, ales proceed to the filtering stage.

If brewers do not use krausening, they typically carbonate the beer near the end of the maturing stage. This may be done with carbon dioxide stored from the fermenting stage, or with gas pumped under pressure into the product.

Exhibit 4   The First Beer Can

The World's FIRST Beer Can

The "official" birthday of the beer can is January 24, 1935. That's the day cans of Krueger's Finest Beer and Krueger's Cream Ale first went on sale in Richmond, Virginia. But the beer can really made its debut some 14 months earlier—just before the repeal of Prohibition. American Can Company had engineered a workable beer can. All that was needed was a brewer willing to take the pioneering plunge. The Gottfried Krueger Brewing Company of Newark, New Jersey, signed on the dotted line in November 1933. By the end of that month, American had installed a temporary canning line and delivered 2,000 Krueger's Special Beer cans, which were promptly filled with 3.2% Krueger beer—the highest alcohol content allowed at the time. Krueger's Special Beer thus became the world's first beer can. The 2,000 cans of beer were given to faithful Krueger drinkers; 91% gave it thumbs up, and 85% said it tasted more like draft than bottled beer. Reassured by this successful test, Krueger gave canning the green light, and history was made.

A photo of two Krueger Special cans appeared in the December 28, 1933, issue of *Brewer's News*, but no current example has been positively verified to exist. The can on the top surfaced briefly in 1985, but its whereabouts remain unknown. The can on the bottom was recreated digitally.

Source: Brewery Collectibles of America. For more information, visit the organziation's Internet site at: www.BCCA.com.

Carbonation is an essential part of the beer-making process because it creates the spritzy, zestful character of beer and the rich, fine collar of foam at the top of a poured beer. Insufficiently carbonated beer is said to be "flat."

At the end of the maturing stage, the beer is sent to a final filtering tank to remove impurities and is readied for packaging.

Packaging

Beer is a perishable product so it must be packaged and shipped to preserve its freshness. Exhibit 4 presents what is thought to be the first beer can. Packaging beer in cans or in amber or brown bottles protects it from becoming "light-struck." Over-exposure to light gives beer a "skunky," sulphur-like aroma, destroying both the taste and aroma of the beer. Exposure to direct sunlight can affect the aroma of beer within minutes.

Beer that is to be canned or bottled is always pasteurized. **Pasteurization** heats the finished, filtered beer (at 140° to 150° F; 60° to 65.5° C) in order to kill bacteria that causes spoiling. The shelf life for most bottled and canned beer is between 110 and 120 days. All imported beers (bottled, canned, or kegged) must be pasteurized because of the lengthy time between shipping and service.

Domestic draft beer is not pasteurized, so it must be kept cool at all times. Storing temperatures for draft beer are 36° F (2° C) to 38° F (3° C). Higher temperatures may cause the beer to turn sour and become cloudy. **Draft beer** is packaged in metal kegs and sold directly to bars and restaurants. Full kegs hold 31 gallons; half-kegs are more popular.

Storing and Handling Beer

The fresher the beer when served, the better it will taste. Beer is generally stored in a cooler behind the bar to serve the needs of daily operations. Extended supplies are stored in a large walk-in refrigerator in the back of the house.

Under ideal storage conditions, canned or bottled beer will remain fresh for up to 120 days. Proper storage protects beer from light, air, high temperatures, and movement. Bottled or canned beers are best stored cold in a dark area where there is little chance of movement or shaking. Vibrations will cause beer to oxidize prematurely and produce a stale, unappealing taste. Bottled beer can be kept at room temperature, but once refrigerated, it should remain chilled until served. Beer should never be frozen. If beer freezes, ingredients break down and separate, forming flakes in the beer that do not dissolve when the beer thaws.

Quality is maintained during storage by using the **first-in, first-out (FIFO)** inventory rotation method. With this method, the beer held in inventory the longest should be the first to be issued for service. As newly received beer enters storage areas, it should be placed behind or under packages already in storage. Marking the date of receipt on every package makes it possible to compare dates of packages used for service and those in storage areas. Beer in service should have been received earlier than those remaining in storage.

Imagine what could happen if the FIFO method is not used at a large resort. Let's say 30 cases of beer arrive in January and are placed in the cooler. That evening, 27 cases of beer are served, leaving 3 cases in the back or bottom of the cooler. The next morning, 30 more cases of beer arrive and that day 29 cases of beer are served. Note that the 3 cases still remain from the previous evening. Over the next few months, the bar continues to serve a little less or a little more beer than it receives. All of a sudden, it's a summer holiday and business is great. The bar sells all the beer that it received by its daily order and begins to sell all that is in stock. Eventually, the staff works all the way down to those three cases that were delivered in January. That beer is now six months old and not fresh enough to be served.

Just like the perishable foods you buy at a grocery store, brewers mark their products with a **freshness date**. While this is helpful, it might not have prevented the problem of the 3 cases of beer going bad in the previous example. Why? Because not all breweries use the same freshness labeling system. For example, some brewers use a **born-on date**. In this case, you may have to add 110 days to the date to determine if it is still fresh enough to serve. Other brewers use a standard expiration date, similar to most food products you buy in grocery stores. Imported brands use a more complicated set of numbers known as the Julian Code, as explained in Exhibit 5. Using the **Julian Code**, the dates on imported beer packages would be interpreted as:

Exhibit 5   Julian Code

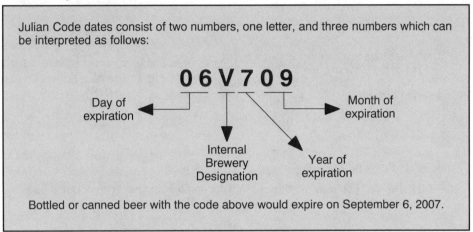

Julian Code dates consist of two numbers, one letter, and three numbers which can be interpreted as follows:

0 6 V 7 0 9

Day of expiration

Month of expiration

Internal Brewery Designation

Year of expiration

Bottled or canned beer with the code above would expire on September 6, 2007.

Julian Code	Expiration Date
04S411	November 4, 2004
28R507	July 28, 2005
13Y601	January 13, 2006
08H705	May 8, 2007
21N810	October 21, 2008

Keg beer is usually stored in a cooler located some distance from the tap where it is dispensed. Gas pressure (carbon dioxide) is applied to the top of the keg, forcing beer out a hose line at the bottom of the keg to the tap. Whenever the tap is opened, gas pressure drives beer out of the keg through the hose line out the tap and into a glass. The hook-up requires an assortment of connectors, hoses, taps, and fittings. Keg and tap systems are diagrammed in Exhibit 6.

The key to this system is setting the proper gas pressure. Too much or too little pressure can cause the beer to foam excessively at the tap. The proper amount of pressure varies with each keg hook-up. The diameter of the hose, the length of the line, the temperature of the beer, and the height of the tap are variables that determine the proper amount of pressure to apply with a particular keg hook-up. Beer suppliers service these systems. Supplier servicing of keg hook-ups involves cleaning the hoses and making sure the carbon dioxide pressure inside the line is appropriate. All keg hook-ups (single keg and multiple keg hook-ups) should be checked before the bar opens so that, if necessary, repair service can be called immediately.

Serving Beer

There are as many kinds of beer glasses as there are styles of beer. Traditionally, lager is served in a pilsner glass. This glass has a V-shaped bottom that enhances the appearance of the beer by displaying a constant stream of bubbles. Ale is

Exhibit 6 Keg and Tap Systems

Draft beer taps are connected to kegs that are out of the view of guests. These connection lines can be quite long depending upon the size of the bar.

Changing Out a Keg

As a bartender, you may need to change out a keg from time to time. Use these instructions for practice.

ONE

Align lug locks on tavern head with lug housing in top of keg; insert tavern head.

TWO

Turn tavern head handle 1/4 turn clockwise; the tavern head is now secured to keg.

THREE

Rotate on/off valve handle 1/4 turn clockwise to open beer and CO_2 ports in keg. The keg is now tapped.

Multi-Keg Systems

Multi-keg draft systems are commonly used in high-volume service situations. WIth several kegs attached to one line, interruptions in guest service are minimal.

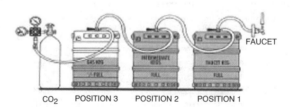

CO_2 POSITION 3   POSITION 2   POSITION 1

Exhibit 7   Samples of Lager and Ale Glassware

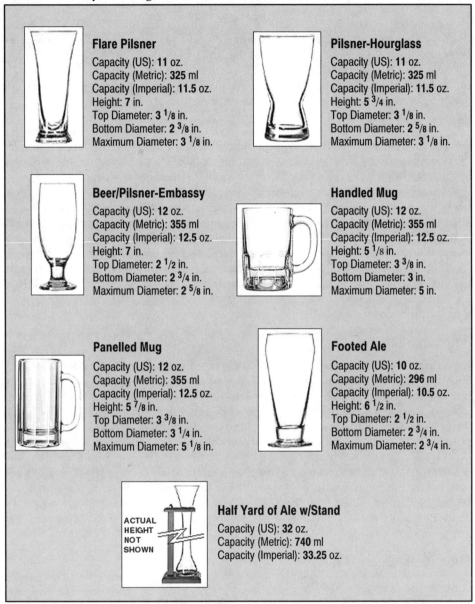

Flare Pilsner
Capacity (US): **11** oz.
Capacity (Metric): **325** ml
Capacity (Imperial): **11.5** oz.
Height: **7** in.
Top Diameter: **3** $^1/_8$ in.
Bottom Diameter: **2** $^3/_8$ in.
Maximum Diameter: **3** $^1/_8$ in.

Pilsner-Hourglass
Capacity (US): **11** oz.
Capacity (Metric): **325** ml
Capacity (Imperial): **11.5** oz.
Height: **5** $^3/_4$ in.
Top Diameter: **3** $^1/_8$ in.
Bottom Diameter: **2** $^5/_8$ in.
Maximum Diameter: **3** $^1/_8$ in.

Beer/Pilsner-Embassy
Capacity (US): **12** oz.
Capacity (Metric): **355** ml
Capacity (Imperial): **12.5** oz.
Height: **7** in.
Top Diameter: **2** $^1/_2$ in.
Bottom Diameter: **2** $^3/_4$ in.
Maximum Diameter: **2** $^5/_8$ in.

Handled Mug
Capacity (US): **12** oz.
Capacity (Metric): **355** ml
Capacity (Imperial): **12.5** oz.
Height: **5** $^1/_8$ in.
Top Diameter: **3** $^3/_8$ in.
Bottom Diameter: **3** in.
Maximum Diameter: **5** in.

Panelled Mug
Capacity (US): **12** oz.
Capacity (Metric): **355** ml
Capacity (Imperial): **12.5** oz.
Height: **5** $^7/_8$ in.
Top Diameter: **3** $^3/_8$ in.
Bottom Diameter: **3** $^1/_4$ in.
Maximum Diameter: **5** $^1/_8$ in.

Footed Ale
Capacity (US): **10** oz.
Capacity (Metric): **296** ml
Capacity (Imperial): **10.5** oz.
Height: **6** $^1/_2$ in.
Top Diameter: **2** $^1/_2$ in.
Bottom Diameter: **2** $^3/_4$ in.
Maximum Diameter: **2** $^3/_4$ in.

ACTUAL
HEIGHT
NOT
SHOWN

Half Yard of Ale w/Stand
Capacity (US): **32** oz.
Capacity (Metric): **740** ml
Capacity (Imperial): **33.25** oz.

Source: Libbey Glass. For more information browse the Internet site at: www.libbey.com.

usually served in a mug. The thick glass of the ale mug keeps the beer cool and the handle of the mug keeps warm hands from affecting the temperature of the ale. Exhibit 7 shows examples of both pilsner glasses and ale mugs. Beer and other alcoholic beverages should never be served in the same type of glass or cup as non-alcoholic beverages. Servers and bartenders need to identify by sight who is consuming alcohol and who is not.

Lager beer is best served in a cold, clean glass at about 41° F (5° C) with an appropriate head, or collar, of foam. Some bars or restaurants will freeze a glass before pouring a draft beer. The idea is that the beer will stay colder longer. However, ice crystals can trap the carbon dioxide from the beer, causing it to retain too much of its carbonation and affecting the taste. To avoid this, many establishments use glasses that are chilled, but not frozen, whether drawing beer from a tap or pouring from a bottle.

Beer contains dissolved carbon dioxide (a gas). When beer is poured, some the gas comes out of solution and forms bubbles. As the bubbles rise to the surface, they combine with other bubbles and increase in size. At the top of the glass, all the bubbles gather to form a frothy collar of foam—the head of the beer.

Most beer drinkers have opinions about the amount of head they like on their beer and the way it should look in a glass. Some beer drinkers also have opinions about the right way to pour various types of beers to produce the proper amount of head appropriate to each beer type. In general, the head produced by pouring a lager should be greater than the half-inch head recommended for pouring ales.

The ingredients and carbonation methods used in the brewing process contribute to the size and stability of the foam produced through pouring. In addition, the amount of head produced is a function of the technique used in pouring and the cleanliness of the glass.

Pouring Beer

If you pour beer slowly down the side of a tilted glass, a smaller head is formed and more carbon dioxide remains dissolved in the beer. If you hold the glass upright and pour straight into the glass, more gas is released and a larger head is formed. Exhibit 8 illustrates one method of pouring beer that results in ¾ inch to 1 inch of creamy head rising to the top of the glass. Exhibit 9 illustrates a method of pouring draft beer. Note that during a pour, the tap is opened quickly and closed quickly. This avoids "pumping" the tap—an action that can build up gas and create too much foam. Also, when beginning to pour, the glass is held an inch below the tap to avoid contact with the nozzle. This prevents the beer from becoming contaminated from bacteria on the tap. Pouring beer to form a perfect collar of foam depends not only on technique, but also on the cleanliness of the glass.

The "Beer-Clean" Glass

A glass may look clean yet have an invisible layer of film or grease residue from smoke, fingerprints, or food in the wash water. Film or grease residue causes the beer's collar of foam to quickly disappear. The carbonation releases and the beer will look and taste flat. A glass may also have an invisible layer caused by soap or grease that causes a false head in which the foam bubbles are large and quickly disappear. Even odors left on glasses from contact with bar towels, or other types of drinks (milk, tea, coffee, soft drinks, juices, etc.) can create an "off" taste in the beer.

Exhibit 8   Pouring a Bottled Beer

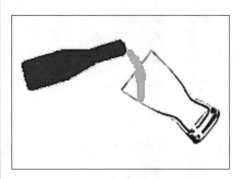 

Start with a "beer-clean" glass in one hand and the bottled beer in the other hand. Hold the glass at a 45° angle tilted toward the bottled beer. Lift the bottle and pour quickly and generously, aiming for the middle of the side of the glass.	When the glass is half full, bring it to an upright position and pour straight down the middle of the glass to produce a 3/4" to 1" foam head.

Some brewing companies recommend the following test for a "**beer-clean**" glass. Dip a glass in clean water. Hold the glass up and turn it upside down. If the glass is beer-clean, a film of water will cover the entire surface of the glass. If the water breaks up into streaks or droplets on the glass, you need to change the procedure for cleaning beer glasses. Check with your beer supplier. The most common procedure for manually washing beer glasses uses a three-compartment sink illustrated in Exhibit 10. Many automatic glass washers operate using this same three-step method that ends with air-drying.

Taste Talk

Bartenders and beverage servers are often asked to describe various styles and brands of beer. Talking about taste can, at first, seem contrived and subjective, but there is a common international language for describing the taste of a wide variety of beer styles. For example, the International Bitterness Unit (IBU) is part of an internationally agreed upon scale for measuring the bitterness of beer. An American lager may have around 10 IBUs, a mild English ale around 20 units, an India Pale Ale may have more than 40 IBUs, and Irish stout (dry stout) may have between 55 and 60 IBUs. While other objective measures exist, most taste talk focuses attention on how the beer appeals to the senses of smell, sight, and taste.

Each style of beer has its own particular aroma, appearance, flavor, and body. The varieties of hops used in making a beer determine its dominant aroma. Some of the more common aromas are described as earthy, herbal, flowery, or citric. A strong malt presence will produce a sweet aroma. Earthy and roasty aromas generally result from roasted malt used making the beer.

Exhibit 9   Pouring a Draft Beer

STEP 1:

Start with a beer-clean glass at a 45° angle, about one inch below the faucet.

STEP 2:

Handle the tap at the bottom. Open the faucet quickly and all the way. After the glass is half full, gradually return it to an upright position.

STEP 3:

Continue allowing the beer to pour straight down the middle to produce a 3/4" to 1" foam head.

STEP 4:

Close the faucet quickly and completely.

Exhibit 10   The "Beer-Clean" Glass

Sink 1—Wash

Place the glass in a sink filled with hot water and a solution of sudsless, non-fat cleaning compound (like dishwasher soap). Use brushes to remove dust, lipstick, or other unsanitary deposits.

Sink 2—Rinse

Allow cold water to run over the glass. Place the bottom of the glass in the water first. This prevents air pockets from forming within the glass. Take the glass out of the sink, bottom first. This "bottom-in, bottom-out" method assures complete rinsing.

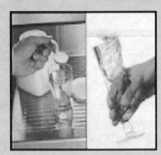

Sink 3—Sanitize

Soak the glass in sanitizing solution—again with a "bottom-in, bottom-out" method. Allow glasses to dry upside down on a wire rack or on a free-draining plastic surface. This allows maximum air flow and odor-free drying.

Each beer style has its own unique appearance. The degree of carbonation determines a beer's sparkle. Lagers are usually golden; pale ales are amber; and, stouts are dark or nearly black. The head, or collar of foam produced when the beer is poured, is also a quality of appearance. Different types of beer produce heads that vary in relation to thickness, foaminess, and how long the head is retained in the glass. Most beers are filtered and should appear clear. However, wheat beers are almost always cloudy when poured.

The flavor of a beer is often described in the same terms as its aroma. Usually, several flavors compete with one another. When they come together to produce an overall effect it is referred to as "balance." If one flavor overpowers the others, the beer is unbalanced. Each type of beer produces its characteristic balance of flavors produced by malt (sweet, earthly, or roasty) and by hops (herbal, flowery, or citric).

The body of a beer is sometimes referred to as the "mouthfeel." An American lager might be described as thin and watery, while a stout might be described as full and chewy. Carbonation affects body.

Unique flavor characteristics to more than twenty different beer styles have been outlined by an independent nonprofit organization called the Beer Judge Certification Program (BJCP). The summaries appearing throughout the appendix to this chapter are fundamental taste characteristics for basic styles of beer that have been adapted from the beer-judging guidelines produced by the BJCP.

By tasting samples of several beers, bartenders and beverage servers are better able to recommend specific types of beers to guests. Tasting beer samples can effectively be incorporated into the training programs for beverage servers and bartenders.

Key Terms

alcohol by volume—A measure of the amount of alcohol in beer; the measure of space the alcohol takes up as a percentage of total space.

alcohol by weight—A measure of the amount of alcohol in beer; the measure of the amount of weight the alcohol has as a percentage of total weight.

ale—A style of beer made with top-fermenting yeast; generally tastes hearty, robust, and fruity.

barley—A cereal grain used in brewing beer; a member of the grass family which also includes wheat, rye, and oats.

beer—An alcoholic beverage obtained through the fermentation of grains. Modern beer is flavored with hops and carbonation.

beer-clean—A term referring to a sanitized glass in which beer will be served. A "beer-clean" glass is free from substances that may chemically alter the beer or otherwise reduce its quality.

born-on date—A type of freshness date used on certain brands of beer; the date on which the beer was produced or "born."

carbonation—The process of infusing carbon dioxide gas into a beverage to produce a sparkling, bubbly liquid as with soda, beer, and sparkling wine.

draft beer—Beer drawn from a tap by means of a keg system.

fermentation—A chemical process in which yeast is added to a sugar source; the yeast breaks down the sugar into alcohol, carbon dioxide, and heat.

first-in, first-out (FIFO)—A storage rotation process in which perishable items are used in the order in which they are received. In storage areas, new items are placed behind or below current items so that current items are used while they are still fresh.

freshness date—A date or code found on beer products to designate the period of time during which the beer is fresh for consumption.

hops—A primary flavoring ingredient in most beers, creating aroma and bitterness; female blossoms of perennial vines.

grain adjuncts—Starches, such as corn and rice, used in place of traditional grains (barley, rye, oats) to lighten the quality of beer.

Julian Code—A type of freshness date found on certain brands of beer; a six-digit code indicating the date upon which the beer is no longer fresh for consumption.

keg—A selling unit of beer; a large metal cylinder containing beer that attaches to a line (hose) in a draft system to be dispensed to the tap; each half-barrel holds 15.5 gallons of beer.

krausening—The addition of partially fermented wort during the maturing stage of beer production to encourage a strong secondary fermentation.

lager—A style of beer made with bottom-fermenting yeast; generally are smooth, elegant, crisp, and clean.

lauter tun—Vessel used to clarify wort after the mashing stage.

malt—Barley or other cereals that are germinated and prepared for conversion into fermentable sugars during beer production.

mash—Ground malt blended with water.

mashing—A stage in the brewing process in which ground malt is combined with water and heated to break down starch into simple sugars that yeast can consume during the fermentation stage.

maturing—A stage in the brewing process in which lagers are pumped into conditioning or aging tanks where the fermented brew is carbonated and then sent to a final filtering tank to remove impurities before packaging.

milling—The first stage in the brewing process in which barley grain is crushed, not ground, to expose the starches found in the kernels, thus preparing the malt for the mashing stage.

pasteurization—The process of heating a liquid to a high temperature and maintaining the heat for a period of time to kill all bacteria and eliminate other impurities.

tap—Part of a keg system; the spout or set of spouts attached to the bar from which draft beer flows; to start the flow of the contents of a keg to the bar spout.

tasting beer—Differentiating styles of beer in terms of aroma, appearance, flavor, and body.

wort—The liquid rich in malt and sugars resulting from the mashing stage of the brewing process.

yeast—A key element in the fermentation process; a living microorganism that converts the sugars contained in the malt into alcohol and carbon dioxide. One species, Saccharomyces cerevisiae, is used to make ale, another species, Saccharomyces carlsbergensis, is used to make lager.

Review Questions

1. How is lager different from ale?

2. What is light beer?

3. Explain the role of malt, hops, and yeast in the beer-making process.

4. How is "mash" different from "wort"?

5. How does beer become carbonated?

6. Why must beverage operations use a first-in, first-out rotation system for storing and issuing beer?

7. What is the "Julian Code"?

8. How do you pour (from a bottle or from a tap) beer into a glass and produce the appropriate collar of foam?

9. What is a "beer-clean" glass?

10. What does is mean when someone says that the taste of a beer is "balanced"?

 Internet Sites

For more information, visit the following Internet sites. Remember that Internet addresses can change without notice. If the site is no longer there, you can use a search engine to look for additional sites. Many alcohol-related sites require users to be of legal drinking age to enter.

Alaskan Brewing Company
www.alaskanbeer.com

All About Beer Online
www.allaboutbeer.com

American Brewer
www.ambrew.com

American Breweriana Association
www.americabreweriana.org

Anheuser-Busch
www.anheuser-busch.com

Association of Brewers
www.beertown.org

Beer History
www.beerhistory.com

Beer Judge Certification Program
www.bjcp.org

Boston Beer Company
www.samadams.com

Modern Brewery Age
www.breweryage.com

Molson
www.molson.com

Chapter Appendix
Beer Styles—Taste Characteristics

AMERICAN LAGER—Standard/Premium/Light
Alcohol Content by Volume: 3.5–5.1 percent
Commercial Examples: Standard: Budweiser, Molson Golden, Kirin, Corona, Fosters; Premium: Michelob; Light: Michelob Light, Bud Light, Miller Lite.

Aroma
Little to no malt aroma. Hop aroma may range from none to light, flowery hop presence. Slight fruity aromas from yeast and hop varieties used may exist.

Appearance
Very pale straw to pale gold color. White head seldom persists. Very clear.

Flavor
Crisp and dry flavor with some low levels of sweetness. Hop flavor ranges from none to low levels. Hop bitterness at low to medium level. Balance may vary from slightly malty to slightly bitter, but is relatively close to even. High levels of carbonation may provide a slight acidity or dry "sting." No fruitiness.

Body
Very light body from use of a high percentage of adjuncts such as rice or corn. Very well carbonated with slight carbonic bite on the tongue.

AMERICAN LAGER—Dark
Alcohol Content by Volume: 4.1–5.1 percent
Commercial Examples: Michelob Dark, Lowenbrau Dark, Beck's Dark, Saint Pauli Girl Dark.

Aroma
Little to no malt aroma. Little or no roast malt aroma since the color is usually derived artificially from the addition of dark caramel brewing syrups. Hop aroma may range from none to light flowery hop presence. Slight fruity aromas may exist from yeast and hop varieties used.

Appearance
Deep copper to dark brown with bright clarity. Foam stand may not be long lasting.

Flavor
Crisp with some low levels of sweetness. Roasted malt flavors, very low to none; often the dark color is from dark caramel brewing syrups rather than roasted malts. Hop flavor ranges from none to low levels. Hop bitterness at low to medium levels. No fruitiness.

Body

Light to somewhat medium body. Smooth, although a well-carbonated beer.

EUROPEAN PALE LAGER—Bohemian Pilsner

Alcohol Content by Volume: 4–5.3 percent
Commercial Examples: Pilsner Urquell, Gambrinus Pilsner, Budweiser Budvar, Staropramen.

Aroma

Rich with a complex malt and a spicy, floral, Saaz hop bouquet.

Appearance

Light gold to deep copper-gold, clear, with a dense, creamy white head.

Flavor

Rich, complex maltiness combined with pronounced soft, rounded bitterness and flavor from Saaz hops. Bitterness is prominent but never harsh, and does not linger. The aftertaste is balanced between malt and hops. Clean, no fruitiness.

Body

Medium-bodied, medium carbonation.

GERMAN AMBER LAGER—Oktoberfest/Maerzen

Alcohol Content by Volume: 4.8–6.5 percent
Commercial Examples: Spaten Ur-Maerzen, Ayinger Oktoberfest-Maerzen, Paulaner Oktoberfest, Wuerzburger Oktoberfest, Hacker-Pschorr Oktoberfest.

Aroma

German (Vienna or Munich) malt aroma. A light toasted malt aroma may be present. No fruitiness or hop aroma.

Appearance

Dark gold to reddish amber color. Bright clarity, with solid foam stand.

Flavor

Distinctive and complex maltiness may include a toasted aspect. Hop bitterness is moderate, and hop flavor is low to none. Balance is toward malt, though the finish is not sweet.

Body

Medium body, with a creamy texture and medium carbonation.

VIENNA LAGER

Alcohol Content by Volume: 4.6–5.5 percent
Commercial Examples: Negra Modelo, Portland Lager, 150 Jahre, Augsburger Red, Leinenkugel Red.

Aroma

Dark German (Vienna or Munich) malt aroma. A light toasted malt aroma may be present. Similar, though less intense than Oktoberfest.

Appearance

Reddish amber to light brown color. Bright clarity and solid foam stand.

Flavor

Soft, elegant malt complexity is in the forefront, with a firm enough hop presence to provide a balanced finish. Some toasted character from the use of Vienna malt.

Body

Light to medium body, with a gentle creaminess. Medium carbonation.

BOCK—Traditional Bock

Alcohol Content by Volume: 6–7.5 percent
Commercial Examples: Aass Bock, Hacker-Pschorr Dunkeler Bock, Dunkel Ritter Bock, Einbecker Ur-Bock.

Aroma

Strong aroma of malt. Virtually no hop aroma.

Appearance

Deep amber to dark brown color. Lagering should provide good clarity despite the dark color. Head retention may be impaired by higher-than-average alcohol content.

Flavor

Rich and complex maltiness is dominated by the grain and caramel flavors of Munich and Vienna malts. A touch of roasty character may be present but is rare. No hop flavor. Hop bitterness is generally only high enough to balance the malt flavors to allow moderate sweetness in the finish.

Body

Medium to full bodied. Low to moderate carbonation.

BOCK—Doppelbock

Alcohol Content by Volume: 7.5–12 percent
Commercial Examples: Paulaner Salvator, Ayinger Celebrator, Spaten Optimator, Tucher Bajuvator, Augustiner Maximator, EKU Kulminator "28," Loewenbraeu Triumphator, Hacker-Pschorr Animator, Old Dominion Dominator.

Aroma

Intense maltiness. Virtually no hop aroma. A fruity aspect to the aroma (often described as prune, plum, or grape) may be present due to reactions between malt, the boil, and aging. A very slight roasty aroma may be present in darker versions.

Appearance

Gold to dark brown in color. Lagering should provide good clarity. Head retention may be impaired by higher-than-average alcohol content.

Flavor

Very rich and malty, infrequently a touch of roastiness. Invariably there will be an impression of alcoholic strength, but this should be smooth and warming rather than harsh or burning. Little to no hop flavor. Hop bitterness varies from moderate to low but always allows malt to dominate the flavor.

Body

Full-bodied. Low carbonation.

BITTER AND ENGLISH PALE ALE—Ordinary Bitter

Alcohol Content by Volume: 3–3.8 percent
Commercial Examples: Henley's Brakspear Bitter, Boddington's Pub Draught, Thomas Hardy Country Bitter, Young's Bitter, Fuller's Chiswick Bitter.

Aroma

Hop aroma can range from moderate to none. Caramel aromas also moderate to none. Should have mild to moderate fruitiness. The best examples have some malt aroma.

Appearance

Medium gold to medium copper-brown. May have very little head due to low carbonation.

Flavor

Medium to high bitterness. May or may not have hop flavor and fruitiness. Crystal malt flavor very common. Balance varies from even to decidedly bitter, although the bitterness should not completely overpower the malt flavor.

Body

Light to medium-light body. Carbonation low, although bottled examples can have moderate carbonation.

BITTER AND ENGLISH PALE ALE—Strong Bitter/English Pale Ale

Alcohol Content by Volume: 4.4–6.2 percent
Commercial Examples: Fullers ESB, Bateman's XXXB, Young's Strong Export Bitter (sold in the U.S. as Young's Special London Ale), Ushers 1824 Particular Ale, Oasis ESB, Big Time ESB, Shepherd Neame Bishop's Finger, Fullers 1845, bottled Bass Ale, Whitbread, Royal Oak, Shepherd Neame Spitfire.

Aroma

Hop aroma high to none. Diacetyl and caramel aroma moderate to none. Moderate fruitiness. Malt aroma apparent.

Appearance

Copper to dark amber-brown. May have very little head.

Flavor

Malt flavors evident. Crystal malt flavor common. Hop flavor ranges from low to strong. Diacetyl and fruitiness moderate to none. Balance varies from even to quite bitter, although malt flavor should not be completely overpowered.

Body

Medium to medium-full body. arbonation low, although bottled pale ales tend to have moderate carbonation.

INDIA PALE ALE

Alcohol Content by Volume: 5–7.8 percent

Commercial Examples: Anchor Liberty Ale, Sierra Nevada Celebration Ale, Brooklyn East India Pale Ale, Tupper's Hop Pocket, Great Lakes Commodore Perry IPA, Samuel Smith's India Ale, Fuller's IPA, Highfalls IPA, Victory Hopdevil, Three Floyds Alpha King.

Aroma

A prominent hop aroma of floral, grassy, or fruity characteristic typical. A caramel-like or toasty malt presence may also be noted, but may be at a low level. Fruitiness may also be detected.

Appearance

Color ranges from medium gold to deep copper, with English versions often darker than American ones. Should be clear, although some haze at cold temperatures is acceptable.

Flavor

Hop flavor is medium to high, with an assertive hop bitterness. Malt flavor should be low to medium, but should be sufficient to support the hop aspect. Despite the substantial hop character typical of these beers, sufficient malt flavor, body and complexity to support the hops will provide the best balance. Fruitiness from the fermentation or hops should add to the overall complexity.

Body

Smooth, medium-bodied, without astringency, moderate carbonation combine, renders an overall dry sensation in the presence of malt sweetness.

PORTER—Robust Porter

Alcohol Content by Volume: 4.8–6 percent

Commercial Examples: Sierra Nevada Porter, Anchor Porter, Great Lakes Edmund Fitzgerald Porter.

Aroma

Roast malt or grain aroma, often coffee-like or chocolate-like, should be evident. Hop aroma moderate to low.

Appearance

Dark brown to black color, may be garnet-like. Clarity may be difficult to discern in such a dark beer. Head retention should be moderate to good.

Flavor

Malt flavor usually features coffee-like or chocolate-like roasty dryness. Overall flavor may finish from medium sweet to dry. May have a sharp character from dark roasted grains. Hop flavor varies widely.

Body

Medium to medium-full bodied. Low to moderate carbonation.

STOUT—Dry Stout

Alcohol Content by Volume: 3.2–5.5 percent
Commercial Examples: Guinness Draught Stout (also canned), Murphy's Stout, Beamish Stout.

Aroma

Coffee-like roasted barley and roasted malt aromas are prominent. Esters low to medium. Hop aroma low to none.

Appearance

Deep garnet to black in color. Clarity is irrelevant in such a dark beer. A thick, creamy, long-lasting head is characteristic.

Flavor

Moderate acidity/sourness and sharpness from roasted grains, and medium to high hop bitterness, provide a dry finish. Balancing factors may include some creaminess and moderate to low fruitiness.

Body

Medium-light to medium body, with a creamy character. Low to moderate carbonation.

STOUT—Sweet Stout

Alcohol Content by Volume: 3–5.6 percent
Commercial Examples: Mackeson's XXX Stout, Watney's Cream Stout, Samuel Adams Cream Stout, Tennent's Milk Stout.

Aroma

Mild roasted grain aromas. Fruitiness can be low to high. Hop aroma low to none.

Appearance
Very dark amber to black in color, which makes clarity essentially unimportant. Creamy head.

Flavor
Dark roasted grains and malts dominate the flavor as in dry stout, though there is medium to high sweetness. Hopping is moderate and tends to be lower than in dry stout, emphasizing the malt sweetness.

Body
Full-bodied and creamy. Carbonation low to moderate.

LIGHT ALE—American Wheat
Alcohol Content by Volume: 3.7–5.5 percent
Commercial Examples: Otter Creek Summer Wheat, Anchor Wheat, Boulevard Wheat, Pyramid Hefe-Weizen.

Aroma
Characteristic of wheat with some graininess. Hop aroma may be high or low but if present will be from American hop varieties.

Appearance
Usually pale straw to gold. Clarity may range from brilliant to hazy. Big, long-lasting head.

Flavor
Light graininess. Hop flavor may be from low to high. Hop bitterness low to medium. Some fruitiness from ale fermentation acceptable; however, the use of a fairly neutral American ale yeast usually results in a clean fermentation.

Body
Light to medium body. Higher carbonation is appropriate.

WHEAT BEER—Bavarian Weizen
Alcohol Content by Volume: 4.3–5.6 percent
Commercial Examples: Paulaner Hefe-Weizen, Pschorr-Brau Weisse, Spaten Club-Weisse, Schneider Weisse, Julius Echter Weizenbier.

Aroma
Vanilla and fruity esters of banana are common. Hop aroma ranges from low to none. Some aroma of wheat may be present.

Appearance
Pale straw to dark reddish-gold in color. A very thick, long-lasting head is characteristic. High protein content of wheat may impair clarity in an unfiltered beer, and clarity can be deliberately cloudy in a Hefe-Weizen from suspended yeast sediment.

Flavor

The soft, grainy flavor of wheat is essential. Hop flavor is low to none and hop bitterness is very low. A tart character from yeast and high carbonation may be present. Fruity esters, most prominently banana, are often present.

Body

The texture of wheat imparts the sensation of a fluffy, creamy fullness that may progress to a surprisingly light finish. A high carbonation level is typical.

Chapter 7 Outline

The Process of Distillation
    Fermentation
    Distillation
    Blending
    Aging
Whiskeys
    Scotch Whisky
    Irish Whiskey
    American Whiskeys
    Canadian Whisky
Vodka
Gin
Rum
Tequila
Brandy
    Distillation
    Aging
    Blending
    Labeling
Liqueurs, Aperitifs, Bitters
Mixology Basics
Judging the Quality of Spirits

Competencies

1. Explain the process of distillation and describe the equipment used to make distilled spirits. (pp. 177–184)

2. Describe the distinguishing characteristics of scotch and identify popular brands and drinks made with scotch. (pp. 184–185)

3. Explain how Irish whiskey differs from American and Canadian whiskeys. (pp. 185–187)

4. Describe the distinguishing characteristics of vodka, gin, rum, and tequila and identify popular brands and drinks made with these spirits. (pp. 187–189)

5. Explain how brandy is produced. (pp. 189–191)

6. Identify the flavors of popular liqueurs. (pp. 191, 193–194)

7. Describe how aperitifs differ from bitters. (pp. 191–192)

8. Identify the glassware, ingredients, and methods for making the twenty most popular mixed drinks at southern resort operations. (pp. 194–202)

7

Spirits

THE TERM "SPIRIT" is often used synonymously with liquor. Spirits have higher alcohol content than beers or wines. The word **proof** refers to the alcohol content of a spirit and is derived from the Latin word *probare,* meaning to prove or test. At one time, there was no reliable way to test the amount of alcohol in a spirit. However, an inventive Englishman discovered that gunpowder mixed with a spirit would fire and that a spirit lower in alcohol content than a certain percentage of water would not fire. The lowest alcohol content at which a spirit would fire when mixed with gunpowder was adopted as the British standard. If a mixture of gunpowder and spirit fired, it was considered *proof* that the spirit had been diluted only to the legal standard. This standard was termed "100 proof"; anything over proof (OP) was over 100 and anything under proof (UP) was under 100. The British retain this system, although the original test of firing to check the content is rarely performed.

In the United States, the strength of alcohol is also measured in terms of proof. The percentage of alcohol in a beverage is one-half the beverage's proof. For example, a 100-proof beverage contains 50 percent alcohol. Most liquors range between 80 and 86.9 proof, except for gin, which ranges from 90 to 94.6 proof. Not all brands of the same liquor have the same percentage of alcohol. For example, vodka may range from 80 proof to 100 proof, and some rum is 151 proof. U.S. law requires that all spirit labels state proof and that imported spirits be labeled in American proof.

Distilled spirits are liquors obtained from the process of distillation. Distilled spirits include whiskeys, vodka, gin, rum, tequila, brandy, and others, or any dilution or mixtures of these, used for human consumption. Distilled spirits do not include mixtures that are half or more wine, such as wines fortified with brandy like sherry or dessert wines. Spirits are generally classified into five main groups:

- Grain spirits

- Plant liquors

- Fruit liquors

- Liqueurs

- Bitters

Spirits made from grains include whiskeys, vodka, and gin. Many plant liquors are produced around the world. However, most are consumed only locally or nationally and, even though they may be consumed by millions (as are Chinese distilled spirits made from sorghum or rice), they are not prominent worldwide. Rum and tequila are the only plant liquors to have attained this status. Brandies are the most important fruit liquors. Liqueurs, or cordials, are made from a base of grain, plant, or fruit spirits or their combination. Aromatic or fruit bitters are highly flavored spirits containing bitter substances such as quinine.

This chapter focuses on the major types of spirits consumed today. After describing the general process of distillation, the characteristics of popular spirits are examined along with unique distillation techniques used to produce them. The fermentation process must be proper for the product and must be controlled to give the unique qualities wanted in the various kinds of beverages. A distilled spirit must be made from the right materials, be properly distilled, and (depending on the spirit) be flavored correctly. Some products need blending to be ready for consumption and many products require a carefully controlled aging process.

After this product review, the chapter explores the basics of **mixology**—the skill of mixing drinks. How many mixed drinks do you suppose a good bartender knows how to make? Probably hundreds. After completing this chapter you will know recipes for twenty of the most requested mixed drinks. But, once you're standing behind the bar, you'll need to know many more recipes. Most beverage operations also offer specialty drinks and you'll need to learn these recipes as well. Offering specialty drinks helps an establishment create a unique experience for guests, often reinforcing its atmosphere and ambience. Another challenge is that new cocktails are being created all the time. Bartenders need to be as contemporary as their guests, so the job of learning new drink recipes really never ends.

The chapter ends with brief guidelines for judging the taste of spirits.

The Process of Distillation

Exhibit 1 outlines the process used to distill the Canadian Mist brand of whiskey. The sections that follow describe the process of distillation in more detail.

Fermentation

Fermentation takes place before distillation. **Fermentation** is a chemical process in which yeast is added to a sugar source. The yeast breaks down the sugar into alcohol, carbon dioxide gas, and heat. During this step, a mash made of water and crushed grain, plant, or grapes is injected with special cultured yeasts. Fermentation takes place at temperatures around 70° to 80°F (21° to 27°C). The process takes from two to four days and the resulting fermented liquid is usually 6 to 7 percent alcohol, although it may go as high as 10 percent. The fermented liquid is often called **wort** (pronounced as "wurt"). Wort, is also referred to as "new beer" because it is made by the same method as beer. In some fermentations, as much as 5 percent of the sugar may be turned into acids, glycerine, and other substances. These fermentation products are called **congeners** which provide flavor and aroma and may be desirable or undesirable, depending upon the type of spirit being produced.

Distillation

Distillation is a process in which a fermented liquid (the wort) is heated to separate the alcohol from it. The liquid is usually mainly water, which vaporizes at 212°F (100°C), while alcohol vaporizes at 176°F (80°C). Thus, by heating a liquid

Exhibit 1   The Distillation Process for Canadian Mist

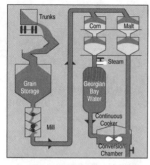

1
Grain Buying and Processing

Corn and barley malt are used to make Canadian Mist. We choose top-quality grains, which we sample and test numerous times to make sure they meet our rigorous quality specifications. We grind the corn and mix it with water and spent-stillage to extract the starch. Then we pressure-cook the corn slurry to make more starch.

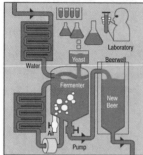

2
Laboratory Testing and Quality Control

The starch is what gives Canadian Mist its light taste. After the corn slurry cools, the enzymes in the ground barley malt convert the starches to sugar. This converted mash is sent to the fermenter, where yeast is added and the process begins. The sugar is converted to alcohol, and the making of Canadian Mist has begun.

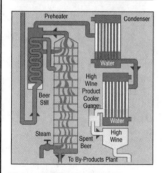

3
Distillation

The fermented grain mash is distilled to remove the alcohol. Canadian Mist is triple-distilled so that its smoothness is without equal. The whisky is vaporized and sent to a condenser. This new whisky is called "high wine."

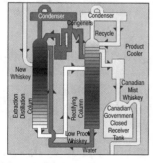

4
Extractive Distillation

The "high wine" is intermingled with water and steam, where some flavor compounds, or congeners, are removed. A controlled amount is left in, however, to give Canadian Mist its distinctive flavor, aroma and taste. This "base whisky" has a high proof that is reduced by pure, clear water from Georgian Bay and put into oak barrels to mellow.

(continued)

Exhibit 1 *(continued)*

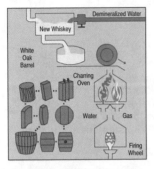

5
Cooperage

At Canadian Mist, we use the finest white oak barrels available. We char them to expose the "red layer" of the wood and impart a smooth, vanilla flavor to the whisky.

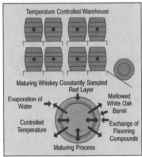

6
Warehousing

Canadian Mist matures in a temperature-controlled facility, so that it can improve year-round, not just in the spring and fall.

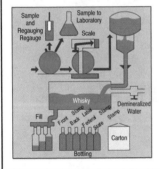

7
Maturity vs. Age

Once Canadian Mist has matured to the peak of perfection, it is bottled, labeled, and taken to your favorite retailer. The resulting whisky is smooth, light-tasting and mellow—great in mixed drinks and cocktails, as well as just over ice or with water.

Cheers!

Source: Canadian Mist. For more information, visit the company's Internet site at: www.canadian mist.com.

containing alcohol above its vaporization point, but not to that of water, the vapor can be captured and cooled to become a liquid separate from the water which never vaporized because the heat was not high enough. The basic parts of a distillation system are the still in which the liquid is heated until the alcohol and its accompanying substances vaporize, and a condenser in which these vapors are cooled down to a liquid state.

Other equipment components include the container into which the distillate is deposited and sometimes a **gin head** through which vapors are passed to pick up flavor. Some spirits are flavored to produce compounded liquors. There are

Exhibit 2   Modern Pot Still with Gin Head on Top

Source: Hiram Walker & Sons, Ltd., Canada.

several ways to incorporate the flavors. Flavoring agents may be added to a brew before distillation so that the essential oils in the flavorings vaporize and come off with the distillate. Another method is to expose the alcohol vapors to the flavoring substances at the top of the still in a gin-head. The spirit may also be percolated over the flavorings or steeped with them (often called maceration).

There are two types of stills: pot stills and continuous stills. Each type is used to produce a distinct kind of distilled product. A **pot still** is a rounded pot with a tapering funnel at the top where rising vapors can be collected and then be carried off to the condenser through a tube. Exhibit 2 shows a modern pot still with a gin head on top. After each distillation, the still must be emptied of spent material and cleaned before being filled with new distilling material. The still is heated from underneath. In some cases, the old method of building a wood fire underneath is used, but most stills today are heated by controlled heat. Distilling temperatures are held down so distillates come off usually at about 110 to 160 proof. This allows more congeners to vaporize with the ethanol, thus heightening the spirit's flavor and body. In pot distillation, it is common to separate the distillate obtained into a first part (head), middle part (heart), and last part (tail). Only the middle part is used to make a spirit. The first and last parts are put back into a liquid about to be distilled and redistilled. Many times the middle part is redistilled. For example, malt scotch is distilled twice, and Irish whiskey is distilled three times. Re-distillation is done to clean and improve product quality.

A **continuous still** is both a vaporizer and condenser. Its condensing system consists of a number of condensing spaces placed at strategic points in the still. Most continuous stills are single towers or cylinders several stories high, but some

Exhibit 3   Continuous Still

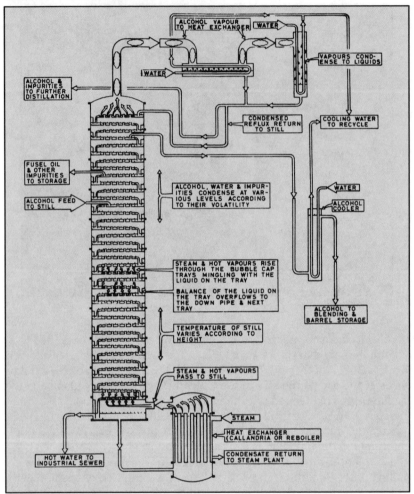

Source: Hiram Walker & Sons, Ltd., Canada.

are set up as two cylinders. Exhibit 3 diagrams a single-tower continuous still. Continuous stills are also called Coffey stills, column stills, or patent stills. Continuous stills are less costly to operate because they can make more alcohol in a given time and require less labor than the operation of pot stills. The process is one in which preheated wort or fermented liquid is introduced at the top of the cylinder while steam to heat it is introduced on the bottom. As the liquid falls, it strikes baffle plates, where it is heated until the alcohol vaporizes. It is then possible to get different temperatures between baffle plates so a much purer alcohol is obtained, because many of the components do not vaporize at exactly the same temperature. These components are condensed at different points in the cylinder and drawn off. The alcohol comes out of the still at 190 proof or slightly below it. The spent liquid falls to the bottom of the cylinder and is drawn off. Thus the process can be continuous, with spent liquid being drawn off at the bottom. Almost all spirits in the United States are made by using the continuous-still method; only some brandies and a few other spirits are distilled by the pot-still method.

Continuous-still products made from grain are called **grain neutral spirits**. Tasteless and colorless, they can be used to make vodka or flavored spirits such as liqueurs and types of gin. They are also used for blending. If a similar spirit is made from a non-grain mash, it must be labeled as a neutral spirit—the word "grain" cannot be used.

Blending

A blending process may be needed to create the desired spirit. Many brands of whiskeys are blends. Blending sometimes involves mixing different types of whiskeys, and sometimes mixing whiskeys of the same type but differing in age or character. The U.S. government refers to blending as **rectification**—blending a spirit with anything other than water. Thus, what is called a blended whiskey in the United States is, by government definition, rectified. Also, when cordials are produced by adding flavors, sugar, and perhaps coloring, the process is rectification. Adding flavor to gin by running it though a gin-head is also considered rectification. In other parts of the world, to rectify generally means to redistill a spirit.

Aging

Spirits under 190 proof are aged in wooden barrels. Aging time varies: some light rums may be aged only a year, while the best brandies may be aged over 20 years. The best scotch is aged for about 15 years. After this, it is apt to take on a woody flavor from the cask. Spirits aged in wood generally mellow with age, losing some of their raw, sharp, and biting characteristics. Aged spirits become smoother. Aging in casks usually decreases the alcohol content of spirits slightly. Spirits evaporate (about 2 percent each year) when aged in casks.

Spirits aged in an oak cask absorb flavor from the wood. Wood also allows a small amount of air to come in contact with the spirit, and there is a slow physical and chemical change that improves quality. Wooden barrels are often charred inside, and the activated charcoal in the charred material changes some of a spirit's constituents. It also adds color. Scotch is often aged in old sherry casks to give it added flavor.

In the United States, **bonded spirits** are those aged in bonded warehouses— warehouses under government supervision. A company placing its spirits in bond gives up control of the product for the storage period, receiving a certificate indicating the company has the quantity and type of spirits described in the certificate. These certificates serve as a type of loan collateral. The company must present the certificate to get back its bonded product. The government will certify that the spirits have been aging in bonded storage for the time they are under bond. A spirit must be stored at least four years in a government-bonded warehouse to be certified as bonded. Spirits labeled as bonded must be produced from a single distillation, be distilled at 160 proof or less, be bottled at 100 proof, and be unblended. Bonding does not guarantee quality. Poor-quality spirits can be bonded. However, when a liquor is bonded, it usually indicates that the aging period improved the original quality of the product.

Whiskeys

The word whiskey comes from the ancient Irish-Gaelic words *uisce beathadh* and the Scottish-Gaelic words *uisge beatha,* meaning "water of life." Somehow *beathadh* and *beatha* were dropped and *uisce* became "whisky," the spelling used by the English, Scots, and Canadians. The Americans and the Irish spell whiskey with an "e," but U.S. government publications use the British form, a vestige of America's colonial heritage. This chapter uses both spellings, depending on the reference (American and Irish, or English, Scottish, or Canadian).

Whiskeys are grain spirits and vary depending on the source of grain, type of fermentation, distillation method, and processing after distillation. The sections that follow focus on the major whiskeys—Scotch, Irish, American, and Canadian.

Scotch Whisky

While commonly referred to simply as "scotch," the product is actually a type of whisky. The U.S. government defines **scotch** as a distinctive spirit from Scotland manufactured in compliance with British laws. If the spirit is a mixture of Scotch whiskies, it must be labeled "Blended Scotch Whisky" or "Scotch—a blend"; unblended malt scotch is labeled "Single Malt Scotch Whisky." U.S. imports must be at least 80 proof (scotch is bottled at 80 to 115 proof).

There are two kinds of scotch: malt and grain. Malt scotch is made from 100 percent barley malt while grain scotch is made from malt combined with unmalted barley and corn or wheat. Malt scotch has a heavier flavor and body than grain scotch because it is pot-distilled and comes off as a fairly low distillate (120 to 140 proof), giving it a number of flavor components. The greater amount of malt also gives it a heavier flavor. Grain scotch is the result of continuous distillation. Because it comes off at 180 to 188 proof, grain scotch has fewer congeners to give flavor, body, and other character to the spirit.

Grain scotch is often blended with malt scotch at a ratio of 40 to 60. Such blends are lighter and more delicate than malt scotch and have increased the popularity of scotch in America and elsewhere. No distillate other than a true malt or grain scotch can be used in a blend.

Scotland's cool climate favors the cultivation of barley, and this grain gives scotch part of its distinctive character. The kind of barley is carefully selected—one of the requirements is that it contain at least 60 percent starch. The barley is cleaned and then placed in warm water to sprout. The sprouting also produces the "malty" flavor which, to some extent, carries over into the spirit. The sprouts are then dried over open peat fires, lending a smoky flavor that also carries over into the spirit. The fermentation period is generally for about 40 hours giving the fermented liquid an alcohol content of 7.5 to 10 percent.

Malt scotch is pot-distilled twice, and only the middle distillate is retained. The first and last distillates (the foreshots and feints) are combined with a new wort for re-distillation. Grain scotch is continuous-distilled once; this method produces a spirit adequate for blending.

While oak aging is important in the production of all whiskeys, it is critical to the production of scotch. Most scotch is aged five or six years. Premium scotch is aged for eight years or more. Scotch usually benefits from aging up to 15 years, after which it can take on a woody flavor from the barrel. Old oak American bourbon barrels are often used, as well as old oak sherry barrels. Scotch matures during this aging, developing smoothness and improved character. While aging may also produce some color, caramel coloring may be added later. A blend labeled with the age of the scotch must indicate the age of the youngest scotch in the blend.

The exact formula used to produce a given scotch blend is kept secret. Every blending company has its own formula, which may include as many as 50 different scotches. This variety is necessary to produce consistent blends, as changing climatic conditions result in slightly different whiskies each year. If a certain malt is not available, a similar one can be substituted from a library stock so that the blender's distinctive flavor is maintained. Thus when a guest orders a particular brand of scotch, he or she always expects the same taste experience. For more information on the making of scotch whisky, visit the Internet sites listed at the end of this chapter—particularly the site of The Scotch Whisky Association.

Popular brands of single malt scotch include Glenfiddich, The Glenlivet, Laphroaig, and Macallan. Popular blends include Chivas Regal, Dewar's, J&B, and Johnnie Walker. Popular drinks made with scotch include: Rob Roy, Rusty Nail, Scotch and Soda, Scotch Sour. Other drinks made with scotch can be found by visiting many of the Internet sites listed at the end of this chapter.

Irish Whiskey

The Irish produce whiskey much the same as the Scots do. There are, however, some differences. The Irish use sprouted barley and other cereals to make wort, and the sprouts are dried in closed kilns, thus avoiding the smokey taste characteristic of scotch whisky. Also, **Irish whiskey** is pot-distilled three times, creating a final spirit that is light and delicate in character. Only the middle distillate is retained, producing a liquor that is very smooth and mellow. The mandatory aging time is three years, but the usual period is five to eight years in old sherry casks. Irish whiskeys are often blended to make them lighter. Blends are labeled "Irish Whiskey—a Blend" or "Blended Irish Whiskey." Popular brands include Bushmill's and Jameson. Popular drinks made with Irish Whiskey are: Irish Coffee, Tipperary, and Nutty Irishman (made with Bailey's Irish Cream which is a combination of Irish whiskey, cream, and chocolate). More recipes for drinks made with Irish Whiskey can be found by visiting many of the Internet sites listed at the end of this chapter.

American Whiskeys

The United States produces three different kinds of whiskey in addition to whiskey blends: bourbon, rye, and corn whiskey. Bourbon is by far the most extensively produced.

Bourbon and Tennessee Whiskey. Bourbon is named for Bourbon County, Kentucky, where it originated. Tennessee Whiskey is a unique type of bourbon invented by the Jack Daniels' distillery. To carry the name "Tennessee Whiskey" the product must be distilled in Tennessee.

Tennessee "bourbon" is often called sour mash whiskey instead of bourbon. **Tennessee whiskey** is filtered through maple charcoal after distillation, which gives a delicate smoothness and flavor. Sour mash is a spirit made from a regular sweet mash brew mixed with some soured old mash brew in a ratio of about two regular to one sour. Federal regulations require that a whiskey labeled "sour mash" have at least one part sour to three parts regular mash. The sour mash gives a heavier body and finer flavor to the bourbon, lending it a bit of sweetness and delicacy. Most bourbons are sour mash, although their labels may not indicate it.

Federal regulations require that **bourbon** be made from a mash containing at least 51 percent corn grain, mixed with other fermentable products such as rice, rye, or wheat. The usual ratio is 60 percent corn, 28 percent rye, and 12 percent barley malt. The grains are ground, cooked into a mash, and fermented. Bourbon is distilled by the continuous method. Most bourbon distillates come off at 110 to 130 proof. Some of the Internet sites listed at the end of this chapter provide online tours of distilleries and provide greater detail on the production of American whiskeys.

Bourbon must be aged at a proof of at least 125 for at least two years in charred oak barrels. Most bourbons are aged four to six years. The barrels help create some of bourbon's distinctive character. Charring produces a reddened, resinous surface on the wood which provides special flavor constituents.

Bourbon has a rich body and the full, distinctive flavor of corn. Most of its color develops during aging, although color may be added. Bourbon is bottled as bottled-in-bond straight, a blend of straights, or a blend of straight bourbon and grain neutral spirits. "Straight" indicates an unblended whiskey of one distillation. Blends must be 20 percent or more straight whiskey. Bottled bourbon has an alcohol content of between 80 to 110 proof.

Popular brands include: Early Times, Jack Daniels, Jim Beam, Old Crow, and Wild Turkey. Drinks made with bourbon are Bourbon Soda, Bourbon Sour, Old Fashioned, Manhattan, Mint Julep, Whiskey Collins, and Whiskey Sour.

Rye. Rye whiskey must be made from 51 percent or more rye grain. Like other American whiskeys, it must not come off distillation at more than 160 proof. Rye whiskey is produced by continuous distillation. It is usually bottled and sold at 80 to 110 proof, although some ryes are higher in alcohol content. Rye must be aged at least two years in new charred oak casks. Pennsylvania and Maryland produce the most rye whiskey.

Corn Whiskey. A whiskey bearing the name "corn" must be made from a mash containing at least 80 percent corn. It is distilled by the continuous method. It need not be aged in charred oak casks and therefore may lack color. Corn whiskey must go into the aging cask (oak) at 125 proof or higher. Its flavor is definitely that of corn, and the body is light.

Canadian Whisky

Canadian whisky is lighter in body and more delicate in flavor than American bourbon. Corn is the primary grain, usually mixed with additional fermentable products such as rye and barley malt. The Canadian government allows distillates to come off 150 to 185 proof, resulting in a spirit light in flavor and body. Canadian whisky is aged primarily in old oak barrels, which help to produce a delicately flavored product. The normal aging time is six years. Canadian whiskies are blends of whisky and grain neutral spirits, modifying the flavor toward the lighter end. They are labeled "Blended Canadian Whisky" or "Canadian Whisky—A Blend." Popular brands include: Canadian Club, Crown Royal, and Seagram's VO. Drinks made with Canadian whisky are Canadian Tea, Canadian Coffee, Crown Safari, and Royal Manhattan. More drinks made with Canadian whisky can be found by visiting some of the Internet sites listed at the end of this chapter.

Vodka

Vodka is a neutral spirit that is distilled or treated after distillation (with charcoal and other materials) so as to be without distinctive character, aroma, taste, or color. Because it lacks flavor and has a soft, mellow character, it mixes better than any other alcohol product. The quality of a vodka depends upon the quality of the grain neutral spirit used to make it. Vodka is distilled at 190 proof. Water is then added and the spirit is bottled at between 80 and 110 proof. Vodka need not be made from grain spirits but almost always is. Some vodka is centrifuged or distilled by a special process to remove congeners; congeners may also be removed by filtering the vodka through a bed of fine sand or other material. However, most vodka is treated by charcoal filtering or by steeping it in charcoal.

Flavorings play an important role in the popularity of vodka. Absolut, a Swedish brand of vodka, produces vodka in several flavors such as citrus (Absolut Citron), jalapeno (Absolut Peppar), and black currant berries (Absolut Kurrant). Many new drinks call for these specific flavorings of vodka. Several sweetened vodkas are on the market, often flavored with orange, lemon, mint, grape, or other ingredients. These products are usually bottled at 70 proof.

Popular brands of vodka include: Absolut, Finlandia, Skyy, Smirnoff, Stolichnaya, and Tanqueray Sterling. Popular drinks made with vodka are: Black Russian, Bloody Mary, Cape Codder, Greyhound, Martini, Salty Dog, Screwdriver, Sea Breeze, and Vodka and Tonic.

Gin

Gin is a compounded spirit. There are basically two kinds of gin: "dry" and "heavy." Dry gin is light in flavor and body; the term "dry" indicates a light, somewhat delicate spirit that mixes well with other substances. Dry gins are often labeled "dry," "extra dry," or "very dry," although there is no real variation among dry gins. Heavy gins are high in flavor and body and carry with them a slight suggestion of malt. They do not make good mixers and are often consumed "neat" over ice.

The Dutch invented gin, but its name derived from the French word *genievre*, meaning "juniper." Dutch (also called Holland or Netherland) gins are heavy and are usually divided into three types—all are heavy: Holland, Geneva (Jenever), and Schiendam. However, the differences between the three are small. Dutch gin is sometimes called schnapps.

Dutch gin is made from a mash containing several grains, usually barley malt, rye, and corn. The resulting brew is distilled into a low-proof substance called malt wine, heavy in body and rich in flavor. The malt wine is pot-distilled at low temperatures so that the resulting distillate of 100 to 110 proof retains its rich flavor and heavy body. During the last distillation, the alcohol vapors pass through juniper berries in a gin head, picking up a heavy juniper flavor. Some distillers may also use other flavoring ingredients (called botanicals) such as coriander, orange peel, lemon peel, anise, cassia, almonds, caraway, cocoa, angelica root, and others. Dutch gins have fewer of these flavorings than gins made in other countries.

English gins are dry. They are produced from grain neutral spirits distilled at 180 to 190 proof. English gins are flavored either by adding juniper berries and other botanicals to the liquor before distillation, or by means of the gin head. English gins vary depending upon the botanicals used.

Some American gins are made by steeping the flavoring ingredients with the final distillate. Some American gins are produced like English gins. Only gins flavored during distillation may be labeled as "distilled gin." American gins have less character than English or Dutch gins because they are produced from a high-proof grain neutral spirit that lacks flavor congeners.

Few gins are aged; if they are, they usually take on a golden color and may be sold as "golden gin." No claim of age can be made for a gin in the United States. American gins must be bottled at no less than 80 proof.

There are several sweet, flavored gins, including mint, orange, lime, or lemon gin. Old Tom is a sweet English gin. Sloe gin is not a gin; it is actually a liqueur flavored with sloe berries, and is usually a heavy pink to reddish color.

Popular brands of gin include: Beefeater, Bombay, Bombay Sapphire, Gilbey's, Gordon's, Schenley, Seagram's Extra Dry Gin, Tanqueray, and Tanqueray 10. Popular drinks made with gin are Gibson, Gimlet, Gin Fizz, Gin and Tonic, Martini, Singapore Sling, and Tom Collins.

Rum

When sugar cane is harvested and converted to sugar, a by-product of the process is molasses. The fermentation and distillation of molasses produces **rum**. The fermented molasses or sugar-cane brew is distilled to 190 proof (160 proof for New England rum). The distillate is aged in uncharred oak casks and thus has little color. Color is added to some products. Most rums are blends, ranging in body and flavor from heavy and pungent to slight and brandy-like, and in color from light to dark. Blending produces a rum distinctive in aroma, taste, body, and color. Rum is usually bottled at 80, 86, or 151 proof. Labels must indicate a rum's area of origin.

There are two basic kinds of rums, light-bodied and heavy-bodied, although there are many variations among them. Light rum (also known as silver or dry rum) is most popular in the United States. Light rum is usually produced by the continuous distillation method and comes off as a high-proof distillate. This method eliminates a number of flavorful congeners but gives a smoother product with only a slight rum flavor. Light rums usually bear a white or silver label. They are mild and slightly sweet in flavor. Most light rums are aged for one year. Most light rums come from Puerto Rico. Cuba, the Dominican Republic, Haiti, Venezuela, Mexico, Hawaii, and the Philippines also produce light rum.

Heavy-bodied, more pungent rums are produced in Jamaica, New England, and Guyana (Demerara, Trinidad, and Barbados). These rums have a heavy bouquet resulting from their basic ingredient, the rich skimmings from sugar boilers. Natural yeast ferments the brew; the result is what is called a product of "spontaneous fermentation," a rather violent and fast process producing many congeners which give a very richly flavored rum. The sediment from a previous brew is often added to help start fermentation, much like the sour-mash process. Much of this rum is often sent to England and other countries for aging and consumption. The label and product are nearly as dark as molasses.

Popular brands of rum include: Barcardi, Captain Morgan, Castillo, Myers, and Mt. Gay. Popular drinks made with run are Bahama Mama, Cuba Libre, Electric Lemonade, Hurricane, Long Beach Tea, Long Island Iced Tea, Mai Tai, Pina Colada, and Strawberry Daiquiri.

Tequila

Only Mexico produces **tequila,** a distinctive liquor distilled from the fermented juice of the blue variety of the agave plant *(tequilon weber cactus).* According to Mexican government regulations, the product may be called tequila only if it is produced in a designated region surrounding the town of Tequila in Jalisco, Mexico. The Mexican government regulates the making of tequila. A tequila label bears the letters DGN if the product conforms to these regulations.

The heart of the agave plant (the *piña*), which may weigh between 50 and 200 pounds, contains a sweet juice called *aguamiel* (honey water). This sap is removed, often fortified with sugar, and then fermented. It is distilled twice, coming off at 104 to 106 proof with many flavoring agents. The distillate is then filtered through charcoal.

When tequila is aged, it develops a gold color. White tequila is a new product shipped without aging; silver tequila is aged up to three years; gold tequila is aged in oak casks for two to four years and may carry the name *muy añejo* (very old). Some tequilas may be artificially colored, so buyers must know what they are buying. Some tequilas are aged quite long and are expensive. More detail on the production of tequila is available from Internet sites listed at the end of this chapter.

Popular brands of tequila include: Don Julio, Herradura, Jose Cuervo, Patron, and Sauza. Popular drinks made with tequila are Brave Bull, Mexican Coffee, Margarita, Tequila Sunrise, and Tequila Sunset.

Brandy

Brandy is the primary liquor made from fruit. The word brandy (short for brandy-wine) comes from the Dutch word *brandewijn* meaning "burnt wine," referring to the fact that the wine was distilled with heat. Any distilled spirit made from fruit or fruit derivatives qualifies as a brandy. However, only a spirit distilled from grapes can be called just "brandy"—if distilled from other fruit, the type of fruit must precede the word "brandy": thus "pear brandy." Cognac and Armagnac are famous brandies from France.

The character of a brandy is influenced by the kind of grapes it is made from, the climate and soil they are cultivated in, cultivation and harvesting methods, fermentation and distillation processes, aging, and blending. Each factor is important and all have an effect on the type and quality of a brandy.

The variety of grape used to make brandy must be low in sugar and rather acidic. It should also produce a fruity wine. The low sugar content means that a lot of wine must be distilled to produce the distillate, increasing the congeners which come over with the alcohol. After careful selection, the grapes are brought to the press where the must (juice) is extracted, then fermented.

Distillation

Brandies are usually marketed at 80 to 84 proof. They can be distilled up to 190 proof. Most American brandy is the result of continuous distillation, but most imports are distilled by the pot method. Brandy must be distilled at fairly low temperatures to produce a low-proof distillate with many congeners. The French regulate the maximum proof of distillates to be used for brandy. The final distillate for cognac cannot be over 144 proof. Pot-distillation is preferred, although some brandies are made by a semi-continuous or continuous method.

Brandy may receive only one distillation, but it is often distilled twice to improve quality. The first distillation is a low proof and thus high in congeners. Only the middle part of the distillate is retained. The first and last parts may be used for other purposes or may be returned to a brew to be redistilled.

Aging

Brandy is aged in special oak casks, from which it extracts flavor. The wood also absorbs some undesirable components from the brandy. In addition, the cask allows a bit of air to seep through, causing a very slow oxidation. Thus the wood is an important factor in a favorable aging process. Aging brandy is stored in special warehouses, where it loses about $2^1/2$ percent of its volume each year. This loss, called the angel's share, can be sizable—up to a fourth of the original distillate in a long aging period.

Aging smooths the flavor out so that it leaves a lingering aftertaste. A rich, aromatic bouquet evolves, which may be slightly musky. Fruitiness ranges from delicate to heavy. Aging also adds a touch of bitterness to some brandies. Brandy turns a beautiful amber-gold during aging; additional coloring is sometimes added later.

Blending

At the end of the aging period, the cellar-master judges the bouquet, quality, character, body, and mellowness of the brandy. This is a complex process from which he or she decides which other brandies are needed to blend with it to produce the desired product. Many master blenders are continuing a family tradition, relying on knowledge handed down from generation to generation. Blending is a venerated occupation requiring tremendous knowledge and skill. Blending is done not only to adjust taste, bouquet, and other qualities, but also to secure a brand's consistency. Brandies of different ages are often blended. Some premium brandies may contain a brandy as young as five years old, as well as a brandy aged for more than twenty years. The younger brandy may be added to give freshness or some other quality needed in the older ones. After blending, the brandy is allowed to rest so the flavors can marry, which may take as long as six months. It is then bottled, after which it does not age.

Labeling

Some brandy producers use special words or letters on labels to indicate quality and other product characteristics. In general, "E" means especial, "F" means fine, "V" means very, "O" means old, "S" means superior, "P" means pale, "X" means extra, and "C" means cognac. However, such designations are not used uniformly, so you need to learn the particular code of a producer or district to understand their labels. For example, at one time the number of stars indicated quality; some very poor brandies today carry three or four stars. Armagnacs and cognacs are generally labeled as shown in Exhibit 4. Popular brands of Cognac include: Courvoisier, Hennessey, Martell, and Remy Martin. Popular brands of Armagnac include: DeMontal, Janneau, Larressingle, and Sempe.

Liqueurs, Aperitifs, and Bitters

Liqueurs, also known as cordials, are compounded spirits flavored in various ways. Liqueurs contain at least $2^1/_2$ percent sugar usually added as syrup; most contain more syrup. The sugar content of a $2^1/_2$ percent sugar liqueur is equivalent to about a half-teaspoon of sugar (eight calories) per two-ounce drink. Liqueurs are flavored with many different substances, including herbs, spices, fruits, mint, coffee, and licorice. The processing method, the quality of the flavorings, and the basic ingredients influence the final quality of each liqueur. Most liqueurs are made from grain-neutral spirits, but there are exceptions—bourbon is used for Southern Comfort, Scotch whisky for Drambuie, Irish whiskey for Irish Mist, and rum for Tia Maria. All liqueurs are usually aged so that the flavor, spirit, and flavorings can marry. Liqueurs are often used as after-dinner drinks. Some (such as Triple Sec) are used as flavoring ingredients for mixed drinks. Exhibit 5 lists many types of liqueurs. Note the variety of locales from which these products originate. Liqueurs listed without a country designation are generally produced by several countries and by multiple commercial distillers. The more popular liqueurs include: Amaretto, Baileys, Chambord, Cassis, Grand Marnier, Kahlua, Malibu, Peach Schnapps, Sloe Gin, Southern Comfort, and Triple Sec. These more popular liqueurs are sorted by flavor in Exhibit 6.

Aperitifs are spirits consumed primarily as appetizers. They may also be mixed with other alcohol products. Many aperitifs, also called "digestives," are

Exhibit 4   Labeling of Armagnac and Cognac

Armagnac:	
VO, VSOP, or Reserve	The youngest brandy in the blend is no less than $4^{1/2}$ years old.
XO, Reserve, Vielle Reserve, Extra, or Napoleon	The youngest brandy in the blend is no less than $5^{1/2}$ years old.
Vintage	Indicates the year distilled (not the year the grapes were grown). The product is not blended with brandies distilled in other years.
Cognac:	
VS or three stars	Average aging period of the brandies in the blend is less than $4^{1/2}$ years.
VSOP, VO, or Reserve	Average age of the blend ingredients is 12 to 20 years; the youngest brandy used is no less than $4^{1/2}$ years old.
Napoleon, VVSOP, XO, Cordon Bleu, Vielle Reserve, Royal, Vieux, or Grand Reserve	Most of the blend is aged 20 to 40 or more years and the youngest is at least $5^{1/2}$ years old.
Grande Fine Champagne or Grande Champagne	Made only from grapes grown in the Grande Champagne area.
Petite Champagne or Petite Fine Champagne	At least 50% of the grapes came from the Grande Champagne area with the remainder grown in the Petite Champagne area.
Vintage	None permitted.

flavored with ingredients that give them a bitter taste. Campari, an Italian liquor, is a well-known aperitif with a very sweet, bitter flavor. It is a rich red and lends a pleasing color to mixed drinks. Amer picon, a brandy, is a similar product produced in the Balkans; it is flavored with quinine, the same substance that gives tonic water its bitter flavor. When quinine was discovered to be a preventive against the malaria virus, it became a popular addition to many mixers, offering the incentive of enjoying a drink while taking your medicine. Amer picon also contains orange and is quite sweet. Fernet branca is another sweet, bitter spirit. It has a reputation of being a good remedy for hangovers. Some aperitifs, including vermouth, are fortified wines; dry vermouth is used in martinis and sweet vermouth in Manhattans. Vermouth is also consumed straight. The fortified wines of Dubonnet and Lillet are both used as mixers and served straight.

Bitters are used only as flavoring ingredients; in many recipes, a dash or two produces just the right flavor. Bitters are usually made from roots, spices, bark, berries, fruit, or herbs steeped in or distilled with a neutral spirit. Bitters have a highly flavorful, aromatic, bitter taste. Some of the better known brands include Angostura, made in Trinidad from a very old secret formula; Abbot's Aged Bitters, made by the same family for years in Baltimore; Peychaud's Bitters, made in New Orleans; and Orange Bitters, made in England from the dried peel of bitter Seville oranges.

Exhibit 5   Types of Liqueurs

Amaretto—(Italy) Made from neutral alcohol, herbs, and apricot pulp kernels. Because the apricot is a relative of the almond, the seed imparts a distinctive almond taste.

Anisette—(Italy) Made from Anise, a dried, ripe fruit that has a definite licorice-like taste.

B&B—(France) Blended liqueur with half Benedictine and half brandy.

Campari—(France) Made from neutral spirits with added herbs, roots, and other aromatic ingredients.

Chartreuse—(France) Subtle blend of 130 different herbs; varieties include yellow and green.

Cassis—(France) Made from black currant berries grown near the Burgundy wine region of France.

Chambord—(France) Delicate and aromatic liqueur made from black raspberries; sweeter than Cassis.

Curacao—(Curacao) Made from the skins of small oranges; comes in red, blue, orange, or triple sec; colors are acquired with food coloring.

Cointreau—(Spain; West Indies) Brand name for one of the finest triple secs, an orange-flavored liqueur.

Crème de Banana—Bright yellow liqueur made by macerating ripe bananas in a pure spirit.

Crème de Cacao (White)—Colorless liqueur with the taste of chocolate; primary flavoring ingredient is the cocoa bean.

Crème de Cacao (Dark)—Dark liqueur that gets its color from percolation through cocoa beans.

Crème de Menthe (White)—Sweet liqueur derived from several varieties of mint, principally peppermint.

Crème de Menthe (Green)—Sweet mint-flavored liqueur made with green coloring.

Crème de Noyaux—Light liqueur that derives its flavor from fruit stones, resulting in an almond flavor.

Drambuie—(Scotland) Scotch-based liqueur with a variety of herbal ingredients; taste is tangy, heathery, and smooth.

Frangelico—(Italy) Hazelnut-based liqueur.

Galliano—(Italy) Honey-sweet liqueur that is bright yellow and packaged in a tall, tapered bottle; named after a military hero.

Grand Marnier—(France) Orange-flavored liqueur with Cognac as its base; blends bitter Haitian oranges with fine French Cognac.

Irish Mist—(Ireland) Blend of honey, herbal ingredients, and Irish whiskey.

Jagermeister—(Germany) Said to originally contain opium, this unusual tasting liqueur derives its flavor from herbs and roots.

Kahlua—(Mexico) Distinctly heavy and sweet; derived from Mexican coffee beans.

Licor 43—(Spain) Made in Spain from 43 different fruits; has a distinctive vanilla taste.

(continued)

Exhibit 5 *(continued)*

Malibu—(Canada) Rum-based spirit with coconut as its flavoring base.

Midori—(Japan) Bright-green melon liqueur with honeydew melons providing the primary flavor.

Peach Schnapps—Peach-flavored liqueur with peach kernel extracts added for a fuller flavor.

Peppermint Schnapps—Clear, pleasant liqueur with the light taste of candy canes; usually less sweet than crème de menthe.

Pernod—(France) Anise-flavored (licorice) liqueur that contains herbs, anise, parsley, coriander, and chamomile.

Sambuca—(Italy) Licorice-flavored liqueur deriving its taste from the fruit of the elder bush; a cousin to anisette.

Sloe Gin—Sweet-flavored and tinted with sloe berries, the fruits of the blackthorn tree; sugar is also added.

Southern Comfort—(America) Peach liqueur with Bourbon added; aged in oak barrels.

Strega—(Italy) Italina coffee liqueur with more than 70 herbs.

Tia Maria—(Jamica) Rum-based beverage flavored with Jamaican Blue Mountain coffee extracts; also has a delicate hint of chocolate flavor; somewhat like Kahlua, but drier and lighter.

Triple Sec—(Curacao) White, dry, orange-flavored liqueur with a distinctive three-stage production process; "Sec" means "dry" in French.

Tuaca—(Italy) Vanilla- and butterscotch-flavored liqueur.

Yukon Jack—(Canada) Close imitator of Southern Comfort; strong, sweetened whiskey with herbs added for flavoring.

Mixology Basics

Mixology is the skill of mixing drinks. One of the greatest challenges facing bartenders is that not all establishments prepare the same drink in exactly the same way. Even the name of certain mixed drinks may vary by regions within a country. There are many variations in recipes, depending upon the operation, the bartender, and the guest. Two different guests may order the same drink and expect different results.

Many books have been published that offer standard recipes for mixed drinks. One of the oldest examples is *Mr. Boston Official Bartenders Guide.* Published by Mr. Boston Distiller Corporation in 1935, the book was an attempt by a major supplier of spirits to standardize the preparation of mixed drinks. The book underwent several editions and can still be found today. Numerous other books have also published standard drink recipes, but variations continue to exist. Why? Probably due to the desire of beverage establishments to differentiate themselves from one another, the creativity of bartenders, and the varying expectations among guests.

Exhibit 6   Popular Liqueurs Sorted by Flavor

Orange
> Curacao, Cointreau, Grand Marnier, Triple Sec

Peach
> Peach Schnapps, Southern Comfort

Chocolate/Cocoa Beans
> Baileys, Crème de Cacao (white), Crème de Cacao (dark)

Coffee
> Kahlua, Strega, Tia Maria

Mint/Peppermint
> Crème de Menthe (white), Crème de Menthe (green), Peppermint Schnapps

Almond
> Amaretto (also apricot), Crème de Noyaux

Licorice
> Anisette, Sambuca, Pernod

Berries
> Cassis, Chambord

Honey
> Galliano, Irish Mist

To ensure consistent service, many large resorts and other hospitality operations develop standard recipes and garnishes for many of the more popular cocktails. As bartenders comply with the standard recipes when preparing drinks, resort guests are assured that the same drink they order at pool, or at the lounge, or at a banquet function will look and taste the same. Similarly, compliance with standard drink recipes developed by a restaurant or hotel chain assures product consistency and meets the expectations of their frequent guests. These frequent guests expect a drink served in one location to be identical to the same drink served at another location. At times, guests may expect or request variations on the standard recipes. This is especially true for international guests and guests from other regions of the country. As you interact with other bartenders and gain experience, you will learn the more commonly requested variations.

Bartenders are responsible for memorizing an establishment's standard recipes for popular drinks. They do not refer to recipe lists during their shifts; they are expected to know the recipes from memory and make them quickly and efficiently. A standard recipe often includes more than just the ingredients. Recipe compliance includes:

- Selecting the right glassware for the type of drink
- Using the right ingredients in the correct amounts
- Making the drink according to the correct method

- Garnishing according to the standard recipe
- Presenting the drink to the guest in a clean glass with a cocktail napkin

Exhibit 7 shows the basic glassware used for most of the more popular mixed drinks. The actual size of glasses used varies from establishment to establishment, depending on guest preferences, standard pour sizes, and the prices charged. The popularity of specific mixed drinks varies from region to region and by the guest preferences of specific markets. Exhibit 7 also lists twenty of the most requested mixed drinks at many southern resort operations. You should know the recipes for these twenty drinks from memory and be able to make the drinks quickly and efficiently. The appendix to this chapter lists sample recipes for these popular drinks and many others as well. Note, these recipes are only samples. As pointed out previously, variations exist among beverage establishments, especially across regions and countries—not only in relation to the names of drinks and their ingredients, but also in relation to the standard pour sizes used. Hundreds more drink recipes can be found by visiting many of the Internet sites listed at the end of this chapter.

The recipes also include instructions on making the drinks correctly. Exhibit 8 defines key terms used in drink preparation. The most basic method for making drinks is the **build method**, which adds ingredients one at a time and in the order and amounts listed on the standard recipe. This method requires that the drink be made and served in the same glass and is used for making many kinds of drinks, especially highballs (the combination of one spirit and one mixer). The order of the build method is ice, spirit, mixer, garnish. While these drinks are not mixed or stirred, they are often served with a swizzle stick, enabling guests to stir them if they wish.

The **stir method** is used for making drinks that are served without ice ("up" or "neat"). Ingredients are mixed and stirred with ice in a mixing glass. The drink is then typically strained into a chilled glass and served. Martinis and gimlets served "up" are made with the stir method. Care must be taken not to overstir the ingredients or the ice in the mixing glass will melt some and dilute the drink. Pitchers of cocktails need at least ten seconds of stirring to mix properly.

The **shake method** is used for making drinks that have ingredients requiring more vigorous mixing than using the stir method. For example, ingredients such as sugar, cream, egg, and some fruit juices do not mix readily with spirits. The drink can be shaken by hand in a shaker or in a shake mixer. After shaking, the drink is strained and poured into the appropriate serving glass and garnished (if required). The **blend method** uses an electric blender to mix drinks which call for solid fruit or ice. Strawberry Daiquiris and frozen Margaritas are examples of blended drinks.

All drinks should be poured for serving as soon as they are made. Standards for garnishing drinks may vary from one beverage operation to another. Exhibit 9 presents sample garnish standards, including preparation instructions and the drinks they go with.

Mixology tools and their frequency of use are described in Exhibit 10. Professional bartenders often purchase some of these tools so that they have them at all times. Most beverage establishments are already supplied with these tools.

Exhibit 7   Basic Glassware and Popular Drinks

Rocks or Martini Glass
Generally used to serve a chilled drink, such as a Screwdriver or a Black Russian.

Collins Glass
Used for drinks served tall and for serving soda and water.

Snifter
Most commonly used to serve brandy, such as Cognac or Armagnac.

Sherry Glass
Used to serve fortified wines, such as Port and sherry.

Name of Cocktail:	**Margarita**
Glassware:	Collins
Ingredients	Ounces
Tequila	$1^{1}/4$
Triple Sec	$^{3}/4$
Sour Mix	3
Lime Juice	$^{1}/2$
Instructions:	*Rim glass with salt. Build in shaker, shake, and pour over ice in glass.*

Name of Cocktail:	**Pina Colada**
Glassware:	Collins
Ingredients	Ounces
Rum	1¼
Pina Colada Mix	4
Instructions:	*Build in glass over ice and shake.*
Garnish:	*Flag*

Daiquiri	Sex on the Beach
Rum Runner	Cosmopolitan
Mai Tai	Manhattan
Martini	Blue Hawaiian
Screwdriver	Bahama Mama
Cuba Libre	Mud Slide
Sea Breeze	Bloody Mary
White Russian	Fuzzy Navel
Long Island Iced Tea	Madras

Exhibit 8   Drink Preparation Terms

blend—To use a machine to mix contents of a drink.

chill—Process of making a drink colder by shaking it with ice, then straining it into a glass without this ice; commonly called "shake and strain."

double—Three-quarter ounces of alcohol added to a 1¼ ounce pour.

dry—Describes a cocktail made with dry vermouth (the drier the drink, the less vermouth used).

fill—To pour liquid to an appropriate drinking level in a glass.

float—To finish off by filling a drink with no more than ¼ ounce of the particular ingredient.

frappe—Describes a drink that is chilled, iced, and poured over crushed ice.

layer—To pour liquor of different densities so they do not mix.

mist—To pour liquor over crushed ice, making a snow cone effect.

mix—To join liquid together in a drink.

muddle—To mash up or pulverize a material, usually fruit.

neat—Liquor poured right out of the bottle; not chilled, iced, or mixed with other liquids.

perfect—Describes a cocktail made with equal parts of sweet and dry vermouth.

splash—A small amount added to a drink (usually water or soda).

tall—Describes a chilled drink that is strained into glassware without ice.

top—To pour liquor on top of a drink.

up—Describes a chilled drink that is strained into glassware without ice.

Judging the Quality of Spirits

Every type of spirit has its own distinguishing characteristics, and within types there are differences that clearly separate products. For example, some rums are light and delicate while others are heavy and robust. These differences are the reasons for consumer preferences. Some people like the smoky flavor of scotch; others prefer vodka. Scotch drinkers may have a preference for one brand over another. Even vodka drinkers can be staunch advocates of one brand, although vodka is supposed to be colorless, odorless, and tasteless.

Evaluating spirit quality is not easy. Spirits are perhaps the most difficult to judge of all alcoholic beverages. A good judge must be able not only to identify the elusive factors that make up quality, but to remember these factors and compare them to a standard.

A glass used to judge spirits should be straight or have slightly outwardly-sloping sides. Only a finger's depth of room-temperature spirit is poured into it.

Exhibit 9   Sample Garnish Standards

Garnish	Handling Instructions	Drinks
Lime Wedge	Squeeze 1/8 of a lime over drink and then drop it in.	Tonic Drinks, Bloody Bull, Cuba Libre, Perrier Water, Bloody Mary
Lime or Lemon Wedge	Place 1/8" slice on rim of glass.	Gimlet, Margaritas, Lime Daiquiri, Bacardi Cocktail, Wine Spritzer, Long Island Iced Tea
Stemmed Cherry	Spear two stemmed cherries with a pick and drop into drink.	Manhattan, Rob Roy
Orange Cherry Flag	Using a pick, spear through one side of an orange wedge. Continue by spearing a stemmed cherry. Finally, spear through the other side of the orange wedge. (A pointed stir stick may be used in place of the pick.)	Collins drink, Sours, Old Fashioned, Side Car, Singapore Sling, Zombie
Pineapple Flag	Spear stemmed cherry first, then place pick through the pineapple rind at an angle.	Piña Colada, Mai Tai, Chi Chi, Planters Punch
Olives	Spear two Large Pimento olives and drop into drink.	Martini
Lemon Peel	Twist peel (rind side down) over drink to allow oil from peel to float on top of drink. Rub lip of glass with outside of peel. Drop into drink.	Martini (on request), Dry and Perfect Manhattan, Perfect Rob Roy, Mists (on request), Kir, Champagne Cocktail
Cocktail Onions	Spear three small onions with a pick.	Gibson

The first thing to do is examine the appearance of the spirit. Watch it as it is poured and note the color. Some spirits carrying a brown or caramel color may be as pale as citron, others will be mellow amber, and others may be brownish with a flash of burnished brass. Vodka must be colorless; gin and tequila should also be colorless unless they are aged. Rums vary in color from clear, light tan, and delicate amber, to an almost blackish brown. Chartreuse, a liqueur, may be green or

Exhibit 10   Mixology Tools

Ice Scoop (high frequency of use)
It's important to use a clean, sanitized ice scoop for moving ice from the well to the glass. Never use your hands or a glass for moving ice to another container. The ice scoop should be kept close at hand at the bar.

Mixing Glass/Shaker Tin (high frequency of use)
The mixing glass is used with the shaker tin to shake the components of a drink. The shaker tin fits over the shaker glass. The combination of the two is referred to as a Boston Shaker. These tools are used frequently and should be kept nearby throughout the shift.

Jigger (frequency of use depends on the kind of bar operation)
The jigger is used for measuring liquor while pouring a drink.

Muddler (low frequency of use)
This is a tool used to mush or pulverize materials (such as fruits) when the drink calls for it or when the guest requests it. Few cocktails today call for using the muddler.

Bar Spoon (moderate frequency of use)
The bar spoon, or layer spoon, is used for stirring drinks. It is sometimes called a layer spoon because it can be used as an effective tool for layering a drink. This type of drink is made by layering liquors of varying densities on top of one another, with the heavier densities at the bottom. Many drinks are stirred, so the bar spoon should be kept at a convenient location.

Strainer (moderate frequency of use)
This is an effective tool for separating the contents of a beverage from the ice in which it was chilled. It goes over the top of the tin, and the strainer is then used to get contents into the glass while holding back the ice. Many drinks are chilled, so this is a tool that is kept in a convenient location.

Salt/Sugar Rimmer (moderate frequency of use)
The salt rimmer or sugar rimmer is used to salt or sugar the rim of the glass. The rimmer should only have a light layer of salt to prevent caking. What makes the salt or sugar stay on the glass? Lime juice. The salt/sugar rimmer is used for drinks such as a Salty Dog and a Margarita. Many cocktails call for salted or sugared rims. Most bartenders keep this tool close by during their shifts.

Blender (moderate frequency of use)
The blender is used to crush ice and blend a frozen drink, such as a strawberry daiquiri. Frozen drinks are fairly popular, so keep the blender is in a convenient location.

Exacto Pour (low frequency of use)
These precisely-measured test tubes allow you to accurately measure liquor pours. It helps a new bartender learn to make pours more exact. This is the tool that is used for testing bartenders who've been given the privilege of free pouring.

(continued)

Exhibit 10 *(continued)*

Garnish Tray (moderate frequency of use)
Time tending a bar is precious. A garnish tray saves the time of marching off to the refrigerator each time a lime wedge or an olive is needed. The garnish tray should be kept near the area at which drinks are made. The tray should be kept cool, covered, and nearby.

Pour Spout (high frequency of use)
The pour spout is a device that fits over bottles of liquor to help control the amount of liquor that comes out of the bottle. Every time you pour liquor, even when using a jigger, you are using a pour spout. This is possibly the most frequently used tool at the bar.

---

yellow. Crème de menthe, another liqueur, comes in white or green. The judge must know what the proper color should be. Part of evaluating appearance is noting clarity and brilliance—two important quality factors.

The next step is to judge body. Body indicators can be observed by rocking the spirit gently in the glass or giving it a gentle whirl and noting how it holds together as it moves. The appearance of rivulets (called "legs") along the sides of the glass also indicates body. Body is judged further when the spirit is in the mouth; the sensation is called "mouthfeel," and should be pleasant. There will be body differences between spirits. For example, a liquor with a high sugar content will have a heavy body while a light vodka will have little or no body, disappearing quickly in the mouth.

The "nose" (aroma or odor) of the beverage is one of the best indicators of spirit quality. Your hand should warm the spirit slightly so the aroma rises in the glass. The swirl should also release it. Put your nose into the glass and sniff, pulling the aroma up into the nostrils. You should detect mellowness, harshness, fruitiness, or other characteristics of the spirit. Is there a proper carryover of the basic ingredients from which the spirit is made? Some spirits made from malt may have a sweetish odor, while spirits made from other grains may have a "dry" aroma. Scotch should smell smoky, but the intensity of this peaty odor is an important factor. The judge matches the odors detected with what he or she knows the spirit should smell like. Odors should blend together smoothly, and the final sensation should be pleasant.

When tasting spirits, some judges like to add a bit of pure room-temperature water (ice lowers the taste sensations and should not be used). The characteristic flavor of the spirit should immediately appear and develop into both taste and odor. It should then fade and disappear. The proof of the spirit makes a difference; high-proof spirits have a bite. Various components should be evident. Is there a muskiness, a flavor of malt, corn, rye, or other ingredient, and is this what it should be?

A liqueur should possess the true flavor of its main flavoring ingredient. Some flavors linger for a time on the palate, while others disappear quickly—a good indicator of the quality of the product is whether what happens is typical of the flavor. The total flavor should be full-bodied, balanced, harmonious, and smooth.

In liqueurs especially, the flavor should be unified (that is, not give way or fall apart) and should continue or last.

Finally, one judges the aftertaste or what is often called the "finish." The aftertaste should echo the spirit's flavor and be harmonious. Everything should be in agreement.

While an expert judge may be able to taste as many as 400 spirits in a day, the average person should not try to taste more than 4 or 5. An expert judge never swallows the spirit. Pure, tasteless, room-temperature water is used often to cleanse the palate. It can be non-sparkling spring water. Some judges also eat a low-salt or no-salt cracker to remove former flavors. Others say they should not be used. Items that have a flavor carryover should not be used to cleanse the palate.

Key Terms

aperitifs—Spirits consumed primarily as appetizers; may be mixed with other alcohol products, and many are flavored with ingredients that give them a bitter taste.

bitters—A type of spirit usually made from roots, spices, bark, berries, fruit, or other herbs steeped in or distilled with a neutral spirit and used primarily as mixed drink ingredients; highly flavorful, aromatic, bitter taste.

blend method—A method for preparing drinks that uses an electric blender to mix drinks which call for solid fruit or ice.

bonded spirit—A spirit (not blended) which has been stored continuously for at least four years in wooden barrels in a warehouse under government supervision and which is bottled at 100 proof; it must all be the product of a single distillation, by the same distiller during a single season and year.

bourbon—An American whiskey produced from a grain mixture containing at least 51 percent corn. Different bourbons use different grain formulas.

brandy—Any distilled spirit made from fruit or fruit derivatives; however, only a spirit distilled from grapes can be called just "brandy"—if distilled from other fruit, the type of fruit must precede the work brandy on the label (as in "pear brandy").

build method—A method of making drinks in which ingredients are poured into the glass in which the drink will be served.

Canadian whisky—Distinctive whisky of Canada, characteristically light, mild, and delicate; most are blended whiskys distilled from mashes of corn, rye, and malted barley, usually aged in used or re-charred white-oak barrels.

condenser—In a distillation system, a container for cooling the alcohol vapor to a liquid state.

congeners—Substances other than alcohol and water (such as acids, glycerine, and others) which are found in new spirit distillates; they provide flavor and aroma and may be desirable or undesirable.

continuous still—A still that acts as a vaporizer and condenser; its condensing system consists of a number of condensing spaces placed at strategic points. Also called a Coffey still, column still, or patent still.

distillation—A process, which takes place in a still, that uses heat to extract the alcohol from a liquid that contains both alcohol and water; when an alcoholic liquid is heated, the alcohol turns into a vapor and rises, leaving the water behind. As these alcoholic vapors cool, they condense back into liquid form, becoming concentrated new distillates.

fermentation—A chemical process in which yeast is added to a sugar source; the yeast breaks down the sugar into alcohol, carbon dioxide, and heat.

gin—A compounded spirit (the basic product flavored by juniper berries) which is usually classified as "dry" or "heavy;" dry gins are light in flavor and body, while heavy gins are heavily flavored and full-bodied.

gin head—In distillation, a device through which vapors are passed to pick up flavor.

grain neutral spirits—A colorless, odorless, and tasteless distilled spirit made from a grain mash; it is produced by continuous distillation until it reaches 190 proof, removing a number of harsh congeners in the process.

Irish whiskey—Distinctive whiskey of Ireland made principally from barley, both malted and unmalted, together with oats, wheat, and sometimes a small proportion of rye.

liqueurs—Flavored, usually sweet alcoholic beverages with an alcohol content higher than fortified wine, but lower than most liquors.

mixology—The art or skill of mixing drinks.

pot still—A round, pot-shaped still with a tapering funnel at the top where rising vapors can be collected and then be carried off through a tube to a condenser.

proof—A method of expressing alcoholic strength or content; in the United States, proof is equal to twice the percentage of alcohol by volume.

rectification—A term that implies a further treatment beyond distillation such as blending, coloring, flavoring, or even redistilling. The U.S. government defines rectification as blending a spirit with anything other than water.

rum—A spirit distilled from the fermented juice of sugar cane or molasses.

scotch—A distinctive whisky from Scotland with at least 80 proof alcohol content, manufactured in compliance with British laws; it is sold and must be labeled as "blended" or "single malt."

shake method—A method of preparing drinks that uses cream, eggs, or fruit juices that cannot be mixed with a spirit to the desired texture by stirring; electric shakers or blenders are more commonly used than hand shakers.

still—The apparatus in which distillation takes place. There are two basic types of stills: (1) the old-fashioned pot still, which generally yields not more than 140 proof alcohol; and (2) the continuous still, which can be used almost continuously day and night and which can easily produce 190 proof alcohol in large volumes.

stir method—A method of making drinks that contain liquors and other ingredients that require stirring with a bar spoon for proper mixture.

Tennessee whiskey—Often called sour mash whiskey instead of bourbon; sour mash is a spirit made from a regular sweet mash brew mixed with some soured old mash brew in a ratio of about two regular to one sour. Federal regulations require that a whiskey labeled "sour mash" have at least one part sour to three parts regular mash.

tequila—A distinctive Mexican spirit distilled from the fermented juice of the blue variety of the agave plant; its fermentation and distillation process is strictly controlled by the Mexican government.

vodka—A clear, colorless, flavorless spirit made by passing highly refined neutral spirits through charcoal, by re-distillation, or by other government-approved processes.

wort—The liquid rich in malt and sugars resulting from the mashing stage of the brewing process.

 # Review Questions

1. How is distillation different from fermentation?

2. How is Scotch whisky different from Irish whiskey?

3. What are popular brands of vodka and popular drinks made with vodka?

4. What are popular brands of gin and popular drinks made with gin?

5. What popular drinks are made with rum?

6. What makes tequila a special kind of spirit?

7. How does the production of brandy differ from the production of whiskey?

8. What are popular brands of liqueurs?

9. Why do drink recipes vary from region to region and even within regions?

10. Why are spirits the most difficult to judge of all alcoholic beverages?

 # Internet Sites

For more information, visit the following Internet sites. Remember that Internet addresses can change without notice. If the site is no longer there, you can use a search engine to look for additional sites. Many alcohol-related sites require users to be of legal drinking age to enter.

General Sites

Adams Beverage Group—industry links
www.beveragenet.net/links/links.asp

Ardent Spirits
www.ardentspirits.com

Bartending Magazine
www.bartender.com

Distilled Spirits Council of the United States
www.discus.org/links/

Pernod Ricard
www.seagram.com

Nightclub & Bar Magazine
www.nightclub.com

Wine and Spirits Wholesalers of America, Inc.
www.wswa.org/public/

The Webtender: An On-Line Bartender
www.webtender.com/browse.html

Scotch

The Scotch Whiskey Association
www.scotch-whisky.org.uk/

Chivas Brothers Limited
www.chivas.com

Dewar's Finest Scotch Whiskeys
www.dewars.com/home/

Glenmorangie plc
www.glenmorangieplc.com

Morison Bowmore Distillers
www.morrisonbowmore.co.uk/

Balantine's Scotch Whiskey
www2.ballantines.com

Whiskey

History of Whiskey
www.history-of-whisky.com/

Jack Daniels Tennessee Whiskey Virtual Tour
www.jackdaniels.com/virtual tour.asp#

James B. Beam Distilling Company—video library on distillation
www.jimbeam.com/jb_web/v5/products/white_label.aspx#

Labrot & Graham Distillery
http://www.woodfordreserve.com/distillery.asp

Malt Advocate Magazing
www.whiskeypages.com

Old Bushmill's Distillery—Three Dimensional VirtualTour
www.bushmills.com

Maker's Mark Distillery, Kentucky Straight Handmade Bourbon Whiskey, Virtual Tour
www.makersmark.com/Flash/Default.asp

Austin, Nichols Distillery Company, Wild Turkey Bourbon, Virtual Tour
www.wildturkeybourbon.com/home.asp

Canadian Mist
www.canadianmist.com

Other Spirits

Beefeaters Gin
www.beefeater.com/LondonDistilled.htm

iVodka.com
www.ivodka.com/index.html

Absolut Vodka, Seagram Associates
www.absolut.com/

Jose Cuervo, Tequilla
www.cuervo.com/

Barcardi, Rum
www.bacardi.com/

Appendix: Sample Drink Recipes

These recipes are only samples. Variations exist among beverage establishments, especially across regions and countries—both with the names of drinks and their ingredients, and the standard pour sizes used.

Name of Cocktail:	**Alabama Slammer**
Glassware:	Collins
Ingredients	Ounces
Amaretto Bols	$3/4$
Southern Comfort	$1/2$
Sloe Gin	$3/4$
Orange Juice	4
Instructions:	*Build in glass over ice and shake.*
Garnish:	*None*

Name of Cocktail:	**Bacardi Cocktail**
Glassware:	Collins
Ingredients	Ounces
Bacardi Light Rum	$1^1/4$
Sour Mix	4
Grenadine	$1/2$
Instructions:	*Build in glass over ice and shake.*
Garnish:	*Lime Wedge*

Name of Cocktail:	**B-52**
Glassware:	Shooter
Ingredients	Ounces
Kahlua	$3/4$
Baileys Irish Cream	$3/4$
Grand Marnier	$1/2$
Instructions:	*Layer in glass in order listed.*
Garnish:	*None*

Name of Cocktail:	**Bahama Mama**
Glassware:	Collins
Ingredients	Ounces
Myers Rum	1
Malibu Rum	1
Pineapple Juice	2
Cranberry Juice	2
Instructions:	*Build in glass over ice and shake.*
Garnish:	*None*

Name of Cocktail:	**Bay Breeze**
	(Hawaiian Sea Breeze)
Glassware:	Rocks

Ingredients	Ounces
Vodka	$1^1/4$
Pineapple Juice	2
Cranberry Juice	2

Instructions:	*Build in glass over ice and shake.*
Garnish:	*None*

Name of Cocktail:	**Bloody Maria**
Glassware:	Collins

Ingredients	Ounces
Tequila	$1^1/4$
Bloody Mary Mix	4

Instructions:	*Build in glass over ice and shake.*
Garnish:	*Lime Wedge*

Name of Cocktail:	**Black Russian**
Glassware:	Rocks

Ingredients	Ounces
Vodka	$1^1/4$
Kahlua	$3/4$

Instructions:	*Build in glass over ice.*
Garnish:	*None*

Name of Cocktail:	**Bloody Mary**
Glassware:	Collins

Ingredients	Ounces
Vodka	$1^1/4$
Bloody Mary Mix	4

Instructions:	*Build in glass over ice and shake.*
Garnish:	*Lime Wedge*

Name of Cocktail:	**Blue Hawaiian**
Glassware:	Collins

Ingredients	Ounces
Light Rum	$1^1/4$
Blue Curacao	$3/4$
Pineapple Juice	3
Sour Mix	1

Instructions:	*Build in glass over ice and shake.*
Garnish:	*None*

Name of Cocktail:	**Cape Codder**
Glassware:	Rocks

Ingredients	Ounces
Vodka	$1^1/4$

Cranberry Juice	4
Instructions:	*Build in glass over ice and shake.*
Garnish:	*Lime Wedge*

Name of Cocktail:	**Cement Mixer**
Glassware:	Shot

Ingredients	Ounces
Baileys Irish Cream	$1^1/_4$
Lime Juice	$^3/_4$

Instructions:	*Serve Baileys and lime juice in separate glasses. Guest drinks them simultaneously.*
Garnish:	*None*

Name of Cocktail:	**Chi-Chi**
Glassware:	Collins

Ingredients	Ounces
Vodka	$1^1/_4$
Pina Colada Mix	4

Instructions:	*Build in blender over ice, freeze, and serve.*
Garnish:	*Flag*

Name of Cocktail:	**Cosmopolitan**
Glassware:	Rocks

Ingredients	Ounces
Vodka	$1^1/_4$
Triple Sec	$^1/_2$
Cranberry Juice	1
Lime Juice	Splash

Instructions:	*Build in shaker over ice. Shake and strain into glass.*
Garnish:	*Lime Wedge*

Name of Cocktail:	**Colorado Bulldog**
Glassware:	Collins

Ingredients	Ounces
Vodka	$1^1/_4$
Kahlua	$^3/_4$
Half & Half	3
Coke	1

Instructions:	*Build in glass over ice, shake, and top with Coke.*
Garnish:	*None*

Name of Cocktail:	**Cuba Libre**
Glassware:	Rocks

Ingredients	Ounces
Light Rum	$1^1/_4$
Coke	4

Instructions:	*Build in glass over ice.*
Garnish:	*Lime Wedge*

Name of Cocktail:	**Daiquiri**
Glassware:	Rocks
Ingredients	Ounces
Rum	$1^1/_4$
Sour Mix	4
Lime Juice	$^1/_2$
Instructions:	*Build in glass over ice and shake.*
Garnish:	*Lime Wedge*

Name of Cocktail:	**Fuzzy Navel**
Glassware:	Rocks
Ingredients	Ounces
Peach Schnapps	$1^1/_4$
Orange Juice	3
Instructions:	*Build in glass over ice and shake.*
Garnish:	*Stirrer*

Name of Cocktail:	**Electric Lemonade**
Glassware:	Collins
Ingredients	Ounces
Vodka	$^3/_4$
Rum	$^3/_4$
Triple Sec	$^1/_2$
Sour Mix	4
Sprite	Splash
Instructions:	*Build in glass over ice, shake, and top with Sprite.*
Garnish:	*Lemon Wedge*

Name of Cocktail:	**Gibson**
Glassware:	Rocks
Ingredients	Ounces
Gin or Vodka	2
Dry Vermouth	$^1/_4$
Instructions:	*Build in glass over ice and shake.*
Garnish:	*Cocktail Onions*

Name of Cocktail:	**Gimlet**
Glassware:	Rocks
Ingredients	Ounces
Gin or Vodka	2
Lime Juice	$^1/_4$
Instructions:	*Build in glass over ice.*
Garnish:	*Lime Wedge*

Name of Cocktail:	**Greyhound**
Glassware:	Rocks
Ingredients	Ounces
Vodka	$1^1/_4$

Grapefruit Juice	4
Instructions:	*Build in glass over ice and shake.*
Garnish:	*None*

Name of Cocktail:	**Grape Crush** (Purple Hooter)
Glassware:	Collins
Ingredients	Ounces
Vodka	$1^1/_4$
Chambord	$^3/_4$
Sour Mix	2
Sprite	Splash
Instructions:	*Build in glass over ice and shake.*
Garnish:	*None*

Name of Cocktail:	**Hairy Navel**
Glassware:	Collins
Ingredients	Ounces
Peach Schnapps	$^3/_4$
Vodka	$1^1/_4$
Orange Juice	4
Instructions:	*Build in glass over ice and shake.*
Garnish:	*None*

Name of Cocktail:	**Harvey Wallbanger**
Glassware:	Hurricane
Ingredients	Ounces
Vodka	$1^1/_4$
Orange Juice	3
Galliano	$^3/_4$
Instructions:	*Build in glass over ice and shake.*
Garnish:	*None*

Name of Cocktail:	**Hurricane**
Glassware:	Collins
Ingredients	Ounces
Rum	1
Myers Rum	1
Orange Juice	1
Pineapple Juice	1
Sour Mix	1
Grenadine	Splash
Instructions:	*Build in glass over ice and shake.*
Garnish:	*None*

Name of Cocktail:	**Hollywood**
Glassware:	Rocks
Ingredients	Ounces
Vodka	$1^1/4$
Chambord	$3/4$
Pineapple Juice	4
Instructions:	*Build in glass over ice and shake.*
Garnish:	*None*

Name of Cocktail:	**Kahlua & Cream**
Glassware:	Rocks
Ingredients	Ounces
Kahlua	$1^1/4$
Half & Half	2
Instructions:	*Build in glass over ice.*
Garnish:	*None*

Name of Cocktail:	**Kamikaze**
Glassware:	Shooter
Ingredients	Ounces
Vodka	$1^1/4$
Triple Sec	$3/4$
Lime Juice	$1/4$
Instructions:	*Build in glass over ice, shake, and strain.*
Garnish:	*Lime Wedge*

Name of Cocktail:	**Killer Kool-Aid**
Glassware:	Collins
Ingredients	Ounces
Vodka	$3/4$
Amaretto Bols	$1/2$
Melon Bols	$3/4$
Cranberry Juice	4
Instructions:	*Build in glass over ice and shake.*
Garnish:	*None*

Name of Cocktail:	**Long Beach Tea**
Glassware:	Collins
Ingredients	Ounces
Vodka	$1/2$
Gin	$1/2$
Rum	$1/2$
Triple Sec	$1/2$
Sour Mix	2
Cranberry Juice	2
Sprite	1
Instructions:	*Build in glass over ice, shake, and top with Sprite.*
Garnish:	*Lime Wedge*

Name of Cocktail: **Lynchberg Lemonade**
Glassware: Collins

Ingredients	Ounces
Jack Daniels	$1^1/4$
Triple Sec	$3/4$
Sour Mix	4
Sprite	Splash

Instructions: *Build in glass over ice and shake.*
Garnish: *None*

Name of Cocktail: **Long Island Iced Tea**
Glassware: Collins

Ingredients	Ounces
Vodka	$1/2$
Rum	$1/2$
Gin	$1/2$
Triple Sec	$1/2$
Sour Mix	3
Coke	1

Instructions: *Build in glass over ice, shake, and top with Sprite.*
Garnish: *Lemon Wedge*

Name of Cocktail: **Madras**
Glassware: Rocks

Ingredients	Ounces
Vodka	$1^1/4$
Orange Juice	2
Cranberry Juice	2

Instructions: *Build in glass over ice and shake.*
Garnish: *None*

Name of Cocktail: **Mai-Tai**
Glassware: Collins

Ingredients	Ounces
Myers Rum	$1^1/4$
Rum	$3/4$
Pineapple Juice	$3/4$

Instructions: *Build in glass over ice and shake.*
Garnish: *Lime Wedge*

Name of Cocktail: **Margarita**
Glassware: Collins

Ingredients	Ounces
Tequila	$1^1/4$
Triple Sec	¾
Sour Mix	3
Lime Juice	$1/2$

Instructions:	Rim glass with salt. Build in shaker, shake, and pour over ice in glass.
Garnish:	Lemon Wedge

Name of Cocktail: **Manhattan**
Glassware: Cocktail

Ingredients	Ounces
Whiskey	2
Dry Vermouth	$^1/_4$

Instructions: *Build in glass over ice and shake.*
Garnish: *Lemon Twist or Stemmed Cherry*

Name of Cocktail: **Martini**
Glassware: Cocktail

Ingredients	Ounces
Gin or Vodka	2
Dry Vermouth	Splash

Instructions: *Build in glass over ice and shake.*
Garnish: *Olives or Lemon Twist*

Name of Cocktail: **Melon Ball**
Glassware: Collins

Ingredients	Ounces
Vodka	$1^1/_4$
Melon Bols	$^3/_4$
Orange Juice	4

Instructions: *Build in glass over ice and shake.*
Garnish: *None*

Name of Cocktail: **Mud Slide**
Glassware: Rocks

Ingredients	Ounces
Kahlua	$^3/_4$
Baileys	$^3/_4$
Vodka	$^1/_2$

Instructions: *Build in glass over ice and shake.*
Garnish: *None*

Name of Cocktail: **Mimosa**
Glassware: Champagne

Ingredients	Ounces
Champagne	4
Orange Juice	2

Instructions: *Pour juice and fill with champagne.*
Garnish: *None*

Name of Cocktail:	**Nuts & Berries**
Glassware:	Collins
Ingredients	Ounces
Frangelico	1
Chambord	1
Half & Half	4
Instructions:	*Build in glass over ice and shake.*
Garnish:	*None*

Name of Cocktail:	**Nutty Irishman**
Glassware:	Collins
Ingredients	Ounces
Baileys Irish Cream	1
Frnagelico	1
Instructions:	*Build in glass over ice.*
Garnish:	*None*

Name of Cocktail:	**Orange Crush** (Perfect John)
Glassware:	Collins
Ingredients	Ounces
Vodka	$1^1/4$
Triple Sec	$3/4$
Orange Juice	4
Sprite	Splash
Instructions:	*Build in glass over ice, shake, and top with Sprite.*
Garnish:	*None*

Name of Cocktail:	**Old Fashioned**
Glassware:	Rocks
Ingredients	Ounces
Whiskey	$1^1/4$
Rock Candy Syrup	$1/2$
Angostura Bitters	Dash
Soda Water	Splash
Instructions:	*Pour rock candy syrup into glass, then bitters, then liquor. Top with soda. Fruit is muddled only upon request.*
Garnish:	*Flag*

Name of Cocktail:	**Pearl Harbor**
Glassware:	Collins
Ingredients	Ounces
Vodka	$1^1/4$
Midori	$3/4$
Pineapple Juice	4
Instructions:	*Build in glass over ice and shake.*
Garnish:	*None*

Name of Cocktail:	**Planter's Punch**
Glassware:	Collins
Ingredients	Ounces
Rum	$1^1/4$
Myers Dark Rum	$3/4$
Pineapple Juice	1
Sour Mix	1
Orange Juice	1
Grenadine	Splash
Instructions:	*Build in glass over ice, shake, and float Myers.*
Garnish:	*None*

Name of Cocktail:	**Pina Colada**
Glassware:	Collins
Ingredients	Ounces
Rum	$1^1/4$
Pina Colada	4
Instructions:	*Build in glass over ice and shake.*
Garnish:	*Flag*

Name of Cocktail:	**Red Snapper**
Glassware:	Collins or Cocktail
Ingredients	Ounces
Crown Royal	1
Amaretto Bols	1
Cranberry Juice	4
Instructions:	*Build in glass over ice and shake.*
Garnish:	*None*

Name of Cocktail:	**Red Death**
	(Red Devil)
Glassware:	Collins
Ingredients	Ounces
Vodka	$1/2$
Amaretto Bols	$1/2$
Southern Comfort	$1/2$
Sloe Gin	$1/4$
Triple Sec	$1/4$
Orange Juice	3
Lime Juice	Splash
Instructions:	*Build in glass over ice and shake.*
Garnish:	*None*

Name of Cocktail:	**Rob Roy**
Glassware:	Collins
Ingredients	Ounces
Scotch	2

Vermouth	$1/4$
Instructions:	*Build in glass over ice.*
Garnish:	*Lemon Twist*

Name of Cocktail: **Rock Lobster**
Glassware: Collins or Cocktail

Ingredients	Ounces
Chambord	1
Amaretto Bols	1
Cranberry Juice	4

Instructions: *Build in glass over ice and shake.*
Garnish: *None*

Name of Cocktail: **Rum Runner**
Glassware: Collins

Ingredients	Ounces
Myers Dark Rum	$3/4$
Blackberry Brandy	$1/2$
Crème de Banana	$1/2$
Orange Juice	2
Pineapple Juice	2
Grenadine	Splash
151 Rum	$1/4$

Instructions: *Build in glass over ice and shake.*
Garnish: *Lime Wedge*

Name of Cocktail: **Rum Collins**
Glassware: Collins

Ingredients	Ounces
Light Rum	$1^1/4$
Sour Mix	5
Soda Water	Splash

Instructions: *Build in glass over ice and top with soda.*
Garnish: *None*

Name of Cocktail: **Rusty Nail**
Glassware: Rocks

Ingredients	Ounces
Scotch	$1^1/4$
Drambuie	$3/4$

Instructions: *Build in glass over ice in order listed.*
Garnish: *None*

Name of Cocktail: **Salty Dog**
Glassware: Rocks

Ingredients	Ounces
Vodka	$1^1/4$
Grapefruit Juice	3

| Instructions: | Rim glass with salt. Build in glass over ice, shake, and pour in glass. |
| Garnish: | None |

| Name of Cocktail: | **Sex on the Beach** |
| Glassware: | Collins |

Ingredients	Ounces
Vodka	$^3/_4$
Peach Schnapps	$^3/_4$
Crème de Cassis	$^1/_2$
Cranberry Juice	2
Orange Juice	2

| Instructions: | Build in glass over ice and shake. |
| Garnish: | None |

| Name of Cocktail: | **Sea Breeze** |
| Glassware: | Rocks |

Ingredients	Ounces
Vodka	$1^1/_4$
Cranberry Juice	2
Grapefruit Juice	2

| Instructions: | Build in glass over ice and shake. |
| Garnish: | None |

| Name of Cocktail: | **Screwdriver** |
| Glassware: | Collins |

Ingredients	Ounces
Vodka	$1^1/_4$
Orange Juice	4

| Instructions: | Build in glass over ice. |
| Garnish: | None |

| Name of Cocktail: | **Singapore Sling** |
| Glassware: | Collins |

Ingredients	Ounces
Gin	$1^1/_4$
Cherry Brandy	$^3/_4$
Sour Mix	2
Grenadine	$^1/_2$
Sprite	1

| Instructions: | Build in glass over ice, shake, and top with Sprite. |
| Garnish: | Flag |

| Name of Cocktail: | **Sloe Gin Fizz** |
| Glassware: | Collins |

Ingredients	Ounces
Sloe Gin	$1^1/_4$
Sour Mix	3

Soda Water	1
Instructions:	*Build in glass over ice, shake, and top with soda.*
Garnish:	*Flag*

Name of Cocktail:	**Sombrero**
Glassware:	Rocks
Ingredients	Ounces
Kahlua	1^1/4
Half & Half	2
Instructions:	*Layer in glass.*
Garnish:	*None*

Name of Cocktail:	**Sours (All)**
Glassware:	Rocks
Ingredients	Ounces
Liquor	1^1/4
Sour Mix	4
Instructions:	*Build in glass over ice and shake.*
Garnish:	*None*

Name of Cocktail:	**Stone Sour**
Glassware:	Rocks
Ingredients	Ounces
Whiskey	1^1/4
Sour Mix	2
Orange Juice	2
Instructions:	*Build in glass over ice and shake.*
Garnish:	*None*

Name of Cocktail:	**Stinger**
Glassware:	Collins
Ingredients	Ounces
Brandy	1^1/4
White Crème de Menthe	^{3}/4
Instructions:	*Build in glass over ice.*
Garnish:	*None*

Name of Cocktail:	**Tequila Sunrise**
Glassware:	Collins
Ingredients	Ounces
Tequila	1^1/4
Orange Juice	4
Grenadine	^{1}/4
Instructions:	*Build in glass over ice in order listed.*
Garnish:	*None*

| Name of Cocktail: | **Texas Tea** |
| Glassware: | Collins |

Ingredients	Ounces
Vodka	$1/2$
Rum	$1/2$
Tequila	$1/2$
Triple Sec	$1/2$
Sour Mix	3
Coke	1

Instructions: *Build in glass over ice, shake, and top with Coke.*
Garnish: *Lemon Wedge*

| Name of Cocktail: | **Tequila Sunset** |
| Glassware: | Rocks |

Ingredients	Ounces
Tequila	$1^1/4$
Pineapple Juice	4
Grenadine	$1/4$

Instructions: *Build in glass over ice in order listed.*
Garnish: *None*

| Name of Cocktail: | **Three Wisemen** |
| Glassware: | Collins |

Ingredients	Ounces
Jack Daniels	$3/4$
Jim Beam	$3/4$
Johnnie Walker Black	$1/2$

Instructions: *Build in glass.*
Garnish: *None*

| Name of Cocktail: | **Toasted Almond** |
| Glassware: | Collins |

Ingredients	Ounces
Amaretto Bols	$1^1/4$
Kahlua	$3/4$
Half & Half	2

Instructions: *Build in glass over ice and shake.*
Garnish: *None*

| Name of Cocktail: | **Tropical Lifesaver** |
| Glassware: | Collins |

Ingredients	Ounces
Malibu	$3/4$
Absolut Citron	$3/4$
Melon Bols	$1/2$
Pineapple Juice	2
Sour Mix	2

| Instructions: | *Build in glass over ice and shake.* |
| Garnish: | *None* |

| Name of Cocktail: | **Tom Collins** |
| Glassware: | Collins |

Ingredients	Ounces
Gin	$1^1/4$
Sour Mix	3
Soda Water	Splash
Instructions:	*Build in glass over ice, shake, and top with soda.*
Garnish:	*Flag*

| Name of Cocktail: | **Vodka Collins** |
| Glassware: | Collins |

Ingredients	Ounces
Vodka	$1^1/4$
Sour Mix	3
Soda	Splash
Instructions:	*Build in glass over ice, shake, and top with soda.*
Garnish:	*Flag*

| Name of Cocktail: | **Vodka Gimlet** |
| Glassware: | Collins |

Ingredients	Ounces
Vodka	2
Lime Juice	$^1/4$
Instructions:	*Build in glass over ice.*
Garnish:	*Lime Wedge*

| Name of Cocktail: | **Wine Spritzer** |
| Glassware: | Collins |

Ingredients	Ounces
White Wine	4
Soda Water	2
Instructions:	*Build in glass over ice.*
Garnish:	*None*

| Name of Cocktail: | **White Russian** |
| Glassware: | Collins |

Ingredients	Ounces
Vodka	$1^1/4$
Kahlua	$^3/4$
Half & Half	2
Instructions:	*Build in glass over ice.*
Garnish:	*None*

Name of Cocktail:	**Woo Woo**
Glassware:	Rocks

Ingredients	Ounces
Vodka	$1^1/4$
Peach Schnapps	$3/4$
Cranberry Juice	3

Instructions: *Build in glass over ice and shake.*
Garnish: *None*

Name of Cocktail:	**Zombie**
Glassware:	Collins

Ingredients	Ounces
Myers Dark Rum	$1^1/4$
Apricot Brandy	$1/2$
151 Rum	$1/4$
Orange Juice	1
Pineapple Juice	1
Sour Mix	1
Grenadine	Splash

Instructions: *Build in glass over ice and shake.*
Garnish: *None*

Chapter 8 Outline

Types of Wine
    Table Wines
    Fortified Wines
    Aperitif and Dessert Wines
    Sparkling Wines
Wine Production
    Pressing
    Fermentation
    Aging
    Fining
    Blending
    Bottling and Corking
    Maturing
    Storage
Making Champagne
Taste Talk
    Look
    Smell
    Taste
    Judging Wine

Competencies

1. Distinguish the various types of wines. (pp. 223–224, 227, 230–231)

2. Identify red varietal wines. (pp. 225–227)

3. Identify white varietal wines. (pp. 228–230)

4. Explain the wine-making process from the pressing of grapes to the storage of bottled wine. (pp. 231–240)

5. Explain how Champagne is made. (pp. 240–243)

6. Describe procedures for tasting and judging wines. (pp. 243–249)

8

Wine Fundamentals

KNOWLEDGE OF WINE IS FUNDAMENTAL to beverage service. Today's guests are more knowledgeable and more sophisticated about wine than ever before and they expect beverage servers to be knowledgeable as well. This chapter reviews various types of wines and describes the basic steps in making wine. **Viniculture**, the study or science of making wines, is a complex and intricate topic on which hundreds of books and thousands of articles have been written. Mastering the basics presented in this chapter will form a foundation of knowledge upon which you can build.

Wine is by far the most complex beverage in the annals of human history: the variety of hauntingly elusive flavors is, by itself, staggering. The methods that produce these flavors are an odd combination of centuries-old nature-dependent processes, stainless steel vats, and computer technology. The subject of wine is further cloaked in mystery and romance and obscured by millions of words written by "experts" in heated disagreement with one another. Getting the fundamentals in one chapter is no easy task.

All grapes are basically vines, members of the *Vitis* genus, *Vitaceae* family. More than 4,000 grape varieties have come from this species. **Viticulture** is the cultivation of grapevines, or the study of grapes. One species of *Vitis* stands out as the great European wine grape—*Vitis vinifera*. This species is generally considered to contain the proper balance of sugar and acid so that it is not required to add sugar or water during fermentation.

North America has its own species, *Vitis labrusca*, that withstands cold winter areas. The vast majority of modern European vineyards consist of selected European *vinifera* vines that are grafted on to a selected American rootstock (*Vitis labrusca*) which is naturally resistant to the deadly, vine-killing phylloxera—a kind of plant lice. In the middle 1800s, phylloxera was carried to Europe on *labrusca* rootstock by some English vintners who thought that the hardy American grapes would prosper in England. Crossing the channel, the phylloxera virtually wiped out all the vineyards in France, Germany, and Italy. The discovery that grafting the branches of the *Vitis vinifera* on to the rootstocks of the *Vitis labrusca* would cancel the destructive power of phylloxera revitalized the shattered European wine industry. Today, virtually all of Europe's vines grow on American roots.

The intricacies of viticulture are beyond the scope of this chapter. However, it is important to note that many wine experts consider *terroir* (the combination of climate and soil in a particular grape-growing region) as the defining feature of the eventual wines that are produced.

While there are thousands of grape varieties, not all are used for making wine. In fact, there are only about fifty grape varieties that impart most of the flavors and taste of wines around the world. This chapter introduces you to the major red and white grape varieties and describes the wines made from them. The final section of the chapter explores the often confusing language of taste and presents a practical wine-tasting vocabulary that you will find useful when describing and serving wine to guests.

Types of Wine

Wine is made from the juice of one variety of grape or from blending the juices of two or more varieties. A wine produced from a single grape variety is called a **varietal** wine. In some countries, such as France, a varietal wine must be made from 100 percent of the grape variety. In the United States, a wine may be identified as a varietal with only 75 percent of the grape variety actually used—with the choice of other grapes left to the winemaker. Examples of names of varietal wines are: chardonnay, riesling, cabernet sauvignon, merlot, and pinot gris. Exhibit 1, Classic Red Wine Grapes, and Exhibit 2, Classic White Wine Grapes, outline fundamental characteristics of major grape varieties used in making varietal and blended wines. The Internet sites listed at the end of this chapter provide more detailed information on these and on many more grape varieties and wines.

Wine made from a blend of wines to resemble a particular wine of an established wine-producing region is called a **generic wine.** Many countries have treaty agreements that protect the names of important wine regions. Examples of names of generic wines are: bordeaux, chablis, chianti, burgundy, beaujolais, and champagne. Blending is a common practice and generic wines are not necessarily inferior to varietals. In fact, a blended wine is often superior in taste to either of the blended components alone. French champagne is almost always a blend of grape varieties. Brand name wines are usually blends which rely on the bottler's reputation for consistency, quality, price, and value. Mateus and Blue Nun are examples of brand name wines.

Basic wine classifications addressed in the sections that follow are:

- Table wines
- Fortified wines
- Aperitif and dessert wines
- Sparkling wines

Table Wines

Table wines make up the largest category of wines and, as the name suggests, include wines primarily suited to accompany food, but not limited to such purpose. Tables wines are referred to as "still" wines. They are not bubbly. Although some table wines may have a very slight carbonation, the amount of carbon dioxide does not disqualify them as table wines. Most table wines are **natural wines**: basically the product of grape fermentation without the addition of alcohol or sugar (beyond a small amount allowed for certain wines under specified

Exhibit 1   Classic Red Wine Grapes

Cabernet Sauvignon
[ka-behr-NAY soh-vihn-YOHN]

Growing Areas
Often called the "king of red grapes," Cabernet Sauvignon is produced throughout the world. The most famous growing area is Bordeaux, France. Needs slightly warmer growing conditions than many other grape varieties. Best growing sites are moderately warm, semi-arid regions with well-drained fields and long growing seasons.

Varietal/Blend
Often blended with Merlot, Cabernet Franc, and Syrah.

Vinification
Fermented in stainless steel or oak. Well rounded, high in tannin content and ages well. Aged in old or new oak. Ranges from medium-bodied to heavier full-bodied.

Flavors
Black currant flavor with hint of mint and cedar.

Merlot
[mehr-LOH]

Growing Areas
One of the world's most popular red grape varieties, Merlot is the most widely planted grape in the Bordeaux region of France and matures in regions cooler than those required for Cabernet Sauvignon. It is grown worldwide, particularly in Italy, Spain, South America, United States, South Africa, Australia, and New Zealand.

Varietal/Blend
Used to soften Cabernet Sauvignon-based wines.

Vinification
As with Cabernet Sauvignon, Merlot is fermented in stainless steel or oak. In some regions, it is cool-fermented when used as a varietal. Lower in tannic bitterness and higher in alcohol content than Cabernet Sauvignon. Also, slightly lower natural acidity than Cabernet Sauvignon and less astringency. Dry, fruity, and usually oak-aged.

Flavors
Similar in flavor to Cabernet Sauvignon, Merlot tends to be softer and mellower with fruity flavors of black currant, black cherry, and mint.

Pinot Noir
[PEE-noh NWAHR]

Growing Areas
One of the oldest grape varieties, Pinot Noir is the primary grape of France's Burgundy region. Difficult to grow, it thrives in a moderately cool climate with warm days and cool nights. Also produced in the United States, Australia, New Zealand, South Africa, Germany, Eastern Europe, and Italy.

Varietal/Blend
Used in most red wines from Burgundy and in the bulk of Champagne production.

(continued)

Exhibit 1 *(continued)*

Vinification
> One of the most difficult grapes to ferment, sometimes oak barrel-fermented. Neither acidic nor tannic, Pinot Noir has a soft, velvety texture. Usually oak-aged. Burgundies are always aged in new oak.

Flavors
> Predominately raspberry, strawberry, and sometimes cherry flavors.

Syrah/Shiraz
[see-RAH]

Growing Areas
> Grown mostly in France and Australia (named as Shiraz and Hermitage), but increasingly in the United States, Algeria, and South Africa.

Varietal/Blend
> Used for blending in Châteauneuf-du-Pape and makes for a fine quality wine as a varietal.

Vinification
> Traditionally fermented at up to 35 degrees Centigrade but now often fermented at cooler temperatures in stainless steel vats. Rich and tannic with a velvety texture. Dry, full, rarely oak-aged, except in Australia.

Flavors
> Fruit flavored, particularly blackberry and raspberry with a peppery overtone.

Sanigiovese
[san-jaw-VAY-zeh]

Growing Areas
> The primary grape of Tuscany, Italy. Thriving in a hot, dry climate, little is grown outside of Italy, with limited production in the United States, Australia, and Argentina.

Varietal/Blend
> Rarely used as varietal, Sanigiovese is blended with most Tuscan red wines and is the basic blend of Chianti.

Vinification
> Short fermentation (3 days) for Chianti. High natural acidity with moderate to high tannins and medium levels of alcohol, produces a spicy, smooth texture. Sweet and sour style, best drunk young and fresh. Usually oak-aged.

Flavors
> Predominant flavors of black and red cherries.

Gamay
[ga-MAY]

Growing Areas
> The Beaujolais grape of Burgundy, France. Virtually all production is in France where the grape flourishes on the granite hills of Burgundy.

Varietal/Blend
> Used as a varietal, it is not blended with other wines.

Exhibit 1 *(continued)*

Vinification
    Usually fermented using carbonic maceration to enhance fruitiness. Low in alcohol and relatively high in acidity with light tannins. Never oak-aged. Best drunk soon after bottling.

Flavors
    Cherry flavors may dominate with hints of raspberries and strawberries.

Zinfandel
[ZIHN-fuhn-dehl]

Growing Areas
    This specialty red wine grape of California is not widely grown in other parts of the world. Some production in Italy (known as Primitivo), South Africa, South America, and Australia.

Varietal/Blend
    Used as a varietal and can be blended with a number of different wines. Also used as a base for sparkling wines.

Vinification
    Modern technology and the lack of confining traditions creates conditions for producing sweetish "blush" wines as well as high-quality, rich reds. Sometimes, fermented using carbonic maceration to enhance fruitiness. Dry, full, usually oak-aged.

Flavors
    Unique black fruit and raspberry flavors with spicy fruitiness.

For audio pronunciations of key wine terms, visit the audio wine dictionary at www.strat splace.com or at www.wineloverspage.com/lexicon.

conditions). Natural fermentation stops when there is no more sugar to convert to alcohol or when the alcohol reaches a specified percentage by volume. In the United States, table wines may have an alcohol content no higher than 14 percent by volume.

On a wine menu, table wines will be further classified by color as *red*, *white*, or *rosé*. However, these colors are approximations: "reds" run from purple to slightly red-tinged brown to clear, light red; "whites" run from clear as water to green-tinged, varying shades of yellow through gold, and light brown. Although rosé wine is generally described by its rose color (light pink to light orange-red), it is made by leaving the skins of red grapes in the fermentation process for a short period, then removing them. Its taste characteristics (which vary widely) are more to the point. Color is an important distinction when wine with the same name comes in both red and white. A Graves is a famous white wine from the Bordeaux district in France; there is a red Graves, however, which is a fine wine but is neither well-known nor particularly important.

Fortified Wines

Fortified wines may range in alcohol content from 14 percent to 24 percent by volume. Alcohol—usually in the form of a brandy distilled from wine—is added to a

Exhibit 2   Classic White Wine Grapes

Chardonnay
[shar-dn-AY]

Growing Areas
> Chardonnay, one of the most popular and versatile of all white grape varieties, is produced in most wine-producing countries throughout the world. The most famous growing area is Burgundy, France. This grape variety adapts to varying climates.

Varietal/Blend
> A quality varietal, Chardonnay is also the major wine blended with Pinot Noir and Pinot Meunier to produce Champagne.

Vinification
> Adaptable to different wine-making techniques: stainless steel fermentation, barrel fermentation, and malolactic fermentation. Different growing soils and varied wine-making techniques produce a range of styles and characteristics. Generally, smooth from a fine balance of sugar and acidity. Also, strong affinity with oak aging that adds depth and flavor.

Flavor
> Often with hints of tropical fruits, with buttery, lemon, and sometimes nutty flavors.

Sauvignon Blanc
[SOH-vee-nyaw*n* BLAH*N*GK]

Growing Areas
> After, Chardonnay, Sauvignon Blanc is the second most popular white wine. It is best grown in cool climates and native to France's Loire Valley region. Countries producing Sauvignon Blanc include: New Zealand, Australia, Chile, Austria, Italy, United States, and South Africa.

Varietal/Blend
> A crisp and tart varietal in Loire, France, and in New Zealand. Often blended with Sémillon in Bordeaux, France, and in many regions around the world to produce elegant, dry wines. Also, a component of the sweet, rich wines of Sauternes and Barsac.

Vinification
> Stainless steel fermentation and usually unoaked. Tangy and sharp when unblended. Softer styles from barrel-fermented Sémillon blends.

Flavor
> Sunny climates produce rich, tropical fruit flavors; cool climates produce sharp, tangy gooseberry flavors with mineral overtones.

Riesling
[REEZ-ling]

Growing Areas
> One of the world's great white wine grapes producing some of the very best white wines. Native of Germany, and suited to the coldest of wine-growing climates, Riesling is produced in Northern France, Northern Italy, Eastern Europe, South Africa, Australia, New Zealand, and the United States.

Varietal/Blend
> Primarily a varietal, occasionally used in blending.

Exhibit 2 *(continued)*

Vinification
> Stainless steel fermented and varied from light and dry to rich and sweet; usually made in dry and semi-dry styles. German-style is sweet and tart; Alsatian-style is bone dry.

Flavor
> Often tastes as it smells. Spicy and fruity with hints of green apple, lime, peaches, apricot, and honey.

Sémillon
[seh-mee-YOHN]

Growing Areas
> Produced worldwide: Native to France's Bordeaux region and found also in Australia, South America, South Africa, eastern Europe, and the United States.

Varietal/Blend
> While mostly a varietal in Australia, Sémillon is blended with Savignon Blanc to produce many of the white wines from Bordeaux, France. Also used in the production of dessert wines.

Vinification
> Stainless steel fermentation and rarely oaked. Blended, produces dry wines or sweet wines.

Flavor
> Often tastes as it smells. Dry, wines have flavors of nectarine and lemon. Sweeter wines have flavors of peaches, apricots, and honey.

Viognier
[vee-oh-NYAY]

Growing Areas
> With limted acreage planted worldwide, Viognier is the primary grape of France's Rhone Valley and is also grown in the United States, Australia, and South America. Low yields and high susceptibility to vineyard diseases make Viognier wines difficult to find and relatively expensive.

Varietal/Blend
> Mainly produced as a varietal, but used as a blend in the United States with Chenin Blanc and Chardonnay. Sometimes used as a blend to add fragrance and soften Syrah.

Vinification
> Stainless steel fermentation, dry, rarely oaked. Dry wines with strong aromatics produce a soft, rich, and luscious style.

Flavor
> Produces rich floral aromatics with flavor hints of apricots, peaches, and pears.

Chenin Blanc
[SHEN-ihn BLAHNGK]

Growing Areas
> Native to the Loire Valley of France and widely grown in South Africa and the United States with some production also in Chile, Australia, and New Zealand.

(continued)

Exhibit 2   *(continued)*

Varietal/Blend
  Used as a varietal and often blended with Chardonnay and Sauvignon Blanc. In
  South Africa, used for fortified wines.

Vinification
  Varied depending on desired style—bone dry, semi-sweet, sweet, or sparkling.
  One of the most versatile of all wine grape varieties. Depending on the wine-making technique, Chenin Blanc is produced as crisp, dry table wines, light sparkling
  wines, dessert wines, and brandy. Usually stainless steel fermentation and
  unoaked.

Flavor
  Often sweet and sour at the same time: floral and citrus aromas with apple and
  pear flavors.

For audio pronunciations of key wine terms, visit the audio wine dictionary at www.strat
splace.com or at www.wineloverspage.com/lexicon.

wine during fermentation. Adding alcohol produces two results: the extra alcohol brings the alcohol content beyond what is naturally possible; the unfermented sugar stays in the wine, producing a sweet wine. Some fortified wines (such as sherry) allow for complete fermentation of the sugar, adding the brandy (and often a sweetener) after fermentation. Port, madeira, and vermouth are other examples of fortified wines.

Aperitif and Dessert Wines

Aperitif wines (from the French, *apéritif,* meaning "appetizer") are wines that are traditionally served before meals as an appetizer or cocktail. They are often fortified and herb-flavored (vermouth, for instance, is both fortified and flavored with herbal ingredients). Dry sherries are often included in this category.

 Dessert wines, as the name implies, are meant to be served after dinner with dessert or *as* dessert. Dessert wines are often fortified—the sweet varieties of sherry ("Cream" and "Oloroso," primarily) and port are examples. Madeira is another. Natural wines, such as some varieties of sauternes and many German wines classified as *Beerenauslese* or *Trochenbeerenauslese*, are sweet wines that are often used as dessert wines.

Sparkling Wines

The alcohol content of sparkling wines is typically 13 percent to 14 percent by volume. Basically, any wine can be made into a sparkling wine by the addition of carbon dioxide gas under pressure. However, sparkling wines are usually made by re-fermentation. An already fermented wine is fermented a second time by the addition of a small bit of yeast and sugar in a tightly sealed container. The resulting carbon dioxide gas from the fermentation is trapped inside and forced into the wine because of the pressure developed. In the classic **champagne method**, the second fermentation takes place in the bottle in which it is sold—a laborious and exacting process which accounts for the high price of the best champagne. Less expensive methods include the *transfer process* (the wine is transferred through a filter to another bottle) and the **Charmat process** (or bulk process) in which the second fermentation takes place in a vat and the wine is later filtered and bottled under pressure. These processes are described in greater detail in a later section of this chapter.

The most famous of the sparkling wines is, of course, champagne. Champagne, by law, can come only from the Champagne district of France. American "champagne" must be identified as "American champagne," "California champagne," or "New York state champagne." The Italian word for "sparkling" is *spumante*; the German word is *Schaumwein* or *Sekt*.

Wine Production

The grape, of course, is the essence of wine. Not only do wine grapes provide a multitudinous variety of wines, but every part of the grape can have an effect on taste. For example, **tannins** produce a dry, sometimes puckery, sensation in the mouth and back of the throat. These astringent substances are found in the seeds, skins, and stems of grapes, as well as in oak storage barrels (especially new oak barrels). Tannins are important in the production of good red wines, providing flavor, texture, and preservative qualities to the wine. Although grapes may appear to be in a range of either red-purples or green-yellows, wine grapes are commonly referred to as either red or black (*noir*) or as green or white (*blanc*), depending on the color of their skins at ripeness.

Red wine is made from red or black grapes. The grapes are crushed and then fermented with the juice, pulp, seeds, and skin for several days. Red and black grapes contain color pigments called **anthocyanins**, which are not soluble in water but are in alcohol. If their skins are left to ferment, as the alcohol forms, the anthocyanins dissolve, creating the red color. As sugar fermentation ends, a wine press separates the liquid from the solid materials which are discarded. Red wine styles range from fruity and refreshing to full-bodied and intense.

Almost all grape juice is initially colorless, therefore, white wine can be made either from green or white grapes or from red or black grapes. The grapes are crushed and pressed immediately to separate the liquid from the solids. After pressing, the skins, seeds, and stems are discarded. White wine styles range from crisp and dry, to spicy and aromatic, to sweet and luscious. Champagne is made from red or black grapes, but the skins are discarded after the grapes are pressed. Pink wines are often made by allowing the skins to be in the ferment for a short time and then removing them.

The basics of fermenting grapes are utterly simple. Squeeze the juice from grapes and yeasts (which grow naturally on grape skins) will cause the juice and skins to ferment. Today, however, wine making is not that simple. Intricate scientific methods are required and complicated equipment is used. Today, new grapes are produced, new varieties of wines are created, and attributes of current wines are changed. To describe all this would take volumes. Exhibit 3 presents a short narrative on wine making from Raymond Vineyard & Cellar, a California winery. Internet sites and search engines listed at the end of this chapter will take you to

Exhibit 3   Wine-Making at Raymond Vineyard & Cellar

Raymond Vineyard & Cellar

Most wineries follow the same basic steps when making wine: the grapes are crushed, the juice is fermented and filtered, and the wine is aged in oak barrels. Although the process can be very similar from one winery to another, the wines can be very different depending on the grapes, on the winemaker's style, on the timing, and on the type of equipment used.

CRUSHING EQUIPMENT:

Speed and flexibility are vital during the crush. The crushing equipment is designed for quick, gentle processing of the ripe fruit. The augers push the grapes into a crusher-stemmer, where the stems are removed. If the grapes are white, the "must" is then pumped into a press to separate juice and skins. If the grapes are red, the "must" is pumped into a fermentation tank with the skins.

PRESSING EQUIPMENT:

Gentle pressing is a key element in wine-making. The Raymond presses are designed to extract a maximum amount of juice with a minimum amount of pressure. This produces clear, intense juice without tannins or flavors from the grape skins.

FERMENTATION:

The conversion from grape juice to wine takes place in these large stainless steel tanks. Each tank is refrigerated and has an individual thermostat, which allows the winemakers to control the time and temperature of each fermentation. A computer monitors all the tanks, 24 hours a day, and will set off an alarm if there are any power failures or problems.

BARREL STORAGE:

After fermentation, the wine is placed into 60 gallon oak barrels for aging. Raymond uses both French and American oak and our wines are aged from 3 months to 2 years. The barrel building is temperature and humidity controlled to provide a perfect environment for our 10,000 barrels.

Source: Raymond Vineyard & Cellar. For more information, visit the company's Internet site at: http:www.raymondwine.com.

thousands of wineries throughout the world. The Internet sites of many vineyards and wineries are very instructive, offering information about their grape-growing and wine-making processes in addition to the wines they produce. The following sections simplify the complex subject of wine making and present a basic outline of the way in which wine is produced today.

Pressing

Harvest season is the best time to visit a winery. In fact it might be the only time to fully appreciate the various stages the wine-making process—seeing the grapes unloaded into presses and experiencing the aroma of grapes and juice during the fermentation process. Most wineries ferment grapes only a few months of the year. The rest of the year, the wine is simply aging.

As they are harvested, grapes are brought to the presses where they are washed and gently crushed to begin the process of removing the juice, which is called **must**. Some of the juice obtained is what is called *free run*. This is the must that runs off after the grapes are crushed but before they are pressed. Most of the must coming from the pressings is retained for wine, but some of it may not be fermented for wine—a portion may be fermented separately and distilled into brandy or used for other purposes, such as making wine vinegar.

Pressing must be done with care, since rough or heavy pressing can extract undesirable components. For example, crushing the seeds or over-crushing the stems can give an excessively bitter wine. In the past, grapes were pressed by bare feet, which gave just about the right pressure and action to remove the juice. However, today's modern presses are more efficient than bare feet in extracting must but tend to leave a higher proportion of solids such as skins, flesh, pips, and dirt in the must. For this reason, the must (especially for white wines) is cleaned before fermentation—by allowing the solids to settle out, by a powerful vacuum filter, or by careful centrifugal pumping.

Fermentation

Almost universally, the first thing wine makers do before fermentation is to add a small dose of **sulfur dioxide** (SO_2) to the must. The amount used is regulated by law. It is used to kill the wild yeasts present on the skins of grapes and thus prevent premature and uncontrolled fermentation; it is also used to prevent oxidation.

The next basic decision required is whether sugar should be added to the must—a process called **chaptalization**. This process is often necessary when weather conditions prevent grapes from ripening fully and developing enough natural sugar to convert into the amount of alcohol prescribed (often by law) for certain wines. In some countries, chaptalization is controlled and some wines may not be allowed to be chaptalized.

All wines also need some acidity. If acid is lacking, the wine maker can blend in grapes with enough acid to make up for any deficiency. During harvest, pickers may also be instructed to pick enough unripe grapes to give the required acidity.

The proper fermentation temperature is different for different kinds of wine, and individual wine makers have sharply differing views on proper temperature. A vigorous chemical process, fermentation develops heat and may have to be controlled so the temperature does not rise too high and develop undesirable substances. Wood and concrete vats are very poor conductors of heat; for this reason alone, stainless steel fermenting vats help reduce fermenting temperatures, the stainless steel being an excellent conductor of heat.

The type of fermentation container can affect how the eventual wine tastes. Stainless steel is a relatively neutral material that does not interact or alter the fresh fruit flavors of a grape as it ferments into wine. However, when making some types of white wines, oak barrel fermentation may be desired. This has the effect of reducing the fruitiness of the eventual wine and adding a hint of roasted nuttiness. Oak barrel fermentation also affects the texture of the eventual wine, making it smoother and denser.

Red wines are fermented at temperatures usually from 70° to 90°F (21° to 32°C) and whites at from 45° to 65°F (7° to 18°C). The lower temperature for whites is used to give a more fresh and fruity flavor to the wine. The usual cold fermentation temperatures are from 65° to 70°F (18° to 21°C) for reds and 44° to 59°F (7° to 15°C) for whites.

Fermentation occurs only as long as there is sugar to ferment. When it is used up, fermentation stops. It also stops when the alcohol content rises to 14 percent, because the alcohol at this point kills the remaining yeast. If sugar remains with alcohol at this percentage, the wine will tend toward sweetness—a wine of 2 percent sugar content is considered sweet.

When skins are left in, a thick cap develops on top of the fermenting wine which hinders fermentation by blocking oxygen. Either this cap must be broken up frequently or wine must be pumped from the bottom and run over the cap so oxygen is available.

Malolactic fermentation (sometimes called "secondary fermentation") can easily occur in the fermentation process. No alcohol is actually produced. This is a bacterial change that converts harsh malic acids into lactic (milk-like) acids and carbon dioxide. Wines undergoing this process become softer and smoother. This process is encouraged in the production of most high-quality red wines and some white wines (Chardonnays, for example). However, malolactic fermentation also reduces the fruitiness of the eventual wine and many white wines need the higher malic acidity to ensure crispness. In these cases, wine makers may use techniques to inhibit malolactic fermentation.

Some wines (primarily reds) are produced by a fermentation process called **carbonic maceration**. Uncrushed grapes are vatted in a sealed chamber and fermentation starts. The oxygen is used up and only carbon dioxide now fills the chamber. Without oxygen, the wine produces less acid and a rich, fruity flavor and brilliant red color. This relatively new process has been particularly successful with wines—such as the Beaujolais Nouveau—which are intended for consumption when very young.

Aging

Aging of wines is the storage of wines that takes place after fermentation, but before bottling. The purpose of **aging** is to allow further chemical reactions with a small amount of air, with suspended particles in the wine, and sometimes, with the storage medium itself (as with oak barrels or casks). Most wines are aged after fermentation, usually by being placed in casks and then stored in a cold area.

During the aging period, suspended material in the wine settles to the bottom of the barrel or vat as sediment or lees. **Lees** are the coarse sediments (dead yeast cells and small grape particles) that accumulate during fermentation and aging. At various times after the settling out of these substances, the clear juice is siphoned off from the lees into another container through a process called **racking**. Racking removes some acidity; the color of the wine becomes more brilliant; and the fermented wine becomes less astringent due to the reduction of tannins. During aging, flavors also blend together and smooth out. Glycerine develops, giving additional smoothness and more body.

Aging wine in small oak barrels is favored for some wines because the wood encourages certain desirable changes in taste and texture. Some aging specifies *new oak* barrels, because new wood imparts stronger wood flavor to the wine; some wine makers scrape the insides of the barrels after many years of use to achieve the effect of "new wood." Wood may actually add tannins, but these tannins are described as "soft" while the tannins in grapes (which partly settle out) are called "hard" and give a harshness to wine. The end result of aging in oak barrels is usually a smoother, softer wine.

Aging today may not always occur in small oak barrels. Instead, huge oak vats may be used. Also, concrete, glass-lined, or stainless steel vats may be used. These may be sealed so there is little oxidation or other changes from the air. Whites and rosés are often aged in vats which are lined with inert materials. Some wine is lost during aging from evaporation and, to keep containers filled, additional wine is added—called *topping off*—to fill the container and prevent excessive oxidation. It is important to prevent excessive oxidation since it can destroy the wine. Another undesirable oxidative change is caused by the fruit fly. It carries a bacterium which, in combination with oxygen, changes alcohol into acetic acid (vinegar). During fermentation and subsequent handling—even through bottling—it is important to keep fruit flies away from the wine.

Aging can develop quality up to a certain point and after that the wine may not improve and may even deteriorate. Most wine is aged just over the winter, and bottling takes place in the spring after the harvest. Other wines are aged several or more years, just as they may be left to ferment over a long period. Some others, like the robust and more stable reds, may be aged in casks for a long time. Aging, in this case, encourages more and more development. In some cases, specific aging times are required by law if certain terms are used on the label.

After a wine is aged, it is possible for wine experts to make a final judgment as to what the quality of the wine will be. Up to this point all indications may point to a great or a good year, but it is only after the wine is aged that the experts make their final determination. In some years, the aged wines may be described as *ordinary*; in a slightly better year, the wine may be said to be *medium*; in a better year, described as *good*; if still better, the wine is described as *great*, and the very best is said to be *exceptional*. Thus the vintage year shown on a label of such wines is important, because a buyer will have a basis for judging the quality and value of the wine without opening a bottle and tasting it. **Vintage year** indicates the year in

Exhibit 4 Comparison of Vintages for the Wine-Growing Regions of France

★ EXCEPTIONAL VINTAGES: 1921, 1928, 1929, 1945 ★										
VINTAGE	Red Bordeaux	White Bordeaux	Red Burgundy	White Burgundy	Côtes du Rhône Growths	Alsace	Pouilly-Loire Sancerre	Anjou Touraine	Beaujolais	Champagne
1947	★	••••	••••		★			★		
1949	★	••••	★		••••			••••		
1955	★	••••	••••	•••	••••			••••		
1959	••••	••••	★	•••	•••	★		★		
1961	★	★	★	••••	••••	••••		•••		
1962	••••	••••	•••	•••	••••	••		•••		
1964	•••	••	••••	•••	••••	•••				
1966	••••	•••	••••	•••	••••	••••				
1967	•••	★	•••	•••	••••	••••				
1969	•	••	••••	••••	•••	•••		••••		
1970	★	•••	•••	★	★	•••		••••		
1971	••••	•••	••••	••••	★			•••		
1973	•••	•••	••	••••		•••		••		
1974	••	•••	•••	•••		••		••		
1975	••••	••••	•	•••	••••	•••		•••		
1976	•••	••••	••••	••••	••••	★		••••		
1977	••	••	••	•••		••		••		
1978	••••	•••	★	••••	★	••		••		
1979	••••	•••	•••	★	••••	••••				
1980	••	••	•••	•••	•••	••	•••	••	••	•
1981	••••	•••	••	•••	•••	••••	••	•••	•••	•••
1982	★	•••	•••	••••	••	•••	••••	••••	•••	•••
1983	••••	••••	••••	••••	•••	★	••••	••••	••••	★
1984	••	••	•••	•••	••	••	••••	•••	••	
1985	**Abundant harvest of very fine quality**									

Average vintage	Medium vintage	Good vintage	Great vintage	Exceptional vintage
•	••	•••	••••	★

These appreciations are based on averages; the exception proves the rule.

Courtesy of Wines of France.

which the wine was fermented. Exhibit 4 shows a vintage chart for wines of France. Note that the wine qualities do not stay the same in the same year between different areas. Thus in 1982, the reds of Bordeaux were the only ones called "exceptional," while other areas obtained only a "medium" rating.

Fining

Fining is a process that removes certain microscopic solids still remaining suspended in the wine after racking. Fining gives the wine more clarity and brilliance; it also removes materials that might give undesirable properties to the wine. Filtering the wine through very fine filters is one way of doing this, and can be very effective since only pure liquid remains. In fact, filters may remove too much, including materials that give a wine special character and taste. For this reason, a vintner may use a fining agent to remove only some suspended particles.

Some fining agents work by carrying negative electrical charges to attract positively charged suspended particles that are undesirable. Others are gels to which flocculent materials attach themselves, causing the combined mass to sink to the bottom. Egg white, colloidal silica, bentonite, gelatin, and even animal blood are some of the products used for fining. Centrifuging can also be used for such clarification.

Blending

Many wines are blends. **Blending** refers to the use of different grape varieties in making one wine, but more often describes the practice of blending different wines (wines from different years or with different taste characteristics) to create one brand of wine. True champagne (from France) is always made from a blend of wines, sometimes from different growers/wine makers, often from different years, almost always from more than one of three specified grape varieties. Many clarets (dry, red Bordeaux wines) are the result of wines purchased at different wineries by *négociants* (wine merchants) and blended by them for a consistent taste.

Traditionally, American wines are blends of different grape varieties. U.S. regulations allow wines to be labeled as a varietal with up to 25 percent from other grapes. (However, the best varietals are 95 percent to 100 percent of the grape specified.)

Blending allows the bringing together of desirable components in different wines to make a better product; it is seldom a dilution of a good wine by a poorer one. One wine may lack the necessary tannins for good taste and keeping qualities, while another wine may have an excess of tannins and be too astringent. By blending the two together, a vinter may produce a very good wine.

Bottling and Corking

By the spring following the fall harvest, most wines are ready for bottling (the fine red wines being a notable exception). Traditionally, this is the time that wine merchants will visit the wineries, sample the wines, and make their purchases. The casks will then be shipped to the bottler's establishment for bottling. More and more wineries, however, are bottling their own wines.

"Estate bottled," which means bottled on the place, has a certain cachet because the wine grower can usually be expected to protect his or her reputation with a high-quality wine. In France, growers who bottle their own wines have a legal right to put *"mis en bouteille au château"* or *"mis en bouteille au domaine"* on

Exhibit 5   Different Bottle Shapes for Different Regions

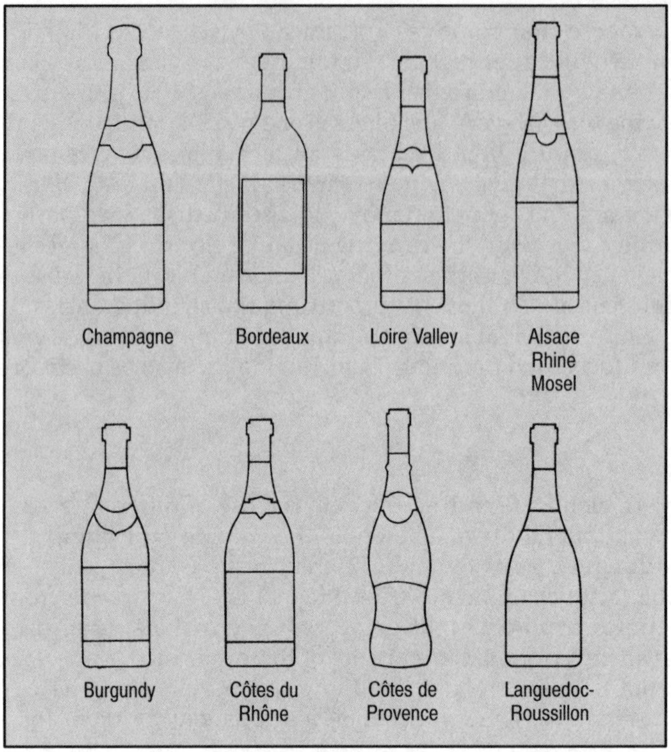

Champagne   Bordeaux   Loire Valley   Alsace Rhine Mosel

Burgundy   Côtes du Rhône   Côtes de Provence   Languedoc-Roussillon

Note that the French Alsace bottle is the same size and shape as that used for the German Rhine and Mosel wines; the Alsace was formerly part of Germany and many of its best wines are made from traditionally German grapes. However, Rhine wine bottles are brown, while Alsace and Mosel bottles are green. (Courtesy of Wines of France.)

their labels. In former years only the very rich vineyards and prominent vintners such as the Rothschild family could afford to have their own bottling plant. Today, portable bottling operations in large vans and trucks can service many less affluent vineyards; the *mis en bouteille* label is no longer synonymous with quality.

Glass is by far the preferred container for holding wine and is often colored to keep the wine from being affected by light. Different shapes are traditionally used for different kinds of wines and especially to signify the wine-growing region (see Exhibit 5). From the bottle shape and color, one can often tell at a glance where the wine comes from and what type it is.

Some sparkling wines of many nations are marketed in standard French bottles and bottle sizes for sparkling wines. Exhibit 6 gives the metric and ounce sizes and the name of the container used for sparkling wines. Most of these bottles must be made of heavy, dark glass and be specially built to withstand the heavy pressures built up by the carbon dioxide gas inside.

Exhibit 6   The Bottle Capacity of Various Champagne Containers

Bottle Name	Bottle Capacity	
	Metric Measure	U.S. Equivalent (oz.)
Nebuchadnezzar	15 L	540.93 (4.23 gal.)
Balthazar	12 L	432.74 (3.38 gal.)
Salmanazar	9 L	324.46 (2.53 gal.)
Methuselah	6 L	216.37 (1.69 gal.)
Rehoboam	4.5 L	156.00 (1.22 gal.)
Jeroboam	3 L	108.19 (3.38 qt.)
Magnum	1.5 L	54.09 (1.69 qt.)
Bottle	750 ml	25.4
Half-bottle	375 ml	12.7
Split	187 ml	6.76

Source: U.S. Bureau of Alcohol, Tobacco, and Firearms.

After bottling, many wines must be left to rest for a time to recover from what is called *bottle sickness*. During this period, the wine stabilizes and regains its full flavor and character.

Cork has been found to be one of the best materials with which to seal a bottle of wine, although some of the new plastic materials do just as well—they probably would be used more if it were not for the fact that cork seems to have some romance attached to it as well as a long tradition in winemaking. Corks often have imprinted on them a logo or some information about the wine such as place of bottling, kind of wine, vintage date, place of production, and so forth.

Special corks must be made for sparkling wines and these must be quite thick with broad bases so the inside pressure does not force them out. In addition, the cork is wired down to the bottle by a helmet called a *muselet*.

Screw-top caps are often used instead of cork or plastic for some wines that do not have to rest on their side, such as sweet dessert and fortified wines. Screw-top caps are sometimes used for sparkling wines. They seem to do quite well.

Maturing

It is often said, "Wines age in the cask, but mature in the bottle." Wine is the only alcoholic product that matures in the bottle. **Maturing** is the term used for aging in the bottle; it is usually associated with complex, full-bodied reds such as a good red Bordeaux or Burgundy, or a wine primarily from a Cabernet Sauvignon or Pinot Noir grape. Different wines mature differently in the bottle. Some mature fast and after that, lose quality. Others can improve up to 50 or more years. However, young white wines can improve with some degree of bottle maturing. Champagne and vintage port are matured almost entirely in the bottle, but tawny port and sherry are fully matured in casks.

A good acid-tannin balance is needed for a wine to continue to improve over a number of years, as one of the finer Bordeaux or Burgundy reds might do. Young reds of good promise start out quite fresh but somewhat harsh and raw in flavor due largely to an overabundance of tannins and acid. They lack smoothness and finesse. Gradually, however, they lose this character and begin to develop a soft mellowness and depth of flavor that begins to approach the characteristics of what might be called "a great wine."

Some wines are not meant to mature for a long time in the bottle. Many German whites lack the staying power to last much over eight years. An ordinary Beaujolais red is a wine that also does not take aging too well. Thus, one must know which wines take age and which ones do not, and to move inventories when the wines in the cellar are beginning to reach a point at which they might begin to go downhill.

Storage

After a shipment of wine is received, it should be carefully stored and allowed to rest. Shipment can cause wines to get "shipping sickness," losing flavor and other quality characteristics. They usually recover after a short rest.

The storage area for wine should not be too dry nor too moist. If too dry, the corks dry out and the wine oxidizes. If too moist, the labels deteriorate and mold may appear. The temperature should be about 55°F (12.8°C) for reds and slightly lower for whites, if possible. Where both reds and whites are stored together 50°F (10°C) should be ideal. Temperatures above 65°F (18°C) can be harmful to wines as are widely and frequently fluctuating temperatures. A steady, cool temperature is best.

The storage area should be lit only when one needs to see. Light is harmful to wine. This is the reason that many wines are put into green, brown, or other colored glass bottles.

Most table wines should be stored on their sides so the wine is always against the cork, preventing it from drying out. Fortified and sparkling wines do not have to be stored on their sides, although some feel sparkling wines have less chance of a dry cork if stored on their sides.

Once stored, a wine should be moved as little as possible. Remove bottles carefully and avoid shaking them. Some wines are best moved some time before service and allowed to rest. One needs to be aware that wine is fragile and must receive proper care to be a good product.

Making Champagne

By law, wine labeled "Champagne" can only come from the triangle formed by the Marne region, Montagne de Reims, and Côte des Blancs. Other laws have been established to strictly control the industry, such as:

- Vineyards that can produce the grapes

- Kinds of grapes

- Growing and pruning methods

- Sugar content of the grapes

- Yield per **hectare**

- Methods of pressing, fermentation, and aging

These controls (and a host of others) have brought about a stable industry, known for its high quality product.

It is of the essence of champagne that it is a blend of wines from many growers. Thus, a considerable quantity of champagne is produced by ***Négociant-Manipulants,*** firms that purchase wines from growers or cooperatives. The label may note this with the letters "*NM*." Other labels may show the following as the producer:

RM	*Récoltant-Manipulant* (vine grower)
CM	*Co-operative de Manipulation* (cooperative)
RC	*Récoltant-Cooperateur* (cooperative for a grower)
SR	*Société de Récoltants* (family-owned firm)
MA	*Marque d'Acheteur* (private brand)

Only three grape varieties can be used to make champagne: the Chardonnay, a white, giving lightness, elegance, and finesse; the Pinot Noir (red), giving body, strength, and fullness of flavor; and the Pinot Meunier (red), giving freshness and youth. If the champagne is made from all white (Chardonnay) grapes, it is called *blanc de blancs* (literally, "white from white"); if it is made from all black (red) grapes (with the skins removed before fermentation), it is called *blanc de noir* (literally, "*white from black*").

The traditional process of making champagne is called *méthode champenoise* (champagne method); the label will often read "**fermented in this bottle**." This method is widely practiced for the making of the highest quality sparkling wines. However, French champagne labels do not carry the designation *méthode champenoise* because, in order to be called "champagne," the wine *must* be made by that method. Only sparkling wines made outside the Champagne region will note the method on the label.

By international law, only France can use the designation "champagne." Sparkling wines produced in the United States, for instance (whether made by the champagne method or not), must be labeled "sparkling" or state specific origin as in "American," "New York State," or "California Champagne." In Germany, sparkling wines are called *Schaumwein, Qualitäts Schaumwein,* or *Sekt* (*Prädikat Sekt* or *Deutscher Sekt*) with different requirements for each classification; in Italy, *spumante*; in Spain, *cava*; in Portugal, *espumante*. In France, sparkling wines produced outside the Champagne region are called *vin mousseux* (foamy) or *pétillant* (crackling—a semi-sparkling wine produced naturally with the malolactic secondary fermentation).

In the spring after the first fermentation, the most important step occurs—the blending of wines in what is known as the *cuvée* for the re-fermentation process which produces the characteristic champagne bubbles. The various wines which will be blended are tasted to judge their flavor and other quality characteristics; as many as 30 or more different wines may be blended to create the desired taste. Blending formulas are carefully guarded secrets, since this is what distinguishes one champagne from others.

The cuvée is then bottled; yeast and some sugar is added and the bottle is plugged with a strong cap. This step in the process is called *le tirage*.

The bottles are now stored in cool (50° to 55°F or 10° to 13°C) chalk caves to slowly ferment, a process called *prise de mousse* (the making of foam). During this second fermentation, more alcohol is made along with carbon dioxide gas which, trapped by the bottle, is forced into the wine. The pressure that builds up is usually 110 psi (pounds per square inch) or 7 1/2 atmospheres. This is the gas that forms the bubbles or sparkle, giving the wine its effervescence. A properly made champagne has fine bubbles that last a long time.

During this second fermentation, the bottles are stored in slanting A-shaped frames called *les pupitres* with the bottle necks down so the yeast and other sediment collect there. To encourage this collection of sediment, a process called *remuage* occurs—professionals (*remueurs*) grab the base of each bottle, giving it a slight shake and turn. Gradually this action causes a plug of sediment to form in the neck of the bottle, so it can be removed later in the *dégorgement* process. Today, *remuage* can be done mechanically by large machines processing thousands of bottles at a time.

As many as three years may be required for this second fermentation, at the end of which time the bottles are brought in from the caves and placed head down into a cold brine (usually propylene glycol) that freezes the sediment in the neck of the bottle to the cork. Then, with a quick motion, an expert removes the cork along with its plug and the clear wine is left in the bottle. This step is called *dégorgement*. The lost volume is now made up with additional wine, sugar and, in some cases, brandy. This last addition is called *le dosage*.

The amount of sugar added in the *dosage* determines the relative dryness or sweetness of the wine. Depending upon the amount of residual sugar, champagne labels indicate:

Extra-brut	Driest	0 to 6 grams of sugar/liter
Brut	Less dry	under 15 grams of sugar/liter
Extra-dry	Some dryness	12 to 20 grams of sugar/liter
Sec	Slight sweetness	17 to 35 grams of sugar/liter
Demi-sec	Sweet	35 to 50 grams of sugar/liter
Doux	Very sweet	over 50 grams of sugar/liter

The wine is quickly corked after *dégorgement*, a wire cage called an *agraffe* (or *muselet*) put over the cork to hold it in the bottle, and foil placed over both. This whole process is called dressing. The bottled champagne is then put into chalk caves to age. From one to five years of aging is required, depending on the quality of wine, but producers usually exceed this requirement. The following summarizes the aging periods:

	Required Aging	Usual Aging
Non-vintage	1 year	3 years
Vintage	3 years	5 years
Prestige Cuvée		8–9 years

Non-vintage Champagne is the most common and usually least expensive champagne. It is made by blending several vintages of champagne, although no vintage date appears on the bottle. Vintage champagne is made with grapes of a single vintage year and is typically considered a higher quality than a non-vintage champagne. Prestige Cuvée is a blend of grapes from the best vineyards in a good year; it is the finest of champagnes and will cost more because of this quality difference.

Occasionally, a vintage champagne will have the letters *"RD"* (*Récemment Dégorgé* or "Recently Disgorged") on the label. This means the wine has aged in contact with its yeast deposits longer than usual (gaining additional flavor) and the *dégorgement* takes place shortly before the wine is sold, ensuring freshness.

A "champagne" made in the United States (or a *Sekt* from Germany) may have on the label **"fermented in the bottle"** (not "in *this* bottle") or "Bottle Fermented," which indicates it is made by the transfer process and not by the traditional *champenoise* method. In the transfer process, the second fermentation takes place "in the bottle" as the label says, but the sparkling wine is then transferred to a vat under pressure for settling, clarifying, and fining, then returned under pressure to the bottles, which have been cleaned and sterilized. A *dosage* is added and the bottle is corked.

Another method of making a sparkling wine is called the "Charmat process," the *"cuvée closé"* process, or "bulk fermentation." The still wine is put into a pressurized tank with sugar and yeast to start the second fermentation. After several weeks of second fermentation, the wine is pumped under pressure into another tank where it is clarified. The *dosage* is then added and the wine is bottled and corked. One of the advantages of the Charmat process, according to some tastes, is that the resulting product has a fresher grape flavor. The Italians use this method almost exclusively for the making of *spumante*. Since this method eliminates a lot of highly professional labor, the wine is less costly. However, the bubbles of carbon dioxide are not as fine nor do they last as long as with the traditional method.

Another method of making a sparkling wine is to carbonate a still wine by forcing carbon dioxide into the wine under pressure. Such a wine is usually lowest in cost and quality. The bubbles are usually coarse and come out of the wine rapidly, giving a flat wine.

Taste Talk

To some people, the language of taste associated with wine is a confusing and seemingly endless list of highly subjective, ambiguous words sprinkled with occasional scientific-sounding terms:

- Acidic
- Balanced
- Bouquet
- Buttery
- Chewy
- Herbaceous
- Oaky
- Tannic

The difficulty of describing the taste of wine arises from the deeper difficulty of language to communicate sensations. This more fundamental difficulty is compounded by the fact that our sense of taste is often dominated by our sense of smell. In fact, most of what we experience as taste is actually the result of our sense of smell. For proof, simply recall how your favorite foods tasted when you had a serious cold. The truth of the matter is—what you can't smell, you won't taste.

The tongue detects four primary flavors: sweet, sour, bitter, and salty. Every flavor experienced by taste in your mouth can be reduced to a combination of these four components. However, the nose knows no such limitation. You are capable of detecting thousands of scents. Putting these scents into words often feels cumbersome and inadequate to the actual sensation you experience. It's no wonder that taste talk seems, at times, forced and stilted—seemingly appropriate only for the secret society of wine connoisseurs. However, while taste is indeed personal and subjective, it can be communicated. A taste vocabulary has been developed to share sensations of flavors and aromas. The appendix at the end of this chapter provides a glossary of common wine tasting terms. The following sections address the look, smell, and taste wine as well as how judges evaluate the taste of wines.

Look

The appearance of the wine is best viewed by looking at the wine against a plain, white background. Pour the wine into a clear wine glass until it is no more than one-third full and hold the glass by the stem. Holding the glass by the bowl will obstruct your full view of the wine and your fingerprints will dull and blur the color of the wine. Also, as wine connoisseurs know, the heat of your hand on the bowl will change the wine's temperature and affect your evaluation of its taste.

Tilt the glass to an approximate 45 degree angle. This enables you to look down on the wine and evaluate it in terms of clarity and color. The wine will have a deeper color in the middle of the glass than at the rim, but the clarity of the wine will stand out. When light passes through quality wines, they appear brilliant and sharp. **Clarity** is determined by the amount of matter you see floating in the wine and is usually a function of how much or how little the wine was refined during production. Both red and white wines should look clear and bright, never hazy or murky.

The color of a wine may be influenced by a number of factors such as the variety of grape from which the wine is made, growing conditions in the vineyard, wine-making techniques, aging, and maturing in the bottle. In general, white wines darken and red wines lighten with age. Young white wines may be nearly colorless or have a yellowish or greenish tinge to them. As they age, they become more typical with a yellow-straw color and mature as gold or deep gold colors. White wines that appear as amber or brown are likely overaged and poor tasting. Young red wines typically appear purple and age to rich red or ruby red. Red wines with mahogany or brown colors are likely past maturity and poor tasting. Young rosé wines are pink or pinkish red and mature to reddish orange. Amber colored rosé wines are likely poor tasting.

Swirling the wine in the glass will give you an indication of the wine's consistency or viscosity. **Viscosity** indicates levels of sugars and alcohol in wine and may range from thin and watery (low viscosity) to thick or syrupy (high viscosity). When swirled in a wine glass, wines with high viscosity tend to cling to the sides of the glass longer than those with low viscosity—developing "tears" or "legs" that drip back down the sides of the glass. Viscosity is a visual clue to the **body** of the wine which is evaluated when experiencing the texture or weight of the wine in the mouth.

Smell

Swirl wine in the wine glass. This agitation releases the aromas. Close your eyes to concentrate on your sense of smell and smell deeply. You'll find that wine does not always smell like grapes. In fact, the most common scents in wine are floral, fruity, spicy, vegetative, or wood odors. While the fruity aromas come from the grapes, the more complex fragrance, the **bouquet** of a wine, results from the fermentation process, aging techniques, and maturing time in the bottle. Hundreds of aromas have been identified and associated with wines. From smell alone, wine experts can identify not only a wine's type of grape but also the wine-making methods used.

The dominant grape used in a wine has distinct aroma and taste characteristics. For example, Pinot Noir typically smells of red fruits (cherries or strawberries) while Cabernet Sauvignon tends to have darker fruit aromas, like black cherries or plums. Some aromas of a wine are the result of wine-making techniques. For example, some yeasts used during fermentation are selected because of the aromas and flavors they create. Also, the wine-maker's fermentation technique affects aroma. In general, cool fermentations give wines with vibrant, fruity aromas; warmer fermentations produce more spicy and earthy aromas and flavors. In addition, wine aged in new oak barrels will absorb elements from the wood that can add aromas and flavors of vanilla, smoke, toast, coffee, and even chocolate.

Taste

While there are only four distinct flavors that the tongue is capable of tasting (sweet, sour, bitter, and salty), there are many taste sensations that you experience when tasting wine. Entire books have been written on tasting wine and on the factors contributing to the varied taste sensations. A basic, instructive, and easy-to-learn system for understanding the many aspects of wine tasting is offered by oregonwines.com. This organization identifies eight primary factors that contribute to taste sensations of wine.

- Sweetness—the amount of residual sugar in a wine, ranging from low (bone dry) to high (sweet).

- Acidity—the amount of citric, malic, and other acids in a wine, ranging from low (flat) to high (biting). A flat wine with too little acidity makes for a bland, uninspiring, flabby wine; too much acidity produces a predominant tart or sour flavor to the wine.

- Tannins—the amount of phenolic compounds, drawn from the skins and pips of grapes, which impart a sharp, bitter flavor to the wine. Signs of higher tannins content in a wine would be if the wine felt chalky or rough in your mouth or if the wine made your mouth pucker. A wine with too little tannins is said to be weak with little structure. A wine with too much tannins produces a taste similar to over-steeped tea.

- Oak—the influence of compounds from oak barrels used to age the wine. Signs of oakiness would be if, when smelling the wine, you detected any aromas of vanilla, wood, or smoke; and, if when tasting the wine, it imparted a buttery, rich flavor.

- Finish—the length and quality of a wine's aftertaste, ranging from brief to long.

- Complexity—how the wine's sweetness, acidity, tannins, and oak affect the wine's overall flavor, ranging from simple to complex.

- Body—how the wine's components affect the intensity and richness of the wine's overall flavor, ranging from weak to potent. Signs of a full-bodied wine would be a strong, potent, fully-developed flavor.

- Balance—how all the other factors balance out, ranging from unbalanced to well-balanced.

Exhibit 7 presents completed tasting stars for types of wine. These tasting stars graphically display fundamental taste characteristics usual to dry white wine, rosé wine, red wine, and sweet desert wine. The star-like format enables a taster to record taste sensations by scoring each factor on a five-point scale ranging from low (closest to the center of the star) to high (farthest from the center of the star). Connecting the dots creates a visual image of the taste sensations and factors. Tasting stars for individual wines vary from these generic patterns. For example, Exhibit 8 presents a completed set of tasting notes for a specific red wine. Note that, while the overall graphic pattern for this particular Pinot Noir is similar to the generic pattern for red wine, differences exist in terms of several taste factors. Systems like the tasting star format enable wine enthusiasts around the world to create and share tasting notes. Oregonwines.com sponsors an online wine club in which members can post their tasting notes, compare them with others, and review notes on wines they have yet to try.

Judging Wine

The objective in judging a wine is to evaluate its quality. Judging wines relies on experience. As your experience in tasting wines grows, you learn to identify various aromatic and taste components of types of wines and to measure their value.

The experienced judge knows how to identify the various sensations and to properly interpret their meaning. All judges should have specific standards by which they judge a specific wine. Each standard may have different elements appropriate to that wine. These elements are judged and their balance evaluated. If there are variations from the standard, these are recorded in the judge's evaluation and a final judgment obtained.

Exhibit 9 shows wine judges at work. Usually, not more than six wines are judged at one time—more might result in tasting fatigue. Low-alcohol and the most delicate wines are selected for judging first. Water and low-salt crackers or

Exhibit 7   Sample Tasting Stars

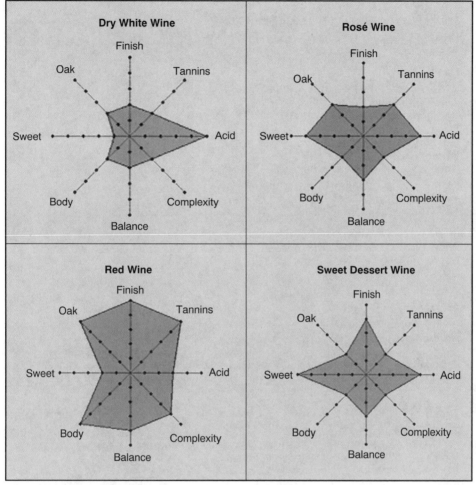

Source: Oregonwines.com. For more tasting information as well as an online tutorial on how to use the star system to develop tasting notes, visit the organization's Internet site at: http://www.oregon wines.com.

bread are sometimes provided to cleanse the palate between judgments. The judging should be in a quiet and well-lighted room. Set a plain, white cloth on the table or surface to be used by the judge, so the wine can be viewed through the glass with the white cloth as backdrop. Use plain, clear, bell-shaped glasses with the top rim smaller than the bowl to help concentrate the bouquet as it rises from the wine. The opening of the glass should be large enough to allow the nose to get into the glass to smell the wine at close quarters. The glass should be large enough to adequately hold the wine and allow it to be swirled.

    The amount of wine poured may vary. Some judges feel a small amount—an ounce or two—is enough, while others may desire more because they feel that they

Exhibit 8 Sample Tasting Notes

Tasting Notes: Winter's Hill 2000 Pinot Noir

Created by	David Anderson
Tasting Date	01/20/2004

Basic Details

Wine Name	Winter's Hill 2000 Pinot Noir
Date Purchased	01/16/2004
Consume By	2005
Price	$18.99
Quantity	1
Winery Name	Winter's Hill Vineyard
Appellation	Willamette Valley
Region	Oregon
Varietal	Pinot Noir
Vintage	2000

Sight

Wine's Color	**Deep Red**
Depth of Color	Deep
Clarity of Color	Crystal
Viscosity	Sheets

Aromas

Aroma Appeal	Neutral
Aroma Categories	- Floral - Spicy
	- Fruity - Woody
Aromas	Aromas include ripe cherry and plum, sweet vanilla and oak, and hints of cinnamon and spice. Very well balanced on the palate. Moderate acids, lingering finish.

Taste

Tasting Star

Sweetness:	Dry
Acidity:	Fresh
Tannins:	Moderately Tannic
Oak:	Oak
Finish:	Lingering
Complexity:	Moderately Complex
Body:	Full-Bodied
Balance:	Well Balanced

Taste Appeal	Attractive
Comments	Very soft, feminine, and subtle. All the qualities of a true Burgunian-style Pinot Noir, but produced in Oregon. Aged 14 months, 2/3 in French Oak, and 1/3 in American Oak. The aging and production imparts a truly soft, gentle bouquet of fruity aromas, gentle flavors, and overall wonderful, subtle, inviting flavor.

Source: Oregonwines.com. For more information, visit the organization's Internet site at http://www.oregonwines.com.

Exhibit 9   Wine Judges at Work

Source: Montreal Passion Vin. For more information, visit the organization's Internet site at: http://www.montrealpassionvin.ca.

are better able to judge the depth of color and also have enough wine to build up a proper aroma in the glass. The wine should be served at a proper temperature.

When tasting the wine, judges will often suck it up with some aggressiveness so there is a spray that pervades the entire mouth. Before swallowing or spitting the wine out, most judges will draw a sharp intake of breath through the mouth over the surface of the wine. This important routine is practiced because the taste buds provide very limited sensations. The taste sensations combined simultaneously with the far more complex odors will offer a more precise record of a wine's "taste." It is not necessary to take a lot of wine to obtain the proper taste sensations. A small amount is adequate. Many judges do not swallow; they spit the wine out after tasting. If the judge consumes some, he or she is doing so to get the throat sensations which can provide a clue to aftertaste.

Some wine experts describe tasting as first an attack, then an evolution or development, and finally a finish. Sweet sensations are evident in the attack, acid and salt in the evolution, and bitter in the finish. In tasting, the judge is looking for a balance between the sweet, the acid, and the bitter components. If they are there in balance, along with proper odor, the wine is apt to be scored high. Variations from what the judge considers a desirable balance can downgrade the wine.

Key Terms

aging—The storage of wines that takes place after fermentation, but before bottling. Allows further chemical reactions with a small amount of air, with suspended particles in the wine, and sometimes with the storage medium itself (as with oak barrels or casks).

anthocyanins—Color pigments in grapes which are not soluble in water but are in alcohol. If grape skins are left to ferment, as the alcohol forms, the anthocyanins dissolve, creating the red color to a wine.

aperitif wine—Wines that are traditionally served before meals as an appetizer or cocktail. They are often fortified and herb-flavored (vermouth, for instance, is both fortified and flavored with herbal ingredients).

acidity—The amount of citric, malic, and other acids in a wine, ranging from low (flat) to high (biting). A flat wine with too little acidity makes for a bland, uninspiring, flabby wine; too much acidity produces a predominant tart or sour flavor to the wine.

blending—The use of different grape varieties in making one wine, but more often describes the practice of blending different wines (wines from different years or with different taste characteristics) to create one brand of wine.

body—The texture or weight of the wine in the mouth; also, how the wine's components affect the intensity and richness of the wine's overall flavor, ranging from weak to potent. Signs of a full-bodied wine would be a strong, potent, fully developed flavor.

bouquet—The complex fragrance of a wine resulting from the fermentation process, aging techniques, and maturing time in the bottle.

champagne method—The original method of making champagne, *méthode champenoise*, in which the second fermentation takes place in the bottle in which it is sold—a laborious and exacting process which accounts for the high price of the best champagne.

carbonic maceration—Uncrushed grapes are vatted in a sealed chamber and fermentation starts. The oxygen is used up and only carbon dioxide now fills the chamber. Without oxygen, the wine produces less acid and a rich, fruity flavor and brilliant red color.

chaptalization—A procedure of adding sugar to grape juice or must prior to or during fermentation to attain the necessary alcohol level. This procedure is often necessary when weather conditions prevent grapes from ripening fully and developing enough natural sugar to convert to the amount of alcohol prescribed (often by law) for certain wines.

Charmat method—Much less expensive than the traditional method of making champagne and other sparkling wines, the second fermentation takes place in a vat and the wine is later filtered and bottled under pressure.

clarity—Determined by the amount of matter you see floating in the wine and is usually a function of how much or how little the wine was refined during production. Both red and white wines should look clear and bright, never hazy or murky.

complexity—How the wine's sweetness, acidity, tannins, and oak affect the wine's overall flavor, ranging from simple to complex.

dessert wines—As the name implies, are meant to be served after dinner with dessert or *as* dessert. Dessert wines are often fortified—the sweet varieties of sherry ("Cream" and "Oloroso," primarily) and port are examples.

fermented in the bottle—The term appearing on a bottle of Champagne or sparkling wine when the transfer process is used; that is, the second fermentation takes place "in the bottle" as the label says, but the sparkling wine is then transferred to a vat under pressure for settling, clarifying, and fining, and then returned under pressure to the original bottles.

fermented in this bottle—The term appearing on a bottle of Champagne or sparkling wine when the traditional champagne method is used; that is, re-fermentation takes place in the bottle in which the Champagne or sparkling wine is sold.

fining—A process that removes certain microscopic solids still remaining suspended in the wine after racking. Fining gives the wine more clarity and brilliance; it also removes materials that might give undesirable properties to the wine.

finish—The length and quality of a wine's aftertaste, ranging from brief to long.

fortified wines—May range in alcohol content from 14 percent to 24 percent by volume. Alcohol—usually in the form of a brandy distilled from wine—is added to a wine during fermentation.

generic wines—Wines made from a blend of wines to resemble a particular wine of an established wine-producing region.

hectare—Pronounced HEHK-tahr and abbreviated as ha. A unit of surface or land equal to 10,000 square meters or 2.471 acres.

lees—The coarse sediment (dead yeast cells and small grape particles) that accumulates during fermentation and aging.

oak—The influence of compounds from oak barrels used to age the wine. Signs of oakiness would be if, when smelling the wine, you detected any aromas of vanilla, wood, or smoke; and if, when tasting the wine, it imparted a buttery, rich flavor.

malolactic fermentation—Sometimes called "secondary fermentation;" can easily occur in the fermentation process. No alcohol is actually produced. This is a bacterial change that converts harsh malic acids into lactic (milk-like) acids and carbon dioxide. Wines undergoing this process become softer and smoother.

maturing—The term used for aging in the bottle; usually associated with complex, full-bodied reds such as a good red Bordeaux or Burgundy, or a wine primarily from a Cabernet Sauvignon or Pinot Noir grape.

must—The juice of freshly crushed grapes that will be fermented into wine; can include pulp, skins, and seeds.

natural wines—The product of grape fermentation without the addition of alcohol or sugar (beyond a small amount allowed for certain wines under specified conditions).

négociant-manipulants—Firms that produce wines from growers or cooperatives, usually blending them for consistency and selling the blend under their own label.

racking—The process of removing the wine from the sediment (lees) at the bottom of a cask or barrel and pouring it into another container, leaving the lees behind.

sulfur dioxide—A sulfur compound widely used in the making of wine to kill the wild yeasts present on the skins of grapes and thus prevent premature and uncontrolled fermentation; it is also used to prevent oxidation and rarely used to stop fermentation.

sweetness—The amount of residual sugar in a wine, ranging from low (bone dry) to high (sweet).

tannins—Phenolic compounds, drawn from the skins and pips of grapes, which impart a sharp, bitter flavor to the wine. A wine with too little tannins is said to be weak with little structure. A wine with too much tannins produces a taste similar to over-steeped tea.

terroir—A French term that refers to the growing environment of a specific area, the total vineyard environment, including the soil and its makeup, chemical qualities, the climate, amount of sun, moisture conditions, and so on.

varietal wine—A wine produced from a single grape variety.

viniculture—The study or science of making wines.

vintage year—The year in which the wine was fermented.

viscosity—Indicates levels of sugars and alcohol in wine and may range from thin and watery (low viscosity) to thick or syrupy (high viscosity).

viticulture—The cultivation of grapevines, or the study of grapes.

Review Questions

1. How are varietal wines different from generic wines?

2. How are table wines different from fortified wines?

3. What roles do tannins and anthocyanins play in the production of red wine?

4. What is "must?"

5. How does malolactic fermentation differ from carbonic maceration?

6. Why are wines aged?

7. How does the Champagne-making technique of *méthode champenoise* differ from the Charmat process?

8. What factors influence the color of a wine?

9. What produces a wine's bouquet?

10. What are tasting notes and how are they used?

Internet Sites

For more information, visit the following Internet sites. Remember that Internet addresses can change without notice. If the site is no longer there, you can use a search engine to look for additional sites. Many alcohol-related sites require users to be of legal drinking age to enter.

Grape Varieties and Varietal Wines

Grapes cultivated in France www.terroir-france.com/wine/grapes.htm and click on any of the grapes listed.

Grapes cultivated in Germany www.deutscheweine.de and click on any of the grapes listed.

Grape Varieties Explained www.grape-varieties.com/index.html

Wine Grape Varieties www.cellarnotes.net/key_grape_varieties.html

Wine Spectator—Varietal Characteristics www.winespectator.com/Wine/Wine_Basics/Wine_Basics_Template/0,1199,1004,00.html

Wine Tidbits—Answers Wine Questions You Never Wanted to Ask www.uncork.com.au/tidbits1.htm

Wine Production

Century Wine www.centurywine.8m.com/winemaking.html

French Wines www.frenchwinesfood.com

About.com wine.about.com/library/bl_making.htm

Terroir France www.terroir-france.com/wine/making.htm

Rutherford Ranch Vineyards—Art of Making Wine www.rutherfordranch.com/presentation/01artofwine.htm

Beringer Vineyards—Wine Making 101 www.beringer.com/wines/winemaking101.jsp

Duckhorn Vineyards—The Business Operations of a Winery www.duckhorn.com/

Wineries

The Wine Guide by Travel Envoy www.travelenvoy.com/wine/wineries.htm

Vine2Wine.com vine2wine.com/Wineries.htm

WineXplore.com www.winexplorer.com/wineries/index.html

Wine Spectator www.winespectator.com/Wine/Wineries/Wineries_Search_Page/0,1161,,00.html

Champagne

A Review of *méthode champenoise* Production, Virginia Polytechnic Institute and State University: www.ext.vt.edu/pubs/viticulture/463-017/463-017.html#L6

Champagne Magic
www.champagnemagic.com/index.htm

Taste Talk

Terroir France—Wine and Aroma
www.terroir-france.com/wine/aromas.htm

Bodegas Piedemonte Winery—Short Wine Tasting Course
www.piedemonte.com

Wine Society of Texas
www.winesocietyoftexas.org/virtual_classroom

Oregonwines.com
oregonwines.com

Decanter Magazine
www.decnater.com

Chapter Appendix
Glossary of Common Wine Tasting Terms

Acid	Tart, citric, or sour taste. In right amount, acid gives wine a longevity and balance; if lacking, wine is said to be flabby or dull.
Aftertaste	Related to the term finish, these are flavors that linger after the wine is tasted and may be described as nonexistent, harsh, hot, short, lingering, soft, or smooth.
Aroma	Smell or odor from a wine that may be described in many ways: appley, chocolately, fresh, fruity, tired, and so on.
Aromatic	Wines with markedly flowery, spicy, or grapy character.
Assertive	Forward, upfront, the wine comes across with a definite flavor and aroma.
Attractive	A pleasant wine to drink usually because of its lighter, fresh style.
Balanced	The wine's various flavors are in correct proportion to give a good flavor; if not balanced, a wine may be described as harsh (too much acid or tannin) or flat (lacking in sufficient flavor and aroma qualities), acidic (too much acid), and so on.
Barnyard	The disagreeable odor of a barnyard.
Bite	Zest or sharpness of flavor from the bitterness of tannins or the intensity of fairly strong acid. If not excessive, acceptable in a wine rich in body, flavor and aroma.

Bitter	One of the four basic tastes; unlike acid which is first felt on the tip of the tongue and saltiness or sweetness which are fully felt in the middle of the tongue, bitterness is tasted in the back of the tongue and even in the first part of the throat. Bitterness in young wines is gradually lost as their tannins precipitate or change with aging.
Body	The feel or weight of the wine in the mouth, described perhaps as heavy, light, weak-in-body, full-bodied, and so on.
Bouquet	The combined aroma or smell of the wine.
Brilliant	A clear wine; not murky or clouded.
Buttery	A wine possessing the smooth flavor associated with butter.
Chewy	So heavy in body as to give the feel that the wine can be chewed; given largely by tannins in the wine.
Character	The wine has distinctive flavor and aroma qualities so that it stands out from other wines.
Corky	Wine tainted by a defective cork giving the wine a musty, or sulfur-like flavor.
Crisp	A wine with a pleasant, fresh, tart flavor.
Closed	A wine that does not release its character well, or a wine that has good flavor but lacks aroma or vice versa.
Clarity	Wines should be clear; see brilliant.
Complete	A balanced wine with a good aftertaste.
Complex	Excellent balance in a wine with many different positive qualities often with compounded flavors.
Concentrated	A wine that has a lot of flavor and aroma that are not spread out.
Delicate	A lightly flavored wine of good quality; often should be consumed after opening the bottle; otherwise much of the flavor will be lost.
Dense	Concentrated aromas and flavors desirable in young wines.
Depth	A wine with layers of aroma and flavor; concentrated aroma and flavors can be described as deep, while a wine lacking depth might be described as weak or shallow.
Developed	A wine that has achieved all of its flavor and aroma qualities and now is considered mature.
Earthy	Describes a desirable clean, earthy smelling and tasting wine often found in red wines, but can also describe the undesirable flavors associated with poorly made wine.
Elegant	A fine wine of excellent balance; a wine of superior qualities.
Empty	Lacking flavor and interest.

Fading	A wine that has "gone over the hill," or that has reached full development and is now losing some of its desirable qualities.
Finish	Wine flavor that lingers after tasting the wine; a long aftertaste usually raises the wine's quality evaluation.
Flabby	Lacking in acidity.
Flinty	A sharp, metallic taste that has the odor of flint striking steel, sometimes found in white wines.
Foxy	A flavor that makes one think of a fox's cage; a wild flavor. See grapey.
Fruity	A fresh, sweetish odor and flavor associated with fruit; some wines will be described as having apple, or cherry, or strawberry, or raspberry, or melon, or a combination of fruit flavors like a lemon-melon flavor.
Fullness	The feel, or weight of a wine in the mouth.
Green	The aroma and flavor of somewhat tart, unripe fruit; desirable in some wines such as those made from the Reisling grape, but an objectionable factor in others.
Grapey	The strong grape flavor found in native American grapes; a flavor related to what is often called foxy, but not resembling it.
Heady	Heavy alcohol odor or flavor.
Herbaceous	The flavor of vegetables, herbs, or spices caused by the development of aldehydes in fermentation and aging.
Legs	Small rivulets that form on the sides of the glass when the wine is swirled; caused by the development of glycerin in the wine as it ferments or ages; is considered a mark of quality because it gives the wine smoothness.
Length	The time taste and aroma sensations last after tasting a wine.
Mouthfeel	The feel of wine in the mouth; related to body and other mouth sensations.
Murky	Not clear, clouded.
Musty	Moldy odor.
Neutral	No outstanding characteristics; a wine that might be described as indifferent.
Nose	The aroma or smell of a wine.
Oak or Oaky	The flavor of oak often derived from aging in oak barrels.
Oxidized	A wine that has gone stale or lost some of its flavor from oxidation.
Palate	The combined factors of flavor and aroma used in tasting.

Peppery	The flavor of pepper often found in the Alsace wine Gewurztraminer; sharper than spicy.
Perfumed	High in delicate fruity odors.
Potent	A wine of strong, intense qualities.
Robust	A full-bodied wine with concentrated, vigorous flavors and aromas.
Round	Having good balance in flavor, aroma, and body.
Short	Lacking in aftertaste.
Simple	A rather ordinary wine whose flavor and aroma qualities are not especially notable and those it has do not make a deep impression. Usually found in young wines.
Smoky	Subtle wood smoke odor resulting frequently from the charred oak barrels used in aging, but in other wines can be caused by the development of the flavor in fermentation and aging; not necessarily an undesirable characteristic.
Soft	A well-rounded wine with mature tannis and little evidence of acidity. Also, could describe a wine lacking in distinctive body, acid, tannins (bitterness), and alcoholic content; and sometimes a wine lacking distinctive characteristics but that retains some smoothness to the palate.
Spicy	Flavors of spice such as anise, bay, cloves, marjoram, mint, pepper, thyme or others often found in wines of some complexity.
Texture	Describes dense, full-bodied wines that give a mouth-filling impression making them seem almost thick.
Thin	Lacking in body, aroma, and flavor.
Tannic	A dry bitterness caused by the presence of tannins; an excessive amount can be caused by over-pressing of grape stems and seeds. Tannin is desirable in wine to help in aging, to give flavor fullness, and to act as a preservative.
Toasty	A flavor found in some white wines brought about by the extraction of wood flavors from barrels used in the wine's making.
Velvety	Smooth, silky mouthfeel and richness obtained in tasting the wine; a good supply of glycerin can be a factor in causing it.

Chapter 9 Outline

French Wine Classification System
    Appellation Contrôlée (AC)
    Vin Délimités de Qualité Supérieure
      (VDQS)
    Vin de Pays
    Vin de Table
Labeling Regulations
Major Wine-Producing Areas
    Champagne
    Alsace
    Loire
    Burgundy
    Bordeaux
    Côtes du Rhône

Competencies

1. Explain the French wine classification system. (pp. 259–263)

2. Define items commonly found on the labels of French wine bottles. (pp. 263–265)

3. Identify the major wine-producing areas of France and the types of wine each produces. (pp. 265–277)

9

Wines of France

W<small>HILE THE NATION OF FRANCE</small> is not the world's largest wine producer, it is perhaps the most important. France leads in the variety of wines produced and has more wines of international reputation than any other nation. It has led the world in the promotion of wine and has marketed its wines in more countries than any other. France was the first nation to classify vineyards and separate wines into various quality ratings, all controlled by a national authority. This system has been copied by a majority of the world's wine-growing nations.

The concept of *terroir* forms the basis for the laws and regulations governing the French wine industry. *Terroir* is a French term that refers to the growing environment of a specific area, the total vineyard environment, including the soil and its makeup, chemical qualities, the climate, amount of sun, moisture conditions, and so on. The physical attributes of soil—texture, porosity, drainage, and depth—are probably more important to growing than the chemical content. Oddly, good wine grapes do not prosper in a rich, loamy soil. Such soil holds too much moisture and nutrients and, consequently, the roots of the vine don't have to develop in their search for moisture. A gravelly or rocky soil provides good drainage, causing vine roots to "chase" after moisture during dry periods. This process ultimately gives the vine the stable root support needed for good grape production. When the French use the term *"gout de terroir"* (taste of the earth), they mean that the terroir of the land on which the grapes were grown is passed on to the grapes grown there.

Hundreds (perhaps thousands) of books have been written on wines of France. How much do you need to know about French wines? Probably at least enough to answer the types of questions that guests may have, such as:

- "How do I know this bottle contains quality French wine?"

- "I bought a bottle of French wine labeled *vin de pays*. Is it any good?"

- "Don't I get the highest quality French wine when the bottle is labeled *mis en bouteille au château*?"

- "Are all Burgundy wines red?"

- "Is Chablis a city in France or just the name of a type of wine?"

- "Why don't you carry a white Beaujolais?"

- "What's the correct pronunciation of Côtes du Rhône?"

The topics covered in this chapter will help you answer these questions and others as well. Also, this chapter provides a foundation for you to build upon as you explore French wines on your own.

Exhibit 1   French Wine Classifications

AC (or AOC)

Appellation d'Origine Contrôlée
(ah-pehl-lah-SYAW*N* daw-ree-JEEN kawn-troh-LAY)

> A wine with this term on the label belongs to the highest classification level of French wines and is strictly regulated by an agency of the French government.

VDQS

Vin Délimité de Qualité Supérieure
(va*n* deh-lee-mee-TAY duh kah-lee-TAY soo-peh)

> A wine with this term on the label belongs to the second-highest level of French wines and indicates a "delimited wine of superior quality." These wines are controlled by regulations similar to AC wines, but they are not as demanding.

vin de pays

(va*n* deu pay-YEE)

> "Country wine" is the third category of French wine after AC and VDQS. The classification applies to simple wines found throughout the country. These wines must also conform to regulations that may include production area, grape variety, yield, and alcohol content.

vin de table

(va*n* deu TAH-bl)

> The lowest category of French wine. Most of these wines simply have the name of the producer on them, and may contain any wine from anywhere.

For any given wine from a specific region, regulations may cover:

- Production area
- Grape variety
- Viticulture standards
- Yield
- Production methods
- Bottling
- Alcohol content
- Taste analysis

For audio pronunciations of key wine terms, visit the audio wine dictionary at www.strat splace.com or at www.wineloverspage.com/lexicon/.

French Wine Classification System

The laws passed in the 1930s in France to regulate its alcoholic beverage industry were given to the *Institut National des Appellations d'Origine* (INAO) for administration. The laws are known under the collective name *Appellation d'Origine Contrôlée*, and the short form stands for ***appellation contrôlée***, which means, literally, "name controlled." Exhibit 1 summarizes the classification system for French wines.

Appellation Contrôlée (AC)

Appellation contrôlée (AC or AOC) on a label means that the wine is among the highest classification of French wines and that whatever appears on the label is strictly regulated by the INAO. Requirements for AC labeling are complex and standards may differ from one major wine region to the next. Although the Appellation d'Origine Contrôlée does not guarantee the quality of a particular wine, it does dictate demanding quality controls that must be met in order for a wine to achieve AC status within the classification system. One or more of the quality control standards listed below must be met to receive the coveted AC label.

Production area. Geography is fundamental to AC classification. The most important geographic areas are still the designated *cru* or growth areas established in 1855. However, since that time the INAO has raised some wines to a higher *cru* rank while dropping others. It has also added some wines while eliminating others. Where the wine comes from is the main point of *appellation d'origine contrôlée*: the more narrowly defined the origin of the wine, the higher the quality is a good "rule of thumb" in selecting quality wines (but is far from foolproof).

- The most precise name in indicating location is the name of a château or vineyard. Thus, a wine bearing the label *Château Margaux* accompanied by the term *appellation contrôlée* means that the grapes were grown at that specific location and the wine is bottled there.

- Labels can state location as that of a defined growing district such as *Appellation Pomerol Contrôlée*. Pomerol is a small area in the Bordeaux region which has a limited number of recognized high-quality vineyards; in any given year such a wine *might* be better than that from a specific château but should definitely be better than the next, broader designation.

- A broader area would be a limited general growing area defined by AC within a wine region such as Bordeaux, and the designation on the label might be *Appellation Bordeaux Supérieur Contrôlée* or *Appellation Premierès Côtes de Bordeaux Contrôlée*. In Burgundy, such a designation might be *Beaujolais Villages*, which includes some 39 villages and is more likely than not to indicate indifferent quality in comparison to a wine from a single town or village.

- The least knowledge of where the grapes were grown and wine was produced under an AC classification is indicated by a label which identifies the wine only by the major wine region it comes from, such as Bordeaux (generally with the *appellation contrôlée* designation directly underneath). Some of these wines can be undistinguished or even poor in quality. However, a number of excellent wines come under this last category. Champagne, for instance, is made from grapes grown anywhere in the Champagne region.

Grape variety. Certain wines can be made only from specific grapes. Thus champagne can be made only from a mixture of Pinot Noir, Pinot Meunier, and Chardonnay grapes. The best Burgundy reds must come from a Pinot Noir, a Beaujolais from the Gamay grape, and a Chablis from the Chardonnay.

Viticulture standards. The grapes must be grown in a manner specified by the law. Only certain kinds of fertilizers and pesticides can be used. Irrigation is prohibited in the *cru* areas. The number of vines per **hectare** (2.471 acres), pruning, and time of harvest are controlled. In fact, very little from the planting of the grapes to the harvest and care of the vines in the winter is not regulated.

Yield. Only a given amount of wine per hectare can be produced in various locations. In most AC areas, the limit is 40 **hectoliters** (4,000 liters) per hectare. However, a complicated system of annual re-assessment can allow considerably more production in certain areas. Yield is most strictly controlled in the *Grand Cru* areas and in the Sauternes area; the yield is limited to 25 hectoliters per hectare for AC designated wines. These restrictions on the amount of wine produced per hectare are rigidly enforced.

Production methods. The manner in which the wine is made is also strictly controlled. Thus, Champagne must be made in a specified manner and labeled accordingly. Sauternes must come from a grape that has developed the **noble rot**, a mold infecting certain grapes in late fall resulting in naturally sweet wines. Fermenting procedures are precisely prescribed for different kinds of wine and for different regions. Such things as adding or taking away acidity depending on how ripe the grapes are at harvest are also controlled.

Bottling. Some appellations, like Alsace and Champagne, stipulate that bottling must take place in the region of production. Even the kind and shape of the bottle may be regulated. Thus, wine from Alsace must be bottled in Alsace and bottled in tall, fluted, greenish glass bottles.

Alcohol content. The minimum alcohol content by volume for different kinds of wine is strictly controlled and specified on the label. Certain wines cannot be made unless the grapes contain at harvest sufficient sugar to produce wine of a specified alcohol content. Some addition of sugar before fermentation to increase alcohol content (**chaptalization**) is permitted, but is strictly regulated. Thus, a chablis can be chaptalized but not above a specified naturally fermented alcohol content.

Taste Analysis. All appellation wines since 1979 have to be submitted to a tasting panel which rejects wines it considers faulty or unrepresentative of the "typical" or historic standard of a particular AC designation. Appellation growers/bottlers can present samples twice and if they fail both times, they lose their right to AC designation for that year. (In a "bad" year, many great châteaux will voluntarily forgo bottling part or all of that year's crop under their AC label, opting instead to sell their grapes to bottlers who will use them in the production of generic or other blended wines.)

Vins Délimités de Qualité Supérieure (VDQS)

In 1945, France instituted a second rank of appellations under the designation *Vins Délimités de Qualité Supérieure* (**VDQS**)—literally, "wines from a specifically defined region of superior quality." While generally ranked below AC wines in quality and consistency of quality, some VDQS wines are superior to some AC wines. Sometimes the reason for a particular wine not getting an AC rating is that it is made from the wrong grape in the right place. It is possible, over time, for a particular VDQS wine to move up to AC ranking or vice versa; some consider VDQS as a "training ground" for AC status.

Vin de Pays

The label *vin de pays* means, literally, "country wine" and such wines must come from the region of production claimed; one or more classic grape varieties are required; yield is controlled and alcohol levels prescribed and on the label. Again, it is possible for a wine in this group to move up or down in rank. This category was created by the government in order to recognize the quality of large, anonymous areas of table wine production and give them some geographical identity. *Vins de pays* do have AC-type limits but are the laxest of the three major designations. There are three levels of *vin de pays*:

- *Vins de Pays Régionaux*—Regional classification covering wide areas, such as the Loire valley

- *Vins de Pays Départementaux*—Classification restricted to smaller areas

- *Vins de Pays de Zone*—Classification covers wines from single communes or small areas within a *département*

Vin de Table

Below the *vin de pays* designation is the *vin de table* or *vin ordinaire* (table or ordinary wines). These very basic wines are virtually unregulated by the government. The grapes may come from anywhere in France and "France" is listed on the label as the only geographic appellation. By law, a grape name or vintage cannot appear on a *vin de table* label.

Labeling Regulations

Exhibit 2 illustrates how to read a French wine label. Regulations govern the labeling of French wines. These regulations specify items that are compulsory, optional, and prohibited. Compulsory label items for a French AC wine include:

- Country of origin

- Appellation of origin

- Quality standard

- Name and address of producer/brand owner

- Bottle content

- Alcohol content

- The term "wine" (for some regions)

- Authenticity seal

Exhibit 2 How to Read a French Wine Label

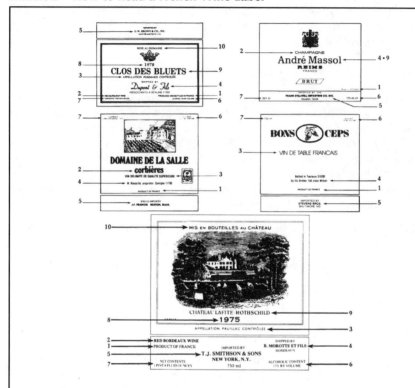

Courtesy of Wines of France.

How to Read a Wine Label

The French government has very strict labeling rules to govern the information given on a bottle of wine.

These sample labels are number coded to show you the information that, by law, must be included on a label:

1. The wine is a product of France.
2. The region in which the wine was produced—for example, Burgundy, Bordeaux, Champagne.
3. The appellation for which the wine qualifies: A.O.C. (Appellation d'Origine Contrôlée), V.D.Q.S. (Vins Délimités de Qualité Supérieure), Vin de Pays, or Vin de Table.

4. The name and address of the shipper, except in the case of Champagne where, usually, the Champagne house (brand) is also the shipper.
5. The name and address of the importer.
6. The alcoholic percentage by volume.
7. The net contents of the bottle.

The following is optional information which may appear on the label:

8. Vintage.
9. Brand name or château name.
10. "Estate bottled," "Château bottled," or similar phrase.

Optional items include: grape variety, vintage, name of the vineyard, the term "Domain," and terms such as "dry," "medium dry," or "sweet." Prohibited items include: the term "wine" (for some regions), sulfites or other additives, and commentaries such as analysis, tasting notes, or approvals. Other labeling regulations apply to the bottler, the vintage, and to the brand or château name.

There are four kinds of bottlers in France. One is a vineyard of no special note bottling its own wines. Another kind is a group of growers and/or vintners (*caves coopératives*) that band together to bottle and even ship their wine. A third is known as a *négociant* or *négociant-éleveur* (merchant or merchant-breeder). The *négociant-éleveur* creates the wine by blending different wines for a distinctive and consistent taste which he or she will offer under the firm's label. He or she may also age the wine before bottling it. Many Bordeaux reds are bottled this way and may carry on the label *mis en bouteille dans nos chais* (put into the bottle in our place or warehouse) or *mis en bouteille par négociant* (bottled by the merchant or firm). These wines can be quite good, but the only guarantee of quality is a merchant's long-standing reputation. The fourth kind of bottler is one who wants the world to know that the wine was produced and bottled on the place where grapes were grown. The bottle will usually state ***mis en bouteille au château***, (bottled at the manor house), ***mis en bouteille au domaine*** (put into the bottle at the place), or ***mis en bouteille à la propriété*** (put into the bottle at the property). Many wine drinkers, especially Americans, have taken the *mis en bouteille au château* as a sign of quality. It's not. Since the advent of mobile bottling "plants" (semi-sterile bottling facilities in large vans or lorries) in the 1960s, many small and undistinguished growers can claim that their wine was bottled at their château or place.

Although the vintage year is optional as far as labeling is concerned, it is a crucial factor when considering wine purchases. It is particularly crucial for the high-quality red Bordeaux wines and some of finer red Burgundies made from the Pinot Noir grape. Such wines mature in the bottle; some are not ready to drink until 7 to 12 years after bottling. Thus, the vintage year can be a decisive purchasing factor.

Although the brand or château name is legally optional, one or the other will always be present on French wine labels.

Major Wine-Producing Areas

Wine is produced in all of France except in its most northern part. Exhibit 3 maps some wine-producing areas and Exhibit 4 offers a pronunciation guide to the major wine-producing areas discussed in this chapter. There are other areas where wines of distinction are produced, but those featured stand out because of the amount and the quality of the wine produced. Each wine-producing region specializes in the production of different types of wines and flavors. Exhibit 5 charts some of the major French areas and lists the types of wines each produces.

Champagne

Champagne is one of France's most famous and finest wines. Champagne was first made at the end of the 17th century by a monk named Dom Perignon and others. It is the wine of love, weddings, births and birthdays, ship christenings, dreams, feasts, and festivals.

By law, wine labeled "Champagne" can only come from the triangle formed by the Marne region, Montagne de Reims, and Côte des Blancs (see Exhibit 6).

Exhibit 3   Major Wine-Producing Areas of France

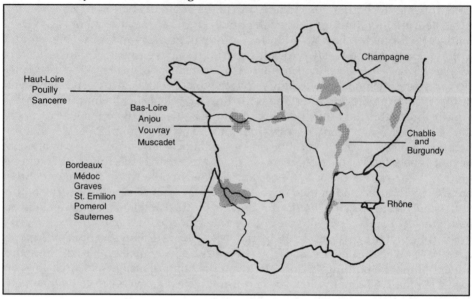

Exhibit 4   Pronunciation Guide—Major French Wine-Producing Areas

Champagne (shah*m*-PAH-nyuh)

Alsace (al-SASS)

Loire (LWAH*R*)

Burgundy (BER-gun-dee)
- **Chablis** (shah-BLEE)
- **Côte d'Or** (koht DO*R*)
- **Beaujolais** (boh-zhuh-LAY)

Bordeaux (bohr-DOH)
- **Médoc** (may-DAWK)
- **Saint-Émilion** (sah*n* tay-mee-LYAW*N*)
- **Pomerol** (paw-muh-*R*AWL)
- **Graves** (G*R*AHV)
- **Sauternes** (soh-TERN; saw-TERN)

Côtes du Rhône (koht deu ROHN)
- **Châteauneuf-du-Pape** (shah-toh-nuhf-doo-PAHP)

For audio pronunciations of key wine terms, visit the audio wine dictionary at www.strat splace.com or at www.wineloverspage.com/lexicon/.

Other laws have been established to strictly control the industry, such as defining the vineyards that can produce the grapes, the kinds of grapes, growing and

Exhibit 5   Types of Wines from Regions in France

Region	Grapes	Wines	Qualities
Burgundy	Pinot Noir, Gamay, and Chardonnay	red, white	dry whites, richly textrued reds
Bordeaux	Cabernet Sauvignon, Cabernet Franc, and Meriot	red, white, and sweet wines	deeply flavored reds, sweet whites
Rhone	Syrah, Cabernet Sauvignon, and Muscat	red, white, and sparkling	earthy, big wines, some wtih a slight fizz
Loire	Sauvignon Blanc, Pinot Noir, and Pinot Gris	rosé, red, white, and sparkling	rich reds and dry whites that go well with shellfish
Alsace	Sauvignon Blanc, Pinot Noir, and Pinot Gris	Riesling and some rosé	sweet wines that are Germanic in flavor
Champagne	Pinot Noir, Pinot Meunier, and Chardonnay	white, red, and champagne	thin and tart, excellent sparkling wines
Beaujolais	Chadonnay and local Gamay	reds, whites, and slightly fizzy wines	fresh tasting, slight fruity flavor

Source: Wine Regions of the World. For more information, browse the Internet site at: www.wine-regions-of-the-world.com/html/france.html.

Exhibit 6   Champagne Territory—France

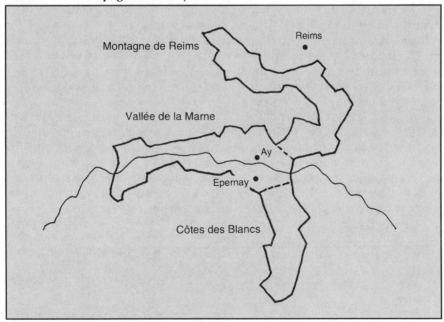

Only wine produced in this area of France, with grapes grown in this area, can legally be called "Champagne." (Courtesy of Food and Wines from France.)

pruning methods, the sugar content of the grapes, yield per hectare, the methods of pressing, fermentation, aging, the method of making the champagne, aging in the bottle and a host of other details. These controls have brought about a stable industry, known for its high quality product.

It is of the essence of Champagne that it is a blend of wines from many growers. Thus, a considerable quantity of Champagne is produced by *Négociant-Manipulants*, firms that purchase wines from growers or cooperatives. The label may note this with the letters "*NM.*" Other labels may show the following as the producer:

RM	Récoltant-Manipulant (vine grower)
CM	Co-operative de Manipulation (cooperative)
RC	Récoltant-Cooperateur (cooperative for a grower)
SR	Société de Récoltants (family owned firm)
MA	Marque d'Acheteur (private brand)

Exhibit 7 illustrates how to read a French Champagne label.

To obtain *Grand Cru* classification, 100 percent of the grapes must come from one of the 12 *Grand Cru* classified villages in the Champagne district; to obtain a *Premier Cru* rating, 90 percent to 99 percent of the grapes must come from one of the 41 *Premier Cru* villages.

Alsace

The Alsace region is in the western part of France along the German border; it is known for its dry, fresh, fruity whites, often sold under the grape variety and not vineyard name (see Exhibit 8). The major grapes used are the Pinot Gris, Pinot Blanc, Riesling, Muscat, Gewürztraminer, and Sylvaner. The Pinot Gris makes a hearty, full-bodied but lightly fruity, dry white wine. The Pinot Blanc produces a wine of good body and delicate lightness and is the primary grape of what are called the Edelzwicker (noble mixture) blends. The Pinot Blanc is also used to produce the excellent dry, fruity, sparkling Crémant d'Alsace.

The widely used Riesling makes a very dry, elegant, and classic white with a light, delicate bouquet. Normally the Muscat produces enough sugar to make a sweet wine, but in the Alsace it does not; the wine is crisp, light, with the typical Muscat grapy, fruity flavor. Gewürztraminer wines are quite fruity and probably exceed all others in spiciness (*Gewürz* means "spicy" in German). Traminer wine belongs to the same family as the Gewürztraminer but is lighter in bouquet and flavor. Sylvaner wines are fresh, light, and fruity whites.

Some late-harvested wines (*Vendange Tardive*—"tardy harvest") are made that resemble the late harvest wines of Germany. The label will read *Sélection des Grains Nobles* for the sweetest. These wines are rich, full-bodied, and sweet with an exotic bouquet.

Loire

The Loire River drains central France, flowing west to the Atlantic Ocean (see Exhibit 9. It is a rich agricultural land, famous for its castles. It has two grape growing areas: (1) Bas-Loire (lower Loire) consisting of Anjou, Saumur, Vouvray

Exhibit 7   How to Read a French Champagne Label

To be sure you are drinking champagne, the proudest of French wines, look for the following information on the label:

1. The word "Champagne" in prominent letters.
2. The brand name of the champagne producer.
3. The phrase "produce of France."
4. The contents of the bottle.
5. The location of the producer in the Champagne Region.
6. The degree of dryness: "brut," "extra-dry," "sec," or "demi-sec."

If the champagne was bottled in a vintage year, the year of the harvest will also appear. The label may also state that the champagne was blended only with Chardonnay grape wines *(blanc de blancs)* or has been allowed to derive a pink color from the skins of red grapes *(rosé)*.

Courtesy of Champagne News and Information Bureau.

(Touraine), and Muscadet de Sèvre-et-Maine, and Haute-Loire (upper Loire) consisting of Pouilly-Fumé and Sancerre. Most of the wines are fresh, light, and delicately fruity and meant to be consumed when fairly young. Only the sweet whites

Exhibit 8   Alsace

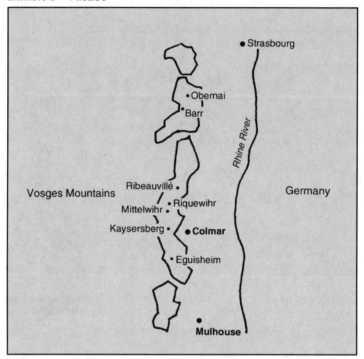

Located on the Rhine River next to Germany, the Alsace produces many traditionally German wines in the French style. (Courtesy of Food and Wines from France.)

Exhibit 9   The Loire Valley

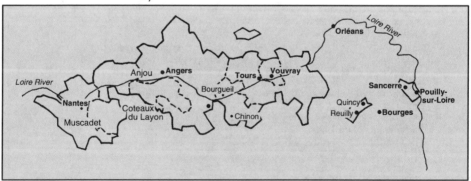

The Loire is noted for its excellent white wines (Vouvray, Muscadet, Saumur) and the well-known rosés of Anjou. (Courtesy of Food and Wines from France.)

age well and keep for a long time. The best known wines of the region are the dry, still, whites of Pouilly-Fumé and Saumur; the white wines, dry or sweet, of

Exhibit 10   Burgundy (Bourgogne)

The heart of Burgundy—the Côte d'Or—produces some of the world's finest wines. (Courtesy of Food and Wines from France.)

Saumur; the still and sparkling white wines of Vouvray; the whites or rosés (the latter mostly sweet) of Anjou; and the dry whites of Muscadet.

Burgundy

Wine was being made in Burgundy (Bourgogne) when it was conquered by the Romans. Today it is rivaled only by the region of Bordeaux as the producer of the world's greatest wines. The Burgundy region lies between the cities of Dijon and Lyon, a distance of some 225 miles (see Exhibit 10). Chablis, the area that produces some of the world's greatest white wines, is considered a part of this region. It is about 75 miles north of Dijon.

If a vineyard produces and bottles its own wine, the label can bear the term *Mise en Bouteille à la Propriété* or *Mise en Bouteille au Domaine*. The label will usually have the name of the *domaine* under this, such as *Domaine Claude Laret*. In some cases, small owners may join together in a cooperative and blend their **musts** together to make wine. If a merchant bottles the wine, the name and location of the bottler will be indicated along with a phrase like *Négociant à Vosne-Romanée* or *Propriétaire à Vosne-Romanée*.

Burgundy has three major wine-producing regions: 1) Chablis, 2) Côte d'Or, which includes Côte de Nuits and Côte de Beaune, and 3) southern Burgundy, which includes Chalonnais, Mâconnais and Beaujolais.

Chablis. The Chablis area, located north of the main Burgundy area, is famous for only one wine, but it is one of the best white wines in the world. It is so popular that vintners in other nations have grown the Chardonnay grape (which, according to French law, must be used to make Chablis) so they could imitate it—they never quite succeed. It is a crisp, fruity, very dry wine with a fresh bouquet and a delicate, refreshing acidity; its color is typically yellow tinged with green.

Côte d'Or. Côte d'Or means "slope of gold," and richly deserves the name, since some of the world's greatest wines come from there. It is divided into two parts: Côte de Nuits in the north and the Côte de Beaune in the south. The best wines of the Côte d'Or are reds which are beautifully balanced between acid and tannins so they last and last. In fact, a good red is not quite that until it has been about 10 years in the bottle. The Côte de Nuits burgundies are full-bodied and carry an elegant, deeply perfumed bouquet. The Côte de Beaune reds have a warm, fragrant bouquet, but are lighter in body and mature more quickly than those of the Côte de Nuits.

In some cases, a village name plus that of the most famous vineyard located in it are combined. This practice allows certain growers or bottlers with inferior wine to trade on the name of a justly famed vineyard. The buyer must beware by knowing more about Côte d'Or vineyards and villages than can be ascertained from labels. Thus, the name Chambolle-Musigny is only an indication that the wine comes from the Chambolle area but does not mean the wine is made from the Musigny vineyard grapes.

By law, all red wines produced in the Côte d'Or must be made from the Pinot Noir grape. The Pinot Noir grape is difficult to bring to successful harvest year after year, but it does better in the Côte d'Or than in other areas. And when it is brought to ripe harvest, it produces magnificent wines.

Côte d'Or Reds. The map of Burgundy shown in Exhibit 10 shows that the northern end of the Côte d'Or where Dijon and Fixin are located is in the shape of a canopy or cap. This area's reds are respectable but are so much overshadowed by those of the more southern areas that we hear little about them. Next in line to the south is the village of Gevrey-Chambertin, from which come nine *Grand Crus*, all bearing the name of Chambertin in some form or another. One must be alert, however, to know which these are, because a wine bearing the name of Gevrey-Chambertin may not be made from any of the famous vineyard grapes but be only an ordinary red made in the village area of Gevrey-Chambertin. South of Gevrey-Chambertin is the village of Morey-Saint-Denis, which has similarly elegant reds. Four Morey-Saint-Denis vineyards hold *Grand Cru* rankings. The next village, Chambolle-Musigny, is noted for reds which are slightly different from those of its more northern neighbors. They are sometimes described as "elegant, delicate, and charmingly feminine." Three of the wines of the area have *Grand Cru* status. Sandwiched in between Chambolle-Musigny and Vosne-Romanée is the tiny village area of Vougeot where the famous *Grand Cru* vineyard, Clos de Vougeot, is located. Today there are more than 80 owners holding the property. The wines of the Vosne-Romanée are rich in flavor and full in body and have a tremendous bouquet. When tasted, they are said to "open up like a peacock's tail in the mouth." The southern end of the Côte d'Or, but the biggest area, is that of Nuits-Saint-Georges.

While it boasts of no *Grand Crus*, it has a flock of *Premier Crus* and its village red wines are of very high quality. The Côte de Beaune starts at the villages of Ladoix-Serrigny and Pernand-Vergelesses. After this, to the south, the first red of note produced is in Aloxe-Corton, a *Grand Cru* of the vineyard Corton. Farther south the area of Savigny-les-Beaunes produces some excellent village reds. Pommard and Volnay to the south of Beaune produce some respected, delicate, soft red wines of elegant quality. Auxey-Duresses is not particularly known for its reds, but the reds bearing the village names are considered good. Similarly, Meursault and Chassagne Montrachet also produce good reds. The reds of Santenay, the last village of importance in Beaune, produces reds called "pleasant and light."

Côte d'Or Whites. The Côte de Beaune is famed for its whites, although they account for less than 20 percent of its total output. The great *Grand Crus* Corton-Charlemagne and Charlemagne come from the village of Aloxe-Corton. Meursault, next in line to the south, produces great whites that are full-bodied, big and round in flavor with a luscious softness. They are dry to the almost crisp stage. Puligny-Montrachet produces only dry whites which are rich in body and flavor and of a green-gold color. It boasts of four *Grand Crus*; since a part of these *Grand Cru* vineyards are in Chassagne-Montrachet, it can also claim these wines as its own.

Southern Burgundy. The middle part of the Burgundy region is made up of the Côte Chalonnaise and Mâconnais. Their reds are of notably good quality, lighter in body and flavor, with less bouquet than the great reds of the Côte d'Or.

Bouzeron Rouge is a respectable wine after about three years maturity. Bouzeron has also been granted the only single village Aligoté white appellation in all of Burgundy.

Mâconnais reds are well thought of, having a fresh, fruity, light flavor and bouquet which comes from the Gamay grape. However, the area's whites are better known than the reds. Montagny produces whites *any* of which, if 11.5 percent or more in natural alcohol, can be labeled *Premier Cru*. Most of the dry whites of the Mâconnais are considered plain with few frills but, because of their highly refreshing, agreeable, and charming quality, are considered a bit above the average.

On the very southern border of the Mâconnais, right next to Beaujolais, are the slopes that produce the famous Pouilly-Fuissé, a richly flavored, pale, golden wine. Other excellent whites are produced in this same area such as Mâcon Blanc, Mâcon Supérieur, Mâcon-Villages, Saint-Véran, Pouilly-Vinzelles, and Pouilly-Loché. Mâcon produces a few good rosés.

Beaujolais. Beaujolais, the most southern part of Burgundy, is the region's largest producer of wine. Here, the Gamay is the grape of choice. Gamay reds have less tannin, less body, and a lively, lighter and more delicate, fruity flavor than the heavier Pinot Noir reds. The wine has a rich, full berry aroma. It is often consumed lightly chilled. It does not improve with age—about three years is enough—so most of the production is consumed young. Beaujolais reds are ranked in one of four quality levels: Cru Beaujolais, Beaujolais Villages, Beaujolais Supérieur, and Beaujolais. First quality is Cru Beaujolais which comes from nine *communes* (villages) in the north: Brouilly, Chénas, Chiroubles, Côte de Brouilly, Fleurie, Juliénas, Morgon, Moulin-à-Vent and Saint-Amour. These nine are part of the group of 35

Exhibit 11   Bordeaux

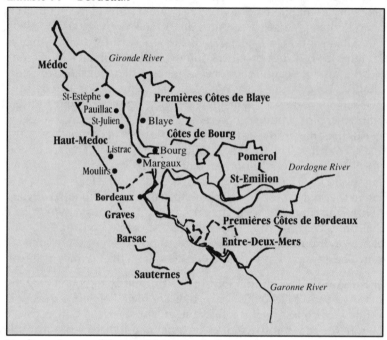

Bordeaux is one of the most important wine regions on earth; it not only produces more wine than other regions of France, but more of France's greatest wines. (Courtesy of Food and Wines from France.)

villages which make up the second ranking: Beaujolais-Villages. Beaujolais Supérieur, the third rank, is only superior to ordinary Beaujolais because it has an extra degree of natural alcohol content. The name of the bottler is often prominently displayed. Some of the new, lighter Beaujolais wines—called Beaujolais Nouveau or Beaujolais Primeur—are hurried to market as early as the third Thursday in November. Beaujolais Nouveau is a very popular wine with a short life—about nine months. It is light, refreshing, lively, and very fruity. Only about one percent of Beaujolais' wine is white. It goes by the name of Beaujolais Blanc and is a fruity, refreshing, wine much like the Saint-Véran white. It should also be consumed young.

Bordeaux

The Bordeaux region is that area of land around the lower Garonne and Dordogne Rivers and some of the area after these two join to form the Gironde River (see Exhibit 11). Reds (the famous clarets), rosés, and whites are produced; the reds are primarily dry while the whites are dry, medium dry, sweet, or very sweet. The Bordeaux region is the most prolific wine producer in France. Reds dominate whites three to one.

The climate favors vine growth—short winters with few frosts and good humidity. The grapes grown to produce the reds are largely the Cabernet Sauvignon and the Cabernet Franc. These give desirable vigor in body and flavor and suffi-cient acid and tannin to give a wine that usually lasts a long time, and improves with age. Merlot grapes are often used to give softness and suppleness while the Malbec and Petit Verdot varieties are used to give wines a proper balance. The major whites grown are Sauvignon Blanc, Muscadelle, and the Sémillon.

Many Bordeaux wines are bottled under the labels of the châteaux which grow the grapes, produce the wine and bottle it. Shippers and bottlers, called *négo-ciants*, may purchase different wines and bottle them, putting their own labels on them. Wine labels may disclose a regional or communal name such as Médoc, Graves, or, simply, Bordeaux. Others may feature a varietal grape name which, by law, requires the contents to be made from 100 percent of that grape.

The most famous AC-defined regions are: Médoc, St-Emilion, Pomerol, Graves, Sauternes, and Barsac. However, some excellent wines also come from dis-tricts such as Cérons, Ste-Croix-du-Mont, Loupiac, Côtes de Bordeaux-Ste-Mac-aire, Prémieres Côtes de Bordeaux, Ste-Foy-Bordeaux, Entre-Deux-Mers, and Graves de Vayres.

Médoc. The most famous parishes (*communes*) in the Médoc are St-Estèphe, Pauil-lac, St-Julien, and Margaux. Their wines are beautiful reds, light bodied and ele-gant, and haunting in fragrance and mellowness. The flavor is delicate and long lasting. Connoisseurs vie to lay down their vintage wines.

St-Estèphe reds have a deep, red color, last a long time and have a succulent and lasting flavor. The reds from this parish are more full-bodied and robust than those of the rest of the Médoc. Their lingering bouquet leaves an impression of pears, apples, peaches, and apricots. They are fairly high in tannin and so last a long time; they mature more slowly than other clarets.

Pauillac, to the south of St-Estèphe, produces reds deep in color and balanced in tannin so they also last a long time. They develop great finesse and an opulent bouquet when mature. The First Growths of the Château Lafite, Château Latour, and Château Mouton-Rothschild are produced here.

St-Julien is next to the south. Its reds are lighter but have excellent harmony and balance. Likewise Moulis and Listrac's dry, fruity reds are light and delicate and mature more quickly than other Bordeaux wines.

Some of the noblest reds of Bordeaux are produced in the parish of Margaux. Its reds are very delicate, yet substantial and full-bodied, lasting a long time. Their great elegance is crowned by a fragrant, lingering bouquet. Château Margaux's First Growth clarets are considered some of the world's finest. Château Palmer, next door, is a Third Growth but its wine often rivals that of its more prestigious neighbor. Other growths of this area are similarly good and often represent bar-gains compared to the price charged for Château Margaux.

St-Emilion. The reds of this district are more full-bodied and robust than the other reds of Bordeaux. They also have a flavor all of their own, with a slightly sweet aftertaste. These wines mature fairly quickly; some of the poorer ones will reach their peak in four years, while others may take eight or more.

Pomerol. While Pomerol is the smallest of the wine districts of the Bordeaux region, Pomerol's wines are far from small. They are substantial wines, more rugged than St-Emilion's but with some of the same flavor characteristics. The finest taste almost creamy; the color is deep and rich. Buyers select Pomerol wines based on the reputation of the châteaux from which they come.

Graves. About a third of the Graves—named for its gravelly soil—wine production is in reds. They are sturdy wines with a body and flavor typical of the Bordeaux clarets. While some should be consumed fairly young, others carry enough tannin to last well from six to eight years.

The whites of Graves are quite dry, having a crisp, lean, clear taste and well balanced between dryness and bitterness. They have a delicate bouquet and a fruity, aldehyde flavor. A few Grave whites are slightly sweet. The whites of the Graves are considered some of the finest whites produced in the world.

Sauternes and Barsac. The most southern wine-producing areas of the Bordeaux are Sauternes and Barsac. They get a lot of sun, and the growing period is long so the grapes can remain on the vines for a long time to develop the "noble rot" and the resulting natural sweetness from the mold growth on the grapes. The wines are mellow, sweet, luscious, and golden in color. They rank among the great sweet wines of the world.

Côtes du Rhône

The Côtes du Rhône wine-growing region starts below Beaujolais and follows the Rhône River south to Avignon (see Exhibit 12). There is good, long summer warmth so the grapes develop full body and solid alcoholic content. The wines are rich and deep in color and show the vigor of the summer climate. The best wine-growing areas are Côte-Rotie, Condrieu, Hermitage, Cornas, St-Péray, St-Joseph, Lirac and Tavel, and Châteauneuf-du-Pape. Excellent whites, reds, and rosés come from this region.

Most of the grapes grown are the Cinsaut and Syrrah varieties which develop a deep red wine, full-bodied, possessing vigor and warmth, with a rich bouquet and luscious, rich, deep taste. Southern Rhône grows other grape varieties such as the Grenache and Clairette. Often wines made from the Syrrah have some white grapes blended in to reduce the deep, almost blackish red color and heavy body that grape gives to wine. The wines of the area usually have a consistent quality which makes them quite dependable. The young reds possess a bit of harshness so they are often aged in the cask several or more years. They mature well in the bottle. The whites of the area also are longer lasting than is usual with whites. This is because of their high alcoholic content as well as other properties.

Perhaps the most famous white—a golden wine with an intense peach-like flavor—comes from the vineyard of Condrieu. A rare golden, fragrant white of full body and flavor comes from the Château Grillet—rare because the vineyard is so small that less than 20 barrels of the wine is made each year. The golden wines of Hermitage and Crozes-Hermitage are dry, with a delicate flavor and fragrance. They are long-lasting. A similar white wine is produced at St-Joseph but it is lighter in flavor and body. It matures more quickly and is not as long-lasting. Some excellent *crémants* (sparkling wines) are also produced in the Côtes du Rhône.

Exhibit 12   Côtes du Rhône

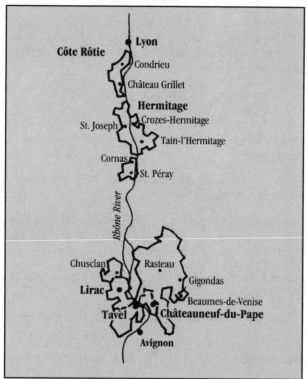

**Stretching north to south along the Rhône River, the
sunny "slopes of Rhône" produce 90 percent red wines,
the famous Tavel and Lirac rosés, and a few interesting
white wines.** (Courtesy of Food and Wines from France.)

Two famous rosés are produced in this area, the Tavel and the Lirac. The
Tavel is made mostly from the Grenache grape and is orange-pink in color. The
flavor is generous, the body medium and the fragrance quite fruity. Lirac rosé is
lighter in body and not as well known. It is also primarily made from the Grenache
grape, has a similar color and about the same high alcoholic content. While the
Tavel is almost as well known as the rosé of Anjou, the Lirac is not, although it
deserves to be. Some good rosés are found under the regional appellation of Côtes
du Rhône.

Châteauneuf-du-Pape. Châteauneuf-du-Pape is perhaps the most famous of the
Côtes du Rhône wines, with a long and distinguished history. Its reds are intensely
Côte du Rhône in character but more pungent, vigorous, and deeper flavored than
others. The Syrrah, Grenache, and Clairette grapes are predominant, but others
may also be used. AC has authorized 13 different grapes that wines bearing the
Châteauneuf-du-Pape label can use. Even some white grapes can be used to reduce
the intensity of the Syrrah grape must.

☞ Key Terms ────────────────────────────

appellation contrôlée (AC)—Literally, "name controlled." A wine with this term on the label belongs to the highest classification of French wines and an agency of the French government strictly regulates it.

chaptalization—A procedure of adding sugar to grape juice or must before or during fermentation to attain the necessary alcohol level. This procedure is often necessary when weather conditions prevent grapes from ripening fully and developing enough natural sugar to convert to the amount of alcohol prescribed (often by law) for certain wines.

cru—Literally, "growth" areas singled out by French government wine regulations as producing the highest quality wines.

grand cru—Literally, "great growth." The meaning of this designation varies among the different wine-producing areas of France. In general, the term identifies the highest ranking vineyards or wine-producing villages.

hectare—Pronounced HEHK-tahr and abbreviated as ha. A unit of surface or land equal to 10,000 square meters or 2.471 acres.

hectoliter—A capacity unit of measure equal to 100 liters, or 26.418 gallons, or 22 Imperial gallons.

mis en bouteille au château—Literally, "bottled at the manor house," it is a term often found on the labels of French wines indicating the origin of the grapes used to make the wine.

mise en bouteille au domaine—Literally, "bottled at the place (or residence)," it is a term often found on the labels of French wines indicating the origin of the grapes used to make the wine.

mise en bouteille à la propriété—Literally, "bottled at the property," usually by the owner of the vineyard, it is a term sometimes found on the label of French wines indicating the origin of the grapes used to make the wine.

must—The juice of freshly crushed grapes that will be fermented into wine; can include pulp, skins, and seeds.

négociant-manipulants—Firms that produce wines from growers or cooperatives, usually blending them for consistency and selling the blend under their own label.

noble rot—A mold, Botrytis cinerea, which infects certain types of grapes in late fall, when morning mists and afternoon sun create ideal growing conditions for the mold; it is called "noble" because it creates some of the greatest naturally sweet wines.

premier cru—Literally, "first growth." The meaning of this designation varies among the different wine-producing areas of France. Premier cru ranks behind areas designated as grand cru. If a wine-producing area does not use a grand cru designation, premier cru may designate the highest ranking vineyards or wine-producing villages.

terroir—A French term that refers to the growing environment of a specific area, the total vineyard environment, including the soil and its makeup, chemical qualities, the climate, amount of sun, moisture conditions, and so on.

vin de pays—Literally, "country wine." French wines with this term on the label must come from the region of production claimed; one or more classic grape varieties are required; yield is controlled and alcohol levels prescribed and are on the label.

vin de table (or vin ordinaire)—Literally, "table wine" or "ordinary wine." These are very basic French wines, virtually unregulated by the government.

Vins Délimités de Qualité Supérieure (VDQS)—Literally, "wines from a specifically defined region of superior quality." A French wine with this term on the label is generally ranked below AC wines in quality and consistency of quality.

vintage—The year of the actual grape harvest and the wine made from those grapes. Since the quality of harvests varies from year to year, vintage is only a general guideline to wine quality. An excellent year for a particular growing region signifies a generally superior quality for that vintage.

Review Questions

1. Explain why the concept of *terroir* forms the basis for the laws and regulations governing the French wine industry.

2. What does it mean for a French wine to be labeled AC?

3. What is the difference between a wine designated as *vin de pays* and a wine designated as *vin de table*?

4. Why don't all French wine labels use the same terminology?

5. By French law, which wine-producing regions can label its wine "Champagne?"

6. What are *négociant-manipulants*?

7. Why are the Burgundy and Bordeaux wine-producing regions famous?

8. Where in France is the "slope of gold?"

9. What is the grape of choice in the Beaujolais wine-producing area of Burgundy?

10. What is meant by the term "noble rot?"

Internet Sites

For more information, visit the following Internet sites. Remember that Internet addresses can change without notice. If the site is no longer there, you can use a search engine to look for additional sites. Many alcohol-related sites require users to be of legal drinking age to enter.

Wine Resources

Decanter Magazine
www.decanter.com

Professional Friends of Wine
winepros.org

The Wine Enthusiast
www.winemag.com

Wine Lover's Page
www.wineloverspage.com/wines/

Wine Spectator
www.winespector.com

Reading Wine Labels

Epicurious
www.epicurious.com/d_drinking
/d08_wines/wine_label/wine_
label_main.html

The Winedoctor
www.thewinedoctor.com/advisory/
labelinterpreter.shtml

Robin Garr's Wine Lovers' Page
www.wine-lovers-page.com/wines/
labels.shtml

Internet Wine Guide.com
www.internetwineguide.com/
structure/abwine/labelreg.htm

Wines of the World

Aboutwines.com
www.aboutwines.com/home/refer
ence/regions/index.html

International Sommelier Guild
www.internationalsommelier.com

Internet Wine Guide.com
www.internetwineguide.com/
structure/ww/worldwide.htm

Cellarnotes.net
www.cellarnotes.net/wine_by_
geographic_origin.htm

Strat's Place
www.stratsplace.com/maps.html

Wine Regions of the World
www.wine-regions-of-the-world.com/
html/regions.html

France

Terroir France: French Wine Guide
www.terroir-france.com/index.html

Good Cooking
www.goodcooking.com/frconnt.htm

The Winedoctor
www.thewinedoctor.com/regional
guides/regionalguideshome.shtml

Chateau Lagrange
www.chateau-lagrange.com

Comte Audion de Dampierre
www.dampierre.com

Chateau Larmande
www.chateau-larmande.com/
eng_index_1024.html

Chapter 10 Outline

Italian Wine Classification System
    Denominazione di Origine Controllata
      e Garantita (DOCG)
    Denominazione di Origine Controllata
      (DOC)
    Vino Tipico
    Vino da Tavola
Labeling Regulations
Major Wine-Producing Areas
    Piedmont
    Lombardy
    Veneto
    Emilia-Romagna
    Tuscany
    Latium
    Sicily

Competencies

1. Explain the Italian wine classification system. (pp. 283–285)

2. Define items commonly found on the labels of Italian wine bottles. (pp. 285–286)

3. Identify the major wine-producing areas of Italy and the types of wine each produces. (pp. 286–292)

10
Wines of Italy

TODAY, ITALY PRODUCES AND CONSUMES more wine than any other country in Europe. Almost every area in Italy produces wine. The climate is warm and the grapes get plentiful sun during the ripening period. The climate may even be too warm—Sicilian and some other southern red grapes may get so much warmth that the wine is fiery and harsh and must be softened by either using white grapes or using special production methods to moderate the flavor.

Only about 40 percent of Italy's grapes are made into wine. A significant quantity is exported to other countries to use as a blending wine. The part that does not leave the country is processed into brandy or made into other commercial products.

Italian Wine Classification System

Italian regulations establish wine-producing regions and a grading system to note wines of "particular reputation and worth." These regulations are known collectively as the *Denominazione di Origine Controllata* (DOC). The name parallels the French *Appellation d'Origine Contrôlée*, but the DOC is at once more complex and less indicative of quality than the AOC. Exhibit 1 summarizes the Italian wine classification system.

Denominazione di Origine Controllata e Garantita (DOCG)

A DOCG rating identifies the highest classification of Italian wines. In addition to meeting standards for a DOC rating, DOCG wines undergo mandatory government testing and tasting before bottling. Wines submitted for DOCG status must have the characteristics historically associated with the wines of their region. Wines granted DOCG status have a government seal of recognition placed over capsules or corks and the labels display the term *Denominazione di Origine Controllata e Garantita*, meaning "Controlled and Guaranteed Denomination of Origin."

Denominazione di Origine Controllata (DOC)

Italy's version of France's *Appellation d'Origine Contrôlée*, is *Denominazione di Origine Controllata (DOC)*, meaning "Controlled Denomination of Origin." A wine classified as DOC must come from the area specified and be made according to the laws for that particular DOC. These laws are usually arrived at on the basis of tradition with input from local producers. A DOC rating does not necessarily identify the "best" wines in a given area, only those wines that conform to

Exhibit 1   Italian Wine Classifications

DOCG

Denominazione di Origine Controllata e Garantita
(deh-NAW-mee-nah-TSYAW-neh dee oh-REE-jee-neh con-troll-AH-tah gah-rahn-TEE-tah)

> Meaning, "Controlled and Guaranteed Denomination of Origin." A wine with this term on the label belongs to the highest classification of Italian wines—the quality guarantee by the Italian government. Government testers examine and taste the wines prior to awarding the DOCG status.

DOC

Denominazione di Origine Controllata
(deh-NAW-mee-nah-TSYAW-neh dee oh-REE-jee-neh con-troll-AH-tah)

> A wine with DOC on its label belongs to the second-highest level of Italian wines, indicating a "controlled wine" meeting specific regulations and standards.

vino tipico

(VEE-noh TEE-pee-koh)

> The third category of Italian wine after DOCG and DOC. The classification (similar to France's vin de pays and Germany's landwein) applies to wines that are officially approved as being representative of their area.

vino da tavola (VdT)

(VEE-noh dah TAH-voh-lah)

> The lowest category of Italian wine, "table wine," is similar to France's vin de table and Germany's tafelwein. While most VdT wines are ordinary, excellent wines can be relegated to this category because producers did not conform to DOC regulations.

For any given wine from a specific region, regulations may cover:

- Production area
- Grape variety
- Viticulture standards
- Yield
- Production methods
- Bottling
- Aging specifications
- Alcohol content
- Taste analysis

For audio pronunciations of key wine terms, visit the audio wine dictionary at www.strat splace.com or at www.wineloverspage.com/lexicon/.

"traditionally popular" characteristics of a defined area. Therefore, the absence of a DOC or DOCG rating on a wine label may not indicate a lack of quality. Many modern Italian winemakers feel compelled to produce a wine by modern methods not approved by some restrictive DOC regulations which are based on historical methods.

The DOC controls claims of geographic origin, permissible grape types, permitted yields, pruning methods, alcoholic strength, and aging requirements. **Chaptalization** (adding sugar during fermentation to raise the level of alcohol) is not permitted; the growing season throughout Italy is long enough and warm enough to provide sufficient ripening for sugar content. Even the weight of the grapes that may be harvested and the percentage of that weight which may be processed per hectare into wine are regulated.

Vino Tipico

Below the DOC and DOCG classifications is the category of *vino tipico* which includes wines considered of good quality and typical of the wine of the regions from which they come. This classification is much like the *vin de pays* of France or the *landwein* of Germany. Wines receiving DOCG, DOC, and *vino tipico* designations meet EEC wine standards.

Vino da Tavola

Below *vino tipico* is *vino da tavola* (wine of the table), which is abbreviated "VdT." This category is also referred to as *vino ordinario* and corresponds to the French *vin de pays* or German *tafelwein*. As in France and Germany, it is that massive category of virtually unregulated wines. These wines may list only the country on their labels. VdT wines may also be known as *vino da pasto*, indicating its appropriateness as an everyday wine for drinking with pasta. Within the *vino da tavola* category is a higher designation, *indicazione geografica tipica (IGT)*. Wines qualifying for this rating may include on their labels the vintage, place of origin, and grape variety. This classification identifies wines regarded as slightly better than common table wines.

Labeling Regulations

Exhibit 2 illustrates how to read an Italian wine label. Regulations govern the labeling of Italian DOC wines. These regulations specify items that are compulsory, optional, and prohibited. Compulsory label items include:

- Country of origin
- Appellation of origin
- Quality standard
- Name and address of producer/brand owner
- Bottle content
- Alcohol content

Optional items include: grape variety, vintage, name of the vineyard, the term "Domain," and terms such as "dry," "medium dry," or "sweet," sulfites or other additives, authenticity seal, and commentaries such as analysis, tasting notes, or approvals. The term "wine" is prohibited.

Italian wine names may be classified as generic (place of origin), such as Cirò Rosso (red), a DOC red wine from Cirò of the province of Calabria, or varietal

Exhibit 2   How to Read an Italian Wine Label

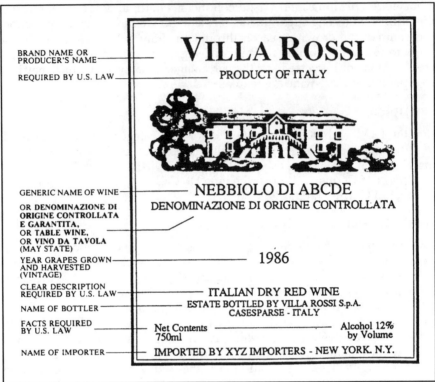

BRAND NAME OR
PRODUCER'S NAME

REQUIRED BY U.S. LAW

VILLA ROSSI

PRODUCT OF ITALY

GENERIC NAME OF WINE

OR **DENOMINAZIONE DI
ORIGINE CONTROLLATA
E GARANTITA,**
OR **TABLE WINE,**
OR **VINO DA TAVOLA**
(MAY STATE)

NEBBIOLO DI ABCDE

DENOMINAZIONE DI ORIGINE CONTROLLATA

YEAR GRAPES GROWN
AND HARVESTED
(VINTAGE)

1986

CLEAR DESCRIPTION
REQUIRED BY U.S. LAW

NAME OF BOTTLER

ITALIAN DRY RED WINE

ESTATE BOTTLED BY VILLA ROSSI S.p.A.
CASESPARSE - ITALY

FACTS REQUIRED
BY U.S. LAW

Net Contents
750ml

Alcohol 12%
by Volume

NAME OF IMPORTER

IMPORTED BY XYZ IMPORTERS - NEW YORK. N.Y.

Courtesy of the Italian Trade Commission.

(grape variety), such as Riesling Italico, a DOC wine from Lombardy. They may be proprietary (special distinctive name), such as Lacrima Christi (literally, "Tears of Christ"). At times one may see a wine with a generic and varietal name such as Lambrusco Grasparossa di Castelvetro which bears the name of the grape, *Lambrusco Grasparossa*, and the place of origin, Castel Vetro (not a "castle" actually, but the name of the 14 communes in the Morela district of the Emilia region which grow and produce this popular wine).

Major Wine-Producing Areas

The DOC (*Denominazione di Origine Controllata*) established 20 wine-producing regions and some 250 wine-growing districts in Italy. Exhibit 3 outlines the DOC regions and Exhibit 4 offers a pronunciation guide. Piedmont, Lombardy, Veneto, Tuscany and Latium are considered the major areas because of either the amount of wine produced or its excellence. Some of the defined districts are large, covering an entire province, while others are only small local communities or just choice vineyards in an area. Exhibit 5 charts some of the major Italian areas and lists the types of wines each produces.

Exhibit 3   Italian DOC Wine Regions

Italian DOC Wine Regions
1. Valle d'Aosta
2. Piedmont
3. Lombardy
4. Liguria
5. Emilia-Romagna
6. Trentino Alto Adige
7. Veneto
8. Fruili-Venezia Giulia
9. Tuscany
10. Umbria
11. Marches
12. Abruzzi
13. Molise
14. Latium (Lazio)
15. Campania
16. Apulia (Puglia)
17. Basilicata
18. Calabria
19. Sicily
20. Sardinia

The Piedmont region is known for its great red wines, but also produces a number of excellent whites. Piedmont is also home to more DOCG wines than any other Italian region and produces Asti Spumante—Italy's answer to French Champagne.

Piedmont

The Piedmont region in northwest Italy descends from the Alps down into the fertile Po River plain. The main wine producing area is in the Hills of Monferrato, where grapes have been cultivated since ancient times. The famous Asti Spumante, Italy's answer to Champagne, comes from this region.

One of the best Piedmont reds is the **Barolo**, a DOCG (*Denominazione di Origine Controllata e Garantita*) wine, made from the Nebbiolo grape. The wine is

Exhibit 4   Pronunciation Guide—Major Italian Wine-Producing Areas

Abruzzo (ah-BROOD-dzoh)
Apulia (ah-POOL-yuh)
Basilicata (bah-see-lee-KAH-tah)
Calabria (kah-LAH-bree-uh)
Campania (kahm-PAH-nyah)
Emilia-Romagna (eh-MEE-lyah raw-MAH-nyah)
Friuli-Venezia Giulia (free-OO-lee veh-HEHT-zee-ah JOO-lee-ah)
Liguria (lee-GOO-ryah)
Latium (LAH-tyum)
Lombardy (LOM-buhr-dee)
Piedmont (PEED-mawnt)
Marches (MAHR-kay)
Molise (MOH-lee-zeh)
Sardinia (sahr-DIHN-ee-uh)
Sicily (SIHS-uh-lee)
Trentino-Alto Adige (trehn-TEE-noh AHL-toh AH-dee-jeh)
Tuscany (TUHS-kuh-nee)
Umbria (UHM-bree-uh)
Valle d'Aosta (VAHL-lay DAWSS-tuh)
Veneto (VEH-neh-toh)

For audio pronunciations of key wine terms, visit the audio wine dictionary at www.strat splace.com or at www.wineloverspage.com/lexicon/.

ruby red in color with amber lights. It is dry, smooth, and velvety in taste, carrying to some tasters the perfume of violet and the taste of roses. It is full-bodied and is at its best when aged six to 20 years. It does, however, cast considerable sediment and often has to be decanted before consumed.

Barbaresco, another DOCG wine, is a rival of Barolo as the best red of the area; it has more smoothness and ages more quickly, but keeps well. It is best when aged six to 15 years. Both Barolo and Barbaresco must be over 12.5 percent in alcohol content.

Other highly respected Piedmont wines are:

- Barbera wines: Barbera d'Alba, Barbera d'Asti, Barbera del Costi Tortonesi, and Barbera del Monterro—all DOC wines.

- Dolcetto wines: Dolcetto d'Aqui, Dolcetto d'Asti, and Dolcetto d'Alba.

- Freisa di Chieri and Freisa d'Asti come from the Freisa grape of Chieri and parts of the provinces of Alessandria, Asti, and Cuneo.

- The Nebbiolo d'Alba has a pleasant bouquet and taste. It can be sweet or dry and is a good keeper.

Exhibit 5   Types of Wines from Regions in Italy

Region	Wines	Flavor	Quality
Piedmont	dark reds, very light whites, and sparkling wines	chewy in substance and wood-like in taste	very high quality, especially the sparkling wines
Valle D'Aosta	light reds and whites	delicate taste and light flavor	good quality but very hard to find outside of Italy
Alto Adige	every style of table wine	light and extremely fresh	high quality wines that do not need to be aged long
Veneto	reds, whites, and some sparkling	nutty, fruity, and sometimes bitter	good quality and pleasing to many wine makers
Tuscany	Chianti and some white wines	tannic and very rich in taste	mostly good quality with a few mediocre wines

Source: Wine Regions of the World. For more information browse the Internet site at: www.wine-regions-of-the-world.com/html/italy.html.

- Asti Spumante, the "champagne" of Italy, carries with it the typical, rich, delicate flavor of the Muscat grape.

- The Vermouth of Turin (Torino or Gran Torino) is famous as an aromatic aperitif wine. It is light golden yellow or dark orange in color with a brilliant shine.

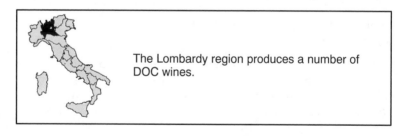

The Lombardy region produces a number of DOC wines.

Lombardy

Valtellina wines, coming from the mountainsides near the city, along the shores of Lake Garda, or on the hillsides of southern Lombardy, are highly regarded. Some of the better known Lombardy wines are:

- The bright ruby red, dry, smooth, and harmoniously flavored Sassella from the vineyards around the old church near Sondrio.

- Sfursat or Sforzato is made from the Nebbiolo grapes also, but some are dried until December which helps to make a wine about 14.5 percent in alcoholic content. It is rich, deep, and somewhat bitter in flavor. It has a heavy bouquet.

The Brescia area produces two wines that have received the DOC rating: the Riviera del Garda Bresciano Chiaretto, a rosé, and the Lugana, a white. Both are best consumed young.

Soave, likely the most popular of the Italian white wines, is produced in the western part of the Veneto region.

Veneto

Many fine wines come from Veneto, especially those from the dusky volcanic hill-sides of Verona, the hillsides of Valdobbiandene flanking Monte Grappa, and the hills of Conegliano in the province of Reviso.

The best known white wine from the vineyards around the city of Verona is the DOC Soave, but the Bianco di Custoza, Gambellara, and Verduzzo del Piave are also DOC-listed white wines. Soave has a light straw color with greenish high-lights, a delicate, fruity, characteristic bouquet, and a dry, suitably acidic, exqui-sitely bitter, well-balanced flavor.

Verona's two DOC reds are the world-renowned Bardolino and Valpolicella. Both have a delicate, characteristic bouquet and smooth, velvety, dry, slightly bit-ter flavor, and are light in body. Neither requires much aging; they are best con-sumed young.

Perhaps the most popular wine from the Emilia-Romagna region is Lambrusco.

Emilia-Romagna

A number of the best wines of this region are made entirely or mostly from the Lambrusco grape. They usually carry the grape name on the label. Many are *friz-zantes* (slightly sparkling) and some may even be fully sparkling wines (*spu-mantes*). Three of the Lambruscos have DOC ratings: Lambrusco di Sorbara from the area of Sorbara and Bomporto, a light bodied, brilliant, ruby red wine with characteristic dry or semi-sweet, slightly tart, fresh and fruity flavor; Lambrusco Reggiano from the Reggiano area; and Lambrusco Grasparossa di Castelvetro.

Tuscany is a region famous for Chianti, Brunello di Montalcino, Vino Nobile di Montepulciano, and acclaimed super-Tuscans.

Tuscany

Florence and Sienna are the main cities in this region, a region famous for Chianti, Brunello di Montalcino, and Vino Nobile di Montepulciano. The three Communes of the ancient League of Chianti, along with some neighboring districts, make what is called Chianti Classico (*classico* is the DOC designation reserved for the area which produces the best wine within a DOC-defined region). Chianti Classico is identified by either a neck label showing a white Della Robbia angel (*putto*) or one showing a black and gold seal with a black cock inside.

The first Chianti was made by using red grapes with some whites added to soften the somewhat harsh, tannic flavor and rich body produced by a wine made only of reds. Today DOC-approved Chianti must be made of 10 percent white grapes, but many Chianti-like wines are being introduced which are made from all red grapes. A wine made by the famous Antinori family called *Tignanello* is made up of 90 percent Sangiovese and 10 percent Cabernet Sauvignon instead of the obligatory white wine. Such wines cannot legally be labeled Chianti.

Chianti has a bright, lively ruby red color, varying in hue and depth according to type. The bouquet is pleasant and the flavor is dry, strong, smooth, velvety and well-balanced. Some Chiantis are best consumed when young; others age well. The best Chiantis are not marketed in the straw-covered flasks but in bottles shaped like Bordeaux wine bottles.

Brunello is a full-bodied, fragrant wine that ages very well—in fact it is best consumed after four to six years of aging. Other DOCs of the region are:

- Vin Santo—a sweet wine of high alcoholic content made somewhat like sherry and tastes somewhat like it.

- Galestro—a delicate white with a distinctive aroma.

- Bianco Toscano—a white dry wine of light body and delicate fruity fragrance.

In the late 1970s some winemakers in the Tuscany region began producing high quality wines of international acclaim. However, because the production methods violated DOC regulations, their wines were relegated to the status of *vino da tavola*, the lowest category in the Italian classification scheme. Some of these wines, referred to as **super-Tuscans**, enjoy a world-wide status and value that exceeds DOC and DOCG wines from the same region.

Latium, a wine-growing area around the city of Rome, is known for Frascati, a dry white wine.

Latium

Latium or Lazio is in south Umbria, the parts surrounding Rome. It is known best for its whites, among which are DOCs like Trebbiano di Aprilla, sweet or dry Frascati, Colli Albani, and Marino. Some good non-DOCs are found bottled under the label of Castelli Romani. Castelli Romani is one of many Italian winemakers who refuse to be restricted by DOC regulations which, they believe, would keep them from making higher quality wines. This region is also the home of the famous Est!

Est!! Est!!! This is a golden wine with a rich, delightful, fruity bouquet and a pleasing, slightly bitter flavor.

The western portion of Sicily produces the vast majority of quality wines in the region.

Sicily

The warm climate and bright sunshine of Sicily produces grapes with good sugar, acidity, and other desirable wine properties. Its most famous wine is **Marsala**, which is amber in color, varying in intensity, with a penetrating, characteristic bouquet and a rich, full, warm, velvety taste. It is sweet and an outstanding dessert wine. Long aging gives it finesse and refinement. Marsala contains from 5 percent to 10 percent sugar and about 18 percent alcohol. "Aromatic" Marsala is a Marsala clarified with eggs and almonds or other ingredients added for additional flavor. The following terms refer to the amount of aging the wine gets:

- Fine—moderately aged
- Superior dry or superior sweet—well-aged
- Virgin or soleras—very old

Corvino (Corvo) is from white grapes grown on Mt. Etna's slopes—a fine, dry, white with a somewhat fiery character. A good red and a sparkling white may also bear this name on the label. Some others of Sicily's best DOCs include Bianco di Alcamo and two reds, Cerasuolo di Vittoria and Etna Rosato.

Key Terms

appellation contrôlée (AC)—Literally, "name controlled." A wine with this term on the label belongs to the highest classification of French wines and is strictly regulated by an agency of the French government.

Barolo—One of the best Piedmont red wines. A DOCG wine made from the Nebbiolo grape.

chaptalization—A procedure of adding sugar to grape juice prior to or during fermentation to attain the necessary alcohol level. This procedure is often necessary when weather conditions prevent grapes from ripening fully and developing enough natural sugar to convert to the amount of alcohol prescribed (often by law) for certain wines.

classico—The Italian designation reserved for the area which produces the best wine within a DOC-defined region.

Denominazione di Origine Controllata (DOC)—The authority that established 20 wine-producing regions in Italy; of these the Piedmont, Lombardy, Veneto,

Tuscany, and Latium are considered the major areas. Also, the term printed on Italian wine labels which ensures that a given wine meets various government requirements, particularly concerning its origin.

Denominazione di Origine Controllata e Garantita (DOCG)—The highest classification for Italian wines. These wines undergo a series of tastings by experts, in addition to meeting DOC standards.

indicazione geografica tipica (IGT)—A class of Italian wines within the *vino da tavola* category identifying wines regarded as slightly better than common table wines. These wines may include on their labels the vintage, place of origin, and grape variety.

Marsala—A famous sweet, fortified wine from Sicily; served as a dessert wine but often noted for its use in cooking (as in veal marsala).

spumante—The Italian word for sparkling wine.

super-Tuscan—High quality wines from Tuscany that, due to production methods outside of regulations established by the DOC, are classified as *vino da travola*.

vini tipici—Italian wines classfied below DOC and DOCG ratings. These wines are considered of good quality and typical of the wine of the regions from which they came. This Italian classification is much like the *vin de pays* of France or the *landwein* of Germany.

vino da tavola (VdT)—Also referred to as *vino ordinario*. Italian wines classified below *vini tipici* and corresponding to the French *vin de pays* or German *tafelwein*. As in France and Germany, it is that massive category of virtually unregulated wines.

Review Questions

1. What is Italy's version of France's *Appellation d'Origine Contrôlée*?

2. What does it mean for an Italian wine to be labeled *Denominazione di Origine Controllata e Garantita (DOCG)*?

3. What is the difference between a wine designated as *vin de table (VdT)* and a wine designated as *indicazione geografica tipica (IGT)*?

4. What are the compulsory items found on the labels of Italian *Denominazione di Origine Controllata (DOC)* wines?

5. How many Italian wine-producing regions are established by the *Denominazione di Origine Controllata (DOC)*?

6. What are some of the wines produced in the Piedmont region of Italy?

7. What kind of Italian wine is "spumante?"

8. What does "Chianti Classico" refer to?

9. What does the term "super-Tuscan" mean?

10. What kind of wine is Marsala and where is it produced?

Internet Sites

For more information, visit the following Internet sites. Remember that Internet addresses can change without notice. If the site is no longer there, you can use a search engine to look for additional sites. Many alcohol-related sites require users to be of legal drinking age to enter.

Wine Resources

Decanter Magazine
www.decanter.com

Professional Friends of Wine
winepros.org

The Wine Enthusiast
www.winemag.com

Wine Lover's Page
www.wineloverspage.com/
wines/

Wine Spectator
www.winespector.com

Reading Wine Labels

Epicurious
www.epicurious.com/d_drinking/
d08_wines/wine_label/wine_l
abel_main.html

The Winedoctor
www.thewinedoctor.com/advisory/
labelinterpreter.shtml

Robin Garr's Wine Lovers' Page
www.wine-lovers-page.com/wines/
labels.shtml

Internet Wine Guide.com
www.internetwineguide.com/
structure/abwine/labelreg.htm

Wines of the World

Aboutwines.com
www.aboutwines.com/home/refer
ence/regions/index.html

International Sommelier Guild
www.internationalsommelier.com

Internet Wine Guide.com
www.internetwineguide.com/
structure/ww/worldwide.htm

Cellarnotes.net
www.cellarnotes.net/wine_by_geo
graphic_origin.htm

Strat's Place
www.stratsplace.com/maps.html

Wine Regions of the World
www.wine-regions-of-the-world.com/
html/regions.html

Italy

Chianti Classico
www.chianticlassico.com/english/
home.htm

Vernon Wines Limited
www.vernonwines.co.uk

The Winedoctor
www.thewinedoctor.com/regional
guides/italy.shtml

Wine Pack
www.wine-pack.com/
italianwines.htm

Chapter 11 Outline

German Wine Classifications
    Qualitätswein mit Prädikat (QmP)
    Qualitätswein bestimmter
        Anbaugebiete (QbA)
    Landwein
    Deutsche Tafelwein (DTW)
    Quality Dry Wines
Labeling Regulations
Major Wine-Producing Areas
    Ahr
    Baden
    Franken
    Hessische Bergstrasse
    Mittelrhein
    Mosel-Saar-Ruwer
    Nahe
    Rheingau
    Rheinhessen
    Rheinpfalz
    Saale-Unstrut
    Sachsen
    Württemberg

Competencies

1. Explain the German wine classification system. (pp. 297–301)

2. Define items commonly found on the labels of German wine bottles. (pp. 301–303)

3. Identify the major wine-producing areas of Germany. (pp. 303–307)

11

Wines of Germany

GERMANY has a shorter growing season and a cooler climate than most of the world's wine-producing countries. The major challenge is getting enough sun and heat in a season to fully ripen the grapes. Consequently, the best wine-producing regions in Germany are those found along the Rhine and Mosel rivers. Here, the best vineyards are found close to the water. These vineyards are steeply sloped and have a high percentage of rock in the soil. The heat of the day is absorbed by the rocks and slowly released at night.

Nearly all the grape varieties that are successful in Germany are white. The Riesling grape variety produces the finest wines in Germany. However, the most widely cultivated grape variety is Müller-Thurgau, a contributor to Liebfraumilch, Germany's most exported (though not necessarily its highest-quality) wine.

German Wine Classifications

In 1971, Germany revised its wine regulations, making them stricter and broader in application. They covered many factors which related not only to general German viticulture conditions but also to specific local conditions. The major points of the 1971 wine regulations are in effect today—along with subsequent revisions. The classification system for German wines, summarized in Exhibit 1, is based on the sugar content of the grapes at the time of harvest.

Qualitätswein mit Prädikat (QmP)

Stiffly translated as "quality wine with special attributes," **QmP** wines are the highest quality German wines. The quality of QmP wines is largely rated by the amount of natural sugar in the grape at harvest. Accordingly, QmP wines are further classified into five categories of quality and natural sweetness. Each QmP wine carries one of the following special attributes on its label:

- *Kabinett*—a wine made from ripe grapes picked at the normal harvest time. These wines are usually the driest and least expensive of QmP wines.

- *Spätlese*—literally, "late picking," which means the grapes are picked up to three weeks later than the official harvest opening and are riper and, consequently, sweeter. The selective picking process can make Spätlese wines quite expensive.

- *Auslese*—literally, "late selected picking," this category uses selected bunches of the very ripest late harvest grapes. (At this point, the wine will retain some

Exhibit 1   German Wine Classifications

QmP

Qualitätswein mit Prädikat
(kvah-lih-TAYTS-vine mitt PRAY-dee-kaht)

A wine with this term on the label belongs to the highest classification level of German wines. Literally, "quality wine with special attributes." The attributes reflect the various stages of ripeness of the grapes when harvested. Six sub-categories with the QmP classification are:

- Kabinett (kah-bih-NEHT)
- Spätlese (SHPAYT-lay-zuh)
- Auslese (OWS-lay-zuh)
- Beerenauslese (BAY-*r*uhn-OWS-lay-zuh)
- Eiswein (ICE-vyn)
- Trockenbeerenauslese (T*R*AWK-uhn-bay-ruhn-OWS-lay-zuh)

QbA

Qualitätswein bestimmter Anbaugebiet
(kvah-lih-TAYTS-vine beh*r*-SHTIHMT-tuhr ahn-B)

A wine with this term on the label belongs to the second-highest level of German wines and indicates "quality wine from designated regions." Sugar may be added during the fermentation of QbA wines, allowing producers to reach the required minimum alcohol level.

Landwein

(LAHNT-vyn)

Literally, "wine of the land." These wines must also conform to regulations and compare well with French wines classified as *vin de pays*.

Deutscher Tafelwein (DTW)

(DOYT-shur TAH-fuh-vyn)

The lowest category of German wine. Labels for these "table wines" will indicate the name of one of Germany's broad growing regions. When used by itself, the word *Tafelwein* on a label indicates that the wine is not German.

For any given German wine, regulations may cover:

- Origin
- Wine name
- Vintage year
- Sugar content
- Grape varieties
- Testing

For audio pronunciations of key wine terms, visit the audio wine dictionary at www.stratsplace.com or at www.wineloverspage.com/lexicon/.

of its natural sweetness after full fermentation.) The best wine from these grapes is sweet and may be categorized as dessert wine.

- *Beerenauslese*—literally, "selected overripe picking," this category uses individual grapes selected for extreme ripeness and concentration, most often grapes which have been infected by the "**noble rot**" (*Edelfaüle* in German)—a mold growth on certain types of grapes resulting in naturally sweet wine. Beerenauslese wines are rare, expensive, and often considered among the world's best dessert wines.

- *Eiswein*—literally, "ice wine." A rare and costly QmP wine made in some years by leaving ripe grapes on the vine until they freeze, then crushing and removing the ice which leaves a heavy concentration of sugar and acid.

- *Trockenbeerenauslese*—literally, "dry grape, special late picking," this is the rarest of the categories. The grapes are left in the field until the *Edelfaüle* dries up the grape to an almost raisin-like state after which the berries are picked individually. Much less juice is obtained, and the harvest conditions are very rare (about one every ten years), so the wine is costly. These wines require a long aging period to be at their best. If properly stored, some can improve for a hundred years or more.

These "attributes" of the QmP label do not necessarily reflect the sweetness of the finished wine. The dryness of a wine is independent of the ripeness level of the grapes upon harvest. If the fementation is interrupted before all sugar is transformed, it will result in a sweeter style of wine. If the fermentation continues until little or no sugar is left, it results in a dry wine.

Depending on the wine-producing region, the quality control standards listed in this chapter must be met to receive the coveted QmP label.

Origin. Labels of QmP wines must show either region, district, cooperative, or vineyard. In some cases the village or township (*Gemeinde*) is given and may be combined with the vineyard: Niersteiner-Auflagen, for example. (Nierstein is the township where the Auflagen vineyard is located. Note the addition of "er" to Nierstein, indicating the wine is from that place, just as one would say "Londoner" for a person living in London.) QbA wines *may* show on the label their origin as region, district, township, cooperative, or vineyard. QmP wines must show vineyard (or *grosslagen*), township, and region, such as:

Bernkasteler-Doktor
Mosel-Saar-Ruwer

Wine Name. Many wines are named for their place of origin. However, in Germany (as in France), many wines are blends and bear a brand or proprietary name. Proprietary names may be used, such as Moselblümchen (now called Moselthaler), Liebfraumilch (Milk of the Blessed Mother), Schwartze Katz (Black Cat), or Hock, after the township of Hochheim in the Rheingau region.

Vintage Year. The **vintage** year is generally considered optional for German wines. However, *Tafelwein*, and *Deutsche Tafelwein* may not include any quality designation on their labels, including vintage year. Although vintage date on a label is no guarantee of quality, certain vintage years are better than others, particularly among wines of QmP designation.

Sugar Content. Often the growing season in Germany is such that the grapes ripen without adequate sugar to make the amount of alcohol prescribed by German regulations for various kinds of wine. Accordingly, the regulations allow limited sugaring (*anreichern*) of the **must** prior to fermentation in QbA wine, Landwein, and Tafelwein, but not in QmP wine. *Anreichern* is, in effect, the same as the French *chaptalization* process.

However, sweetening *after* fermentation is not only allowed but is more the rule than not in Germany; the result, when done properly, is an exceptional fruitiness characteristic of the best German wines. The finished wine is sweetened by adding some unfermented grape must. Only a small quantity is usually added.

Grape Varieties. The labels for all wines except Tafelwein must give the grape name. If the label for one of the quality level wines indicates the wine is a varietal wine, 85 percent of the grapes used to make the wine must be that grape. It is possible to indicate two kinds of grapes as a varietal combination; in this case both grapes must make up 85 percent of the grapes used, but no ratio of the combination is set. If the label gives a subregion, a village, or vineyard name, 85 percent of the grapes must come from there. These grape sources may be indicated as from five defined regions: Rhein, Mosel, Oberrhein, Neckar, and Main.

The Riesling grape is the premier grape of Germany—it is the great grape for the great German wines and no hybrids or other variety has yet surpassed it. However, its slow (and thus late) ripening characteristics which undoubtedly bring about its great taste characteristics are also, sometimes, its downfall. Many German wines are made from grapes which ripen earlier and thus avoid being wiped out by killing frosts in the fall. Among the other popular grape varieties are the Sylvaner, Müller-Thurgau, Weissburgunder (French Pinot Noir), Kerner, and Gutedel.

Testing. To be sure a wine meets the QmP or QbA standard, three bottles of the wine must be submitted to regulatory authorities for testing. If approved, the wine is given a certified number called *Amtliche Prüfungsnummer* (usually abbreviated on a wine label as "A.P. Nr."). If a wine does not meet a particular standard, it may be put into a lower classification—a QmP wine dropped to a QbA classification, for instance, or an *auslese* re-classified as a *spätlese*.

Qualitätswein bestimmter Anbaugebiete (QbA)

Literally, "quality wine from designated regions," **QbA** wines are in the second quality ranking. The basic legal difference between QbA and QmP wines is that *chaptalization* is permitted. That is, sugar may be added to the must to help the QbA wines ferment to required alcohol levels. To qualify as a QbA wine, the wine must come from one of the 13 quality wine regions and not contain wine from any other region. A local panel tests the wine to ensure that it embodies the typical character of an approved grape variety of the region. Wines awarded QbA status are assigned an official test number (A.P. Nr.) that is printed on the label along with the name of the wine-producing region. The required sugar and alcohol levels vary from one wine-producing region to another. These wines are generally consumed within the first few years after production.

Landwein

This "wine of the land" was reclassified from common table wine to recognize some qualitative differences in large regional areas. Production is subject to only a few regulations. *Landwein* corresponds nicely with the French *vins de pays* classification.

Deutscher Tafelwein (DTW)

Deutscher tafelwein (table wine) is a blended wine that compares with vin de pays of France and is usually consumed young and domestically. It is prohibited from claiming any vineyard origin; it may or may not indicate its origin by giving a township name. Look for Deutscher Tafelwein on the label if you want a good German table wine; it means all of the grapes have been grown in Germany. Tafelwein without the "Deutscher" designation is relatively uncontrolled, often using grapes from Italy.

Quality Dry Wines

In 1977 the Germans received approval from the EEC to market two types of wines with a designated standard of sugar content; one was *trocken* (dry) with a maximum residual sugar content of 0.9 percent (9 g/L) and the other was *halbtrocken* (half-dry) with a maximum residual sugar content of 1.8 percent (18 g/L). Limits of the acid-sugar ratio in these wines were also set. German producers asked for these classifications because many consumers of German wines have expressed a preference for a wine drier than the quality sweet wines—something similar to the wines of Alsace—wines which would more appropriately accompany food.

Labeling Regulations

Labeling is strictly controlled and considerable information is required on a German wine label so consumers can know what they are getting. Exhibit 2 illustrates how to read a German wine label. Labeling regulations specify items that are compulsory, optional, and prohibited. Compulsory label items for a German QmP wine include:

- Country of origin
- Appellation of origin
- Quality standard
- Name and address of producer/brand owner
- Bottle content
- Alcohol content
- Analysis, tasting notes, approvals

Exhibit 2   Reading German Wine Labels

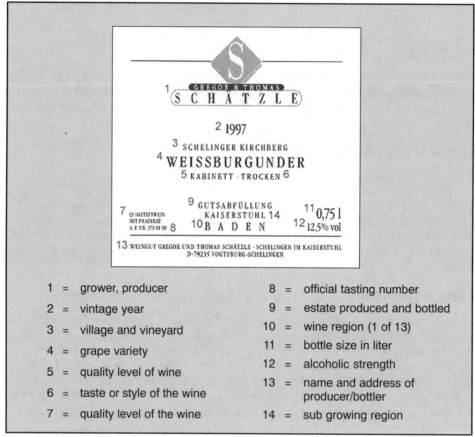

1	=	grower, producer	8 =	official tasting number
2	=	vintage year	9 =	estate produced and bottled
3	=	village and vineyard	10 =	wine region (1 of 13)
4	=	grape variety	11 =	bottle size in liter
5	=	quality level of wine	12 =	alcoholic strength
6	=	taste or style of the wine	13 =	name and address of producer/bottler
7	=	quality level of the wine	14 =	sub growing region

Source: Peter Ruhrberg's German Wine Page. For more information about German wine, visit the Web site at: www.winepage.de.

Optional items include: grape variety, vintage, name of the vineyard, authenticity seal, the term "Domain," and terms such as "dry," "medium dry," or "sweet," Prohibited items include: the term "wine" and sulfites or other additives. Other labeling regulations apply to the bottler, the vintage, and to the brand or château name.

The grower, producer, and bottler is not always the same person. There are about 100,000 grape growers in Germany, yet only about a fourth as many producers. If the label indicates *Erzeugerabfüllung* (estate-bottled), it assures you that the grapes were grown and the wine was produced by one and the same grower or cooperative of growers (*Winzergenossenschaft*). The grower or collective group of growers is responsible for and guarantees the quality of the wine. The bottler or shipper whose name is on the label assumes responsibility for the wine's quality, and this fact is identified on the label by the term, *abfüllung*.

An effervescent wine resembling champagne is made by the Germans and, under 1986 regulations, must be made from German grapes. The label will give the name of *Deutscher Sekt*, but in the United States it may be labeled German Sekt. The label should give an A. P. number. Also one may find on the label the letters b. A. which indicates the wine was produced from grapes from the area named on the label. If only *Deutscher Sekt* appears, the grapes may come from any German area. In the past, much of Sekt was made from grapes imported from Italy or France. This is still done and the label will indicate this by having on it only the term *Sekt*. Sparkling Hock and sparkling Moselles are prominent among *Sekt* wines. Most German sparkling wines tend to be sweeter than their French counterparts.

Major Wine-Producing Areas

There are thirteen designated wine regions in Germany. As shown in Exhibit 3, most of these regions are in the southwestern part of the country. Exhibit 4 offers a pronunciation guide for the thirteen regions. The German designated wine-producing regions are subdivided as follows:

> 13 Regions or *Anbaugebiete* (AHN-bow-geh-beet) within the country
> 43 Districts or *Bereichen* (beh-RIKH-ehn) within the 13 regions
> 150 General sites or *Grosslagen* (GROSS-lah-gehn) across the 43 districts
> 2,600 Vineyards or *Einzellagen* (I'n-tsuh-lah-gehn) throughout the country

As with the château designation in French labeling, the smaller the unit, the higher the quality is likely to be. *Einzellagen* corresponds to the French *châteaux*.

Only five of the designated wine-growing areas of Germany produce wines that are found commonly in the United States: these are the wines of the regions of Mosel-Saar-Ruwer, Rheingau, Rheinhessen (Hessen), Rheinpfalz (Palatinate), and Nahe. These five are grouped together in the central Rhine River area.

Ahr

One of the smallest German wine regions, Ahr's vineyards extend along the steep hillsides that line the Ahr River as it flows into the Rhine south of Bonn. In spite of its northern location, the vast majority of wines produced are red. Most of the wine is consumed locally.

Baden

The southernmost of Germany's wine regions, Baden's climate helps create wines with typically higher alcohol content and less acidity than other German regions. Soil conditions range from gravel, limestone, and clay, to volcanic stone near the famous Kaiserstuhl, an extinct volcano. The climate and soil enables Baden to produce a diverse range of wines.

Franken

Just east of Frankfort, Franken's vineyards are on hilly slopes of the Main River and its tributaries. Franken's climate can be cold and the area is planted mainly with white grapes. Traditionally, most Franken wines are bottled in a squat, green or amber flagon called a *Bocksbeutel*.

Exhibit 3   German Wine Regions

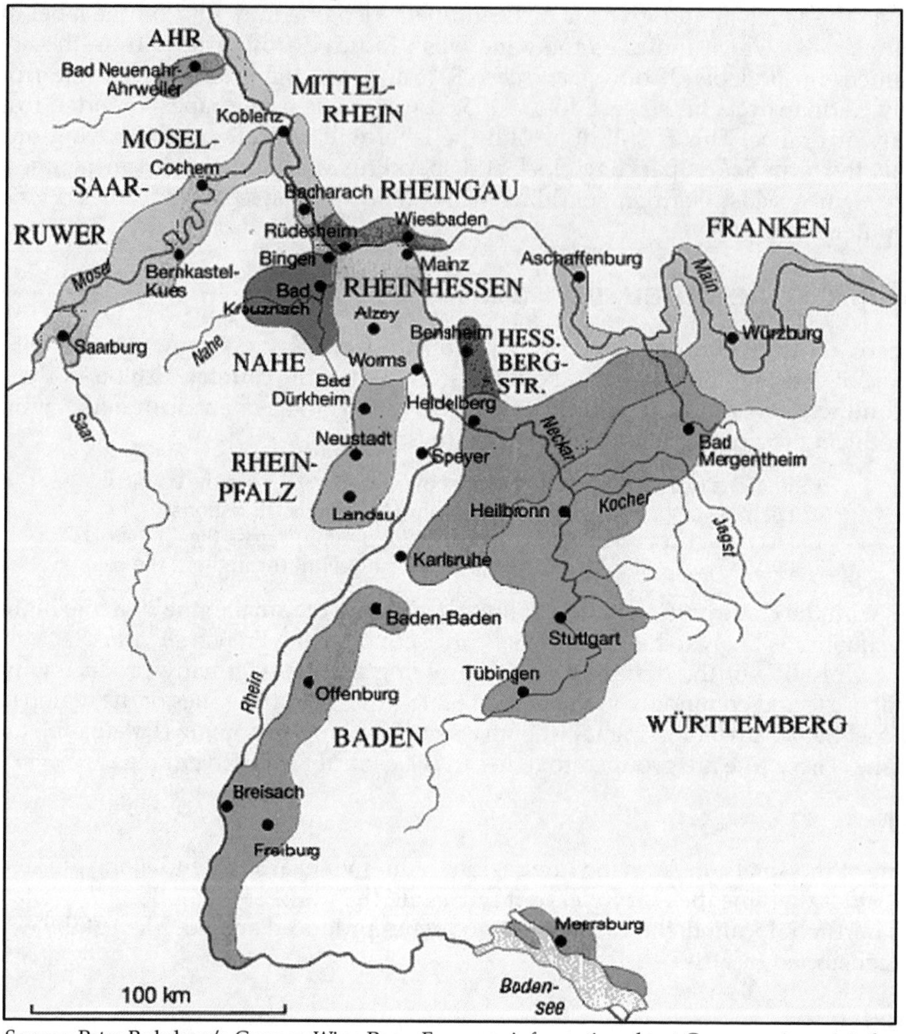

Source: Peter Ruhrberg's German Wine Page. For more information about German wine, visit the Web site at: www.winepage.de.

Hessische Bergstrasse

One of the smallest of the German regions, Hessische Bergstrasse begins north of Darmstadt and runs south to Heidelberg. Over half of the vineyard area is planted with Riesling. Most wines produced here are consumed locally.

Mittelrhein

Another small German region, Mittlerhein lies along the Rhine with steep, terraced vineyards below medieval castles and ruins. Riesling predominates.

Exhibit 4   Pronunciation Guide—Major German Wine-Producing Areas

Ahr (AHR)

Baden (BAHD-uhn)

Franken (FRAHNG-kuhn)

Hessische Bergstrasse (HEH-see-shuh BEHRK-strah-suh)

Mittelrhein (MIHT-uh-rine)

Mosel-Saar-Ruwer (MOH-zuhl sahr ROO-vay*r*)

Nahe (NAH-uh)

Rheingau (RINE-gow)

Rheinhessen (RINE-hehs-uhn)

Rheinpfalz (RINE-fahlts)

Württemberg (VU*R*T-uhm-beh*r*k)

Saale-Unstrut (ZAHL oon-sht*r*uht)

Sachsen (ZAHKH-zuhn)

For audio pronunciations of key wine terms, visit the audio wine dictionary at www.strat splace.com or at www.wineloverspage.com/lexicon/.

Mosel-Saar-Ruwer

The soil of the Mosel-Saar-Ruwer region is high in slate and stones which capture heat in the day and lose it slowly during the night. The great Riesling grape predominates in this region, producing excellent wines of light alcoholic content (8 percent to 10 percent), with light, crisp body, and a dry, fragrant flavor. The best wines come from middle Mosel areas such as Piesport, Bernkastel, Zeltingen, and Erdener Treppchen.

Nahe

Nahe sits between Rheinpfalz and Alsace. Its wines resemble those of the Rheingau but often carry more fruity bouquet and flavor with a somewhat earthy flavor. The best wines will come from the vineyards located in the villages of Bad Kreuznach, Niederhausen an der Nahe, and Schloss Böckelheim.

Rheingau

The Rheingau area is northwest of the Rhine River bend as it moves toward Koblenz and includes the adjoining west bank of the Main River, where it flows into the Rhine. The wines come in tall, slim, brown bottles. Rheingau wines are delicate and have a light body and flavor, a fragrant bouquet, and a brilliant sparkle, but some may be a bit austere and hard. They are light in alcohol and may vary in quality from year to year, depending on seasonal and climatic conditions. The labels will usually have the name of the village or township with the Schloss name or just the name of the vineyard. The best wines of the area usually come from the villages of Eltville, Erbach, Geisenheim, Hallgarten, Hattenheim, Hochheim (the home of Hock), Johannisberg, Kiedrich, Oestrich, Rauenthal, Rüdesheim, and Winkel. The famous Schloss Johannisberg, Schloss Vollrads, Rüdesheimer Schlossberg, Marcobrunn, and Steinberg wines come from this area.

Rheinhessen

The Rheinhessen is located on the inner side of the Rhine River where it meets the Main River. Its wines are like those of the Rheingau but are a bit softer and richer. They are apt to have a slightly higher alcoholic content and a heavier bouquet and flavor.

The famed proprietary wine called "**Liebframilch**" (Milk of the Blessed Mother) was originally a Hessian wine, but today regulations allow this blended wine to be made in the Rheingau, Rheinhessen, Rheinpfalz, and Nahe. Liebfraumilch is, legally, a QbA from the four regions mentioned and from three grape varieties: Riesling, Sylvaner, and Müller-Thurgau. The name "Liebfraumilch" cannot be on a label larger than the name of the region. The original Liebfraumilch does not carry the name. Instead, it will be sold under the name of one of the famous vineyards—Liebfrauen, Stift, or Kirchenstück—that surround the Church of Our Beloved Lady (*Liebfrauenkirche*) in the city of Worms. The other imitators are apt to be good if they come under the name of a good shipper and from Nierstein, Nackenheim, or Oppenheim, but many poor Liebfraumilchs are marketed in the United States.

Rheinpfalz

South of Hessia is the Rheinpfalz (Palatinate) region where the grapes develop greater sugar content and the resultant wines are not as dry as most German wines. They also tend to be higher in alcohol. The Mittel-Haardt area between Neustadt and Bad Dürkheim produces the best wine, especially around Wachenheim, Forst, Deidesheim, Ruppertsberg, Bad Dürkheim, Kallstadt, Leistadt, and Königsbach. The better wines have a delicate flavor, rich fruitiness, soft bouquet, and great delicacy. They are less crisp and harsh than the Rheingau wines. In good years, many of the *Beerenauslese* and *Trockenbeerenauslese* wines come from here. The poorest wines from this area are coarse, lack flavor, and may taste heavily of soil (described as *bodeneschmack*).

Saale-Unstrut

Formerly under control of the East German government and west of Leipzig, Saale-Unstrut wines are improving as vineyards and wine-making facilities become upgraded.

Sachsen

Sachsen's vineyards are on the slopes of the Elbe River. This easternmost wine region in Germany is, like Saale-Unstrut, attempting to improve its vineyards and wine-making facilities.

Württemberg

The largest red wine region in Germany, Württemberg includes the cities of Stuttgart and Heidelberg. Most of the vineyards lie along the Neckar rivers and extend from the Tauber River valley to south of Stuttgart. There are many small vineyards in the region with over half of the planted acreage in red varieties.

🗝️ Key Terms

chaptalization—A procedure of adding sugar to grape juice or must prior to or during fermentation to attain the necessary alcohol level. This procedure is often necessary when weather conditions prevent grapes from ripening fully and developing enough natural sugar to convert to the amount of alcohol prescribed (often by law) for certain wines.

Deutscher tafelwein (DVT)—German table wine. A blended wine that compares with *vin de pays* of France and is usually consumed young and domestically. It is prohibited from claiming any vineyard origin; it may or may not indicate its origin by giving a township name.

halbtrocken—A German word for "half-dry" or "medium dry," referring to wines that are sweeter than *trocken* wines. German regulations cite requirements for residual sugar and total acidity.

landwein—Literally, "wine of the land." This German wine classification recognizes some qualitative differences among table wines in large regional areas. It corresponds nicely with the French *vins de pays* classification.

Liebfraumilch—A popular German white wine grown in several specified German wine regions, from a combination of grape varieties specified by government regulations.

must—The juice of freshly crushed grapes that will be fermented into wine; can include pulp, skins, and seeds.

noble rot—A mold, Botrytis cinerea, which infects certain types of grapes in late fall, when morning mists and afternoon sun create ideal growing conditions for the mold; it is called "noble" because it creates some of the greatest naturally sweet wines.

Qualitätswein bestimmter Anbaugebiete (QbA)—Literally, "quality wine from designated regions," QbA wines are in the second quality ranking of German wines. The basic legal difference between QbA and QmP wines is that sugar may be added to the must to help the QbA wines ferment to required alcohol levels.

Qualitätswein mit Prädikat (QmP)—Stiffly translated as "quality wine with special attributes," QmP wines are the highest quality German wines. The quality of QmP wines is largely rated by the amount of natural sugar in the grape at harvest.

sekt—Ordinary sparkling wine from Germany.

trocken—German word meaning "dry." According to German regulations, a wine labeled *"trocken"* must meet strict requirements regarding residual sugar and total acidity.

vintage—The year of the actual grape harvest and the wine made from those grapes. Since the quality of harvests varies from year to year, vintage is only a general guideline to wine quality. An excellent year for a particular growing region signifies a generally superior quality for that vintage.

Review Questions

1. What are the challenges facing German wine producers?

2. What does it mean for a German wine to be labeled QmP?

3. What is the difference between a wine designated as *landwein* and a wine designated as *Deutscher tafelwein*?

4. Why don't all German wine labels use the same terminology?

5. What is the difference between a wine labeled *"trocken"* and a wine labeled *"halbtrocken?"*

6. What kind of German wine is "sket?"

7. How are the thirteen designated wine-producing regions of Germany subdivided?

8. What is the German classification for Liebfraumilch?

9. What kind of wines are produced in the Mosel-Saar-Ruwer region of Germany?

10. What do the German wine-producing regions of Saale-Unstrut and Sachsen have in common?

Internet Sites

For more information, visit the following Internet sites. Remember that Internet addresses can change without notice. If the site is no longer there, you can use a search engine to look for additional sites. Many alcohol-related sites require users to be of legal drinking age to enter.

Wine Resources

Decanter Magazine
www.decanter.com

Professional Friends of Wine
winepros.org

The Wine Enthusiast
www.winemag.com

Wine Lover's Page
www.wineloverpage.com/wine/

Wine Spectator
www.winespector.com

Reading Wine Labels

Epicurious
www.epicurious.com/d_drinking/
d08_wine/wine_label/wine_
label_main.html

The Winedoctor
www.thewinedoctor.com/advisory/
labelinterpreter.shtm

Robin Garr's Wine Lovers' Page
www.wine-lovers-page.com/wine/
labels.shtml

Internet Wine Guide.com
www.internetwineguide.com/
structure/abwine/labelreg.htm

Wines of the World

Aboutwines.com
www.aboutwines.com/
home/reference/regions/index.htm

International Sommelier Guild
www.internationalsommelier.com

Internet WineGuide.com
www.internetwineguide.com/struc
ture/ww/worldwide.htm

Cellarnotes.net
www.cellarnotes.net/wine_by_
geographic_origin.htm

Strat's Place
www.stratsplace.com/maps.htm

Wine Regions of the World
www.wine-regions-of-the-world.
com/html/regions.htm

Germany

The German Wine Society Online
www.germanwinesociety.org

The German Wine Institute
www.deutscheweine.de/

GermanWine.de
www.germanwine.de/english/

Peter Ruhrberg's German Wine Page
www.winepage.de/

The Winedoctor
www.thewinedoctor.com/regional
guides/germany.shtml

Chapter 12 Outline

Spain
    Spanish Wine Classification System
    Labeling Regulations
    Major Wine-Producing Areas
Portugal
    Portuguese Wine Classification System
    Labeling Regulations
    Major Wine-Producing Areas

Competencies

1. Explain the Spanish wine classification system. (pp. 311–313)

2. Identify items commonly found on the labels of Spanish wine bottles. (pp. 313–314)

3. Explain the solera system of aging sherry produced in the Jerez region of Spain. (pp. 314–317)

4. Explain the Portuguese wine classification system. (pp. 317–318)

5. Identify items commonly found on the labels of Portuguese wine bottles. (pp. 318–319)

6. Describe the different types of port produced in the Douro region of Portugal. (pp. 319–321)

Wines of Spain and Portugal

Spain

WHILE, IN THE PAST, SPAIN was known primarily for sherry, many types of Spanish wines have grown in quality over the past 30 years. Today, many wines have acquired a solid international reputation. The country's varied geography contributes to the variety of wines produced. Also, the steady sunshine of its general climate can raise the sugar levels in grapes, making it possible to produce some wines with high alcohol content. Spain has the largest amount of vineyard land of any country in the world but the average yields are low, leaving Spain third in the world in terms of tonnage of grapes produced. Since joining the European Union in 1986, Spain has refined its regulations governing the wine industry.

Spanish Wine Classification System

In 1972, Spain established new regulations to control its alcoholic beverage industry. Collectively, these regulations are referred to as *Denominaciones de Origen (DO)*, "destination of origin." The law and its enforcement were modeled after the French *appellation contrôlée (AC)* system. There are more than fifty DO wine areas in Spain. Each region has its own governing body that may enforce stricter regulations than those enforced federally by the DO.

Regulatory councils in each region collect wine samples every year from winemakers (*bodegas*) and send them to the region's *Consejo Regulador* (Control Board) for analysis and classification. If a wine passes the examination, a special number is assigned which can be placed on the back of every bottle of that lot. All wine exports must be sent to the *Consejo* to be examined; the cases are then wax sealed to assure they remain authentic. Exhibit 1 summarizes the Spanish wine classification system discussed below.

Denominación de Origen Calificada (DOCa). This highest category of Spanish wines has, so far, been awarded only to wines from the Rioja wine-producing region. Wines labeled as "qualified designation of origin" must meet stricter standards than wines designated as DO.

Denominación de Origen (DO). This "designation of origin" category parallels the French *Appellation d'Origine Contrôlée* classification. However, the standards for Spanish DO wines do not appear to be as high as the standards for French AC wines. Almost fifty percent of Spanish wines qualify for DO designation, while only about twenty-five percent of French wines achieve an AC status. Wines

Exhibit 1   Spanish Wine Classifications

DOCa

Denominación de Origen Calificada

[deh-naw-mee-nah-THYON deh aw-REE-hen kah-lee-fee-KA-da]
> "Qualified designation of origin" is the highest category for Spanish wines.

DO

Denominación de Origen (DO)

[deh-naw-mee-nah-THYON deh aw-REE-hen]
> A Spanish wine with DO, "destination of origin," on its label meets require-
> ments of the European Economic Community's highest wine classification.

vino de la tierra

[BEE-noh theh lah TYEH*R*-*r*ah]
> This is the Spanish term for "country wines," a new category that's equiva-
> lent to the French category of *vin de pays* and the German classification of
> *landwein*.

vino de la mesa

[BEE-noh theh MAY-sah]
> The lowest classification of Spanish wines, "table wine," is made from
> unclassified wine-producing areas and/or from various blends. This desig-
> nation is similar to France's *vin de table*, Germany's *tafelwein*, and Italy's
> *vino da tavola*.

For any given DO wine from a specific region, regulations may cover:

- Production area
- Grape variety
- Viticulture standards
- Yield
- Production methods
- Aging specifications
- Alcohol content

For audio pronunciations of key wine terms, visit the audio wine dictionary at www.strat
splace.com or at www.wineloverspage.com/lexicon/.

within the DO category can be further classified in relation to the amount of time
the wine ages in tanks, wood, or in bottles. These classifications are *crianza*, *reserva*,
and *gran reserva*. The rules for labeling wines within these categories are defined
by the governing body of each DO. If a DO has no rules governing these designations, the following federal standards apply:

Crianza wines must receive a minimum of two years aging either in a
tank, an oak barrel, or a bottle. Many of the DOs require that wine age in
oak barrels for at least one of the required years.

Reserva wines must have a minimum of three years of aging, with at least
one year in oak barrels. Rosé and white reserves require a minimum of
aging of two years, with at least six months in oak.

Exhibit 2   Reading Spanish Wine Labels

1. Bodega: The name of the vineyard. In this case, the vineyard is
   Martinez Bujanda.

2. Region: The location where the
   grapes have been grown. This
   label shows that the grapes were
   grown in the Rioja region, the
   largest and best-known area for
   grape growing in Spain.

3. Varietal: The type of grape used
   to make the wine. Here, Garna-
   cha grapes were used. Other
   popular varietals in Spain include
   Tempranillo, Graciano, Mazuelo,
   Viura, Malavasia, Xarello, and
   Parellada.

4. Vintage: The year the wine was
   made. The wine in this bottle
   dates back to 1990.

Source: Coleción Internacional del Vino-USA. For more information, visit the company's Internet site at: www.civusa.com.

Gran Reserva red wines must age for five years (with two of those years in wooden barrels) and white and rosé wines must age for four years (six months in wood).

Vino de la Tierra. This category of wines directly below DO classification is equivalent to the French category of *vin de pays* and the German classification of *landwein*.

Vino de la Mesa. The lowest classification of Spanish wines, "table wine," is made from unclassified wine-producing areas and/or from various blends. This designation is similar to France's *vin de table*, Germany's *tafelwein*, and Italy's *vino da tavola*.

Labeling Regulations

Exhibit 2 illustrates how to read a Spanish wine label. Regulations govern the labeling of Spanish DO wines. These regulations specify items that are compulsory, optional, and prohibited. Compulsory label items include:

- Country of origin
- Appellation of origin
- Quality standard

- Name and address of producer/brand owner
- Bottle content
- Alcohol content
- The term "wine" (for some regions)

Optional items include: grape variety, vintage, name of the vineyard, the term "Domain," and terms such as "dry," "medium dry," or "sweet," and an authenticity seal. Sulfites or other additives are prohibited and, for some regions, the term "wine."

A significant difference between the wine industry in Spain and France is that the Spanish wine producers, the powerful *bodegas*, are generally more important than vineyards or estates. They buy the best grapes from local farmers to supplement the grapes they grow themselves. Estate bottling (estates which produce all the grapes and bottle their own production) is not a factor. Only one vineyard is featured on all the sherries made in Spain. And only one estate, Castillo Ygay, is prominent in wine-producing area of Rioja.

Major Wine-Producing Areas

Today, the DO *(Denominaciones de Origen)* has established more than fifty wine-growing regions and each has specific regulations. Exhibit 3 outlines the DO regions and Exhibit 4 offers a pronunciation guide for some of the major regions. The *Instituto Nacional de Denominaciones de Origen* (**INDO**) was set up to provide regions with assistance in producing and marketing their products and in conforming to the regulations. The federal INDO system appoints a *Consejo Regulador* for each appellation (DO), and this local body establishes and enforces regulations regarding varietals, cultivation, vinification, and aging procedures. The *Consejo Regulador* also registers vineyards and *bodegas*, monitors stocks from vineyard to bottle, and tests before approving for export.

Rioja. One of the main growing regions is **Rioja**, about 200 miles southwest of Bordeaux. Rioja wines are often favorably compared to French wines from Bordeaux and Burgundy. Rioja is the only region in Spain whose wines are awarded *Denominación de Origen Calificada (DOCa)* status. Rioja has three growing areas: Rioja Alta, over 2000 feet above sea level, Rioja Alavesa, about 1500 feet above sea level, and Rioja Baja, around 1000 feet high. Alta and Alavesa's wines are usually exported; Baja's wines are a bit harsher, higher in alcohol, and mostly for local consumption. All the Rioja areas have much sun and warmth during the growing season, so the grapes develop considerable sugar, resulting in wines of fairly high alcohol content. The red Riojas will be full bodied, balanced in acid with a rich, full flavor, fruity bouquet, and fairly high tannin content. Some are apt to be fiery. The reds are basically of two types: a *tinto* which may be considered Spain's answer to a Burgundy-type wine—deep, full red in color, with a heavy body and full flavor; the other kind is a *rioja* which is lighter in body and flavor and might be compared to a Beaujolais, only heavier in body and flavor. The whites will also have a rich, fruity bouquet, high alcohol content and rich, full flavor, but are less likely to have some of the harshness sometimes displayed by the reds.

Exhibit 3   Wine Regions of Spain

Source: Coleción Internacional del Vino-USA. The names appearing in boxes with arrows are wineries operated by the company. For more information, visit the company's Internet site at: www.civusa.com.

Catalonia. Another region producing good quality wines is **Catalonia**, especially around the area of Penedés, near Barcelona. The winemaker of note here is Bodega Torres, operated by the Torres family for over three centuries, but fully modernized with stainless steel fermenting vats, and planting traditional grapes such as the Pinot Noir, Cabernet, Chardonnay, and Gewürztraminer. Its reds age well, carrying a good balance of acid-tannin-alcohol. They are heavy in body and full in flavor with a velvety feel in the mouth. Their Gran Coronas Black Label is pure Cabernet and carries a fruity bouquet reminiscent of blackberries.

Jerez. Spain's most famous wine is **sherry**, production of which is limited by the INDO to a wine-growing region of **Jerez** in the southwestern part of Spain known as Andalusia. Jerez is short for the full name of the region, *Jerez-Xérèx-Sherry y Manzanilla de Sanlúcar de Barrameda.*

Sherry is a fortified wine. Fortified wines have higher levels of alcohol than that produced with natural yeast fermentation. These wines are "fortified" to higher alcohol content by adding brandy or neutral spirits. Only wine of Spanish origin can truly be labeled sherry; all the imitators must mention the place of origin on the label, such as California sherry.

Exhibit 4   Pronunciation Guide—Some Spanish Wine-Producing Areas

> **Almansa** (ahl-MAHN-suh)
>
> **Catalonia** (katl-OH-nee-uh)
>
> **Condado de Huelva** (kohn-DAH-doh day-WAYL-bah)
>
> **Jerez** (heh-RETH)
>
> **La Mancha** (lah MAHN-chah)
>
> **Navarra** (nah-VAHR-RAH)
>
> **Penedès** (pay-NAY-dahss)
>
> **Priorato** (pryaw-RAW-tah)
>
> **Rias Baixas** (REE-ahs bi-SHAHS)
>
> **Ribera del Duero** (ree-BEHR-ah del DWAY-roh)
>
> **Rioja** (ree-OH-hah)
>
> **Rueda** (roo-AY-dah)
>
> **Tarragona** (tah-rah-GAW-nuh)
>
> **Valdepeñas** (bahl-deh-PEH-nyahss)
>
> **Valencia** (vuh-LEHN-shee-uh; bahl-LEHN-thyah)
>
> **Yecla** (YAY-klah)

For audio pronunciations of key wine terms, visit the audio wine dictionary at www.strat splace.com or at www.wineloverspage.com/lexicon/.

Aging is accomplished by the *solera* **system**, an elaborate blending of sherries of similar character according to individual *bodega* formulas and guided by Spanish law. Rows of casks are stacked in tiers—usually ten tiers maximum and three minimum. The casks are outside so they are exposed to the full effects of the Spanish sun and warmth. After sufficient aging, sherry from the bottom casks is removed for bottling and wine from the next higher tier is added to the bottom casks, wine from the third tier added to fill up the second tiers, and so on, with new wine topping off the casks in the highest tier. By law, only 33% can be removed from the bottom cask each year. Because there are fewer casks as the tiers go up, more than 33% is removed from the upper tiers, so casks in the top tier will often require about 80% new wine to be completely filled.

Casks are also not tightly bunged so air can enter, encouraging the growth of *flor*, a thin, yeasty, whitish film that forms over the wine, slowing the process of oxidation and helping to give sherry its typical flavor. The longer the sherry remains in contact with the *flor*, the finer the sherry. These finer sherries are, in fact, called *finos*. Some heavier sherries, however, develop little or no *flor* (or are given a stronger dose of fortifying spirit which discourages *flor*) and produce *oloroso* type sherries. A third, rare class of sherry—*palo cortado*—combines the depth and body of an *oloroso* with the finesse of a *fino*.

All sherries are fermented dry, i.e., all the grape sugar is turned into alcohol during fermentation. While coloring sometimes takes place after aging (with a tasteless, blackish wine called *vino de color*), aging in wood darkens color. All sherries come from the cask dry at 13 percent to 14 percent alcohol but are sweetened, made deeper in color, or given a higher alcohol content by addition. Sherry is sweetened by the addition of a heavy grape syrup or *dulce*, a sweetening wine often made from the sweet Muscat grape especially for blending. Alcohol can be increased to 15 percent, even over 20 percent, by adding brandy made from the last pressings of grapes. The following classifies sherries according to their dryness or sweetness:

Manzanilla	Pale and light bodied; somewhat acid and salty flavor; very dry, fine sherry
Fino	Very pale color; more body but less dry than Manzanillas; light body; distinctive, soft, nutty flavor
Amontillado	Dry, golden color with fuller body than finos
Amoroso	Golden to light amber; medium dry; some body
Oloroso	Amber to light brown or tan color; full body; sweet; full, well-balanced, nutty flavor; delicate, rich aroma
Cream	Deep tan to brown; full body; rich, full flavor; very sweet; rich bouquet

Beyond solera blending, most sherry is also a further blend of finos, olorosos, coloring, sweeteners, sometimes a little unaged, young wine for freshness, and extremely old, wood-aged sherry used as a flavoring agent. The particular blending formulas not only create the *Amontillados* and cream sherries, but produce the distinctive taste associated with a particular *bodega* or brand.

Portugal

Portugal is the world's seventh largest wine-producing nation. While **port** is the country's most famous wine, some authorities claim that the greatest wine of Portugal is Moscatel de Setúbal, rated along with some of the greatest dessert wines of the world as "out of this world." It is made from Muscat grapes and is less fortified than port. It is excellent both young and aged.

Perhaps Portugal's greatest world-wide marketing success was created by Mateus with its semi-sweet, semi-sparkling rosé. The phenomenal success of Mateus led to many other companies producing similar wines. The rosés are made from grapes anywhere in Portugal and made much like rosés anywhere with the red skins in contact with the fermenting must for only a short time.

Portuguese Wine Classification System

Portugal was actually the first nation to regulate its wine industry. Almost 180 years before the French adopted the *appellation d'origine contrôlée* system, Portugal regulated wine production through a "demarcated region" (*Região Demarcada*) system. However, control was allowed to lapse and until very recently, one had to look to the brand name of a bottler as the sole indication of quality. Joining the European Economic Community has helped to change that situation, and today,

Exhibit 5   Reading Portuguese Wine Labels

From the Port House of **Fonseca** comes this **Vintage Port** from **1991**. Port vintages are generally declared three or four times each decade, depending on the quality of the wines produced that year. In non-declared years (Fonseca chose to declare 1992 in favor of 1991), if quality is sufficient, some vintage wine will still be made, and Fonseca calls this wine **Guimaraens.** Vintage Port must be aged in oak for at least two years, and indeed this label tells us that the wine was **Bottled in 1994.** Beneath this there is some information regarding the producer, revealing that Fonseca, like all the top Port houses, has offices in **Oporto.**

Source: The Winedoctor. For more information, visit the Internet site at: www.thewinedoctor.com/advisory/labelinterpreter.shtml.

areas of production have been redefined and production regulated by a *Denominação de origem* system.

The highest category of Portuguese wines is ***Denominação de Origem Controlada (DOC)***. Wines of lesser quality may be labeled ***Indicação de Proveniencia Regulamentada (IPR).*** The classification system requires that all exports bear the government seal of guarantee (*selo de garantia*). The term *reserva* indicates a high quality, aged wine from a good harvest. The term *garrafeira* indicates that the wine is the merchant's best—a cut above a *reserva*, aged in the bottle as well as the barrel. Some of the more well-known exporters of *garrafeira* wines are: Aliança, Arealva, Aveleda, Garcia, Gatao, Gazela, Mesa do Presidente, and Ouro do Minho. Wines are either *verde* (young) or *maduro* (mature).

Labeling Regulations

Exhibit 5 explains some of the information found on Portuguese wine labels. Regulations govern the labeling of Portuguese DOC wines. These regulations specify items that are compulsory, optional, and prohibited. Compulsory label items include:

- Country of origin
- Appellation of origin
- Quality standard
- Vintage
- Name and address of producer/brand owner
- Bottle content

- Alcohol content

- Authenticity seal

Optional items include: grape variety, name of the vineyard, the term "Domain," and terms such as "dry," "medium dry," or "sweet," sulfites or other additives, and commentaries such as analysis, tasting notes, or approvals. The term "wine" is prohibited.

Major Wine-Producing Areas

Exhibit 6 reproduces an online, interactive map of the wine-producing regions of Portugal. Most of Portugal's wine is produced in the northern part of the country, known as the **Minho**, where the wine known as *vinho verde* (literally, "green wine") is made—the "green" refers to the youth of the wine and not its color. The whites are a pale lemon color and the reds, a light ruby. The wine is clean, crisp, and refreshing with a slight spritz or fizziness.

Dão is the biggest and most prosperous producer of *vinho maduro* wines. It also produces some excellent fruity, medium-bodied reds, that are smooth and soft to drink even though young. Some very good dry whites also come from the region.

The Portuguese islands of Madeira, Porto Santo, and Desertas are known for only one wine—**Madeira**. It is made from the Rhine Riesling grape. The grapes develop considerable sugar, and fermentation is stopped midway by the addition of brandy. The result is a sweet fortified wine.

Bucelas produces crisp, dry reds with a fairly high tartness. Bairrada makes excellent rich, dark, full-bodied and full-flavored reds which are high in alcohol. Its whites are delicate, moderate in body, with just a touch of sweetness or the sensation of it.

Portugal's most famous wine is port, as it is known in English or porto, as it is known in other countries. It is one of the original trinity of great processed wines which includes champagne and sherry. Although the wines are made inland in the **Douro** wine-producing area, most go for aging and shipping to the seaport of Oporto.

Today, port is one of the most strictly regulated of all wines—every stage of its production is overseen and controlled. In a few places, crushing is still accomplished by bare feet; however, new crushing machinery is now commonplace. Fermentation takes place in closed, concrete tanks where natural carbon dioxide keeps bubbling up, breaking up the cap, and causing the juice to churn in contact with the skins.

When fermentation has reached the stage where half the sugar has been used up, the partially fermented juice is poured into a barrel containing one-fourth brandy. Fermentation stops immediately upon contact with the brandy as the alcohol kills the remaining yeast cells. Port ends up at 18 percent to 22 percent alcohol and is moved to shippers' lodges where it is stored, aged, and blended much like sherry. Barrel aging must be for at least three years; what is called "vintage" port can be wood-aged two years, but must be bottle-aged for many more.

Exhibit 6   Wine Regions of Portugal

This interactive map is available from the Portuguese Trade Commission at their Internet site: www.winesofportugal.org. Clicking on areas of the map provides information about wine-producing regions in Portugal.

A ruby port is the youngest port; a tawny port is so called because aging for a long time (six to eight years) in the barrels causes a degeneration of the red pigments which turn a brownish purple. The ultimate port—a vintage port—is not blended but produced from the grapes of an exceptionally good year. About three out of ten years qualify. As mentioned earlier, vintage port is only aged in the barrel for two years; its significant aging takes place in the bottle where it must be aged 15 to 20 years, but many shippers won't put it on the market until it is at least 25 years old. The wine needs many years of bottle aging to reduce its harshness; adding many more years serves to make it, at its best, one of the world's great wines. In this impatient age, the slow bottle aging process is often replaced by late bottling. Late bottled vintages ("LBVs" or just "Vs") are aged in the barrel for six years before bottling and are ready to drink much sooner than the vintage ports. Some quality ruby ports which come from close to vintage years are aged for four or five years in the cask and are ready to drink when bottled; these ports are referred to as "vintage character" or "vintage reserve."

Key Terms

bodegas—Winemakers in Spain.

Bucelas—A wine-producing area in Portgual.

Catalonia—A major wine-producing region in Spain.

Consejo Regulador—The Spanish control board set up as the enforcement agency for Denominaciones de Origen (DO).

crianza—Spanish wines achieving DO designation that receive a minimum of two years aging either in a tank, an oak barrel, or a bottle.

Dão—A wine-producing region in Portugal that is the biggest and most prosperous producer of *vinho maduro* wines.

Denominação de Origem Controlada (DOC)—The highest wine category of Portuguese wines.

Denominaciones de Origen (DO)—Regulations controlling the alcoholic beverage industry in Spain. The law and its enforcement were modeled after the French AC system. There are over fifty DO wine areas in Spain. Each region has its own governing body that may enforce stricter regulations than those enforced federally by the DO.

Denominación de Origen Calificada (DOCa)—This highest category of Spanish wines. Wines labeled as "qualified designation of origin" must meet stricter standards than wines designated as DO.

Douro—A wine-producing region in Portugal famous for port.

gran reserva—Spanish red wines achieving a DO designation that must age for five years (with two of those years in wooden barrels) and white and rosé wines must age for four years (six months in wood).

Indicação de Proveniencia Regulamentada (IPR)—Portuguese wines of lesser quality than those categorized as Denominação de Origem Controlada (DOC).

Instituto Nacional de Denominaciones de Origen (INDO)—Provides Spanish wine-making regions with assistance in producing and marketing their products and in conforming to the regulations the Denominaciones de Origen (DO) establishes.

Jerez—A wine-growing region in the southwestern part of Spain in which sherry is produced.

Madeira—A fortified wine from Portugal's Madeira Island.

Minho—A wine-producing region in northern Portugal where the wine known as *vinho verde* (literally, "green wine") is made—the "green" refers to the youth of the wine and not its color.

port—The famous fortified sweet wine from Portugal.

reserva—Spanish wines achieving a DO designation that have a minimum of three years of aging, with at least one year in oak barrels. Rosé and white reserves require a minimum of aging of two years, with at least six months in oak.

Rioja—One of the main wine-growing regions in Spain. The only region whose wines are awarded Denominación de Origen Calificada (DOCa) status.

sherry—Spain's most famous wine whose production is limited by INDO to the wine-producing area of Jerez. All imitators must mention the place of origin on the label, such as California sherry.

solera system—An elaborate blending of sherries of similar character according to individual bodega formulas and guided by Spanish law.

vino de la mesa—The lowest classification of Spanish wines, "table wine," is made from unclassified wine-producing areas and/or from various blends. This designation is similar to France's *vine de table*, Germany's *tafelwein*, and Italy's *vino da tavola*.

vino de la tierra—This category of Spanish wines directly below DO classification is equivalent to the French category of *vin de pays* and the German classification of *landwein*.

Review Questions

1. What is Spain's version of France's *Appellation d'Origine Contrôlée*?

2. What does it mean for a Spanish wine to be labeled *Denominación de Origen Calificada (DOCa)*?

3. What is the difference between a wine designated as *vino de la tierra* and a wine designated as *vino de la mesa*?

4. What are the compulsory items found on the labels of Spanish *Denominación de Origen (DO)* wines?

5. Why is the Rioja wine-producing region of Spain famous?

6. How is sherry aged with the solera system?

7. What is the difference between Portuguese wines designated as *Denominação de Origem Controlada (DOC)* and those labeled as *Indicação de Proveniencia Regulamentada (IPR)*?

8. What are the compulsory items found on the labels of Portuguese *Denominação de Origem Controlada (DOC)* wines?

9. What is *vinho verde* and where is it produced?

10. What are the different types of port produced in the Douro region of Portugal?

Internet Sites

For more information, visit the following Internet sites. Remember that Internet addresses can change without notice. If the site is no longer there, you can use a search engine to look for additional sites. Many alcohol-related sites require users to be of legal drinking age to enter.

Wine Resources

Decanter Magazine
www.decanter.com

Professional Friends of Wine
winepros.org

The Wine Enthusiast
www.winemag.com

Wine Lover's Page
www.wineloverspage.com/wines/

Wine Spectator
www.winespector.com

Reading Wine Labels

Epicurious
www.epicurious.com/d_drinking/
d08_wines/wine_label/wine_
label_main.html

The Winedoctor
www.thewinedoctor.com/advisory/
labelinterpreter.shtml

Robin Garr's Wine Lovers' Page
www.wine-lovers-page.com/wines/
labels.shtml

Internet Wine Guide.com
www.internetwineguide.com/
structure/abwine/labelreg.htm

Wines of the World

Aboutwines.com
www.aboutwines.com/home/refer
ence/regions/index.html

International Sommelier Guild
www.internationalsommelier.com

Wine Regions of the World
www.wine-regions-of-the-world.com/
html/regions.html

Cellarnotes.net
www.cellarnotes.net/wine_by_
geographic_origin.htm

Strat's Place
www.stratsplace.com/maps.html

Wine Regions of the World
www.wine-regions-of-the-world.com/
html/regions.html

Spain

The Best Spanish Wines
www.bestspanishwines.com

Coleción Internacional del Vino
www.civusa.com

The Winedoctor
www.thewinedoctor.com/regional
guides/spain.shtml

Dominio Buenavista Vineyards in
Spain
www.dominiobuenavista.com/
index.htm

Bodegas Santa Catarina
www.santa-catarina.com

Portugal

The Winedoctor
www.thewinedoctor.com/regional
guides/portugal.shtml

Portugese Trade Commission
www.winesofportugal.org

Internet Guide to the Wines of Spain
www.filewine.es/english/default.htm

Roteiro Gastronomico de Portugal
www.gastronomias.com/wines/
e-inicio.htm

The Portuguese Wine Store—Wines
from Portugal
www.portuguesewine.com/
default.asp

Chapter 13 Outline

Competencies

1. Explain the wine classification system in the United States. (pp. 327–328)

2. Define items commonly found on the labels of United States wine bottles. (pp. 328–330)

3. Identify the major wine-producing areas of the United States and the types of wine each produces. (pp. 330–339)

13

Wines of the United States

THE FIRST WINE IN THE UNITED STATES is thought to have been made from Scuppernong grapes by the Huguenots in Florida in 1564. Records also show that missionaries were making sacramental wine in New Mexico in 1609. The first commercial winery was built in 1793. California's wine industry began around 1824. Today, there are more than 3,000 wineries in all 50 states. The top wine-producing states are: California, New York, Washington, and Oregon. California produces more than 90 percent of the total volume.

The United States has been a bit more lenient than European countries in its regulation of the wine industry. The wine producer can decide which particular grape to grow in an area, the time of harvest, the time of aging, the aging process, the kind of fining, and other factors often controlled in other countries. **Chaptalization** is permitted except in California. The relative lack of regulations has given the industry the liberty to experiment and to conduct extensive research and development which has brought about a highly scientific, modern wine industry. Thus the United States can better control the kind of wine produced as well as its quality.

United States Wine Classification System

Regulations and standards set by **The Bureau of Alcohol, Tobacco, Firearms and Explosives (ATF)**, a division within the Department of Justice, define appellations of origin and labeling requirements to provide consumers with truthful and adequate information about wine. The ATF does not grade quality levels of wine, but rather sets standards of identity for wine. The label of a United States wine may display any one of the following appellations of origin:

- A single state ("California")
- Two or three contiguous states ("Washington/Oregon")
- A county ("Napa County")
- Two or three counties within the same state ("Napa County/Sonoma County")
- A viticultural area ("Napa Valley")
- More than one viticultural area ("Napa Valley/St. Helena")

An **American Viticultural Area (AVA)** is a "delimited grape growing area" recognized and defined by the ATF as meeting evidentiary requirements that focus primarily on geographical factors (such as climate, soil, elevation, and

Exhibit 1   Reading a United States Wine Label

Clos du Val is one of California's top wineries, and all of their wine labels bear an image of The Three Graces—Aglaia, Euphrosyne, and Thalia—based on a Leo Wyatt engraving designed around George Petel's statue (created in 1624). The vintage, 1988, is clearly declared. In this region, "reserve" is a poorly defined term, denoting some special selection or aging in oak. The region of origin (or AVA—the U.S. equivalent of the French appellation system) is Napa Valley, one of the best.

Source: The Winedoctor. For more information, visit the Internet site at: www.thewinedoctor.com/advisory/labelinterpreter.shtml.

others) distinguishing the viticultural features of that area from those of surrounding areas. A petition to become recognized as a viticultural area will generally include documents from soil experts, engineers, meteorologists, and even historians to support the claims of distinguishing features. The ATF has established more than 145 viticultural areas. For a complete listing of AVAs sorted by name, size, or state, visit the Internet site of The Wine Institute at: www.iwineinstitute.com/ava/default.asp.

AVAs can be huge, with the Ohio River Valley AVA covering 26,000 square miles including parts of Indiana, Kentucky, Ohio, and West Virginia. AVAs can also be very small, such as Cole Ranch that covers less than a quarter square mile. Most AVAs, however, are more reasonably sized. While AVA is not a quality designation by the ATF, it is beginning to become so to some consumers and to those wine-producing areas that aspire to the AVA status.

Labeling Regulations

United States regulations require that American wine labels give the name of the wine and an appellation of origin. Exhibit 1 examines how to read parts of a United States wine label. Exhibit 2 presents a fictitious wine label depicting a vintage-dated, varietal, estate-bottled AVA wine.

If an AVA is indicated on the label, 85 percent of the wine must come from there. If two or three places of origin are given, 85 percent of the wine must be made from grapes grown in these areas, and the percentage coming from each must be given. If a wine is estate-bottled, 100 percent of the grapes used must come from there. States may have stricter regulations. For example, California requires that 100 percent of the grapes used to produce a wine with any kind of "California" appellation (state, county, or AVA) be from there. Generally, state and county appellations require that 75 percent of the grapes used to produce the wine must be grown in the state or county listed on the label.

Exhibit 2   United States Wine Labeling Regulations

The Present

Click on the different text portions of the fictitious Carissa Vineyards label for regulatory reference to some of the mandatory label information.

Nowadays...

Like Chardonnay is to table wine, not all appellations are viticultural areas. Appellations can be the name of a state, or the names of up to three contiguous states (and for a while, we were arguing about what "contiguous" really meant); the name of a county or up to three counties within the same state (counties don't have to be "contiguous" but have to use the term "County," e.g., "Napa County" and not "Napa," is required), the name of a country, or the name of a viticultural area (and in some cases the name of two viticultural areas, but don't get me started just yet).

Specific federal regulations can be found elsewhere on our Web site (in our Federal Library), but for a quick read, take this link to 27 CFR 4.25a and then come on back.

CARISSA VINEYARDS

Estate Bottled

1993

Merlot

Los Carneros

GROWN, PRODUCED AND BOTTLED BY
CARISSA VINEYARDS
NAPA, CALIFORNIA
Alcohol 13.5% by volume

Source: The Wine Institute. Access this fictitious vineyard label at: www.wineinsitute.org/ava/use/thepresent.htm. Click on different parts of the label and this site provides you with relevant labeling regulations of the United States.

Wine names may be based on grape variety (varietal) or on the type of wine (generic) or be a proprietary name such as "Rancho Yerba Buena," "Royal Occasion," or "Premium Red." A wine with a varietal name such as "Cabernet Sauvignon" must be made from grapes of which 75 percent must be Cabernet Sauvignon. A wine made from a *Vitis labrusca* variety is made from grapes of which only 51 percent needs to be from that variety.

A vintage date may be given, but there is no requirement that it must be on the label. A wine carrying a vintage date must be made from grapes of which 95 percent came from the harvest of that year; the 5 percent allowance is for wines used for topping and blending.

Generic wines such as "Burgundy" or "Chablis" can be made from any grape or grape mixture, but must state origin as in "California Burgundy." Proprietary wines need not meet any specific grape percentage requirements.

Alcohol content by volume must be stated and a 1.5 percent variation from the stated content is allowed. If a wine is between 7 percent and 14 percent alcohol, the label may omit the percentage and just say "table wine" or "light wine." The alcohol content by volume standard for sherries is between 17 percent and 20 percent; for port the standard is between 18 percent and 20 percent. Both have a tolerated variance of 1 percent from the stated content.

Labels must also state the amount of wine in the container and the presence of **sulfites**. A small percentage of the population can experience severe allergic reactions to sulfur compounds and asthma sufferers can have adverse reactions as well. Some sulfur is naturally occurring in the environment, in grapes, and in nearly all fruits and vegetables. Even without the addition of sulfur, yeast fermentation produces a certain level of sulfur naturally. Wine that contains 100 parts per million or more of sulfites, must say on its label, "Contains Sulfites."

Any alcoholic beverage bottled or imported for sale and distribution must have a government health warning on its label, stating that drinking alcoholic beverages can cause birth defects, impair the ability to drive a car or operate machinery, and cause health problems.

Labels on wine imported into the United States must meet certain standards. The label must indicate that it is the product of the country where it originated and must show the importer's name and location. The percentage by volume of alcohol, net contents, and name of the wine with some kind of description indicating what it is must be given. The presence of sulfites must be noted.

California

California has led all other states in the amount of wine produced, in varieties of wine, and in developing a major industry in winemaking. Its wines are of the highest quality and compete with the best in the world. It is fortunate in having a climate and soil that furthers grape growth. The climate has historically been consistent year after year and there is adequate rainfall, or, if not, adequate water for irrigation purposes. The climate is usually so reliable and the production of sugar in grapes so consistent that chaptalization is forbidden in California.

California has a variety of climates, from the desert south to the northern coastal regions near San Francisco. Wine grapes do well in almost all of California's climatic conditions, but the best wines grow in the famed Napa Valley, where cool nights and morning fog ameliorate the hot summer days and keep the many grape varieties from ripening too soon. Following is a discussion of the main grape varieties grown in California. It should be noted, however, that most California wines are blends of different grape varieties. By law, a named varietal need make up only 75 percent of the grapes used in that wine, and some of California's best wines are not varietals, but blends.

Main Grape Varieties (Red)

The Cabernet Sauvignon grape prospers in California and it is that state's most widely grown grape. It is partial, however, to Napa Valley where it is the primary grape used in the production of a red claret-type wine that rivals those of Bordeaux. It develops a complex flavor of cedar, cassis, and black currants and produces a wine that is balanced in tannins and acid, is full-bodied, and ages into a smooth, brilliant, deep ruby red with a very fragrant bouquet. The best Cabernets are aged in American, French, or Yugoslavian oak barrels, with much discussion about the merits of the taste characteristics of each.

The **Zinfandel** is another popular red grape variety in California. The grape is a sort of bastard since no one knows its parentage. Some think it derives from a spore from the Italian Primitivo grape that was brought to California. It makes a light and fruity red somewhat like a Beaujolais, a more intense, heavier-bodied and complex red, a delicate, spicy rosé, or a nearly-white wine. All wines made from it carry the typical spicy, raspberry flavor and aroma.

The Merlot grape was originally brought to California to be used in blending, especially with the musts of the Cabernet Sauvignon. But by using the carbonic maceration method, a refreshing, well-balanced red with mouth-filling roundness and softness was produced that made it a wine of its own and worthy of bottling. Many say it is much like the wines of the Pomerol in Bordeaux.

The Pinot Noir grape is not too well suited to California's climate, but it does well in certain areas, especially Carneros. It makes a full-bodied, full-flavored red that has a cherry-like aroma and flavor and a silky, satiny, almost oily feel in the mouth. It is the grape used to make the generic wine called Burgundy.

The Gamay and Gamay Beaujolais are used to make a light-bodied, refreshing, fruity wine. The Gamay makes a slightly heavier-bodied wine than the Gamay Beaujolais. Both are used to make good rosés.

The Petite Sirah grape makes a wine of rich, deep red color, with good body and a fresh, spicy, berry-like flavor and aroma. Because it is well-balanced with acid and tannins, the wine ages very well.

The Barbera grape is used more for blending (to provide a good natural acidity to red table wines) than as a varietal wine. However, some Barbera wines are marketed which have a medium to dark color, with a fruity taste and a natural tartness that gives a zestful quality to the wine.

Main Grape Varieties (White)

California makes a large quantity of high quality white wines but, with the heavier market demand today for these, producers are moving to step up production even more. The best white and most white wine produced comes from the Chardonnay grape that does well in many places in California, but loves the Alexander Valley. One excellent Chardonnay varietal wine is made by fermenting in stainless steel to obtain the luscious, crisp, apple aroma and flavor, and then aging in small oak barrels to develop greater complexity of flavor. A quite different Chardonnay results when the fermentation takes place in a barrel and the fermentation process is continued over a long time. The flavor of wine produced by this process is complex and considered by some the more desirable of the two processes. The California Chardonnays hold their flavor for about six to seven years.

The Chenin Blanc grape makes a wine that is light, delicate, slightly acidic and fruity with a hint of melon in its aftertaste. A dry Chenin Blanc that is given oak-cask aging makes a good table wine, while a slightly sweeter version is served as a refreshment wine.

The Sauvignon Blanc is perhaps California's second most popular white vari-etal wine. Sometimes it is identified on labels as Fumé Blanc. The wine has great depth with a full, lively, peppery, fruity flavor. A blend with the Sémillon grape is also popular.

The Johannisberg Riesling, sometimes called the White Riesling, does well in California making a delicate, light, slightly tart and slightly sweet, zestful white that is touched with a hint of spring flowers and autumn peaches. It can be left to develop the "noble rot" to make a sweet, full-bodied, full-flavored, high alcohol wine reminiscent of the German *Spätlese* or *Auslese*. The label will note "late har-vest" or "selected late harvest."

California vintners have developed a variety of the Gewürztraminer grape that has a fruity, flowery, spicy aroma and flavor with a touch of sweetness. It is delicate and light as is typical of the wines made from this grape.

The French Colombard is a grape grown in France primarily to produce cognac. California's vintners have been able to take this grape and make from it a fresh, fruity light- to medium-bodied wine with a slight bit of sweetness balanced by acidity.

The Pinot Blanc grape is used to make unique, dry, crisp, delicate, medium-bodied wines and heavier, oak-aged wines. It is also used to make California champagne.

California's vintners make their rosés by cold fermentation to preserve the freshness and fruitiness of the grape. Many different grape varieties are used for rosés. They can vary from a dry, crisp wine to a slightly sweet one. The Zinfandel and the Gamay grapes are used to make a popular wine called the pink rosé (or, sometimes, Zinfandel white or Gamay white). The distinct character of the grape comes through, giving a pleasant, wholesome wine.

California makes its champagne by four methods, the traditional champagne method, the bulk fermentation (Charmat) process, the transfer process, and forced carbonation for the lower-priced ones. The traditional grapes of the French Cham-pagne are often used—Pinot Noir and Chardonnay—but other grape varieties such as the Pinot Blanc are also used.

Vintages

Europe's climate is such that the quality of the harvest (and the subsequent wine production) can vary greatly in quality from year to year and from growing region to growing region. This gave rise to the labeling of "vintage year" and the development of quality evaluations of the different regional wines according to their quality for that year. California's remarkably consistent climate, however, produces grapes of about equal ripeness year after year; vintage labeling thus does not convey such crucial information about quality. California uses vintage labeling more to indicate wines of special character and style.

Growing Regions

California's wine-growing regions are usually divided into four major areas: the North coast, consisting of Mendocino County, Lake County, Napa Valley, and Sonoma County; the North-Central coast, consisting of Livermore, Santa Clara and Monterey Counties; the South-Central coast, consisting of San Luis Obispo and Santa Barbara; and the Central Valley, another way of referring to the San Joaquin Valley.

While Mendocino County is the most northern of these growing areas, it is not necessarily the coldest; some excellent wines such as the full-bodied reds are made from the Cabernet, Pinot Noir, Zinfandel, and Petite Sirah grapes. Some of the better known wineries are Parducci, Fetzer, Cresta Blanca and Weibel.

Lake County gets its name from Clear Lake which lies within its boundaries; the best vineyards are located near the lake. Lake County is not particularly known for its fine wines, but the famous Guenoc vineyard, currently the only vineyard given an AVA (American Viticulture Area) designation, is located here.

Napa Valley has a large number of famous wineries such as Stony Hill, Chappellet, Schramsberg, Clos du Val, Stag's Leap, Robert Mondavi, Inglenook, Louis M. Martini, Beaulieu, Beringer, Charles Krug, Freemark Abbey, and Sterling. Wines of almost any kind are produced with the major emphasis on wines made from the Cabernet Sauvignon grape. The Napa Valley is so well thought of as an ideal vineyard location, that Moët and Chandon located their Domaine Chandon winery there in 1973, producing an excellent California champagne. Mumm's of Rheims followed by locating its winery there. Exhibit 3 presents an online, interactive map of the AVAs in Napa Valley.

Sonoma County is known for both its whites and its reds. The Cabernets of Kenwood Winery are highly respected. The Chardonnay of Château St. Jean has a similar reputation. The Sebastiani winery is located there, and one of its wines is an especially good Barbera. Los Carneros ("The Sheep Place"), a good wine producer, straddles Napa and Sonoma County, and therefore, wines from its wineries may use the name of Sonoma County, Napa Valley, or Los Carneros on the label as the area of production. The Pinot Noir grape does well there as does the Chardonnay; wines from these two grape varieties are especially good from this area. Exhibit 4 presents an online, interactive map of the AVAs in Sonoma County.

The Livermore area is best known for its whites; the Wente Brothers and Concannon vineyards are located there. The high-gravel slopes drain into the east side of San Francisco Bay. Much of the land of this area has been taken out of grape production and sold for home sites. If this trend continues, some wonderful dry, crisp whites, as well as sweet whites, will disappear from the market.

Santa Cruz, Santa Clara, and Monterey Counties lie south of San Francisco Bay. Famous vineyards such as Mirassou, Almadén, Jekel, Taylor, Paul Masson, and Martin Rey are located there.

The San Joaquin Valley produces 80 percent of California's wine. It is a huge area, 400 miles long, fertile, and flat, and a producer not only of wine grapes, but

Exhibit 3   Napa Valley AVAs

During the early decades of winemaking in the Napa Valley, grapes were often planted in patchwork pattern vineyards in which many varieties were mixed. But experience has since shown the wisdom of matching grapes with locations whose microclimates and soils are best suited to particular grape varieties.

Within the Napa Valley, regions have emerged that possess distinct microclimates and terrains, imprinting recognizable characteristics on the grapes grown within them.

Vintners and growers within these regions delineate the boundaries of these growing areas, giving them names that reflect their regional designations, or *appellations*.

Data supporting a proposed American Viticultural Area, or AVA, is submitted to the government, which decides whether the proposed appellation designation will be granted.

The Napa Valley is itself an appellation. Within the Napa Valley appellation exists 13 subappellations, or AVAs, including: Atlas Peak, Chiles Valley District, Diamond Mountain District, Howell Mountain, Los Carneros, Mt. Veeder, Oakville, Rutherford, St. Helena, Spring Mountain District, Stags Leap District, Yountville, and Wild Horse Valley—as well as the pending Oak Knoll District.

This interactive map is available from Napa Valley Vintners Association at the Internet site: www.napavintners.com. Clicking on areas of the map provides information about specific wine-producing regions.

grapes for raisins and table grapes. Grapes like the Emerald Riesling and the Ruby Cabernet do well in the hot, dry summers. The huge Gallo vineyards and winery (Gallo accounts for one out of every three bottles of California wine production) are located there. Still wholly owned by the Gallo brothers, Ernest and Julio, Gallo also buys grapes from all over the state, particularly the types of grapes that do not do so well in the warm valley vineyards. Two other huge wine corporations— Guild with its Tavola and Winemaster brands and ISC with its Colony, Italian Swiss Colony, Petri Lejon, and Jacques Bonet brands—are located in the San Joaquin Valley. Another large winery, Franzia, is also located there.

The San Joaquin Valley not only grows grapes for its own production but it grows grapes for many other wineries in the state and even ships out of the state. The northern part of the valley near Sacramento is noted for producing the best quality wine of the area. Some respected wines come from the vineyards around Madera such as Almadén, Papagni, Fixin, and Quady.

Certain areas of southern California are too warm to produce anything but some very good dessert wines and some fair table wines. Wineries like Brookside,

Exhibit 4   Sonoma County AVAs

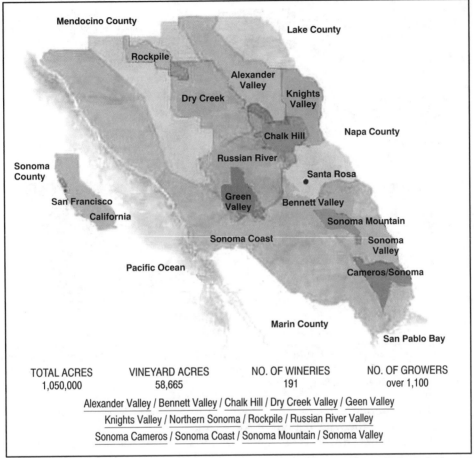

TOTAL ACRES	VINEYARD ACRES	NO. OF WINERIES	NO. OF GROWERS
1,050,000	58,665	191	over 1,100

Alexander Valley / Bennett Valley / Chalk Hill / Dry Creek Valley / Geen Valley
Knights Valley / Northern Sonoma / Rockpile / Russian River Valley
Sonoma Cameros / Sonoma Coast / Sonoma Mountain / Sonoma Valley

This interactive map is available from Sonoma County Grape Growers Association at the Internet site: www.sonomagrapevine.org. Clicking on areas of the map provides information about specific wine-producing regions.

Rancho California (Temecula), Callaway, and San Pasqual have good reputations. In table wines, whites rather than reds are the better wines.

Most of California's sherries are not made by the traditional *solera* method. Instead, they are heated to give them a nutty, sherry-like flavor and deepened color. However, some sherries are made by the traditional method and are considered good products. California brandies are well thought of, but are considered more suitable for mixed drinks than the traditional after-dinner drink.

New York

New York is another state in which wine making had early beginnings. Early colonists found an abundance of grapes suitable for winemaking there and, while

Exhibit 5   New York Wine Regions

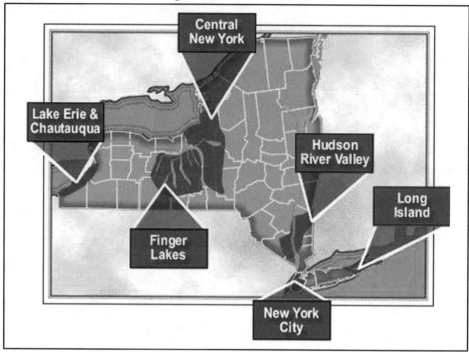

This interactive map is available from New York Wine and Grape Foundation at the Internet site: www.nywine.com. Clicking on areas of the map provides information about specific wine-producing regions.

some grapes produced fair wines, others did not. Exhibit 5 presents an online, interactive map of the wine regions of New York.

Over the years, growers created hybrids and developed clones from the native varieties that made a better product. The primary wine grape of this area is one or more varieties of **Vitis labrusca** along with some *Vitis vinifera-Vitis labrusca* hybrids. A few *vinifera*, those that have been found able to stand the more rugged winters that occur there, are grown, but the roots need to be covered by more than a foot of earth after harvest to be safe from the hardest frosts.

The major *Vitis labrusca* varieties used in New York state are the Delaware, the Elvira, and the "Riesling," which has some characteristics of the grape after which it is named but is much like the Elvira. The Catawba is another *labrusca* which is widely grown in Ohio as well as New York and is desirable for the making of sparkling wine.

The main producing regions are the Finger Lakes District which lies south of Syracuse and Rochester. Long, narrow lakes such as Lake Seneca, Keuka, and Canandaigua help to moderate the winters.

Long Island has been suitable for some *Vitis vinifera* varieties and is becoming prominent. A fairly large area west of Buffalo along the Lake Erie shore is another area of some significance.

Exhibit 6 Washington Wine Facts

National rank:	2nd in premium wine production in the United States
Number of wineries:	240+
Number of wine grape growers:	300+
Varieties produced:	15 varietals
Leading red varietals:	Merlot, Cabernet Sauvignon, Syrah, Cabernet Franc, Sanglovese
Leading white varietals:	Chardonnay, Riesling, Sauvignon Blanc, Semillon, Viognier
Record harvest:	2002, with 109,750 tons
Wine production:	17 million gallons or 64.3 million liters
Average hours of summer sunlight:	17.4 hours per day, about 2 hours more than California's prime growing region
Grapevine acreage:	28,000
Ratio of red to white:	57% red/43% white
Total economic impact on Washington State:	$2.4 billion
Total retail value:	$725.4 million

Source: Washington Wine Commission. For more information, visit the Internet site at: www.washingtonwine.org.

Washington and Oregon

The State of Washington is now a significant wine producer. The major Washington AVAs are:

- Yakima Valley
- Walla Walla Valley
- Columbia Valley
- Puget Sound
- Red Mountain

Vineyards existed before 1900, but it was not until about 1960 that growers realized that the *vitis vinifera* prospered, especially in the Yakima Valley and along the banks of the Columbia River. Washington's summers and summer days are long and although there is usually adequate rainfall, most vineyards are irrigated. The nights are cool. This favors the growth of grapes that make good whites. Exhibit 6 presents statistics on the wine industry in Washington.

Oregon is another serious but small producer of wines. Its climate is slightly milder than Washington's but rather similar otherwise. While Oregon has been making wines for a long time, it was not until recently that it seriously entered into such making. There are more than 250 wineries and more than 40 varietal wines produced, with an almost even split of white wine to red wine production. The major varieties produced are: Pinot Noir, Pinot Gris, Cabernet Sauvignon, Chardonnay, Gewürztraminer, Merlot, Müller-Thurgau, Pinot Blanc, Riesling, Sauvignon Blanc, Sémillon, and Syrah.

Other States

Other areas where wine is produced or where there is a promise of developing some significance are: Virginia, Maryland, Pennsylvania, West Virginia, Kentucky, Massachusetts, Georgia, Tennessee, Ohio, Michigan, Colorado, Missouri, Arkansas, Texas, Arizona, and New Mexico. Access information about these states through the Internet sites provided at the end of this chapter.

Virginia has grown from 6 wineries in 1979 to more than 80 wineries today. The major AVAs in Virginia are:

* Monticello
* Northern Neck (George Washington's birthplace)
* Rocky Knob
* Shenandoah Valley
* Eastern Shore
* North Fork of Roanoke

The major *vitis vinifera* varieties produced are: Chardonnay, White Riesling, Cabernet Sauvignon, Pinot Noir, Gewürztraminer, Cabernet Franc, Sauvignon Blanc, Merlot, and Viognier. Concord, Deleware, Niagara, and Norton are the major American varieties produced.

With incredible growth over the past two decades, Texas now ranks the country's fifth wine-producing state and has more than 50 wineries. Texan AVAs include:

* Bell Mountain
* Fredericksburg in the Hill Country
* Texas Hill Country
* Escondido Valley
* Texas High Plains
* Davis Mountain
* Messila Valley

The major *vitis vinifera* varieties produced are: Cabernet Sauvignon, Chardonnay, Chenin Blanc, Merlot, Riesling, and Sauvignon Blanc.

Most of Michigan's quality wine grapes are grown on the western side of the state, within twenty-five miles of Lake Michigan. The weather effects of the Great Lakes protects the vines with snow in winter, retards budding in early spring (avoiding frost damage), and extends the growing season by up to four weeks. The thirty-nine wineries in Michigan make many styles of wine—from dry to sweet (including ice wine), and from sparkling to fortified wines. The four AVAs in Michigan are:

- Leelanau Peninsula

- Old Mission Peninsula

- Lake Michigan Shore

- Fennville

The majority of Michigan's wine grapes are *vitis vinifera* varieties such as: Chardonnay, Riesling, Pinot Noir, Pinot Gris, and Cabernet Franc. Less than 5 percent of Michigan wine is made from American varieties.

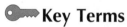 **Key Terms** ─────────────────────────────

American Viticultural Area (AVA)—A "delimited grape growing area" ATF (Bureau of Alcohol, Tobacco, Firearms and Explosives, a division within the United States Department of Justice), recognizes and defines as meeting evidentiary requirements that focus primarily on geographical factors (such as climate, soil, elevation, and others) distinguishing the viticultural features of that area from those of surrounding areas.

Bureau of Alcohol, Tobacco, Firearms and Explosives (ATF)—A division within the United States Department of Justice that enforces regulations defining appellations of origin and labeling requirements to provide consumers with truthful and adequate information about wine. The ATF regulates the qualification and operations of distilleries, wineries, and breweries, as well as importers and wholesalers in the industry.

chaptalization—A procedure of adding sugar to grape juice or must before or during fermentation to attain the necessary alcohol level. This procedure is often necessary when weather conditions prevent grapes from ripening fully and developing enough natural sugar to convert to the amount of alcohol prescribed (often by law) for certain wines.

Napa Valley—Famous wine-producing area of California.

Sonoma County—Famous wine-producing region of California.

sulfite—A sulfur compound found in wines and other foods, it is dangerous to the health of a relatively small proportion of people allergic to it; the United States federal government requires that the presence of sulfites in excess of 100 parts per million in foods and beverages be noted on the label.

Vitis labrusca—A variety of grape vine, native to North America, which thrives in colder areas and which is resistant to phylloxera.

Zinfandel—The most extensively planted red grape in California. All wines made from it carry the typical spicy, raspberry flavor and aroma.

Review Questions

1. What are the different appellations of origin that could be displayed by a wine from the United States?

2. What does it mean for an area in the United States to be designated as a viticultural area?

3. What does a consumer know when "AVA" is displayed on the label of a wine from the United States?

4. What is the alcohol content by volume permitted on wines from the United States?

5. Why are wines from the United States labeled with "Contains Sulfites?"

6. Why is chaptalization forbidden in California?

7. Why do so many grape varieties grow well in California?

8. What are Napa Valley and Sonoma County famous for?

9. Why does the state of New York grow varieties of the *vitis labrusca*?

10. What are the major wine-producing areas of the state of Washington?

Internet Sites

For more information, visit the following Internet sites. Remember that Internet addresses can change without notice. If the site is no longer there, you can use a search engine to look for additional sites. Many alcohol-related sites require users to be of legal drinking age to enter.

Wine Resources

Decanter Magazine
www.decanter.com

Professional Friends of Wine
winepros.org

The Wine Enthusiast
www.winemag.com

Wine Lover's Page
www.wineloverspage.com/wines/

Wine Spectator
www.winespector.com

Reading Wine Labels

Epicurious
www.epicurious.com/d_drinking/
d08_wines/wine_label/wine_
label_main.html

The Winedoctor
www.thewinedoctor.com/
advisory/labelinterpreter.shtml

Robin Garr's Wine Lovers' Page
www.wine-lovers-page.com/
wines/labels.shtml

Internet Wine Guide.com
www.internetwineguide.com/
structure/abwine/labelreg.htm

Wines of the World

Aboutwines.com
www.aboutwines.com/home/
reference/regions/index.html

International Sommelier Guild
www.internationalsommelier.com

Internet Wine Guide.com
www.internetwineguide.com/
structure/ww/worldwide.htm

Cellarnotes.net
www.cellarnotes.net/wine_by_
geographic_origin.htm

Strat's Place
www.stratsplace.com/maps.html

Wine Regions of the World
www.wine-regions-of-the-
world.com/html/regions.html

California

Travel Envoy Wine Guide
www.travelenvoy.com/wine/
wineries.htm

Wineries Around the World
vine2wine.com/Wineries.htm

Wineries Around the World
www.winereader.com/wineries.php

United States Wineries
The Wine Enthusiast Magazine
www.winemag.com/domestic
links.cfm

United States Wineries
www.winezealot.com/ineratings.
php?op=allwineries

United States Wineries
wine.about.com/cs/wineriesus

California Wineries
www.winexplorer.com/wineries/
index.html

Napa Valley Vintners Association
www.napavintners.com

Sonoma County Grape Growers
Association
www.sonomagrapevine.org/index.
html

Wine Institute—The Voice of
California Wines
www.wineinstitute.org/Welcome.
html

Colorado

Colorado Wines
www.coloradowine.com

Illinois

Illinois Wines
www.illinoiswine.org

Indiana

Indiana Wines
www.indianawines.org/index.cfm

Michigan

Michigan Wines
www.michiganwines.com

Missouri

Missouri Wines
www.missouriwine.org

New Jersey

Wines of New Jersey
www.newjerseywines.com

New Mexico

New Mexico Wine Growers
www.nmwine.net

New York

New York Wine and Grape
Foundation
www.nywine.com

New York Wines
www.fingerlakeswinecountry.com

North Carolina

North Carolina Grape Council
www.ncwine.org

Ohio

Ohio Wine Producers Association
www.ohiowines.org

Oregon

Oregon Wine Advisory Board
www.oregonwine.org

Washington

Washington Association of Wine
Grape Growers
www.wawgg.org

Washington Wine Commission
www.washingtonwine.org

Washington Wineries
www.thewineguru.com/washington
links.htm

Wisconsin

Wisconsin Wollersheim Winery
www.wollersheim.com/vineyard2.html

The Cayuga Wine Trial
www.cayugawinetrail.com

The Keuka Wine Trail
www.keukawinetrail.com

The Seneca Lake Wine Trail
www.senecalakewine.com

Pennsylvania

Pennsylvania Wines
www.pennsylvaniawine.com

Texas

Texas Wines
www.agr.state.tx.us/wine/index.htm

Virginia

Virginia Wines
www.virginiawineguide.com

Walla Walla Vinters
www.wallawallavintners.com

Walla Walla Wine Alliance
wallawallawine2.pageland.com/
index.html

Chapter 14 Outline

Argentina
Australia
Austria
Bulgaria
Canada
Chile
Cyprus
Greece
Hungary
New Zealand
Romania
Russia
South Africa

Competencies

1. Identify the major wine regions in Argentina and Chile as well as the kinds of wines they produce. (pp. 345, 351)

2. Explain how regulations governing wine production in Australia differ from those in Austria and Bulgaria. (pp. 345–350)

3. Identify the best known wines from Cyprus and Greece. (p. 351)

4. Identify the best known wines from Hungary and Romania. (pp. 352–353)

5. Identify the primary wine regions of New Zealand. (pp. 353–354)

6. Explain the role of the South African Wine and Spirit Board in the regulation of wine production. (pp. 355–356)

14

Wines of Other Countries

THE AMOUNT OF WINE produced in the world each year is immense. Wine is produced worldwide in any temperate area where there are 120 or more frost-free days with fairly warm summers and not overly cold winters. In the last 50 years many countries not traditionally known as wine producers have developed sizable wine industries and are exporting their wines around the world. At almost any important wine competition today, you can observe a great many nations offering a wide variety of excellent quality wines. Nor is it unusual to see some country not particularly noted for its wines walk off with some of the highest awards. This chapter provides a short summary of other wine-producing nations, along with some indication of the quality and the distinctive characteristics of their major wines.

Argentina

Argentina is the world's fifth largest wine producer and is also one of the world's largest wine consumers. Exceeded in consumption only by the French, Italians, and Portuguese, there is little wine left for export. Almost all the wine-producing areas are in arid zones with temperate climates. **Cuyo** is the main wine-growing region, including the provinces of Mendoza and San Juan. Exhibit 1 illustrates items found on a wine label from the Cuyo region. The Mendoza vineyards on the eastern side of the Andes mountain range are at higher altitudes than those of most other wine-growing countries. Rainfall is minimal and fields must be irrigated. Wine production in the San Juan province exceeds that of combined production of California's regions of Napa and Sonoma. Argentina's main grapes are the Criolla and the Malbec, but plantings of the Cabernet Sauvignon and Pinot Noir are gaining ground. In the cooler northern area, Reisling and Chardonnay grapes are producing acceptable white wines. Regulations governing wine production require that wines labeled with a varietal name must contain 90 percent of that varietal.

Australia

The first grape vines were brought to Australia by Governor Phillip in 1788 and planted at Farm Cove. Under amateur care, the vines did poorly and it was not until 1801 that Dr. William Redfern established a successful planting southwest of Sydney. He used the wine he produced as a medicine and other doctors followed suit. Wine production continued in earnest when it was found that grapes prospered in Hunter Valley and Upper Hunter and in a number of areas south of a straight line running from Sydney to Adelaide. For the most part, these areas

Exhibit 1 Reading Argentine Wine Labels

An image of the producer's wine cellars dominates the label. The producer is Bodega y Cavas de Weinert, as declared in the text near the foot of the label, abbreviated to BCW just beneath the picture. The wine is their Gran Vino, Weinert's top wine, named Cavas de Weinert after the winery. The vintage is 1986. The phrase "cepaje procedente de la region de Lujon de Cuyo" tells us that the wine originates from the Lujon de Cuyo vineyards, and "envasado en origen," bottom right, shows that the wine has been bottled at the estate. Beneath the name of the domain, in very small type, are contact details, revealing the estate to be located in San Martin 5923 in Mendoza.

Source: The Winedoctor. For more information, visit the Internet site at:www.thewinedoctor.com/advisory/labelinterpreter.shtml.

Exhibit 2 Reading Australian Wine Labels

This imposing label comes from the Henschke winery, which, as the information near the foot of the label tells us, is in Keyneton, South Australia. The text on either side of the Henschke coat of arms tells us that the estate has been in existence since 1868. The wine here is Mount Edelstone, coming from the vineyard of the same name, in the 1991 vintage. This wine is a Shiraz, although the label does not tell us this. The label proudly declares the wine as Produce of Australia, and also reassures us that the wine has been Estate vintaged and bottled, meaning that the wine has been produced and bottled on the estate.

Source: The Winedoctor. For more information, visit the Internet site at: www.thewinedoctor.com/advisory/labelinterpreter.shtml.

produce grapes of highest quality. Fortunately, the wine growers and wine producers were highly knowledgeable in viticulture and wine production and soon Australia was producing a tremendous amount of wines equal in quality to the wines of any other region of the world. Exhibit 2 illustrates items found on an Australian wine label.

Australia is the world's tenth largest wine producer and the world's twelfth largest wine consumer. There are more than 1,100 wineries in Australia with the majority of wine produced in the southern regions. Australia has succeeded as an

Exhibit 3   Wine Regions of Australia

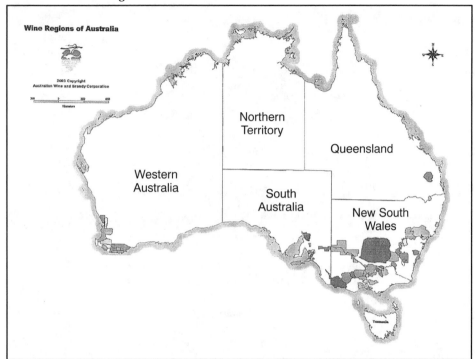

Source: Australian Wine & Brandy Corporation. For more information, visit the company's Internet site at: www.awbc.com.au.

innovator, experimenting with new technologies and unconventional wine-producing methods. This is made possible by considerably less bureaucracy and regulation governing its wine industry in comparison to older and more established wine-producing countries. The official description of an Australian wine zone, region, or area is a **Geographical Indication (GI)**. Exhibit 3 maps the major wine-producing areas of Australia. While similar to the appellation naming system used in other countries, the GI description is far less restrictive in relation to viticultural practices and wine-making techniques.

Australia is one of the primary countries of the world that markets wines with two grape blends (Sémillon/Chardonnay) identified on a label. The variety representing the greater portion of the wine is named first. Otherwise, laws require that wines labeled with a varietal name must contain 85 percent of that varietal. The most successful grape varietal is the Shiraz (also known as Syrah). Other varietals include Cabernet Sauvignon, Merlot, Chardonnay, Semillon, and Riesling.

Austria

While Austrian wines are not well known, some excellent wines come from there. By far, the good whites exceed the reds. Austria passed the world's strictest wine

Exhibit 4   Reading Austrian Wine Labels

County of Origin	Österreich (Austria)
Appellation of Origin	Zöbinger Heilingenstein
Producer	Weingut Schloss Gobelsburg Langenlois-Österreich
	Category: Gutsabfüllung
Bottle Content	75 cl
Alcohol Content	12,5 (12.5%) vol
Vintage	1997

Source: Internet Wine Guide.com. For more information, visit the Internet site at: www.internetwine guide.com.

regulations in 1985 and 1986. While we cannot hope to cover the regulations in detail, we can outline their primary thrust. They provide for four classes of wine, *Tafelwein*, *Qualitätswein*, *Kabinett*, and *Prädikatswein* (the latter divided into *Spätlese*, *Auslese*, *Eiswein*, *Beerenauslese*, *Ausbruch*, and *Trockenbeerenauslese*). While the categories are similar to those of the German classification, in most cases Austrian requirements are stricter.

If a vineyard, village, or commune is mentioned on the label, 100 percent of the grapes must come from that area (see Exhibit 4). However, if vintage or grape variety is stated on the label, only 85 percent is required. In order to receive the Austria Wine Seal, wines must meet two tests: 1) a laboratory test to check for

Exhibit 5   Wine Regions of Austria

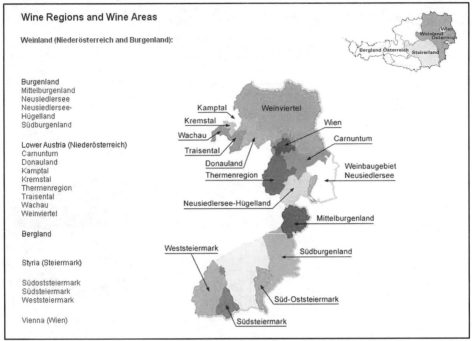

Wine Regions and Wine Areas

Weinland (Niederösterreich and Burgenland):

Burgenland
Mittelburgenland
Neusiedlersee
Neusiedlersee-
Hügelland
Südburgenland

Lower Austria (Niederösterreich)
Carnuntum
Donauland
Kamptal
Kremstal
Thermenregion
Traisental
Wachau
Weinviertel

Bergland

Styria (Steiermark)

Südoststeiermark
Südsteiermark
Weststeiermark

Vienna (Wien)

This interactive map is available for Wines of Austria at the Internet site: www.austrian. wine.co.at. Clicking on areas of the map provides information about specific wine-producing regions.

sugar, alcohol, acid, and other properties; and 2) a taste test in which six judges check a sample.

The grapes grown are much like those of Germany. However, wines made from the German Riesling grape bear *Rheinriesling* on the label. If *Riesling* alone is on the label, the poorer Italian Riesling grape is used. Exhibit 5 maps the wine-producing regions of Austria. The main growing region is in eastern Austria. Some of the best wines are Ruster Ausbruch, a sweet wine between a *Beerenauslese* and a *Trockenbeerenauslese*, the Grüner Veltliner, Lenz-Moser, and most wines coming from the famous Esterhazy vineyards.

Bulgaria

For many years, Bulgaria has been a large producer of wines, but they have not been of particularly high quality. A major change of its viticulture industry came about in 1978 when Bulgaria established a set of very high standards to meet EEC requirements. Now, its wines are beginning to compete in quality with those of other European countries. Bulgarian wines classified as **DGO (Declared Geographical Origin)** must be labeled with one of the twenty-six approved wine-producing regions. The main regions are found all through central and southeast

Exhibit 6   Peller Estates—A Canadian Winery

Source: Peller Estates, Niagara-on-the-Lake, Ontario. For more information about the company and its wines, visit the Internet site at www.andreswines.com.

Bulgaria. A few scattered and small producing centers are also found in the north and west. Bulgaria's climate is conducive to good grape growth. The main grapes are the Cabernet Sauvignon, Merlot, and Chardonnay. A high quality, fruity, vigorous, well-balanced claret is made from the Cabernet.

Canada

The primary wine-producing areas of Canada are the provinces of British Columbia and Ontario. The Niagara Peninsula in southern Ontario has 45 local wineries with a total of 19,000 acres of vineyards and produces over 75 percent of all Canadian wines. One of these wineries is featured in Exhibit 6.

Icewine (*Eiswein* in German) has become a specialty of the area. Ontario summers ensure high sugar content in the grapes and the winters provide a "natural" icewine harvest. With icewine production, the grapes are left on the vine until after the first frost. The grapes are harvested after they have been frozen in the vineyard. In Ontario and in Germany, icewine is defined as naturally frozen. No artificial freezing method is permitted for wines with the term "icewine" on the label. The grapes are pressed while frozen, leaving a highly concentrated juice, very high in acids, sugars, and aromatics.

Chile

Chilean wines are of high quality and are popularly priced. Chile's location (between the 30th and 40th parallels of the southern hemisphere) affords it a climate equal to the best growing regions of the northern hemisphere. Chile's main wine producing region is around Santiago. Excellent Cabernet Sauvignons are made; they are fruity, with good tannin-acid balance, deep color, and good body. They are long-lasting wines. The white wines are also good, since the producers changed over to refrigerated fermentation and improved methods of aging. Exhibit 7 shows some of the modern wine-making technology used at the Santa Rita winery. Chile has five distinct grape-growing regions. The Aconcagua and Central Valley (Maipo) regions are the main producers of exported wines, with the exception of Chardonnay wines produced in the Casablanca region. The major grapes are Cabernet Sauvignon, Merlot, Camenere, Syrah, Chardonnay, and Sauvignon blanc.

Cyprus

Cyprus makes a considerable amount of its wine from native grapes. Its wines are good and all types are made. One of the best-known wines is the **Commandaria** made from dried red and white grapes which gives a very sweet wine, sweeter than port or some of the richer, fortified wines. By law, Commandaria has a certification of origin that stipulates types of grapes as well as regions and methods of production. After the importation of the Palomino grape, sherry was made which is of good to high quality.

Greece

Greece was probably the first European country to make wine an important drink. Vines from Asia found their way to Greece in ancient times, and wine became a national drink, often diluted with water. Today a large quantity of wine is still being produced but most of it is locally consumed. Good quality whites, reds, and rosés are produced. Much of the whites and some rosés are flavored with resin during fermentation which gives a resinous, turpentine-like flavor to the wine. The Greeks like *retsina,* as they call it, because it goes well with the oily, spicy food they often eat. The Greek Islands also produce wine. Sweet ones predominate. Some fairly good sherries are made in the islands.

Exhibit 7   Santa Rita—A Chilean Winery

Santa Rita plays a leading role in the Chilean wine industry, combining modern technology throughout its winemaking, a large installed capacity for aging wine, and the expertise mastered through years of wine producing.

In the past few years, Santa Rita has invested in new technology, such as the latest horizontal pneumatic press technology, stainless steel vats with temperature control systems, and spira-flow equipment to control grape temperatures before fermentation.

These innovations have propelled Santa Rita to the forefront in top-class wine production, receiving international recognition for the quality of its wines.

Source: Santa Rita. For more information about the company and its wines, visit the winery's Internet site at: www.santarita.com.

Hungary

The Riesling grape grows well in Hungary and some excellent whites are made from it. They are rich in flavor and light in body and almost golden in color. The climate is such that the grapes develop much sugar and so many sweet whites are made. The most famous of the Hungary sweet wines is the **Tokaji Aszú**, a wine referred to as "the wine of kings and the king of wines." Some fine reds and good rosés are also produced.

The main grape growing region is on the northern shore of Europe's largest lake, Lake Balaton. To the northwest is the Ezeno Ator region; and farther to the west, the Matralia Eger. The famed Tokaji region is in the far Northwest. A few significant vineyards are in the southern part near Yugoslavia.

The Riesling and Furmint grapes are the primary grapes from which dry, delicate, whites are produced. Similar wines are produced in the Ezeno Ator. However, the district of Eger is more widely known for its noble, rich, red Bikaver (Blood of the Ox). The wine is a deep, red color and much like a fine Bordeaux except richer in flavor, heavier in body, and a bit fiery in nature. The alcoholic content is high and the wine holds its age well.

Tokay wine is made largely from the Furmint grape which is allowed to stay on the vines until it develops the "noble rot" (*aszú* is Hungarian for grapes infected with noble rot—a mold infecting grapes that produces a naturally sweet wine).

New Zealand

New Zealand also has a prospering viticulture industry. The first grapes were planted by missionaries in 1819. Exhibit 8 maps the major wine-growing regions of New Zealand. These fall between the 35th and 45th parallels, which puts it in the same region as Europe's vineyards. However, three regions (Marlborough, Hawke's Bay, and Ginsborne) produce 90 percent of New Zealand's grapes. Exhibit 9 explains some of the items found on a wine label from the Marlborough region. New Zealand's reds, made from its Cabernet Sauvignon, are of high quality and its whites are nearly so. The country is gradually developing an export trade in wines.

Romania

Romania produces a significant amount of wine which is not known outside the country. One wine for which it is justly famed, **Cotnari**, is a dessert wine—delicate in body and flavor, with great fragrance and holding power in the mouth much like Tokay. It comes from the part in Moldavia that was left in Romania after the Russians took the greater part after World War II. This is also the area from which most of Romania's better wines come. Most are whites. Two good whites come from Transylvania: one called Tîrnave, a light, slightly sweet white; and the other called Perla.

Murfatlar is another area known for its sweet, pale, golden brown wine made from the muscat grape. Focsani is Romania's biggest wine producer but nothing of world renown comes from there, although many of the wines are considered respectable.

Russia

Russia has a modern set of regulations governing the industry, and these meet the regulations of the EEC. From best to last, qualities are: *kollektsionye*, which is a wine from selected areas and named varieties with two years aging in the bottle; *named*, a wine of some maturity with a named place of origin; and *ordinary*, a wine similar to *vin ordinaire* in France. If a grape name is put on the bottle, 85 percent of the grapes must be of that variety. A majority of the grapes used are *vitis vinifera* varieties common in Europe.

Exhibit 8   Wine Regions of New Zealand

This interactive map is available from TiZwine.com at the Internet site: www.tiz wine.com. Clicking on areas of the map provides information about wine-producing areas of New Zealand.

The main producing region is a long area stretching from Moldavia near Romania (it was once part of Romania) westward to the Caspian Sea. This takes it through the Ukraine down through Crimea and all through the huge land mass that sits between the Black and Caspian Seas. It is the second largest amount of land devoted to the wine grapes in the world. Excellent dry reds, whites, and rosés are made, as well as sweet wines. A lot of the wines produced in the wine growing

Exhibit 9   Reading New Zealand Wine Labels

New Zealand has made its mark with Sauvignon Blanc, and this variety is prominently declared on the label. This wine is from Cloudy Bay, an estate renowned for its Sauvignon, which is in a well-known wine producing region called Marlborough on the South Island. The hills depicted on the label are the mountains of the South Island, visible from the Cloudy Bay vineyards. The label declares that the wine has been produced and bottled by Cloudy Bay, and gives the location of the winery in Blenheim.

Source: The Winedoctor. For more information, visit the Internet site at: www.thewinedoctor.com/advisory/labelinterpreter.shtml.

area along the Caspian Sea are very sweet. Excellent sparkling whites and reds are also produced, as well as sherries, ports and aromatic wines; even a good imitation of a Madeira can be found.

South Africa

At one time Britain favored the wine industry of South Africa because it wanted wines that could compete with those of Europe, and South Africa's wines met this requirement. However, quality dropped and today, South Africa is seeking to bring the reputation of its wines back to their former prominence. In 1972, new regulations were set up and defined regions of origination were established. These laws conform to EEC regulations and the South African Wine and Spirit Board administers them. This Board certifies wines that meet **Wine of Origin** standards. Strict control is exercised during pressing, blending, and bottling stages. Wines meeting these standards display a certification seal. The seal guarantees the trustworthiness of all information and claims made on the label. Regulations govern the labeling of South African wines. These regulations specify items that are compulsory, optional, and prohibited. Compulsory label items include:

- Country of origin
- Appellation of origin
- Quality standard
- Name and address of producer/brand owner
- Bottle content
- Alcohol content
- The term "wine"

Exhibit 10   Wine Regions of South Africa

This interactive map is available from Wines of South Africa at the Internet site: www. wosa.co.za. Clicking on areas of the map provides information about wine-producing areas of South Africa.

- The term "domain"
- Authenticity seal

Optional items include: grape variety, vintage, name of the vineyard, terms such as "dry," "medium dry," or "sweet," and commentaries such as analysis, tasting notes, or approvals. Sulfites or other additives are prohibited.

The main grape used for reds is the Pinotage, a cross between the Cinsaut and Pinot Noir grapes. Some straight Pinot Noirs and Cabernet Sauvignon are also grown. The main grape grown for the whites is the Chenin Blanc, called Steen in South Africa. It makes excellent dry and sweet whites as well as sherry. The Sémillon and a type of Riesling are also grown for whites. The Palomino is grown for sherry making. Some sweet wines are made from the Muscadel and the Muscat of Alexandria.

Exhibit 10 maps the wine regions of South Africa. The main vineyards are the Olifante and Lower Orange along the Olifants River, a spotted coastal area, and the Breede River Valley, Worcester, Paarl, Robertson, Stellenbosch, Malmesbury and Montagu. Most of the exports go to Canada and to Great Britain.

Key Terms

Commandaria—A very sweet dessert wine produced in Cyprus that is made from a variety of dried, raisined grapes.

Cotnari—A famous Romanian dessert wine.

Cuyo—The main wine-growing region in Argentina.

Declared Geographical Origin (DGO)—Bulgarian wine classification system that also identifies twenty-six approved wine-producing regions.

Geographical Indication (GI)—The official description of an Australian wine zone, region, or area.

Icewine—A specialty of Canadian wines in Ontario. Grapes are left on the vine until after the first frost and pressed while frozen, leaving a highly concentrated juice, very high in acids, sugars, and aromatics. Also produced in Germany as Eiswein.

retsina—A Greek wine, made for over 3,000 years, with a turpentine-like flavor created by treatment with resin from pine trees during fermentation.

Tokaji Aszú—A famous sweet wine from Hungary made by an elaborate blending process from wines made from grapes infected with the noble rot.

Wine of Origin—A South African wine designation certifying that the wine has met strict standards during pressing, blending, and bottling stages.

Review Questions

1. What is the main wine-growing region of Argentina?

2. What does "Geographical Indication (GI)" mean in relation to Australian wines?

3. Austrian wine regulations are stricter than those of what European country?

4. How is Canadian icewine made?

5. What country produces Commandaria? Retsina? Tokaji Aszú? Cotnari?

6. What does "Wine of Origin" mean in relation to South African wines?

Internet Sites

For more information, visit the following Internet sites. Remember that Internet addresses can change without notice. If the site is no longer there, you can use a search engine to look for additional sites. Many alcohol-related sites require users to be of legal drinking age to enter.

Wine Resources

Decanter Magazine
www.decanter.com

Professional Friends of Wine
winepros.org

The Wine Enthusiast
www.winemag.com

Wine Spectator
www.winespector.com

Wine Lover's Page
www.wineloverspage.com/wines/

Reading Wine Labels

Epicurious
www.epicurious.com/d_drinking/
d08_wines/wine_label/wine_
label_main.html

Robin Garr's Wine Lovers' Page
www.wine-lovers-page.com/wines/
labels.shtml

Internet Wine Guide.com
www.internetwineguide.com/
structure/abwine/labelreg.htm

The Winedoctor
www.thewinedoctor.com/advisory/
labelinterpreter.shtml

Wines of the World

Aboutwines.com
www.aboutwines.com/home/
reference/regions/index.html

Cellarnotes.net
www.cellarnotes.net/
wine_by_geographic_origin.htm

International Sommelier Guild
www.internationalsom
melier.com

Strat's Place
www.stratsplace.com/maps.html

Internet Wine Guide.com
www.internetwineguide.com/
structure/ww/worldwide.htm

Wine Regions of the World
www.wine-regions-of-the-world.com/
html/regions.html

Wines of Other Countries and Areas

Argentina

Argentine Wines
www.argentinewines.com

Wines of Argentina.com
www.winesofargentina.com

Australia

National Wine Center of Australia
www.wineaustralia.com.au

Australian Wine & Brandy
Corportation
www.awbc.com.au

Australian Wine and Beer
www.australianwineandbeer.com

Austria

Austrian Wines
www.austrian.wine.co.at/eindex.html

Austrian Wineries
wine.about.com/cs/austrian

Canada

Canadian Wines
www.canwine.com

Andres Wines, Ltd.
www.andreswines.com

Hillebrand Estates Winery
www.hillebrand.com/hillebrand/
default.htm

Canadian Wineries
wine.about.com/cs/canada

The Viticultural Roundtable of
Southwestern Ontario
www.ontariograpes.com

Chile

Chilean Wineries
wine.about.com/cs/winerieschile

Greece

Greek Wineries
wine.about.com/cs/greek/

The Roads of Greek Wines
w4u.eexi.gr/~oinos/ENGEO.HTM

A Window on Cyprus
www.windowoncyprus.com/
wines+.htm

New Zealand

New Zealand Wines
www.nzwine.com/intro

New Zealand Wine Regions
www.tizwine.com/regions

New Zealand Wines and Wineries
www.winesofNZ.com

South Africa

Wines of South Africa
www.wosa.co.za

Wine Routes of South Africa
www.wine.co.za/routes/default.aspx

South African Wineries
wine.about.com/cs/wineriessafrica

Index

Wake Technical Community College
9101 Fayetteville Road
Raleigh, NC 27603-5696

DATE DUE

	WITHDRAWN		

JUL   '06